AF840365

FEDERALISM AND THE RIGHTS OF PERSONS WITH DISABILITIES

This book shines a light on the still unexplored relationships between federalism and disability rights. It investigates how the UN Convention on the Rights of Persons with Disabilities (CRPD) is implemented by different federal systems around the world.

It analyses the effects that the obligations undertaken under the CRPD have on federal governance and on the constitutional division of powers within 14 federal systems, including those in Germany, Canada, Brazil, India, the UK and Italy. The book also considers the trends and patterns of disability rights governance in federal systems and looks at the future developments of comparative disability federalism.

Volume 29 in the series Hart Studies in Comparative Public Law

Hart Studies in Comparative Public Law

Recent titles in this series:

Entick v Carrington
250 Years of the Rule of Law
Edited by Adam Tomkins and Paul Scott

Administrative Law and Judicial Deference
Matthew Lewans

Soft Law and Public Authorities
Remedies and Reform
Greg Weeks

Legitimate Expectations in the Common Law World
Edited by Matthew Groves and Greg Weeks

The Dynamics of Exclusionary Constitutionalism
Mazen Masri

Constitutional Courts, Gay Rights and Sexual Orientation Equality
Angioletta Sperti

Australian Constitutional Values
Edited by Rosalind Dixon

Human Rights in the UK and the Influence of Foreign Jurisprudence
Hélène Tyrrell

The Nordic Constitutions
Edited by Helle Krunke and Björg Thorarensen

Regulation in India
Design, Capacity, Performance
Edited by Devesh Kapur and Madhav Khosla

New Media and Freedom of Expression
Rethinking the Constitutional Foundations of the Public Sphere
András Koltay

Why Religious Freedom Matters for Democracy
Comparative Reflections from Britain and France for a Democratic 'Vivre Ensemble'
Myriam Hunter-Henin

The Role of Monarchy in the Modern Democracy: European Monarchies Compared
Edited by Robert Hazell and Bob Morris

Responsible Government and the Australian Constitution:
A Government for a Sovereign People
Benjamin B Saunders

Federalism and the Rights of Persons with Disabilities

The Implementation of the CRPD in Federal Systems and its Implications

Edited by
Delia Ferri
Francesco Palermo
and
Giuseppe Martinico

•HART•
OXFORD • LONDON • NEW YORK • NEW DELHI • SYDNEY

HART PUBLISHING

Bloomsbury Publishing Plc

Kemp House, Chawley Park, Cumnor Hill, Oxford, OX2 9PH, UK

1385 Broadway, New York, NY 10018, USA

29 Earlsfort Terrace, Dublin 2, Ireland

HART PUBLISHING, the Hart/Stag logo, BLOOMSBURY and the Diana logo are trademarks of Bloomsbury Publishing Plc

First published in Great Britain 2023

Copyright © The editors and contributors severally 2023

The editors and contributors have asserted their right under the Copyright, Designs and Patents Act 1988 to be identified as Authors of this work.

All rights reserved. No part of this publication may be reproduced or transmitted in any form or by any means, electronic or mechanical, including photocopying, recording, or any information storage or retrieval system, without prior permission in writing from the publishers.

While every care has been taken to ensure the accuracy of this work, no responsibility for loss or damage occasioned to any person acting or refraining from action as a result of any statement in it can be accepted by the authors, editors or publishers.

All UK Government legislation and other public sector information used in the work is Crown Copyright ©. All House of Lords and House of Commons information used in the work is Parliamentary Copyright ©. This information is reused under the terms of the Open Government Licence v3.0 (http://www.nationalarchives.gov.uk/doc/open-government-licence/version/3) except where otherwise stated.

All Eur-lex material used in the work is © European Union, http://eur-lex.europa.eu/, 1998–2023.

A catalogue record for this book is available from the British Library.

A catalogue record for this book is available from the Library of Congress.

Library of Congress Control Number: 2023933023

ISBN: HB: 978-1-50996-243-3
ePDF: 978-1-50996-245-7
ePub: 978-1-50996-244-0

Typeset by Compuscript Ltd, Shannon

To find out more about our authors and books visit www.hartpublishing.co.uk. Here you will find extracts, author information, details of forthcoming events and the option to sign up for our newsletters.

Preface

THIS VOLUME EXPLORES the advancement of the human rights of persons with disabilities in federal systems. In doing so, it considers how federal systems facilitate or hinder the implementation of the United Nations Convention on the Rights of Persons with Disabilities (CRPD), or are affected by it in the way they operate. Most importantly, this volume adopts an innovative comparative constitutional perspective, by investigating whether and how the CRPD has impacted on the constitutional design of federal systems, and the extent to which it has affected the distribution of competences between different levels of government. In consequence, this volume is positioned at the intersection of the fields of international human rights law and comparative constitutional law, using comparative federalism as lens of analysis of the implementation of the CRPD.

The editors of this work conceptualised the project on which it is based in 2021, 15 years after the adoption of the CRPD by the UN. This was a fitting point in time to recapitulate and reflect on the implementation and impact of a core human rights treaty on the material constitution of federal states. Further, while international treaties often operate with consideration of the federal characteristics of a participating state, the CRPD provides, in Article 4(5), that its obligations 'extend to all parts of federal States without any limitations or exceptions'. This makes the CRPD an excellent case study of how international human rights treaties impact on federal systems and, conversely, how federal systems can respond to the challenges of implementing and adhering to human rights conventions. The case study is all the more interesting given that the CRPD recognises, in Article 33, the significance of intergovernmental coordination for the full realisation of the rights that it protects.

Despite burgeoning scholarship on the CRPD, there has been a gap in examining it from a federal perspective. The editors of this collection – who bring together expertise in disability law, federalism and constitutional law – have collated a range of contributions that illustrate how the 'transformative potential' of the CRPD has also 'transformed' the interrelations between national and sub-national entities. Most of the chapters suggest that the Convention has augmented the power of the centre, limiting the contribution of sub-national entities or leaving it obscure. Nevertheless, while authors from diverse constitutional traditions may approach the issue differently, most of the chapters also show that experiential federalism has produced successful strategies at the sub-national level that have influenced harmonisation at the centre, as that has occurred. In addition, as might be expected, the chapters by authors from European countries tend to show that the impact of international law on federal arrangements and the material constitution of federal states may be further affected by supranational law. The European Union, itself party to the CRPD, has been an obvious catalyst for this dynamic. On the whole, the volume highlights the significance of interactions between levels of government in multi-level systems, but it also demonstrates that these dynamics deserve more attention than they generally get.

The volume understands federalism broadly and adopts a non-formalistic and functional approach to the coexistence of multiple levels of government that have some degree of organisational autonomy and jurisdictional authority. Such a broad understanding allows the authors to better appreciate how the distribution of powers responds to the protection and promotion of the rights of people with disabilities. It also raises questions about the federal toolkit itself and its implications for the 'transformative potential' of the CRPD, and the quest for inclusive equality. The distribution of governmental powers among different levels of government, which is a characteristic of federal systems, facilitates diversity, but may be detrimental to the equal enjoyment of human rights of persons with disabilities, as several contributors seem to suggest. Even so, federalism has other advantages, in terms of checks and balances and as a potential tool for local responsiveness and for the protection of intersectional identities, where disability is intertwined with ethnic, linguistic, religious and gender differences. In this respect, this volume calls for further investigation as to whether federalism can become a key to implement the capacious view of equality and the protection of diversity that the CRPD envisages.

Transformation and change are never easy or quickly achieved. They begin, however, with the re-conceptualisation of previously held beliefs and the development of new modes of thought. Progress in ideas and attitudes ultimately takes form through policy and legislation and can produce enduring structural change. Whether the CRPD has the power to trigger transformation, and how the processes it has put in train evolve, remain to be seen. Nevertheless, this volume marks the beginning of an exciting opportunity to observe the structural impact of international disability law on federal systems. In doing so, it heralds the emergence of a new subfield – that of comparative disability federalism – to be further studied in greater depth and detail.

Cheryl Saunders
Melbourne, 31 October 2022

Acknowledgements

THIS VOLUME IS the result of a long journey and marks an important collaborative effort. It was first conceived of at a very difficult moment at the outset of the Covid-19 pandemic, and then commenced in 2021. In spite of some delays along the way, we have thoroughly enjoyed the collaboration with fellow colleagues around the world who contributed to this volume. Most authors joined us at the very beginning of this project, and some others came on board at a later stage, but all of them have greatly supported us as editors. First and foremost, we would like to warmly thank them for believing in this project that seeks to connect federal studies, and more broadly constitutional studies, with disability law. We feel this is a first step and more research is due.

Special thanks go to Ms Eva Krolla (Maynooth University), who provided invaluable editorial assistance. Her kindness, patience and attention to detail have been key to bringing the book to completion. Our thanks go also to Ethan Smith and Matthew McKenna who provided editorial help in the final phase of the project and supported a linguistic review of the volume. Finally, we are indebted to Kate Whetter and the whole publishing team at Hart Publishing for believing in this project, as well as for their advice and support throughout the process.

Delia Ferri, Francesco Palermo and Giuseppe Martinico
Maynooth-Verona-Bolzano/Bozen-Pisa, 31 October 2022

Contents

Contributors

Paolo Addis is Postdoctoral Fellow in Constitutional Law at the Dirpolis (Law, Politics and Development) Institute at Scuola Superiore Sant'Anna Pisa (Italy). He teaches Comparative Legal Systems at the University of Pisa.

Francisco J Bariffi is CONEX-Plus Postdoctoral Fellow at Carlos III University in Madrid (Spain) and Deputy Director of the Human Rights Centre at National University of Mar del Plata (Argentina). He is also Coordinator of the Latin-American Network on the UN Convention on the Rights of Persons with Disabilities (www.redcdpd.net).

Jonas-Sébastien Beaudry is Associate Professor, jointly appointed to the Faculty of Law and the Institute for Health and Social Policy at McGill University (Canada), and a member of the Quebec Bar. His research focuses on human rights, ethics and disability theory.

Paloma Breit holds a BA in Humanities (UFABC) and an MBA in Innovation, Technology and Information for Business (UFSCAR) (Brazil). She is an autistic woman working in a technological company designing solutions for the inclusion of Persons with Disabilities.

Peter Bußjäger is Professor of Public Law at the Department of Public Law, State and Administrative Theory, University of Innsbruck (Austria) and the Head of the Institute of Federalism in Innsbruck.

Tinashe C Chigwata is the Head of Multilevel Government at the Dullah Omar Institute for Constitutional Law, Governance and Human Rights, University of the Western Cape (South Africa).

Beza Dessalegn is Assistant Professor of Law at Hawassa University (Ethiopia).

Amita Dhanda is Professor Emerita at NALSAR University of Law, Hyderabad (India).

Daniel Dumont is Professor of Social Security Law at Université Libre de Bruxelles (Belgium), Lawyer and Philosopher. Between 2014 and 2016 he was Vice-President of the Belgian Society for Labour and Social Security Law. His research focuses on Social Protection Systems, Employment and Vocational Training Policies.

Delia Ferri is Professor of Law at the School of Law and Criminology, Maynooth University (Ireland) and Co-Director of the MU Assisting Living and Learning (ALL) Institute.

Yonatan T Fessha is Professor of Law and Research Chair in Constitutional Design in Divided Societies at the University of the Western Cape (South Africa).

Naomi Ghys is Mandate Assistant in Social Security Law and Researcher at the University of Antwerp (Belgium).

Freek Louckx is Professor of Law at the University of Antwerp and the Vrije Universiteit Brussel (Belgium). He teaches on Fundamental Social Rights, Social Security Law and Legal Aspects of the Organisation of Health Care.

Giuseppe Martinico is Professor of Comparative Public Law at the Scuola Superiore Sant'Anna Pisa (Italy) and Director of the Sant'Anna Legal Studies (STALS) Programme.

Kasey McCall-Smith is Senior Lecturer in Public International Law at the Law School of the University of Edinburgh (United Kingdom) and Director of the Global Justice Academy. She is also Executive Chair of the Association of Human Rights Institutes (AHRI).

Matteo Monti is Postdoctoral Researcher in Comparative Constitutional Law at the Department of Political Science of Luiss Guido Carli Rome (Italy). He holds a PhD in Law from Sant'Anna School of Advanced Studies.

Robert D Nanima is Associate Professor at the Faculty of Law, University of the Western Cape (South Africa) and a Research Fellow at the Dullah Omar Institute for Constitutional Law, Governance and Human Rights.

Francesco Palermo is Professor of Comparative Constitutional Law at the University of Verona (Italy) and Head of the Institute for Comparative Federalism at Eurac Research, Bolzano/Bozen (Italy).

Maribel González Pascual is Professor at the Universitat Pompeu Fabra (Spain) and Senior Legal Advisor at the Cabinet of the Ministry on Territorial Policies.

Gilberto MA Rodrigues is Associate Professor at the Federal University of ABC (UFABC) and Head of the Graduate Programme in International Relations in São Paulo (Brazil). He coordinates the CNPq research group – Nucleus for the Study of Federalism and Local Government.

Irene Spigno is the General Director of the Inter-American Academy of Human Rights of the Autonomous University of Coahuila (Mexico), where she is Professor of Human Rights Law and Comparative Constitutional Law.

Neža Šubic is a Legal Officer at the European Commission. Previously, at the time of writing her contribution for this volume, she was a Postdoctoral Researcher at the School of Law and Criminology, Maynooth University (Ireland) working on the ERC-funded project 'Protecting the Right to Culture of Persons with Disabilities and Enhancing Cultural Diversity through European Union Law: Exploring New Paths'.

Felix Welti is Professor for Social and Health Law, Law of Rehabilitation and Disability at the University of Kassel (Germany) and Board Member of the German Association of Rehabilitation Sciences (DGRW).

Abbreviations

AC	*Arresten van het Hof van Cassatie* (Judgments of the Court of Cassation) – Belgium
ADA	Americans with Disabilities Act
ADI	*Acción Directa de Inconstitucionalidad* (Direct Action of Unconstitutionality) – Brazil
AfD	*Alternative für Deutschland* (Alternative for Germany)
AGG	*Allgemeines Gleichbehandlungsgesetz* (General Equal Treatment Act) – Germany
AJPTLRI	Amhara Justice Professionals Training and Legal Research Institute – Ethiopia
ANC	African National Congress – South Africa
ANDIS	*Agencia Nacional de Discapacidad* (National Disability Agency) – Argentina
ASMK	*Arbeits- und Sozialministerkonferenz* (Conference of Ministries for Labour and Social Affairs) – Germany
ASVG	*Allgemeines Sozialversicherungsgesetz* (General Social Insurance Act) – Austria
BAG	*Bundesarbeitsgericht* (Federal Labour Court) – Germany
BAGüS	*Bundesarbeitsgemeinschaft überörtlicher Träger der Sozialhilfe* (Social assistance bodies) – Germany
BBB	*Bundesbehindertenbeirat* (Federal Disability Council) – Austria
BBG	*Bundes-Behindertengesetz* (Federal Law on Persons with Disabilities) – Austria
BEinstG	*Behinderteneinstellungsgesetz* (Employment of Persons with Disabilities Act) – Austria
BFSG	*Barrierefreiheitsstärkungsgesetz* (Accessibility Strengthening Act) – Germany

BGBl	*Bundesgesetzblatt* (Federal Law Gazette) – Austria
BGG	*Behindertengleichstellungsgesetze* (Disability Equality Acts) – Germany
Bgld GPB-A-G	*Burgenländisches Gesundheits-, Patienten- und Behindertenanwaltschaftsgesetz* (Burgenland Health, Patients' and Disabled Persons' Ombudsman Act) – Austria
BGStG	*Bundes-Behindertengleichstellungsgesetz* (Federal Law on the Equality of Persons with Disabilities) – Austria
BMG	*Bundesministeriengesetz* (Federal Ministries Act) – Austria
BMSGPK	*Bundesministerium für Soziales, Gesundheit, Pflege und Konsumentenschutz* (Federal Ministry for Social Affairs, Health, Care and Consumer Protection) – Austria
BRD	*Bundesrepublik Deutschland* (Federal Republic of Germany)
BSG	*Bundessozialgericht* (Federal Social Court) – Germany
BTHG	*Bundesteilhabegesetz* (Federal Participation Act) – Germany
BVerfG	*Bundesverfassungsgericht* (Federal Constitutional Court) – Germany
BVergG 2018	*Bundesvergabegesetz 2018* (Federal Procurement Act 2018) – Austria
B-VG	*Bundes-Verfassungsgesetz* (Federal Constitution) – Austria
CA	Constitutional Amendments
CAF	*Comitê de Articulação Federativa* (Federative Articulation Committee) – Brazil
CC	Constitutional Court – Belgium
CCI	Council of Constitutional Inquiry – Ethiopia
CCOHR	Continuing Committee of Officials on Human Rights – Canada

CDU/CSU	*Christlich Demokratische Union Deutschlands/ Christlich-Soziale Union* (Christian Democratic Union of Germany/Christian Social Union)
CE	*Constitución Española* (Spanish Constitution)
CEDAW	Convention for Elimination of Discrimination Against Women
CERMI	*Comité Español de Representantes de Personas con Discapacidad* (Spanish Committee of Representatives of People with Disabilities)
CESCR	United Nations Committee on Economic, Social and Cultural Rights
CF-88	*Constituição da República Federativa do Brasil de 1988* (Federal Constitution of Brazil 1988)
CFR	Charter of Fundamental Rights of the European Union
CHRC	Canadian Human Rights Commission
CHT	Canada Health Transfer
CI	*Costituzione Italiana* (Italian Constitution)
CIADDIS	*Convención Interamericana para la Eliminación de Todas las Formas de Discriminación contra las Personas con Discapacidad* (Inter-American Convention on the Elimination of All Forms of Discrimination against Persons with Disabilities)
CJEU	Court of Justice of the European Union
CN	*Constitución de la Nación Argentina* (National Constitution of Argentina)
CNDH	*Comisión Nacional de los Derechos Humanos* (National Human Rights Commission) – Mexico
CNJ	*Conselho Nacional de Justiça* (National Council of Justice) – Brazil
CNMP	*Conselho Nacional do Ministério Público* (National Council of the Public Prosecutor's Office) – Brazil
CO	Concluding Observations of the CRPD Committee
COE	Council of Europe

COHOM	Working Party on Human Rights of the Council of the European Union
CONACYT	*Consejo Nacional de Ciencia y Tecnología* (National Council for Science and Technology) – Mexico
CONADE	*Conselho Nacional dos Direitos da Pessoa Portadora de Deficiencia* (National Council for the Rights of People with Disabilities) – Brazil
CONADIS	*Comisión Nacional Asesora para la Integración de las Personas con Discapacidad* (National Advisory Commission on the Integration of Persons with Disabilities) – Argentina
CONADIS	*Consejo Nacional para el Desarrollo y la Inclusión de las Personas con Discapacidad* (National Council for the Development and Inclusion of Persons with Disabilities) – Mexico
CONAPRED	*Consejo Nacional para Prevenir la Discriminación* (National Council to Prevent Discrimination) – Mexico
CONFENEN	*Confederação Nacional dos Estabelecimentos de Ensino* (National Confederation of Educational Establishments) – Brazil
COPIDIS	*Comisión para la Plena Participación e Inclusión de las Personas con Discapacidad* (Commission for the Full Participation and Inclusion of Persons with Disabilities) – Argentina
CRPD	Convention on the Rights of Persons with Disabilities
CRPD Committee	Committee on the Rights of Persons with Disabilities
CSJN	*Corte Suprema de Justicia de la Nación* (Supreme Court of Justice of the Nation) – Argentina
CST	Canada Social Transfer
CUD	*Certificado Único de Discapacidad* (Single Disability Certificate) – Argentina
DA	Democratic Alliance – South Africa
DBR	*Deutscher Behindertenrat* (German Disability Council)
DDA	Disability Discrimination Act 1995 – United Kingdom

DDR	*Deutsche Demokratische Republik* (German Democratic Republic)
DF	*Distrito Federal* (Federal District) – Brazil
DIM	*Deutsches Institut für Menschenrechte* (German Institute for Human Rights)
DIPD	*Decreet betreffende de inclusie van personen met een handicap* (Decree on the Inclusion of Persons with Disabilities) – Belgium
DPCM	*Decreto del Presidente del Consiglio dei Ministri* (Decree by the President of the Council of Ministers) – Italy
DPOs	Disabled People's Organisations
DWYPD	Department of Women, Youth and Persons with Disabilities – South Africa
EAA	European Accessibility Act – European Union
ECHR	European Convention on Human Rights
ECNI	Equality Commission for Northern Ireland
ECSR	European Committee of Social Rights
ECtHR	European Court of Human Rights
EDF	European Disability Forum
EDS	European Disability Strategy 2010–2020 – European Union
EFF	Economic Freedom Fighters – South Africa
EHRC	Equality and Human Rights Commission – United Kingdom
EPRDF	Ethiopian People Revolutionary Democratic Front
EPWCSAH	*Reglementair deel van het Waals Wetboek van Sociale Actie en Gezondheid* (Executive Part of the Walloon Code on Social Action and Health) – Belgium
EqA	Equality Act 2010 – United Kingdom
ERC	European Research Council

ESDC	Employment and Social Development Canada
EU	European Union
FDP	*Freie Demokratische Partei* (Free Democratic Party) – Germany
FEAPD	Federation of Ethiopian Associations of Persons with Disabilities
FIO	*Federación Iberoamericana del Ombudsman* (Ibero-American Ombudsman Federation)
FPFA	*Decreet houdende de persoonsvolgende financiering voor personen met een handicap en tot hervorming van de wijze van financiering van de zorg en de ondersteuning voor personen met een handicap* (Flemish Personal Finance Act) – Belgium
FRA	European Union Agency for Fundamental Rights
FSPA	*Decreet Vlaamse sociale bescherming* (Flemish Social Protection Act) – Belgium
F-VG	*Finanz-Verfassungsgesetz* (Financial Constitutional Act) – Austria
GBER	General Block Exemption Regulation – European Union
GG	*Grundgesetz* (Basic Law) – Germany
GTP	Growth and Transformation Plan – Ethiopia
HoF	House of Federation – Ethiopia
HoPR	House of Peoples Representatives – Ethiopia
HRA 1998	Human Rights Act 1998 – United Kingdom
IBGE	*Instituto Brasileiro de Geografia e Estatística* (Brazilian Institute of Geography and Statistics)
ICC	International Criminal Court
ICD	International Classification of Diseases
ICF	International Classification of Functioning, Disability and Health
ICIDH	International Classification of Impairments, Disabilities and Handicaps

ILO	International Labour Organization
IMNI	Independent Mechanism for Northern Ireland
IMSS	*Instituto Mexicano del Seguro Social* (Mexican Social Security Institute)
INADE	*Instituição Nacional dos Direitos das Pessoas com Deficiência* (National Institution for the Rights of Persons with Disabilities) – Brazil
INADI	*Instituto Nacional contra la Discriminación, la Xenofobia y el Racismo* (National Institute to Combat Discrimination, Xenophobia and Racism) – Argentina
INE	*Instituto Nacional Electoral* (Federal Electoral Institute) – Mexico
KB	*Koninklijk Besluit* (Royal Decree) – Belgium
K-ChG	*Kärntner Chancengleichheitsgesetz* (Carinthian Act of Equality of Chances) – Austria
KMK	*Kultusministerkonferenz* (Conference of Educational Ministers) – Germany
LGIPD	*Ley General para la Inclusión de las Personas con Discapacidad* (General Law for the Inclusion of People with Disabilities) – Mexico
LMAPDs	Labour Market Agreements for Persons with Disabilities – Canada
LMDAs	Labour Market Development Agreements – Canada
MA	*Monitoringausschuss* (Federal Monitoring Committee) – Austria
MEC	Provincial Members of the Executive Council – South Africa
MOLSA	Federal Ministry of Labour and Social Affairs – Ethiopia
MPF	*Ministério Público Federal* (Federal Public Prosecutor's Office) – Brazil
MRE	*Ministério das Relações Exteriores* (Ministry of Foreign Affairs) – Brazil

NA	National Assembly – South Africa
NAP Disability 2012–2020	*Nationaler Aktionsplan Behinderung 2012–2020* (National Action Plan on Disability 2012–2020) – Austria
NAP Disability 2022–2030	*Nationaler Aktionsplan Behinderung 2022–2030* (National Action Plan on Disability 2022–2030) – Austria
NARBSA	National Building Regulations and Building Standards Act of 1977 – South Africa
NCoP	National Council of Provinces – South Africa
NGEU	Next Generation European Union (Plan)
NHRI	National Human Rights Institution
NHRPH	*Nationale Hoge Raad Personen met een Handicap* (National High Council for Persons with Disabilities) – Belgium
NI Act	Northern Ireland Act
NI Executive	Northern Ireland Executive
NIHRC	Northern Ireland Human Rights Commission
NIMCC	National Implementation and Monitoring Coordinating Committee – Ethiopia
NLTA	National Land and Transport Act – South Africa
NPA	National Plan of Action of Persons with Disabilities – Ethiopia
Nö. MTG	*Niederösterreichischer Monitoringgesetz* (Lower Austrian Monitoring Act) – Austria
OAB	*Ordem dos Advogados do Brasil* (Brazilian Bar Association)
OAS	Organization of American States
ODI	Office for Disability Issues – Canada
OHCHR	Office of the United Nations High Commissioner for Human Rights

ÖAR	*Österreichischer Behindertenrat*, formerly known as *Österreichische Arbeitsgemeinschaft für Rehabilitation* (Austrian National Council of Disabled Persons)
ÖBB	*Österreichische Bundesbahnen* (Austrian Federal Railways)
Oö. ADG	*Oberösterreichisches Antidiskriminierungsgesetz* (Upper Austrian Anti-Discrimination Act) – Austria
Oö-ChG	*Oberösterreichisches Chancengleichheitsgesetz* (Upper Austrian Equal Opportunities Act) – Austria
OP-CRPD	Optional Protocol to the Convention on the Rights of Persons with Disabilities
ORF	*Österreichischer Rundfunk* (Austrian Broadcasting Corporation)
ÖVP	*Österreichische Volkspartei* (Austrian People's Party)
OSDP	National Office on the Status of the Disabled People – South Africa
PEPUDA	Promotion of Equality and Prevention of Unfair Discrimination Act – South Africa
PFDC	*Procuradoria Federal dos Direitos do Cidadão* (Federal Prosecutor's Office for the Rights of the Citizen) – Brazil
PGR	*Procurador-Geral da República* (Attorney General of the Republic) – Brazil
PIP	Personal Independence Payment – United Kingdom
PNRR	*Piano Nazionale di Ripresa e Resilienza* (National Recovery and Resilience Plan) – Italy
PNS	*Pesquisa Nacional de Saúde* (National Health Survey) – Brazil
PR	Proportional Representation
PRASA	Passenger Rail Agency of South Africa
PRTR	*Plan de Recuperación, Transformación y Resiliencia* (National Recovery and Resilience Plan) – Spain

PSDB	*Partido da Social Democracia Brasileira* (Brazilian Social Democracy Party)
PSED	Public Sector Equality Duty – United Kingdom
PWDA	Persons with Disabilities (Equal Opportunity, Protection of Rights and Full Participation) Act – India
RIO clause	Regional Integration Organisation clause
RPDA	Rights of Persons with Disabilities Act – India
RV	*Regierungsvorlage* (Government Bill) – Austria
RW	*Rechtskundig Weekblad* (Legal Weekly) – Belgium
SAHRC	South African Human Rights Commission
SAIR	*Bijzondere Wet tot hervorming der instellingen* (Special Act on Institutional Reform) – Belgium
SCJN	*Suprema Corte de Justicia de la Nación* (Supreme Court of Justice of the Nation) – Mexico
SGB	*Sozialgesetzbuch* (Social Code) – Germany
S. GBG	*Salzburger Gleichbehandlungsgesetz* (Salzburg Equal Treatment Act) – Austria
SHRC	Scottish Human Rights Commission
SNDPD	*Secretaria Nacional dos Direitos da Pessoa com Deficiência* (National Secretariat for the Rights of Persons with Disabilities) – Brazil
SPD	*Sozialdemokratische Partei Deutschlands* (Social Democratic Party of Germany)
StBHG	*Steiermärkisches Behindertengesetz* (Styrian Disability Act) – Austria
STF	*Supremo Tribunal Federal* (Supreme Federal Court) – Brazil
S. THG	*Salzburger Teilhabegesetz* (Salzburg Participation Act) – Austria
STJ	*Superior Tribunal de Justiça* (Superior Court of Justice) – Brazil
Strategy 2021–2030	Strategy for the Rights of Persons with Disabilities 2021–2030 – European Union

SUS	*Sistema Único de Saúde* (Unified Health System) – Brazil
TADG 2005	*Tiroler Antidiskriminierungsgesetz* 2005 (Tyrolean Law on Anti-Discrimination) – Austria
TEU	Treaty on the European Union
TFEU	Treaty on the Functioning of the European Union
TSE	*Tribunal Superior Eleitoral* (Superior Electoral Court) – Brazil
TTHG	*Tiroler Teilhabegesetz* (Tyrolean Law on Participation and Inclusion Rights) – Austria
UKIM	United Kingdom Independent Mechanism
UN	United Nations
UNCRC	United Nations Convention of the Rights of the Child
UNGA	United Nations General Assembly
UNHRC	United Nations Human Rights Council
UNIA	*Interfederaal Gelijkekansencentrum* (Interfederal Centre for Equal Opportunities and Combating Racism and Discrimination) – Belgium
UPIAS	Union of Physically Impaired Against Segregation – United Kingdom
UPSC	Union Public Service Commission – India
V ADG	*Vorarlberger Antidiskriminierungsgesetz* (Vorarlberg Anti-Discrimination Act) – Austria
VfSlg	*Sammlung der Erkenntnisse und Beschlüsse des Verfassungsgerichtshofes* (Collection of Judgements of the Constitutional Court) – Austria
WAD	Web Accessibility Directive – European Union
W ADG	*Wiener Antidiskriminierungsgesetz* (Vienna Anti-Discrimination Act) – Austria
WCSAH	*Waals Wetboek van Sociale Actie en Gezondheid* (Walloon Code on Social Action and Health) – Belgium
WDAs	Workforce Development Agreements – Canada

WHO	World Health Organization
WIPO	World Intellectual Property Organization
WPRPD	White Paper on the Rights of Persons with Disabilities – South Africa
WZG	*Web-Zugänglichkeits-Gesetz* (Web Accessibility Act 2019) – Austria

Figures and Tables

Introduction

Conceptual and Methodological Approaches

DELIA FERRI, FRANCESCO PALERMO AND GIUSEPPE MARTINICO

I. STATE OF THE ART AND CORE AIMS OF THE VOLUME

THE YEAR 2021, when this project started, marked the 15th anniversary of the adoption of the United Nations (UN) Convention on the Rights of Persons with Disabilities (CRPD), together with its Optional Protocol (OP-CRPD), by the UN General Assembly in 2006. The CRPD, which entered into force in 2008, less than two years after its approval, is the first international human rights treaty that seeks to ensure the protection and promotion of the rights of persons with disabilities on an equal basis with others. It does not aim to create new rights, but it 'extends existing human rights to take into account the specific experience of persons with disabilit[ies]'.[1] Irrespective of the fact that it imposes onerous obligations on States Parties, requiring them to ensure equal participation of persons with disabilities in political, economic, social and cultural life by accommodating their difference, the CRPD enjoys a high number of ratifications at the global level. It has become a global normative standard and has sketched the roadmap of current disability policy worldwide.[2]

Much attention has been paid to the CRPD as a core human rights treaty[3] within the broader realm of international human rights law.[4] Disability law

[1] F Mégret, 'The Disabilities Convention: Human Rights of Persons with Disabilities or Disability Rights?' (2008) 30 *Human Rights Quarterly* 494.

[2] A Broderick and D Ferri, *International and European Disability Law. Text, Cases and Materials* (Cambridge University Press, 2019).

[3] See commentary by I Bantekas, MA Stein and D Anastasiou, *The UN Convention on the Rights of Persons with Disabilities: A Commentary* (Oxford University Press, 2018).

[4] See eg G De Beco, *Disability in International Human Rights Law* (Oxford University Press, 2021); P Blanck and E Flynn (eds), *Routledge Handbook of Disability Law and Human Rights* (Taylor & Francis Group, 2017); G de Beco, 'The Indivisibility of Human Rights and the Convention on the Rights of Persons with Disabilities' (2019) 68 *International & Comparative Law Quarterly* 141–60; EJ Kakoullis and K Johnson (eds), *Recognising Human Rights in Different Cultural Contexts: The United Nations Convention on the Right of Persons with Disabilities (CRPD)* (Palgrave Macmillan, 2020).

scholars have also investigated how the obligations set out in the CRPD have been fulfilled by selected States Parties in distinct domains, such as, inter alia, education[5] or mental health.[6] In that connection, several contributions have analysed changes in policymaking and legislative advancements driven by the Convention.[7] Other scholarly work has questioned the extent to which the CRPD can act as a driver to improve the lives of people with disabilities.[8] Comparative work on the implementation of the CRPD by domestic courts has been edited by Waddington and Lawson;[9] however, very little research has been undertaken on the impact that the CRPD has had on constitutional structures and, even less so regarding the division of powers in federal systems.[10]

The scant scholarship on the interrelation between federalism and disability law for the most part predates the CRPD and is characterised by the absence of a human-rights approach to disability.[11] In many instances, work related to federalism and the rights of persons with disabilities concerns the United States. In 1993, Percy published a piece on the Americans with Disabilities Act (ADA) and its pre-empting effects on states and local governments.[12] He explored the evolution of regulatory federalism through the lens of disability rights, suggesting that the federal level had, in substance, acquired a dominant

[5] G de Beco, J Lord and S Quinlivan (eds), *The Right to Inclusive Education in International Human Rights Law* (Cambridge University Press, 2019); J Biermann, *Translating Human Rights in Education: The Influence of Article 24 UN CRPD in Nigeria and Germany* (University of Michigan Press, 2022).

[6] P Weller, *New Law and Ethics in Mental Health Advance Directives: The Convention on the Rights of Persons with Disabilities and the Right to Choose* (Routledge, 2013).

[7] G de Beco (ed), *Article 33 of the UN Convention on the Rights of Persons with Disabilities: National Structures for the Implementation and Monitoring of the Convention* (Martinus Nijhoff Publishers, 2013). See also D Ferri and A Broderick (eds), *Research Handbook on EU Disability Law* (Edward Elgar, 2020).

[8] E Flynn, *From Rhetoric to Action: Implementing the UN Convention on the Rights of Persons with Disabilities* (Cambridge University Press, 2011).

[9] L Waddington and A Lawson, *The UN Convention on the Rights of Persons with Disabilities in Practice. A Comparative Analysis of the Role of Courts* (Oxford University Press, 2018).

[10] Following a functional and non-formalistic approach to the ever-lasting issue of defining federalism (see F Palermo and K Kössler, *Comparative Federalism. Constitutional Arrangements and Case Law* (Hart Publishing, 2017)), the term 'federal system' is used to indicate all those constitutional systems in which at least two political tiers of government exist, thereby combining self-rule and shared rule and thus making use (to a greater or lesser extent) of the federal toolkit. Accordingly, the term federal system (or federal state/country) is used not only to denominate fully fledged federal states, defined as such by the respective constitution, but also regional or devolved states or multilevel polities such as the European Union. What justifies the inclusion of such systems in the broader category is that, like fully fledged federations, they are constitutionally unitary states, subordinated to the national constitution and with constitutionally entrenched political autonomy of the subnational units. See also below, section III of this introduction.

[11] D Cameron and V Fraser (eds), *Disability and Federalism: Comparing Different Approaches to Full Participation* (Institute of Intergovernmental Relations, 2001). See also MJ Prince, 'Canadian Federalism and Disability Policy Making' (2001) 34 (4) *Canadian Journal of Political Science/Revue Canadienne De Science Politique* 791.

[12] S Percy, 'ADA, Disability Rights, and Evolving Regulatory Federalism' (1993) 23 *Publius: The Journal of Federalism* 87–106.

role in producing and enforcing norms on non-discrimination on the ground of disability, reducing the authority of state and local governments to create and implement their own disability rights measures. In 2001, Gottesman[13] focused on the Supreme Court's cases on the ADA and, in particular, on *University of Alabama Board of Trustees v Garret*, in which the Court declared the ADA unconstitutional insofar as it allowed private citizens to recover damages against the states in cases of discrimination on the ground of disability.[14] Alongside recent US scholarship that has commented on (and criticised) the failure to ratify the CRPD,[15] scholars have lately attempted to engage with federalist approaches. In particular, Barsky discussed the extent to which local and state governments have supported the CRPD and subtly 'implemented' it, even in absence of ratification.[16] He identified a form of 'an uncooperative' federalism whereby 'many cities and counties have denounced the Senate's refusal to ratify the CRPD through resolutions and other expressive policies' and states 'have also enacted measures to push the Senate in the direction of ratification'.[17] Further, he posits that several states have enacted legislation to support the exercise of legal capacity, signalling 'to the rest of the world that U.S. subnational entities are committed to the international causes of disability justice and human rights',[18] arguing that the CRPD exerted important influence on the United States' guardianship reforms and stimulating federal coordination.

The potential of the CRPD to impact on the federal structure, even in a country, such as the United States, that has not ratified it, emerges blatantly in Barsky's piece, and raises important research questions which have not yet been addressed. In that regard, this volume aims to fill an ostensible gap in literature. It investigates how the CRPD is implemented by different components of federal systems, in a selected number of federal or federal-like countries, by examining the role of the national vis-à-vis subnational entities in the implementation of the Convention, with the view of understanding whether the ratification of the CRPD has had an impact on federal governance and what such impact has been.

Comparative federal studies have consistently highlighted that, in federal systems, the autonomy of subnational entities is constrained (at least to a certain degree) by the protection of fundamental rights enshrined at the

[13] MH Gottesman, 'Disability, Federalism, and a Court with an Eccentric Mission' (2001) 89 *Georgetown Law Faculty Publications and Other Works* 31–107. For an analysis of previous case law, see also RC Hartley, 'The New Federalism and the ADA: State Sovereign Immunity from Private Damage Suits after Boerne' (1999) 24 *NYU Review of Law & Social Change* 67.

[14] *University of Alabama Board of Trustees v Garret* (99–1240) 531 US 356 (2001) 193 F3d 1214.

[15] AS Kanter, 'Let's Try Again: Why the United States Should Ratify the United Nations Convention on the Rights of People with Disabilities' (2019) 35 *Touro Law Review*.

[16] BA Barsky, 'Dual Federalism, Constitutional Openings, and the Convention on the Rights of Persons with Disabilities' (2022) 24 *Journal of Constitutional Law* 345–411.

[17] Ibid 350.

[18] Ibid 351.

federal level.[19] It has also been observed that the respect of international obligations undertaken by federal governments can trigger a centralising dynamic in the exercise of legislative powers.[20] Palermo and Kössler also suggested that it is necessary for federal studies to look more carefully at *policies*, including how they are managed on the basis of legal norms and how they are interpreted by courts.[21] Along these lines, this volume looks at disability policies, and at their development further to the ratification of the CRPD. It, hence, engages with the way in which federal systems have managed the 'complexities' arising from the CRPD, with a view of understanding whether the protection and promotion of disability rights mandated by the Convention has increased the exercise of federal powers and provoked a sort of federal pre-emption, or whether the national and subnational entities have exercised their autonomous powers to the fullest extent. In that vein, the volume aims to explore whether national measures aimed to implement the CRPD have or have not abridged the powers of national and subnational entities.

After having highlighted the core aims of this volume and how they situate in current literature, this introductory chapter moves on to provide an overview of the core tenets of the CRPD. It does not aim to give a comprehensive overview of the Convention. Rather, it focuses on its most notable features and its inherent novelties. It then explains the concept of federalism embraced by the volume. Notably, the substantive understanding of federalism adopted by this volume allows for the inclusion of countries, and even supranational organisations such as the EU, that refrain from classic federal terminology in their constitutions, but work according to the federal principle by combining self-rule and shared rule.[22] Finally, the chapter presents the methodological approach and the overall structure adopted. Being premised on the idea of addressing a diverse readership, the volume blends constitutional theory, legal and policy analysis.

II. THE UN CONVENTION ON THE RIGHTS OF PERSONS WITH DISABILITIES: NOVELTIES AND COMPLEXITIES

A. The Genesis of Disability Rights and the Long Road Towards the CRPD

Disability has traditionally been considered a mere individual deficit, deriving from a disease hampering physiological or cognitive functioning,[23] and conceived

[19] F Palermo and K Kössler, *Comparative Federalism. Constitutional Arrangements and Case Law* (Hart Publishing, 2017) 321.
[20] Ibid.
[21] Ibid.
[22] DJ Elazar, *Exploring Federalism* (University of Alabama Press, 1987) 5.
[23] C Drum, 'Models and Approaches to Disability' in C Drum, G Krahn and H Bersani (eds), *Disability and Public Health* (American Public Health Association/American Association on Intellectual and Developmental Disabilities, 2009).

of as a personal tragic destiny. This 'medical model' of disability, which considered people with disabilities unable to participate in society as the result of their own impairments, began to be confronted by disability activists in the 1960s, both in the United States[24] and in the United Kingdom.[25] In the 1970s, the British Union of Physically Impaired Against Segregation (UPIAS) elaborated the idea that society disables people with impairments. UPIAS distinguished the 'impairment' itself from the social 'situation' of people with impairments,[26] the latter giving rise to a 'disability'. On the basis of UPIAS' manifesto, Michael Oliver, probably the best-known UK disabled academic, further expounded a conception of disability as a societal construction, currently termed the 'social model of disability'.[27]

The 'social model of disability' and its countless academic elaborations[28] and critical accounts[29] have stimulated the international development of disability rights as a key element of the UN's work.[30] From 1970 to 1980, according to Degener and Begg, persons with disabilities became recognised as 'subjects of rehabilitation',[31] while tentative signs of a rights-based approach to disability became evident, for example, in the Declaration on the Rights of Disabled Persons.[32] Degener and Begg note that, from 1980 to 2000, persons with disabilities became 'objects of human rights',[33] and the 1993 (non-binding) Standard Rules on the Equalization of Opportunities for Persons with Disabilities[34]

[24] For an historical account, see P Blanck et al., *Disability Civil Rights Law and Policy: Case and Materials*, 3rd edn (West Publishers, 2014) 4–8; F Pelka, *What We Have Done: An Oral History of the Disability Rights Movement* (University of Massachusetts Press, 2012); JI Charlton, *Nothing About Us Without Us: Disability Oppression and Empowerment* (University of California Press, 1998); I Zola, *Missing Pieces: A Chronicle of Living with a Disability* (Temple University Press, 1982); LJ Davis, *Enabling Acts: The Hidden Story of How the Americans with Disabilities Act Gave the Largest US Minority Its Rights* (Beacon Press, 2015).

[25] H Meekosha and A Jakubowicz, 'Disability, Political Activism, and Identity Making: A Critical Feminist Perspective on the Rise of Disability Movements in Australia, the USA and the UK' (1999) 19 *Disability Studies Quarterly* 393–404.

[26] Union of Physically Impaired Against Segregation (UPIAS), *Fundamental Principles of Disability* (The Disability Alliance, 1976) 4.

[27] Inter alia M Oliver, *Understanding Disability: from Theory to Practice* (Macmillan Education, 1996).

[28] Among many others, see E Barnes, 'Constructing Disability' in E Barnes (ed), *The Minority Body: A Theory of Disability* (Oxford University Press, 2016).

[29] For a critique of the social model, see T Shakespeare, *Disability Rights and Wrongs* (Routledge, 2006). See also J Morris, *Pride Against Prejudice: Transforming Attitudes to Disability: A Personal Politics of Disability* (Women's Press, 1991) 10.

[30] A Kanter, *The Development of Disability Rights under International Law: From Charity to Human Rights* (Routledge, 2017).

[31] T Degener and A Begg, 'From Invisible Citizens to Agents of Change: A Short History of the Struggle for the Recognition of the Rights of Persons with Disabilities at the United Nations' in V Della Fina, R Cera and G Palmisano (eds), *The United Nations Convention on the Rights of Persons with Disabilities: A Commentary* (Springer, 2017) 2.

[32] UN Declaration on the Rights of Disabled Persons, 09 December 1975, UN General Assembly (UNGA) Resolution 3447.

[33] Degener and Begg (n 31) 4.

[34] UNGA, 'UN Standard Rules on the Equalization of Opportunities for Persons with Disabilities', Resolution 48/96, Annex of 20 December 1993.

represented a momentous political commitment to realising equality for persons with disabilities. The new millennium represented a crossroads, in that 'international disability policy became a rights-based policy',[35] and a binding treaty to ensure equal rights to persons with disabilities was indicated as the key objective to be achieved. An Ad Hoc Committee was set up in December 2001 by the UN with the mandate to draft a comprehensive international convention.[36] This Ad Hoc Committee released the text of the CRPD, which, as mentioned above, was formally adopted by the UN on 13 December 2006, entering into force on 3 May 2008.

B. The Transformative Potential of the CRPD

It is often highlighted that the CRPD ushered in a new era of disability rights. With its Preamble, which is quite long and detailed, and 50 articles, it '[forges] new ground and requires new thinking'.[37] The OP-CRPD, accompanying the Convention, enables any individual in a State Party to the Convention to bring a claim in respect of an alleged violation of his/her rights through submitting an individual communication to the UN Committee on the Rights of Persons with Disabilities (CRPD Committee), the treaty body attached to the CRPD. The OP-CRPD also entrusts the CRPD Committee with the power to launch *ex officio* inquiries into 'grave and systematic' violations of the rights provided for in the Convention.

The transformative potential of the CRPD is linked to the fact that it recasts disability as a social construct and abandons the outdated medical model of disability. In doing so, the Convention focuses on the removal of barriers to ensure the equal exercise and enjoyment of rights by persons with disabilities and their full participation in society. In this connection, the CRPD is said to encapsulate the social-contextual model of disability.[38] In fact, Article 1 CRPD acknowledges that 'disability results from the *interaction* between persons with impairments and attitudinal and environmental barriers that hinder their full and effective participation in society on an equal basis with others' (emphasis added).[39] Notably, Article 1 CRPD

[35] Degener and Begg (n 31) 4.

[36] The General Assembly renewed the mandate of the Ad Hoc Committee four times from 2002 to 2005 (Resolutions 57/229 of 18 December 2002, 58/246 of 23 December 2003, 59/198 of 20 December 2004 and 60/232 of 23 December 2005).

[37] N Pillay, *The Convention on the Rights of Persons with Disabilities* (Training Guide, Professional Training Series No 19, United Nations Publication, 2014).

[38] The term 'social-contextual model' was used by A Broderick, *The Long and Winding Road to Equality and Inclusion for Persons with Disabilities* (Intersentia, 2015) 77. Several authors still refer to the CRPD as embracing the social model of disability (inter alia, A Arstein-Kerslake, *Restoring Voice to People with Cognitive Disabilities. Realizing the Right to Equal Recognition before the Law* (Cambridge University Press, 2017) 72).

[39] See also Preamble para (e) CRPD.

allows for a dynamic approach that can facilitate adaptations over time and in different socio-economic settings, and does not set forth any distinction between different categories of disability.

The novelty of the CRPD also arises from the embedment of the 'human rights model of disability', which has been elaborated by Degener.[40] Without engaging in a thorough discussion of this model, it suffices here to recall some of its core features. Degener argues that this model emphasises the human dignity of persons with disabilities, and 'encompasses both sets of human rights, civil and political as well as economic, social and cultural rights'. She suggests, inter alia, that the human rights model values impairments as part of human diversity, paying attention to intersectional discrimination. Further, the human rights model 'offers room for minority and cultural identification'.[41]

Skarstad and Stein contend that the CRPD embraces a human rights approach to disability and claim that the CRPD 'precipitated a dramatic sea change in the relative human rights empowerment of persons with disabilities by recognizing their equal dignity, autonomy, and worth, and by ensuring their equal enjoyment of all human rights and fundamental freedoms'.[42] In a similar vein, Celik suggests that 'the CRPD brings a new dimension to the perception of "human" in the legal arena, through challenging the very liberal notions attached to it; by bringing a solid insight into the concepts of dignity and traditional autonomy'.[43] In fact, the transformative potential and the innovative character of the CRPD is enshrined in its normative principles that include respect for human dignity, non-discrimination and equality, accessibility, and participation. The foregoing principles, read jointly, endeavour to ensure inclusion, redress disadvantage, and address stigma.

The principle of non-discrimination has been described as the 'leitmotif' of the CRPD,[44] as it cuts across both civil and political rights, such as the right to legal capacity, and economic, social and cultural rights, such as the right to education. Article 2 CRPD provides a broad definition of discrimination on the ground of disability, stating that such discrimination comprises the denial of reasonable accommodation, whereby reasonable accommodation is any 'necessary and appropriate modification and adjustments', 'where needed in a particular case, to ensure to persons with disabilities the enjoyment or exercise on an equal basis with others of all human rights and fundamental

[40] T Degener, 'A New Human Rights Model of Disability' in V Della Fina, R Cera and G Palmisano (eds), *The United Nations Convention on the Rights of Persons with Disabilities: A Commentary* (Springer, 2017) 41.

[41] Ibid.

[42] K Skarstad and MA Stein, 'Mainstreaming Disability in the United Nations Treaty Bodies' (2018) 17 *Journal of Human Rights* 1.

[43] E Celik, 'The Role of CRPD in Rethinking the Subject of Human Rights' (2017) 21 *The International Journal of Human Rights* 933–95.

[44] O Mjöll Arnardóttir, 'A Future of Multidimensional Disadvantage Equality' in O Mjöll Arnardóttir and G Quinn (eds), *The UN Convention on the Rights of Persons with Disabilities: European and Scandinavian Perspectives* (Martinus Nijhoff Publishers, 2009) 41.

freedoms'. The duty to provide reasonable accommodation must be distinguished from accessibility, which, as noted above, is another core principle of the Convention.

Article 9 CRPD requires States Parties to take appropriate measures to ensure that people with disabilities have access to environments, facilities, information and services on an equal basis with others. Accessibility duties are generalised and group-based, as well as anticipatory (*ex tunc*).[45] Moreover, Article 4(1) CRPD includes an array of obligations that are linked to the realisation of the principle of accessibility. These encompass the duty to engage in or promote the research and development of new technologies[46] and the requirement for States Parties to provide accessible information.[47] The CRPD Committee identifies accessibility as an essential 'precondition' for the enjoyment of other human rights and as 'a means to achieve *de facto* equality for all persons with disabilities'.[48] The principle of participation and inclusion of people with disabilities in society is also a core feature of the Convention. In fact, the CRPD requires the involvement of persons with disabilities in society, and in all spheres of policymaking.[49] Ensuring participation of persons with disabilities is particularly important for fostering awareness-raising and promoting respect for the rights and dignity of persons with disabilities.[50]

The normative principles of respect for human dignity, non-discrimination and equality, accessibility, and participation converge in the concept of inclusive equality, which is embodied in the CRPD. This concept, which is said to go beyond that of substantive equality,[51] embraces four intertwined dimensions: a fair *redistributive* dimension, which refers to the need to address socioeconomic disadvantages; a *recognition* dimension, which requires the combatting of stigma and recognition of dignity and intersectionality; a *participative* dimension, which necessitates the recognition of the social nature of people with disabilities as members of society; and an *accommodating* dimension, which entails making space for difference as a matter of human dignity.[52]

[45] CRPD Committee, 'General Comment No. 2 on accessibility' (2014) CRPD/C/GC/2; See also CRPD Committee, 'General Comment No. 6 on equality and non-discrimination' (2018) CRPD/C/GC/6, paras 23 *et seq*.

[46] Art 4(g) CRPD.

[47] Art 4(h) CRPD.

[48] CRPD Committee, 'General Comment No. 5 on living independently and being included in the community' (2017) CRPD/C/GC/5, para 40.

[49] CRPD Committee, 'General Comment No. 7 on the participation of persons with disabilities, including children with disabilities, through their representative organizations, in the implementation and monitoring of the Convention' (2018) CRPD/C/GC/7.

[50] Ibid para 76.

[51] CRPD Committee, 'General Comment No. 6' (n 45); See also T Degener and M Uldry, 'Towards inclusive equality: 10 years Committee of the Rights of Persons with Disabilities' (German Federal Ministry of Labour and Social Affairs, 2018).

[52] CRPD Committee, 'General Comment No. 6' (n 45), para 11.

Articles 10 to 30 CRPD enumerate specific rights that the Convention promotes and protects. These encompass civil, political, economic, social and cultural rights. Among these provisions, central to the CRPD is the right of persons with disabilities to legal capacity (ie, the capacity to be a holder of rights and the capacity to act under the law) enshrined in Article 12.[53] This Article also imposes on States Parties the obligation to provide persons with disabilities with adequate supports in the exercise of their legal capacity, in order to enable them to make decisions that have legal effect. Support provided in the exercise of legal capacity must respect the rights, will and preferences of a person with a disability, and it should never amount to substitute decision-making.[54] While Article 12 has been quite 'controversial',[55] it has also been deemed revolutionary in that it challenges the traditional approaches to legal capacity and guardianship systems.[56] Closely related to Article 12 is Article 19 CRPD, which contains the right to live independently and be included in the community, prohibiting institutionalisation and segregation of persons with disabilities.

In particular, although not exclusively, Article 24 on the right to education, Article 25 on the right to health, Article 27 on the right to work, Article 28 on the right to social protection and Article 30 CRPD on the right to participation in cultural life, place, to different degrees, a focus on the inclusion and participation of persons with disabilities in society. Kayess and French suggest that these provisions oblige States Parties to incorporate 'disability sensitive measures into mainstream service delivery' and to ensure 'the provision of necessary specialist services and special measures in a manner that facilitates the inclusion and participation of persons with disability within the general community'.[57]

Article 4(2) CRPD reiterates the traditional distinction between rights that are subject to immediate implementation (ie civil and political rights) and those that are to be realised progressively (ie economic, social and cultural rights). It recognises that States Parties are allowed to realise socio-economic rights progressively, with a view to achieving their full protection and promotion over time, because the realisation of such rights is often heavily dependent on the availability of resources. However, as argued by Stein,[58] the CRPD blurs the

[53] C de Bhailís and E Flynn, 'Recognising Legal Capacity: Commentary and Analysis of Article 12 CRPD' (2017) 13 *International Journal of Law in Context* 6.

[54] CRPD Committee, 'General Comment No. 1 Article 12: Equal recognition before the law' (2014) CRPD/C/GC/1, para 17.

[55] Among many others, see M Scholten and J Gather, 'Adverse Consequences of Article 12 of the UN Convention on the Rights of Persons with Disabilities for Persons with Mental Disabilities and an Alternative Way Forward' (2018) 44 *Journal of Medical Ethics* 226; and A Pearl, 'Article 12 of the United Nations Convention on the Rights of Persons with Disabilities and the Legal Capacity of Disabled People: The Way Forward?' (2013) 1 *Leeds Journal of Law and Criminology* 1, 7.

[56] P Cuenca Gómez et al., 'The Impact of Article 12 of the Convention on the Rights of Persons with Disabilities on Qatar's Private Law' (2017) 9 *The Age of Human Rights Journal* 81, 82.

[57] R Kayess and P French, 'Out of Darkness into Light? Introducing the Convention on the Rights of Persons with Disabilities'(2008) 8 *Human Rights Law Review* 31.

[58] MA Stein, 'Disability Human Rights' (2007) 95 *California Law Review* 75.

distinction between these traditional categories of rights and has 'compounded the different categories of rights' throughout its provisions.[59] For example, several CRPD rights which fall under the traditional category of socio-economic rights (eg, the right to education) encompass reasonable accommodation obligations (which need to be immediately realised), while civil and political rights in the CRPD require positive measures and expenditure on the part of states. In doing so, the Convention emphasises the interconnectedness between civil and political rights and socio-economic rights.

C. The Implementation of the CRPD and its Complexities

Overall, the CRPD can be considered 'the single most exciting development in the disability field in decades'[60] and a 'catalyst for change'.[61] To effect that change, the CRPD itself recognises that implementation and monitoring are essential.

States Parties are required to adopt legislative, administrative, financial, judicial and all other necessary measures to ensure the realisation of the object and purpose of the CRPD. They must review and amend national laws and policies to ensure compliance with the CRPD. Article 4(1)(c) CRPD requires that States Parties mainstream disability in all their policies, and Article 4(1)(d) CRPD obliges States Parties to ensure that public authorities and institutions act in compliance with the Convention. As it is typical for international treaties, there are no specific references in these provisions to the role of the national and subnational levels of governments. Also, there is no definition of 'public authorities and institutions' in the CRPD itself, as these will be identified at the domestic level, in light of the constitutional arrangements of that country, following the still predominant 'federal blindness' approach of international law.[62] However, those provisions must be read in conjunction with Article 4(5) CRPD, which affirms that the obligations laid out in the Convention 'extend to all parts of federal States without any limitations or exceptions'. The latter norm is designed to ensure that both subnational and federal authorities fulfil their implementation obligations under the Convention.

[59] G de Beco, 'The Indivisibility of Human Rights and the Convention on the Rights of Persons with Disabilities' (2019) 68 *International and Comparative Law Quarterly* 141.

[60] de Bhailís and Flynn (n 53) 7, citing G Quinn, 'A Short Guide to the United Nations Convention on the Rights of Persons with Disabilities' in G Quinn and L Waddington (eds), *European Yearbook on Disability Law: Volume 1* (Intersentia, 2009) 89.

[61] L Arbour, 'Statement by Louise Arbour UN High Commissioner for Human Rights on the Ad Hoc Committee's Adoption of the Convention on the Rights of Persons with Disabilities' (New York, 5 December 2006).

[62] *Föderalismusblindheit* – see HP Ipsen, 'Als Bundesstaat in der Gemeinschaft' in E von Caemmerer, HJ Schlochauer and E Steindorff, *Probleme des Europäischen Rechts. Festschrift für Walter Hallstein zu seinem 65. Geburtstag* (Klostermann, 1966) 248.

The CRPD, as with other international treaties, includes a specific Regional Integration Organisation clause (RIO clause) specifically aimed at accommodating the European Union's (EU) peculiar legal nature and allowing it to ratify the Convention. Article 44 CRPD defines a 'Regional integration organization' as 'an organization constituted by sovereign States of a given region, to which its member States have transferred competence in respect of matters governed by the present Convention'. Interestingly, Article 44 also provides that the RIO must 'declare, in their instruments of formal confirmation or accession, the extent of their competence with respect to matters governed by the present Convention'. While the division of powers which is internal to a federal state remains entirely a domestic matter, the sharing of competences between the EU and its Member States acquires relevance, but only in the context of international responsibility.[63]

Notably, the CRPD recognises that the full realisation of human rights depends on appropriate governance mechanisms. It obliges States Parties to put in place structures at the domestic level with a view to facilitating the implementation of the Convention and to monitor such implementation. Article 33 CRPD sets forth the obligations to: designate one or more focal points to implement the CRPD (Article 33(1) CRPD); give due consideration to the establishment of a mechanism to coordinate the implementation process (Article 33(1) CRPD); and put in place a structure to protect, promote and monitor the implementation of the Convention (Article 33(2) CRPD). In addition, Article 33(3) CRPD requires States Parties to involve civil society, in particular disabled people's organisations (DPOs) in monitoring processes. Quinn suggests that Article 33 in its entirety is a key innovation, with the potential to transform the 'majestic generalities' of the Convention into concrete reform at the domestic level.[64]

The focal point must be set up within the government for matters relating to the implementation of the Convention, and resources must be allocated to carry out its function and collaborate with persons with disabilities.[65] However, Article 33(1) CRPD leaves a margin of discretion to the State Party on whether to create a single focal point or multiple focal points (both horizontally – by creating multiple focal points in the national government, and vertically – by creating focal points at the subnational level), although Manca suggests that, during the negotiations on the CRPD, a strong preference for

[63] On RIO clauses and Declarations of Competence, see inter alia A Delgado Casteleiro, 'EU Declarations of Competence to Multilateral Agreements: A Useful Reference Base?' (2012) 17 *European Foreign Affairs Review* 491.

[64] G Quinn, 'Resisting the "Temptation of Elegance": Can the Convention on the Rights of Persons with Disabilities Socialise States to Right Behaviour?' in O Mjöll Arnardóttir and G Quinn (eds), *The UN Convention on the Rights of Persons with Disabilities: European and Scandinavian Perspectives* (Martinus Nijhoff Publishers, 2009) 215, 217.

[65] Office of the United Nations High Commissioner for Human Rights (OHCHR), 'Thematic study by the Office of the United Nations High Commissioner for Human Rights on the structure and role of national mechanisms for the implementation and monitoring of the Convention on the Rights of Persons with Disabilities' (2009) A/HRC/13/29.

multiple focal points was expressed.[66] Aichele even maintains that Article 33 CRPD could be read as imposing an obligation on federal states for each of the governments to have a focal point.[67] In fact, during the drafting process, federal states had 'pointed out that it would be in the interests of their regions to be equipped with focal points that would enable them to ensure their inner sovereignty'.[68]

Article 33(1) CRPD also requires States Parties to 'give due consideration to the establishment or designation of a coordination mechanism within government to facilitate related action in different sectors and at different levels'. The establishment or designation of a coordination mechanism is not a legal obligation, however, and the distinction between the functions of the focal point and the coordination mechanism remains vague and blurred. Nonetheless, in decentralised states, the establishment of the coordination mechanism should be of vital importance to ensure the smooth implementation of the Convention across different levels of government. In that regard, taking into account previous research,[69] this volume investigates whether traditional institutional forms of territorial participation have been replicated into the focal point, and whether the coordination mechanism in Article 33 CRPD acts as a 'transmission belt' between the national and the subnational entities' governments.

It is evident that the CRPD necessitates States Parties to intervene on their governance structures. By including provisions such as Article 4(5) and Article 33(1), the drafters of the CRPD were somewhat mindful of the particular challenges that the implementation of the CRPD brings about in federal systems, where competences on pivotal areas, such as eg accessibility, are shared between national and subnational levels. However, these provisions have not prevented gaps in the implementation. Furthermore, a lack of coordination has progressively emerged in federal systems and has been highlighted by the CRPD Committee in its Concluding Observations on States Parties reports. A recent report, written by Wooding for the European Blind Union, indicates the lack of coordination as an issue in some of the federal countries examined. A shortage of coordination efforts between cantons was reported with regard to Switzerland, while in Belgium the 'complexity of governing arrangements made effective participation [of persons with disabilities] problematic'. In a more general fashion, '[l]ack of coordination was evident, where

[66] L Manca, 'Article 33: National Implementation and Monitoring' in V Della Fina, R Cera and G Palmisano (eds), *The United Nations Convention on the Rights of Persons with Disabilities: A Commentary* (Springer, 2017) 591.

[67] Ibid 989.

[68] V Aichele, 'Article 33 National Implementation and Monitoring' in I Bantekas, MA Stein and D Anastasiou (eds), *The UN Convention on the Rights of Persons with Disabilities: A Commentary* (Oxford University Press, 2018) 985.

[69] de Beco (n 7).

not enough focal points were present at the various levels of government or across ministries'.[70]

Article 33(2) CRPD obliges States Parties to create 'a framework, including one or more independent mechanisms, as appropriate, to promote, protect and monitor implementation' of the Convention. What may constitute a framework is not defined in Article 33(2). Nevertheless, this provision requires States Parties to designate or establish one or more bodies as part of the framework.[71] The framework should include 'one or more independent mechanisms' that comply with the 'Principles relating to the Status of National Institutions for the Promotion and Protection of Human Rights (NHRIs)' (also known as the Paris Principles),[72] which sketch out the responsibilities, composition and working methods of NHRIs, placing emphasis on independence and pluralism. The responsibilities of the independent mechanisms within the framework include: awareness-raising activities to ensure that a human rights approach to disability is adopted; the power to deal with individual claims related to violations of the rights provided for in the CRPD; and the assessment of the extent to which the CRPD has been effectively implemented.

As noted above, Article 33(3) CRPD establishes that 'civil society, in particular persons with disabilities and their representative organizations, shall be involved and participate fully in the monitoring process'. This provision tallies with Article 4(3) CRPD which requires in a general fashion close consultation with, and active involvement of, disabled people, through their representative organisations, in the development and implementation of legislation and policies and in all decision-making processes concerning issues relating to persons with disabilities. These norms are considered to stem from the participatory process that characterised the negotiation of the CRPD and reflect the slogan of the disability rights movement 'Nothing About Us Without Us'. On the whole, the CRPD demonstrates that the full realisation of human rights of persons with disabilities only passes through a participatory approach to implementation and monitoring.

III. FEDERALISM AS A THEORETICAL FRAMEWORK

Federalism and related concepts are some of the most studied topics in social, political and legal sciences and beyond. In fact, federalism is at the heart of one

[70] S Woodin, 'Monitoring of the Rights of Blind and Partially-Sighted People in Europe: An Analysis of the European Blind Union CRPD Database – Article 33: National Implementation and Monitoring' (European Blind Union, 2019).

[71] Ibid.

[72] Annex to the UN General Assembly, 'National institutions for the promotion and protection of human rights' (1993) A/RES/48/134. The Paris Principles provide a short set of minimum standards for National Human Rights Institutions (NHRIs), organised under four headings: 1. Competence and responsibilities; 2. Composition and guarantees of independence and pluralism; 3. Methods of operation; 4. Additional principles concerning the status of commissions with quasi-[judicial] competence.

of the most pressing challenges in the history of mankind: how to order public life and how to limit, organise and regulate power in a way that guarantees freedom and efficiency, unity and plurality, autonomy and coordination. At the same time, defining federalism and classifying federal states has always been a matter of contention and is ultimately impossible.[73] In 1994, Elazar estimated that about half of around 180 sovereign states in the world were federal or had some form of federal arrangement,[74] whereas, just a few years later, another leading scholar in the field, Ronald Watts, determined that only 23 fully fledged federal states existed in the world.[75] As a matter of fact, federalism is deeply contextual about how to achieve the ideal goal of, as put by Wheare, 'dividing powers so that the general and regional governments are each, within a sphere, co-ordinate and independent'.[76] What really matters from a legal perspective is the practical purpose of federalism as a set of measures and instruments that balance unity and diversity, autonomy and integration, self-rule and shared rule.[77]

The volume adopts a comparative federalism perspective. In line with the most recent studies,[78] we adopt a non-formalistic and functional approach to federalism. Rather than trying to define federal countries by identifying abstract markers of the federal idea, we look at when and how instruments of the federal toolkit[79] are used to address relevant constitutional issues: in our case, the protection of the rights of persons with disabilities and the implementation of the CRPD. This is why we generally speak of *federal systems*[80] (or federal countries/states) as institutional manifestations of federalism, and we do so irrespective of whether the very countries define themselves as federal, regional, devolved or otherwise. We are conscious of the slippery meaning of federalism or federalisation processes. In fact, they often have different – indeed the opposite – resonance in diverse political realms. In formerly unitary states like Italy, Spain, Belgium and the United Kingdom, the process of federalisation has implied surrendering some autonomy to certain minorities or groups, in order for them to achieve some sort of self-governing status within their own territorial subdivision. Federalisation is therefore increasingly used as an instrument for recognising and accommodating national diversity.[81] In the context of

[73] See A Gamper, 'A "Global Theory of Federalism": The Nature and Challenges of a Federal State' (2005) 6 *German Law Journal* 1297.

[74] See DJ Elazar, *Federal Systems of the World: A Handbook of Federal, Confederal and Autonomy Arrangements* (Longman, 1994) XVI.

[75] See RL Watts, *Comparing Federal Systems*, 2nd edn (McGill-Queen's University Press, 1999); and RL Watts, 'Typologies of Federalism' in J Loughlin, J Kincaid and W Swenden (eds), *Routledge Handbook of Regionalism and Federalism* (Routledge, 2013) 19.

[76] See KC Wheare, *Federal Government* (Oxford University Press, 1947) 11.

[77] Elazar, *Exploring Federalism* (n 22) 5.

[78] Inter alia Palermo and Kössler (n 10); and P Popelier, *Dynamic Federalism. A New Theory for Cohesion and Regional Autonomy* (Routledge, 2021).

[79] Palermo and Kössler (n 10) 5.

[80] Following, inter alia, Elazar (n 74); Watts, *Comparing Federal Systems* (n 75); and M Burgess, *Comparative Federalism: Theory and Practice* (Routledge, 2006); Palermo and Kössler (n 10).

[81] E Cloots, G De Baere and S Sottiaux (eds), *Federalism in the European Union* (Hart Publishing, 2012).

multinational states, federalism hence refers to increased self-governing powers for subnational entities and, accordingly, more legal diversity. By contrast, the epithet 'federal' and the term federalisation when used in relation to the EU appear to indicate more unity, uniformity throughout the Union, at the expense of the autonomous powers of its Member States.

From a structural perspective, federal constitutions set out how the power between the subnational units and the centre is distributed. From a process perspective,[82] comparative federalism literature highlights the importance of horizontal and vertical coordination in policy areas like education, health, and, especially, welfare issues.[83] Both aspects are relevant in this volume. The question is thus not a definitional controversy on federalism as an abstract term, but rather a comparative analysis of how constitutional instruments taken from the federal toolkit are used in order to accommodate the rights of persons with disabilities in the interplay of different levels of government. While the (predominantly centralising) impact of fundamental rights guarantees on federal governance has been studied widely, the specific case of the rights of persons with disabilities has not. The book aims at casting light on the impact of the CRPD and of rights of persons with disabilities and the territorial setting, and its main research question is whether, and to what extent, such a centripetal dynamic is to be observed also with regard to the rights of persons with disabilities, whether the Convention has limited or enhanced the margin of manoeuvre of subnational entities, or whether the impact has not been relevant, and why.

Cognisant of the nuances accompanying federalism, this volume's quandaries revolve around how the distribution of powers responds, in different federal systems, to the common challenge of providing a legal framework for the co-management of the rights of people with disabilities, and to the obligations rising from the CRPD. The following chapters provide an analysis of intergovernmental relations in this area and, where appropriate, of constitutional adjudication. Both are, beyond the mere text of the constitution, decisive in defining the roles of national and subnational governments. Indeed, the analysis of broad subject matters regarding both their legal foundation in the distribution of powers and actual policy-making appears to emerge, in the context of an era of pluralism, as the most crucial challenge for research on federalism. As to the actual use of autonomous powers within the limits of national homogeneity, particular emphasis is placed on the potential of self-government, not only for single subnational entities, but also on potentially beneficial spill-over effects of policy innovation to other jurisdictions.

This presumed advantage of so-called competitive, experimental or laboratory federalism was emphasised with reference to the United States example by

[82] CJ Friedrich, *Trends of Federalism in Theory and Practice* (Praeger, 1968).

[83] TO Hueglin and A Fenna, *Comparative Federalism: A Systematic Inquiry* (University of Toronto Press, 2015).

James Bryce as early as the late nineteenth century.[84] Today, however, this rationale is even more associated with an often-quoted statement from a dissenting opinion by US Supreme Court Justice Louis Brandeis in 1932: 'It is one of the happy accidents of the federal system that a single courageous state may, if its citizens choose, serve as a laboratory, and try novel social and economic experiments without risk to the rest of the country'.[85] Brandeis's laboratory argument boils down to the claim that multiple experiments at a smaller scale are more likely to produce good policies than one single nationwide effort. If such experiments fail, damage would be limited to a single jurisdiction. However, if they prove successful, they could be emulated by other jurisdictions.

Whether federal systems are able to fulfil this role seems to depend on certain practical preconditions. First, the rationale of experimental federalism presupposes substantial legislative autonomy because, otherwise, there is just no room for experimenting with policies that are genuinely a subnational entity's own to be then emulated by others. Administrative federalism in a very pure and extreme form, with subnational entities merely putting into practice nationally devised policies, seems therefore unlikely to make federal systems laboratories of innovation. Second, this rationale assumes that subnational entities are willing to bear the costs of inventing something new that others might then benefit from. Third, it presupposes that economic, social and political contexts are sufficiently similar to enable a transfer of innovation from one jurisdiction to another.[86]

Moreover, one should be cautious not to overestimate experimental federalism as the driving force behind a linear development towards more progressive societies. Just as subnational entities are not always the proponents of democratic reform but sometimes its opponents,[87] they have sometimes also inhibited more progressive policies in other areas. This is because federalism, while being an idea, is not ideological, but rather a set of instruments; therefore, it is neutral with regard to ideology in terms of policy-making at the various levels of government and just enables greater congruence of policies with subnational preferences. Therefore, it also provides opportunities for conservative forces in subnational entities to resist the progressive agenda of a national government. From a historical perspective, this arguably applied to the United States, Canada and Australia in the late nineteenth and early twentieth centuries, with national governments attempting to achieve quick countrywide adaption in response to

[84] Bryce suggests that: 'Federalism enables a people to try experiments in legislation and administration which could not be safely tried in a large centralized country. A comparatively small commonwealth like an American State easily makes and unmakes its laws; mistakes are not serious, for they are soon corrected; other States profit by the experience of a law or a method which has worked well or ill in the State that has tried it'. J Bryce, *The American Commonwealth* (Macmillan, 1893) 353.

[85] *New State Ice Co v Liebmann* 285 US 262 (1932).

[86] TO Hueglin and A Fenna, *Comparative Federalism: A Systematic Inquiry* (Broadview Press, 2006) 347.

[87] One may think, inter alia, of racial segregation in the US or of women's suffrage in Switzerland.

industrialisation-related social and economic change. At that time, 'it seemed that the judiciary, backed by conservative business interests, was intent on using the division of powers to create a governmental no-go area and thereby enforce a regime of laissez-faire'.[88] The flipside of the theory that subnational entities are laboratories facilitating innovation is also reflected in numerous examples, such as racial segregation in the United States.

This leads to the conclusion that federalism – rather, the federal toolkit – has the potential to both promote and limit the enjoyment of rights and the effectiveness of policies, depending on the use that is made of them. Taking the angle of a relatively recent area of study and of policy-making such as the rights of persons with disabilities, the book looks at how such potential is used in practice in a number of representative countries having faced particularly interesting challenges in this area.

IV. METHODOLOGY

The volume does not intend to replicate existing academic work on the implementation of the CRPD. Rather, it aims to focus on the effects of that implementation on federal structures and powers. With that in mind, along the conceptual lines indicated in the previous section, the volume includes a range of chapters on selected countries, which are considered as representative test studies.

A. The Selection of Case Studies

Those countries have been selected on the basis of three criteria, deploying what Hirsch defines 'inference-oriented research design and case selection'.[89] First, we looked at the ratification date of the CRPD, with the aim to include States Parties that ratified the CRPD at least 10 years ago, in order to be able to evaluate trends in the implementation of the CRPD across a relatively long timespan. Secondly, we included countries that can be qualified as federal systems as identified above, ie countries with at least two tiers of government, where division of legislative powers is constitutionally guaranteed. Finally, we included countries for which there is preliminary evidence of complexities in the implementation of the CRPD, signalled by the CRPD Committee in their Concluding Observations, by literature, as well as by DPOs' reports. Furthermore, the volume embraces a global approach by looking at countries from different geographical areas,

[88] Hueglin and Fenna (n 86) 342.

[89] R Hirschl, 'The Question of Case Selection in Comparative Constitutional Law' (2005) 53 *American Journal of Comparative Law* 125–55.

including countries that belong to what is often termed the 'Global South',[90] even though it does not engage directly with the academic discourse related to development and disability. It also ensures a balance when it comes to the nature of the legal system: the volume in fact includes countries with a common law tradition, such as India and the United Kingdom, and states that are usually qualified as responding to a civil law tradition. Further, it encompasses jurisdictions with diverse approaches to international law, ie traditionally monist or dualist or characterised by a mixed approach.

On the basis of the criteria indicated, the federal systems selected are: Austria, Belgium, Germany, Italy, Spain, the United Kingdom, the EU, Canada, Mexico, Brazil, Argentina, India, South Africa and Ethiopia. Given that the CRPD has not yet been ratified by the United States, this country is not included in the analysis. Despite the global reach of the book, the somewhat predominant focus on European countries is justified due to their comparative relevance for the issue at stake. Not only is Europe a region with a high number of federal systems, but it has also dedicated significant attention to disability policies. Therefore, the interplay between federalism and disability law is of special evidence in the European continent.

Even though, as noted above, the peculiar and non-state legal nature of the EU is actually recognised by the CRPD, by virtue of the RIO clause, the volume deliberately chooses to include the EU as a case study. It does so on the basis of a wealth of literature that has analysed the process of European integration through the lens of federalism.[91] Furthermore, taking into consideration that several key principles of EU law are typically federal,[92] a chapter on the EU supports and enriches the comparative analysis, as well as the functional approach to federalism.

On foot of such comparative research design, the selected case studies have been grouped and presented in the book following both a geographic and a comparative logic. The first part is devoted to European cases, including the EU which, as a *sui generis* (federal) system, is placed in the beginning, for reasons of both content (its ratification of the CRPD) and method (it proves that the federal toolkit operates also in non-state organisations). After the chapter on the EU, authored by Ferri and Šubic, the other European examples are ordered by the historical duration of the federal experience. The chapter on Germany (authored by Welti), is followed by chapters on Austria (written by Bußjäger), Italy (authored by Addis and Monti), Spain (written by González Pascual), and Belgium (authored by Ghys, Louckx and Dumont). A chapter on the United Kingdom, by McCall-Smith, closes this initial part on European examples.

[90] The term 'Global South' is used to refer to post-colonial territories (R West-Pavlov, 'Toward the Global South' in R West-Pavlov (ed), *The Global South and Literature* (Cambridge University Press, 2018) 1.

[91] Among others Burgess (n 80).

[92] R Schütze, *From Dual to Cooperative Federalism. The Changing Structure of European Law* (Oxford University Press, 2009).

countries, on which legal debate has been topical, or on which recent reforms have been undertaken. In this respect, each chapter reflects the distinct expertise of the authors, but also the constitutional tradition of the country considered.

Furthermore, while the book, in overall terms, is informed by both a human-rights perspective on disability, each chapter embeds the perspective (which does not necessarily reflect that of the editors) of the author. This entails that, while the volume for the most part uses 'people-first language' (ie 'persons/people with disabilities') compliant with the terminology used in the CRPD, some authors refer to 'disabled persons/people' consistent with the terms adopted in national legislation. In addition, while the overall volume embeds a substantive, rather than formal, understanding of federalism, authors defined the country's federal arrangement according to their own appreciation of the system. As a consequence, chapters adopt a federal terminology which better reflects each country's characteristics and constitutional approach. For example, the German and Austrian chapters use the term *Land/Länder* to indicate the constituent sub-national units. More generally, each chapter adopts a terminology that best reflects the constitutional understanding of federalism of the country in question. Equally, chapters typically refer to legislation and other regulatory acts in a way that reflects the constitutional articulation of the sources of law in that country (law, statute, etc). Consistent with this, some chapters (eg Austria and Germany) use the wording 'Paragraph' or 'Section' (eg India and South Africa), instead of 'Article', where appropriate and when referring to national legislation in line with relevant national practice. Most authors refer to primary and secondary sources in the language of the country in question and, unless indicated otherwise, provided the translation for the quotations included in the chapter.

The chapters in this volume were finalised, for the most part, at the beginning of August 2022. Thus, the volume covers legal developments that occurred up until that time.

1

The European Union
Federal Trends in Disability Rights

DELIA FERRI AND NEŽA ŠUBIC*

I. INTRODUCTION

THE UNITED NATIONS (UN) Convention on the Rights of Persons with Disabilities (CRPD) aims to ensure that persons with disabilities can participate on an equal basis with others in all areas of life. It covers a broad spectrum of rights, which partly fall within the remit of European Union (EU) competence and partly within that of the Member States. The CRPD has been ratified by both the EU, by means of Council Decision 2010/48/EC of 26 November 2009,[1] and all its Member States. From an EU legal perspective, the CRPD has become an integral part of EU law and, accordingly, provisions of EU secondary law must, as far as possible, be interpreted in a manner that is consistent with the Convention.[2] Even though the CRPD is hierarchically superior to secondary legislation, this does not automatically make EU provisions breaching the Convention invalid. The validity of EU secondary law can only be assessed vis-à-vis an international provision if the latter is capable of displaying direct effect: in *Z v A Government Department*, the Court of Justice of the European Union (CJEU) held that 'the provisions of [the] Convention are not, as regards their content, provisions that are unconditional and sufficiently precise … and that they therefore do not have direct effect in [EU] law'.[3]

* This contribution has been written within the remit of the project 'Protecting the Right to Culture of Persons with Disabilities and Enhancing Cultural Diversity through European Union Law: Exploring New Paths – DANCING', funded by the European Research Council (ERC) under the European Union's Horizon 2020 research and innovation programme (Grant Agreement No 864182). The information and views set out in this article are those of the authors and do not necessarily reflect the official opinion of the European Commission.

[1] Council Decision concerning the conclusion, by the European Community, of the United Nations Convention on the Rights of Persons with Disabilities [2010] OJ L23/25.

[2] Joined Cases C-335/11 and C-337/11 *HK Danmark* ECLI:EU:C:2013:222, para 32.

[3] Case C-363/12 *Z v A Government Department* ECLI:EU:C:2014:159, para 90.

Being a mixed agreement, which both the EU and its Member States are a party to,[4] the CRPD must be implemented ensuring close mutual cooperation.[5] However, mixity is both legally challenging and politically sensitive in light of the *sui generis* quasi-federal nature of the EU system.[6] While the EU's accession to the CRPD has been heralded as a historical advance in protection of disability rights,[7] little has been said on whether the burgeoning of disability legislation and policy at the EU level has provoked a progressive erosion of Member States' competences. This chapter addresses this gap in the literature and interrogates the extent to which the implementation of the CRPD has affected the division of powers between the EU and its Member States. Echoing Lenaerts' words,[8] it investigates the balance 'between unity and diversity' in the EU. This chapter uses federalism as a lens of enquiry, acknowledging that while federalisation can often be 'seen as an instrument for recognising and accommodating, rather than transcending, national diversity', when it comes to the EU, it 'appears to signify more unity, uniformity and (formal) equality throughout the Union, at the expense of the autonomous powers of its territorial subdivisions (i.e. the Member States)'.[9]

Further to these introductory remarks, section II examines the legal nature of the EU and its federal elements. It also gives an overview of the division of competences related to disability, in light of the EU's Declaration of Competence annexed to the Council Decision on the conclusion of the CRPD.[10] Section III goes on to discuss the 'Europeanisation' of the concept of disability, while section IV focuses on the three main areas identified by the overall volume: equality, accessibility and participation. It first addresses the role of the EU in protecting persons with disabilities from discriminatory treatment. It then explores the importance of Article 114 of the Treaty on the Functioning of the European Union (TFEU) in supporting the adoption of accessibility legislation. Finally, it examines the extent to which the EU has used its supporting competences to enhance participation of persons with disabilities in society. Section V

[4] M Chamon, 'Negotiation, Ratification and Implementation of the CRPD and its Status in the EU Legal Order' in D Ferri and A Broderick (eds), *Research Handbook on EU Disability Law* (Edward Elgar, 2020).

[5] Opinion 1/94 ECLI:EU:C:1994:384, para 108.

[6] D Ferri, F Palermo and G Martinico, 'Introduction: Conceptual and Methodological Approaches', in this volume.

[7] D Ferri and A Broderick, 'Introduction to the Research Handbook on EU Disability Law' in Ferri and Broderick (n 4) 1.

[8] K Lenaerts, 'EU Federalism in 3-D' in E Cloots, G De Baere and S Sottiaux (eds), *Federalism in the European Union* (Hart Publishing, 2012).

[9] E Cloots, G De Baere and S Sottiaux, 'Introduction: Federalism's Janus Face' in Cloots, Baere and Sottiaux (n 8).

[10] A Code of Conduct, which sets out the division of tasks between the EU and the Member States based on competence, was also agreed in 2010. Code of Conduct between the Council, the Member States and the Commission setting out internal arrangements for the implementation by and representation of the European Union relating to the United Nations Convention on the Rights of Persons with Disabilities [2010] OJ C340/11.

looks at the implementation of Article 33 CRPD at the EU level, discussing the ostensible lack of coordination with Member States in that regard. Section VI provides some concluding remarks.

II. THE *SUI GENERIS* QUASI-FEDERAL NATURE OF THE EUROPEAN UNION AND ITS CROSS-CUTTING COMPETENCES ON DISABILITY

A. The Legal Nature of the EU

This chapter (and indeed the whole volume) is premised on the, still contested,[11] idea of the EU as a constitutional quasi-federal entity.[12] The concept of a 'Constitution' proved to be too controversial to be explicitly mentioned in the Treaties.[13] However, the Treaties and the Charter of Fundamental Rights (CFR) are in fact deemed to be the EU's Constitution, as the CJEU recalled in *Wightman*,[14] recasting the classic *Les Verts*.[15] Even before the 1990s, scholarship referred to the European constitutionalisation process, or to the EU as a constitutional entity.[16] According to von Bogdandy, the Treaties 'constitutional character manifests itself especially clearly in the founding principles'.[17] Constitutional readings of the EU, while being varied, concur in denying the state-like nature of the EU. In that connection, several authors agree that the EU is not and will not become a federal state.[18] However, as indicated in the introduction to this volume, federalism entails 'a set of measures and instruments that balance unity and diversity, autonomy and integration, self-rule and shared rule', and is thus not necessarily wedded to statehood. In that regard, it has been highlighted that the EU possesses both elements of a federation and others of a confederation.[19] Federal elements are present in the legal principles

[11] D Marco and JM Agustin, 'European Constitutional Imagination: A Whig Interpretation of the Process of European Integration?' (2021) 243 *iCourts Working Paper Series*.

[12] F Palermo, 'What Does The EU Tell Us About Federalism?' *50 Shades of Federalism* (2019).

[13] NW Barber, M Cahill and R Ekins (eds), *The Rise and Fall of the European Constitution* (Hart Publishing, 2019).

[14] Case C-621/18 *Wightman* ECLI:EU:C:2018:999, para 44.

[15] Case 294/83 *Les Verts* ECLI:EU:C:1986:166, para 23.

[16] GF Mancini, 'The Making of a Constitution for Europe' (1989) 26 *Common Market Law Review* 595; G Martinico, *The Tangled Complexity of the EU Constitutional Process. The Frustrating Knot of Europe* (Routledge, 2012). For an earlier discussion, see E Stein, 'Lawyers, Judges and the Making of a Transnational Constitution' (1981) 75 *The American Journal of International Law* 1.

[17] A von Bogdandy, 'Founding Principles' in A von Bogdandy and J Bast (eds), *Principles of European Constitutional Law*, 2nd edn (Hart Publishing, 2010) 13.

[18] F Palermo and K Kössler, *Comparative Federalism. Constitutional Arrangements and Case Law* (Hart Publishing, 2017) 62. This did not prevent scholars from using federal language in relation to the EU, see G Martinico, 'The Federal Language and the European Integration Process: the European Communities Viewed from the US' (2016) 53 *Politique européenne* 38.

[19] Palermo and Kössler (n 18) 64; R Schütze, *From Dual to Cooperative Federalism: The Changing Structure of European Law* (Oxford University Press, 2009).

underpinning the EU's constitutional structure,[20] as well as in its institutional set up and in some foundational principles of EU law. Those elements juxtapose with significant 'non-federal' characteristics,[21] such as the general reliance on the Member States to implement and enforce EU law, a lack of power to levy taxes, and a blurred European identity.[22] However, as Burgess notes, '[i]f we are to understand the contemporary EU as a federal model, it is vital that we are sensitised to the peculiarities and idiosyncrasies of European integration'.[23]

As early as in 1963, the CJEU declared in *Van Gend en Loos* that the EU 'constitutes *a new legal order* of international law for the benefit of which the states have limited their sovereign rights, albeit within limited fields, and the subjects of which comprise not only Member States but also their nationals'.[24] This led the CJEU to find that EU law can have direct effect in the legal systems of Member States, and, in another seminal case, *Costa v Enel*, that EU law prevails over national law (principle of primacy).[25] While these two principles are still not explicitly set out in the Treaties, they are – at least from the perspective of EU law[26] – firmly embedded in the EU's constitutional structure. In addition to these principles, many other 'federal'-like principles are now contained in the Treaties, in particular the principle of loyal cooperation,[27] and the principles of conferral,[28] subsidiarity and proportionality,[29] but also of pre-emption and implied powers.

[20] A von Bogdandy, 'Neither an International Organization Nor A Nation State: The EU as a Supranational Federation' in E Jones, A Menon and S Weatherill (eds), *The Oxford Handbook of the European Union* (Oxford University Press, 2012); JHH Weiler, 'Federalism without Constitutionalism: Europe's Sonderweg' in K Nicolaidis and R Howse (eds), *The Federal Vision: Legitimacy and Levels of Governance in the United States and the European Union* (Oxford University Press, 2001) 55–56.

[21] Palermo and Kössler (n 18) 62.

[22] K Lenaerts, 'Federalism: Essential Concepts in Evolution – The Case of the European Union' (1997) 21 *Fordham International Law Journal* 746, 747; EA Young, 'A Comparative Perspective' in R Schütze and T Tridimas (eds), *Oxford Principles of European Law: Volume I* (Oxford University Press, 2018) 157–71. In this light, the EU has been considered as a multinational federation. H Dumont, 'The European Union, a Plurinational Federation *in Sensu Cosmopolitico*' in M Seymour and AG Gagnon (eds), *Multinational Federalism: Problems and Prospects* (Palgrave Macmillan, 2012).

[23] M Burgess, *Comparative Federalism: Theory and Practice* (Routledge, 2006) 227; S Rehling Larsen, *The Constitutional Theory of the Federation and the European Union* (Oxford University Press, 2021).

[24] Case 26/62 *Van Gend en Loos* ECLI:EU:C:1963:1. Emphasis added.

[25] Case 6/64 *Costa v Enel* ECLI:EU:C:1964:66.

[26] Admittedly, not all (highest) national courts accept the 'absolute' and 'unconditional primacy' of EU law over national constitutional law, but in practice conflicts arise very rarely. See M Claes, 'The Validity and Primacy of EU Law and the Cooperative Relationship between National Constitutional Courts and the Court of Justice of the European Union' (2016) 23 *Maastricht Journal of European and Comparative Law* 151.

[27] Art 4(3) Treaty on the European Union (TEU); K Lenaerts and JA Gutiérrez-Fons, 'A Constitutional Perspective' in Schütze and Tridimas (n 22) 118–20.

[28] Ibid 112.

[29] Art 5 TEU. Lenaerts, for example, notes that '[t]he constitutional embedding of the division of powers between the central authority and the component entity' is one of the 'main characteristics of federalism'. Lenaerts (n 22) 775.

In elaborating on the quasi-federal nature, scholars have argued that asymmetry is the cypher that characterises the EU. In that regard, Palermo notes that EU competences are often exercised by means of Directives that bind Member States in regard to the outcome but allow them to 'tailor implementation to their specific situation, with this becoming an element of asymmetry'.[30] Other elements of asymmetry derive from systems such as enhanced cooperation, the mechanism of differentiated integration,[31] and soft law.

Alongside a discussion on the processes of constitutionalisation, federalisation and integration, scholars have also extensively elaborated on the phenomenon of Europeanisation. The latter term is used to refer to an array of phenomena that span from 'the mutual influence of the EU and its member states, to interactions within and between member states driven by the EU, and to the effect of the EU on EU applicant states',[32] but broadly address the deepening of the EU influence over domestic law.[33]

B. The Division of Competences from a Disability Perspective

The Treaty on the European Union (TEU) explicates the values and objectives of the EU. It does not explicitly mention disability, but states in Article 2 that '[t]he Union is founded on the values of respect for human dignity, freedom, democracy, equality, the rule of law and *respect for human rights*, including the rights of persons belonging to minorities', and refers to a society in which 'non-discrimination' among other values prevails. Article 3(1) TEU affirms that the EU's aim is 'to promote peace, its values and the well-being of its peoples'. In addition, it lists a number of goals that the EU must pursue, including the long-standing market integration goal. Although these provisions do not confer competences to the EU, they require that the EU ensures the protection of fundamental rights and equality, when exercising its powers.[34] Further, Article 6 TEU provides for the protection of fundamental rights in the EU context, and confers to the CFR constitutional value. The CFR lists disability as one of the grounds on which discrimination must be prohibited, and affirms that 'the Union recognises and respects the right of persons with disabilities to benefit from measures designed to ensure their independence, social and occupational integration and

[30] F Palermo, 'Federalism and the European Union: Asymmetry, Policies and some Recurring Federal Dilemmas' in J Kincaid (ed), *A Research Agenda for Federalism Studies* (Edward Elgar, 2019) 198.

[31] G Martinico, 'Asymmetry as an Instrument of Differentiated Integration: The Case of the European Union' (2016) 18 *European Journal of Law Reform* 139.

[32] S Dosenrode, 'Europeanization' in F Laursen (ed), *Oxford Encyclopedia of European Union Politics* (Oxford University Press, 2021).

[33] See generally CM Radaelli, 'The Europeanization of Public Policy' in K Featherstone and CM Radaelli (eds), *The Politics of Europeanization* (Oxford University Press, 2003).

[34] E Howard, 'EU Equality Law: Three Recent Developments' (2011) 17 *European Law Journal* 785.

participation in the life of the community'.[35] The latter provision is intended to guide the EU institutions when they legislate, but it does not oblige them to act and is not directly enforceable.[36]

The TFEU distinguishes between three types of EU competences: exclusive, shared and supporting competences.[37] In areas of exclusive competence, the EU alone can legislate. Areas of exclusive competence comprise, among others, customs union, competition rules and monetary policy. In areas of shared competence, both the EU and its Member States are able to legislate, but Member States can exercise their own competence where the EU does not act or has decided not to exercise its competence. Fields of shared competence include the rules related to the internal market, but also social policy albeit with regard to limited aspects connected to the exercise of free movement rights. Where the EU has supporting competences, it can only intervene to support, coordinate or complement the action of its Member States, and EU legislation must not entail the harmonisation of national laws. Fields such as culture or health are included among the array of supporting competences.

Disability is not listed among areas of competence as such, but Article 19 TFEU confers upon the EU the competence to combat discrimination on the basis inter alia of disability. The TFEU also contains – in Article 10 – a horizontal provision, which supports the mainstreaming of non-discrimination within all EU policies and actions. Alongside Article 19 TFEU, as noted by Waddington, 'the full range of competences of both the EU and the Member States are engaged' in the context of the CRPD.[38] Chamon contends the following examples of areas of EU competence as relevant for the CRPD: social policy, research and development, internal market as cases of shared competences; and culture and education as cases of supporting competences.[39] Waddington points to transport and internal market as examples of areas in which legislative measures containing disability-specific references have been adopted.[40] Article 114 TFEU, which allows the EU to adopt approximating measures with the objective of 'the establishment and functioning of the internal market', has been an important legal basis for the adoption of disability-related legislation. Ferri and Broderick also highlight that disability issues span across the whole spectrum of EU competences and have been regulated within the remit of labour

[35] Art 26 Charter of Fundamental Rights (CFR).

[36] T Lock, 'Rights and Principles in the EU Charter of Fundamental Rights' (2019) 56 *Common Market Law Review* 1201.

[37] Arts 2–6 Treaty on the Functioning of the European Union (TFEU).

[38] L Waddington, 'The European Union and the United Nations Convention on the Rights of Persons with Disabilities: A Story of Exclusive and Shared Competences' (2011) 18 *Maastricht Journal of European and Comparative Law* 431, 438.

[39] Chamon (n 4) 55.

[40] Waddington (n 38) 434.

law, freedom of movement, transport, copyright law, accessibility of goods and services, standardisation, public procurement, public services, state aid, structural and investment funds, consumer law and asylum law.[41]

C. The Division of Competence between the EU and its Member States and the CRPD

In the process of negotiation and ratification of the CRPD, the EU addressed the scope of its own competences to implement the CRPD at several junctures. The Council Decision concerning the conclusion of the CRPD sets out (only) Articles 13 EC (now Article 19 TFEU) and 95 EC (now Article 114 TFEU) as the legal bases for joining the CRPD.

In line with Article 44 CRPD, the EU submitted a Declaration of Competence in the form of an Annex to the Council Decision. This Declaration indicates the EU's competences in the areas covered by the CRPD. It lists State Aid and the Common Customs Tariff as relevant exclusive competences, as well as its own public administration.[42] It further notes combating discrimination on the ground of disability, free movement of goods, persons, services and capital, agriculture, transport by rail, road, sea and air transport, taxation, internal market, equal pay for male and female workers, trans-European network policy and statistics, as relevant shared competences.[43] However, in respect of those areas, to the extent that provisions of the CRPD or legal instruments adopted in its implementation affect EU common rules, the EU has exclusive competence.[44] On the other hand, when common rules exist but are not affected, the Member States retain competence to act. The latter instance seems, however, rather unlikely to occur. The CJEU (in particular in the context of ratification of international agreements) has tended to recognise that when EU rules have been adopted they are likely to be affected by international instruments and undermined by different implementing approaches at the national level.[45] Lastly, relating to supporting competences, the Declaration mentions EU policies and strategies on employment, education, vocational training, economic and social cohesion, and development cooperation policy and economic, financial and technical cooperation with third countries, as also potentially relevant to the CRPD.[46] An appendix listing pieces of EU legislation is attached with the intention to 'illustrate the extent of the area' of EU competence. Differently from the Declaration, the list of measures is not designed around the three categories

[41] Ferri and Broderick (n 7).
[42] Para 1 of Annex 2 to the Council Decision (n 1).
[43] Ibid para 2 of Annex 2.
[44] Ibid.
[45] Opinion 3/2015 ECLI:EU:C:2017:114.
[46] Para 3 of Annex 2 to the Council Decision (n 1).

of EU competence, but rather lists specific areas which correspond to (certain) CRPD provisions (ie, accessibility; independent living and social inclusion; work and employment; personal mobility; access to information; statistics and data collection; international cooperation),[47] and legislative measures adopted by the EU that are relevant to these areas.

The Declaration, as well as the attached list, have been considered rather 'unhelpful'[48] both for the purpose of defining the scope of international responsibility (which is the aim of the Declaration), and for internal purposes (even though the Declaration is not intended for the EU and Member States).[49] Additionally, the comprehensiveness of the list has been questioned by scholars[50] and by the CRPD Committee in its Concluding Observations to the Initial Report of the EU, with repeated (yet unheeded) requests for an update of the Declaration.[51]

III. THE PROGRESSIVE 'EUROPEANISATION' OF THE SOCIAL-CONTEXTUAL UNDERSTANDING OF DISABILITY

Disability-related provisions had been mainstreamed across different fields of EU legislation (eg, transport,[52] lifts,[53] public procurement,[54] electronic communications networks and services)[55] before the conclusion of the CRPD. However, none of these pieces of legislation explicitly engaged with the concept of disability. Only in 2005, in the infamous case of *Chacón Navas*,[56] did the CJEU attempt, for the first time, to define disability with reference to application of Directive 2000/78/EC of 27 November 2000 establishing

[47] Waddington (n 38) 443.

[48] Chamon (n 4) 61.

[49] Waddington (n 38) 443.

[50] Ibid 444; JW Reiss, 'Innovative Governance in a Federal Europe: Implementing the Convention on the Rights of Persons with Disabilities' (2014) 20 *European Law Journal* 107, 114.

[51] CRPD Committee, 'Concluding Observations on the Initial Report of the European Union' (2015) CRPD/C/EU/CO/1, paras 16–17.

[52] See eg Regulation 1899/2006 on the harmonisation of technical requirements and administrative procedures in the field of civil aviation [2006] OJ L377/1; Directive 2006/87/EC laying down technical requirements for inland waterway vessels [2006] OJ L389/1; Regulation 1370/2007 on public passenger transport services by rail and by road [2007] OJ L315/1; Regulation 1371/2007 on rail passengers' rights and obligations [2007] OJ L315/14; Regulation 1107/2006 concerning the rights of disabled persons and persons with reduced mobility when travelling by air [2006] OJ L204/1.

[53] Directive 95/16/EC on the approximation of the laws of the Member States relating to lifts [1995] OJ L213/1.

[54] Directive 2004/17/EC coordinating the procurement procedures of entities operating in the water, energy, transport and postal services sectors [2004] OJ L134/1; Directive 2004/18/EC on the coordination of procedures for the award of public works contracts, public supply contracts and public service contracts [2004] OJ L134/114.

[55] See eg Directive 2002/22/EC on universal service and users' rights relating to electronic communications networks and services (Universal Service Directive) [2002] OJ L108/51.

[56] Case C-13/05 *Chacón Navas* ECLI:EU:C:2006:456.

a general framework for equal treatment in employment and occupation (hereafter 'Employment Equality Directive').[57] The Luxembourg judges established that the concept of 'disability' must be 'given an autonomous and uniform interpretation' and that it is not possible to refer to the laws of the Member States.[58] They adopted a narrow interpretation of disability, based on the medical model, distinguishing the concept of sickness from that of disability.[59] Namely, the CJEU argued that 'the concept of "disability" must be understood as referring to a limitation which results in particular from physical, mental or psychological impairments and which hinders the participation of the person concerned in professional life'.[60] As noted by Waddington, the CJEU focused on the individual 'impairment', irrespective of the role played by environmental barriers. Quinn and Flynn suggested that the Court opted for a definition of disability inflicting the lowest financial burden on Member States in effecting that same definition.[61]

The numerous critical voices raised against the outdated medical approach to disability adopted in *Chacón Navas*[62] did not lead to any immediate overruling, nor to the adoption of a broader prescriptive definition of disability. A paramount 'paradigm shift'[63] only occurred in 2013, when the Court released its decision in the *HK Danmark* case.[64] For the first time, the CJEU, interpreting the Employment Equality Directive in light of the CRPD, attempted to align the definition of disability to the social-contextual model of disability that underpins the Convention. It held that:

> if a curable or incurable illness entails a limitation which results in particular from physical, mental or psychological impairments which in interaction with various barriers may hinder the full and effective participation of the person concerned in professional life on an equal basis with other workers, and the limitation is a long-term one, such an illness can be covered by the concept of 'disability' within the meaning of Directive 2000/78.[65]

In almost all subsequent decisions in the field of non-discrimination on the ground of disability and in connection with the interpretation of the Employment Equality Directive, the CJEU recalled the conceptualisation embedded in

[57] Directive 2000/78/EC establishing a general framework for equal treatment in employment and occupation [2000] OJ L303/16.

[58] *Chacón Navas* (n 56) para 40.

[59] L Waddington, 'Equal to the Task? Re-Examining EU Equality Law in Light of the United Nations Convention on the Rights of Persons with Disabilities' (2013) 4 *European Yearbook of Disability Law* 169.

[60] *Chacón Navas* (n 56) para 43. The same definition is included in Case C-303/06 *Coleman* ECLI:EU:C:2008:415.

[61] G Quinn and E Flynn, 'Transatlantic Borrowings: The Past and Future of EU Non-Discrimination Law and Policy on the Ground of Disability' (2012) 60 *American Journal of Comparative Law* 23.

[62] Among others L Waddington, 'Case C-13/05, *Chacón Navas v Eurest Colectividades* SA, judgment of the Grand Chamber of 11 July 2006' (2007) 44 *Common Market Law Review* 487.

[63] Opinion of AG Wahl in *Z v A Government Department* ECLI:EU:C:2013:604, para 88.

[64] *HK Danmark* (n 2).

[65] Ibid para 41.

Article 1(2) CRPD.[66] Outside the remit of the Employment Equality Directive, in *Glatzel*,[67] the CJEU also interpreted the reference to disability in Article 21 of the Charter in light and in compliance with the CRPD.[68]

The progressive embracement of a social-contextual model oriented view of disability by the CJEU (although more formal than substantial)[69] aligns with a similar trend detectable in policy documents – such as the European Disability Strategy 2010–2020 (EDS)[70] and the Strategy for the Rights of Persons with Disabilities 2021–2030 (Strategy 2021–2030)[71] – and in the overall EU policy discourse, with institutions and bodies referring to Article 1(2) CRPD in their work.[72] In that connection, we can identify a horizontal 'Europeanisation', meaning the diffusion of the social-contextual concept of disability among different actors at the European level and across different dimensions of the EU governance of disability.

EU legislation has also progressively embedded definitions of disability that reproduce, wholly or partially, Article 1(2) CRPD. In the 2014 General Block Exemption Regulation (GBER),[73] a definition of 'workers with disabilities' quotes almost verbatim the wording of the CRPD, albeit leaving the door open to different national definitions. The Web Accessibility Directive (WAD)[74] refers to the CRPD conceptualisation of disability in its non-binding preamble.[75] The European Accessibility Act (EAA),[76] in a similar fashion to the WAD, mentions the CRPD in its preamble,[77] but most notably reproduces the text of Article 1(2) CRPD in Article 3 on Definitions. More general references to external barriers as a cause of disability are included in other pieces

[66] Among others Case C-397/18 *Nobel Plastiques Ibérica* ECLI:EU:C:2019:703, para 41; Case C-485/20 *HR Rail* ECLI:EU:C:2022:85, para 34.

[67] Case C-356/12 *Glatzel* EU:C:2014:350.

[68] See D Ferri, 'The Unorthodox Relationship between the EU Charter of Fundamental Rights, the UN Convention on the Rights of Persons with Disabilities and Secondary Rights in the Court of Justice Case Law on Disability Discrimination' (2020) 16 *European Constitutional Law Review* 275.

[69] L Waddington, 'Saying all the Right Things and Still Getting it Wrong: The Court of Justice's Definition of Disability and Non-Discrimination Law' (2015) 22 *Maastricht Journal of European and Comparative Law* 576.

[70] Commission, 'European Disability Strategy 2010–2020: A Renewed Commitment to a Barrier-Free Europe' (EDS) COM(2010) 636 final.

[71] Commission, 'Union of Equality: Strategy for the Rights of Persons with Disabilities 2021–2030' COM(2021) 101 final (Strategy 2021–2030).

[72] Eg the European Union Fundamental Rights Agency (FRA), for example in its report on 'Violence Against Children with Disabilities: Legislation, Policies and Programmes in the EU' (Publications Office of the European Union, 2015).

[73] Regulation 651/2014 declaring certain categories of aid compatible with the internal market in application of Articles 107 and 108 of the Treaty [2014] OJ L187/1.

[74] Directive 2016/2102 on the accessibility of the websites and mobile applications of public sector bodies [2016] OJ L327/1.

[75] Recital 12 Web Accessibility Directive (WAD).

[76] Directive 2019/882 on the accessibility requirements for products and services [2019] OJ L151/70.

[77] Recital 3 European Accessibility Act (EAA).

of legislation, such as the so-called Marrakesh Directive,[78] implementing the Marrakesh Treaty to Facilitate Access to Published Works for Persons Who Are Blind, Visually Impaired, or Otherwise Print Disabled. In that regard, we identify a vertical effect of 'Europeanisation', with a visible progressive shift towards the EU level when it comes to the definition of disability.

The CJEU had already highlighted the need for an EU autonomous concept of disability in EU non-discrimination law long before the conclusion of the CRPD. However, the CRPD has determined a spill-over effect in several other areas of EU law, from state aid to the broader remit of internal market legislation. The EAA is exemplary in that Member States will not be able to derogate from the definitions included in Article 3, and will not be able to adopt narrower or medically oriented views of disability in transposing legislation. Undoubtedly, Member States still have some leeway within the remit of social policy or with regard to legal capacity (although they should still align to Article 1(2) CRPD having ratified the Convention in their own capacity). However, there is a progressive erosion of their space to adopt diverse conceptualisations of disability. On the whole, the Europeanisation of the concept of disability, while asymmetrical, shows, to varying degrees, a push towards a more centralised governance, or towards more 'unity'.

IV. THE IMPLEMENTATION OF THE CRPD IN SELECTED KEY AREAS: A PUSH TOWARDS HARMONISATION?

A. EU Non-Discrimination Legislation

As noted above, combatting discrimination on the ground of disability is an area of shared competence. In that regard, Broderick and Watson note that 'the EU is not bound to implement in their entirety all provisions of the CRPD that relate to discrimination',[79] but both the EU and its Member States are obliged to take implementation measures in combination.[80]

The Employment Equality Directive, adopted in 2000, remains the main piece of legislation that addresses discrimination, inter alia, on the ground of disability. The Directive prohibits direct and indirect discrimination as well as harassment on the listed grounds and sets out minimum requirements, allowing Member States to adopt broader and more protective non-discrimination

[78] Directive 2017/1564 on certain permitted uses of certain works and other subject matter protected by copyright and related rights for the benefit of persons who are blind, visually impaired or otherwise print-disabled and amending Directive 2001/29/EC on the harmonisation of certain aspects of copyright and related rights in the information society [2017] OJ L242/6.

[79] A Broderick and P Watson, 'Disability in EU Non-Discrimination Law' in Ferri and Broderick (n 4) 121.

[80] L Waddington and A Broderick, 'Disability Law and the Duty to Reasonably Accommodate Beyond Employment: A Legal Analysis of the Situation in EU Member States' (European Commission, 2018) 44.

legislation.[81] The material scope of the Directive is limited to the employment field, albeit broadly interpreted to cover conditions of access to employment or self-employment, employment and working conditions, or access to vocational training and membership, as well as involvement in an organisation of workers or employers, or a professional organisation, and to the benefits provided by such bodies.[82] However, Article 3 establishes that Member States may introduce exceptions to the prohibition of discrimination on the ground of disability with regard to the armed forces. It is also worth recalling that Article 5 imposes a duty on employers to provide reasonable accommodation for persons with disabilities, while Article 7 allows Member States to adopt positive actions, ie:

> specific measures to prevent or compensate for disadvantages experienced by disabled persons, and to maintain or adopt measures relating to health and safety at work, or measures aimed at creating or maintaining provisions or facilities for safeguarding or promoting their integration into the working environment.[83]

As yet, the CJEU has interpreted the Employment Equality Directive in light of and in compliance with the CRPD in a rather comprehensive and extensively commented line of cases.[84] On the whole, the CRPD has contributed to a broadening of the personal scope of application of the Directive, by offering a definition of disability that attempts to align with the letter of Article 1(2) CRPD. The CRPD has also supported a more robust application of Article 5. Most recently, in *HR Rail*,[85] the CJEU confirmed that the purpose of reasonable accommodation is that of eliminating the barriers that hinder the full and effective participation of people with disabilities in employment, as it had stated in *HK Danmark*.[86] In *Commission v Italy*, the Luxembourg judges also held that this obligation to adopt reasonable accommodation measures applies to all employers, and national laws cannot create exceptions to exempt certain categories of employers.[87] The Court has adopted a wide approach to the Employment Equality Directive's personal scope. This is evident in *VL*,[88] where the Luxembourg judges held that the prohibition of discrimination on the grounds of disability also applies in relation to differential treatment of two groups of disabled people. The Court, referring to the *ratio* of the Directive, suggested that the protection granted by it 'would be diminished if it were to be considered that a situation where such discrimination occurs within a group of persons, all of whom have disabilities, is, by definition, not covered by the

[81] Art 8(1) of the Employment Equality Directive.
[82] Ibid Art 3(1).
[83] Broderick and Watson (n 79) 126.
[84] L Waddington and A Lawson, 'The Unfinished Story of EU Disability Non-Discrimination Law' in A Bogg, C Costello and ACL Davies (eds), *Research Handbook on EU Labour Law* (Edward Elgar, 2016).
[85] *HR Rail* (n 66) para 44.
[86] *HK Danmark* (n 2).
[87] Case C-312/11 *European Commission v Italian Republic* ECLI:EU:C:2013:446.
[88] Case C-16/19 *VL v Szpital Kliniczny* ECLI:EU:C:2021:64.

prohibition of discrimination laid down thereby'.[89] In that regard, Xenedis argues that the Court extended 'the protection to intragroup discrimination and thus broaden[ed] the pool of rights holders'.[90] This extensive interpretation does not seem strictly related to the CRPD. Rather, it appears linked to a teleological approach in the application of the Directive.

Further, as noted by Xenedis, employment, occupation and vocational training 'are entry points for multi-dimensional demands that extend beyond the scope of material and distributive disadvantage, and include grievances relating to participation in social life and recognition of diversity and difference'.[91] In that regard, from a disability perspective, notable are *Tartu Vangla*[92] and *Komisia*,[93] whereby the CJEU addressed the discrimination faced by prison officers and jurors respectively. While the organisation of justice falls within the competence of Member States, as argued elsewhere, EU non-discrimination legislation is pragmatically used to advance the right of access to justice of persons with disabilities in the EU.[94]

On the whole, while the CRPD as such has not been the single cause for extending the reach of existing EU non-discrimination legislation, it has supported this trend. The need to comply with the CRPD has not, however, been a sufficiently strong driver for the adoption of new non-discrimination legislation. A proposal for a horizontal non-discrimination Directive[95] to tackle discrimination outside the labour market has been under discussion at EU level since 2008. The proposed Directive should extend protection on the ground of, inter alia, disability to the fields of social protection, including social security, healthcare and social housing; education; and access to, and supply of, goods and services, including housing.[96] Scholars tend to concur on the fact that the eventual adoption 'would serve to bring the content of EU non-discrimination law somewhat closer to the requirements set out in the CRPD'.[97] Due to the requirement of unanimity in the Council, the proposal has yet to be adopted. As evidenced in parliamentary debates, challenges concern the division of

[89] Ibid para 35.

[90] R Xenidis, 'The Polysemy of Anti-Discrimination Law: the Interpretation Architecture of the Framework Employment Directive at the Court of Justice' (2021) 58 *Common Market Law Review* 1649, 1657.

[91] Ibid 1653.

[92] Case C-795/19 *Tartu Vangla* ECLI:EU:C:2021:606.

[93] Case C-824/19 *Komisia za zashtita ot diskriminatsia* ECLI:EU:C:2021:862.

[94] D Ferri and L Urzel, 'The Role of the Employment Equality Directive in Advancing Access to Justice for Persons with Disabilities in the European Union' (2022) *European Yearbook on Human Rights*.

[95] Commission, 'Proposal for a Council Directive on Implementing the Principle of Equal Treatment Between Persons Irrespective of Religion or Belief, Disability, Age or Sexual Orientation' COM(2008) 426 final.

[96] Ibid Art 3.

[97] Broderick and Watson (n 79) 138. See S Favalli and D Ferri, 'Defining Disability in the European Union Non-Discrimination Legislation: Judicial Activism and Legislative Restraints' (2016) 22 *European Public Law* 541.

competences, legal certainty and the financial implications of the proposal, in particular in relation to reasonable accommodation outside the workplace.[98] After almost 14 years of stalling, and in spite of the Commission's renewed commitment to bring this forward,[99] the adoption of such a piece of legislation seems highly unlikely. However, if it were to happen, this will support a centralising dynamic in the implementation of the CRPD in the EU.

B. The Internal Market as Gateway for Accessibility Legislation

Since the ratification of the CRPD, accessibility has become a priority field of action for the EU. While accessibility of different means of transportation had been addressed extensively by EU legislation long before the CRPD,[100] a portfolio of legislative and other instruments to improve access for people with disabilities to an array of goods and services and implement the CRPD was envisaged in the EDS. The WAD and the EAA have represented the most significant tools in this portfolio, and the Strategy 2021–2030 indicates that the Commission 'will pay close attention to [their] correct implementation and evaluation'.[101] Both the WAD and the EAA are based on Article 114 TFEU, whereby access to goods and services for persons with disabilities are considered essential to the creation of a 'deeper and fairer' internal market.

The WAD was adopted in 2016 with the aim to 'approximate the laws, regulations and administrative provisions of the Member States relating to the accessibility requirements of the websites and mobile applications of public sector bodies, thereby enabling those websites and mobile applications to be more accessible to users, in particular to persons with disabilities'.[102] In essence, it provides that Member States shall ensure that public sector bodies' websites and mobile applications are accessible,[103] unless this imposes a 'disproportionate burden' upon public sector bodies.[104] Given that the WAD entails minimum harmonisation, 'Member States may maintain or introduce measures in conformity with Union law which go beyond the minimum requirements' established by the Directive.[105]

The EAA provides for accessibility of a range of key products and services, such as computers, smartphones, tablets, TV sets, banking ATMs and services, payment terminals, e-books and e-readers, e-commerce websites and mobile

[98] See eg European Parliament debate from 22 October 2019.
[99] Strategy 2021–2030 (n 71).
[100] See generally E Varney and A Pearson, 'Disability in EU Transport Legislation' in Ferri and Broderick (n 4).
[101] Strategy 2021–2030 (n 71).
[102] Art 1(1) WAD.
[103] Art 4 WAD.
[104] Recital 39 of the Preamble and Article 5 WAD.
[105] Art 2 WAD.

applications and ticketing machines, and check-in machines. It places a range of accessibility obligations on manufacturers, authorised representatives, importers, distributors and service providers,[106] and applies equally to economic operators from the public and private sectors.[107] Similarly to the WAD, Article 14 of the EAA establishes that accessibility requirements do not apply where they would impose a disproportionate burden on the economic operators concerned. This provision includes an additional limit in that accessibility requirements would not apply when they cause significant change in the product or service at stake that results in the fundamental alteration of its basic nature.

The WAD and the EAA tally with an array of other EU legislative instruments that for the most part predate the CRPD, or have been recast or amended after the ratification of the Convention, and address accessibility, such as the Directive that harmonises laws related to radio equipment[108] or the Audio-Visual Media Services Directive.[109] The latter was most recently amended in 2018,[110] and requires, in Article 7, Member States to ensure that audio-visual media services are made accessible for persons with disabilities. Most of those instruments have been based on Article 114 TFEU. In that regard, while the extensive use of this legal basis is certainly not a novelty and has given rise to a debate on the competence creep,[111] it can be safely argued that the CRPD has provoked a 'quantitative shift' in the adoption of new harmonising legislation addressing accessibility. Even when the approach adopted is that of minimum harmonisation, the capacity for Member States to conduct an autonomous policy to increase access appears rather limited.

C. Participation of Person with Disabilities: Soft Law, 'Mutual Recognition' as Stepping Stones Towards an EU 'Centralised' Approach

Participation is a general principle of the CRPD, and is mentioned at various junctures of the Convention.[112] Given such a cross-cutting nature of participation

[106] Art 7 *et seq* EAA.

[107] Recital 57 EAA.

[108] Directive 2014/53/EU on the harmonisation of the laws of the Member States relating to the making available on the market of radio equipment and repealing Directive 1999/5/EC [2014] OJ L153/62.

[109] Directive 2010/13/EU on the coordination of certain provisions laid down by law, regulation or administrative action in Member States concerning the provision of audio-visual media services (Audio-Visual Media Services Directive) [2010] OJ L95/1.

[110] Directive 2018/1808 amending Directive 2010/13/EU [2018] OJ L303/69.

[111] S Garben and I Govaere, 'The Division of Competences between the EU and the Member States: Reflections on the Past, the Present and the Future' in S Garben and I Govaere (eds), *The Division of Competences Between the EU and the Member States: Reflections on the Past, the Present and the Future* (Hart Publishing, 2017).

[112] See Arts 3 (General principles), 19 (Living independently and being included in the community), 24 (Education), 26 (Habilitation and rehabilitation), 29 (Participation in political and public life), and 30 (Participation in cultural life, recreation, leisure and sport) CRPD.

for the purpose of the CRPD, an array of EU shared and supporting competences are relevant. Although measures adopted by the EU on accessibility, for example in the area of transport, are an important part of guaranteeing inclusion of persons with disabilities in society, this section focuses on what the Commission itself has identified as pertaining to participation as priority area of action in the EDS, ie free movement rights, community-based living, and participation in cultural and sporting activities.[113] In all those areas the EU has considered its role subsidiary to that of the Member States, making extensive use of soft law, funding, and pilot projects limited to a number of Member States.[114]

The new Strategy 2021–2030 does not contain a specific section on participation, however the theme of participation runs across its priorities. While measures on participation for the most part maintain a 'soft' nature, centralising tendencies can be observed even in relation to most sensitive areas. Most notably, the Commission proposes to create a European Disability Card with a view to 'expand the scope of the mutual recognition of disability status in areas such as labour mobility and benefits related to conditions of service provision'.[115] This measure builds on the pilot European Disability Card (which was not only voluntary in terms of the participation of Member States, but also restricted mainly to areas of culture, leisure, sport and transport)[116] and the European Parking Card; the scope of application of the newly proposed Card seems much broader, extending into highly sensitive areas for the Member States such as social security. While it may be argued that mutual recognition is a tool to avoid integration through harmonisation,[117] the more recent experience of applying it in areas of significant differences among Member States – such as criminal law – has shown that some level of basic comparability among national laws must exist in order for its successful and legitimate application,[118] and adopting mutual recognition measures can, in fact, in turn lead to a need for further approximating measures to support mutual recognition.[119] Thus, the introduction of the principle of mutual recognition into the area of disability might not only require recognising decisions on disability status adopted in one Member State in other Member States, but could also lead to calls for approximation in

[113] EDS (n 70) 5.

[114] For example, the Commission adopted the 'Inclusion and Diversity Strategy' which promotes the participation of young people with disabilities in Erasmus+ youth mobility projects, and taking funding and awareness-raising initiatives in relation to participation in sports. See European Commission, 'Commission Staff Working Document Evaluation of the European Disability Strategy 2010–2020' SWD(2020) 289 final, 24–25.

[115] Strategy 2021–2030 (n 71) 6.

[116] See Commission, 'EU Disability Card' (2021) www.ec.europea.eu.

[117] C Janssens, *The Principle of Mutual Recognition in EU Law* (Oxford University Press, 2013) 258; M Möstl, 'Preconditions and Limits of Mutual Recognition' (2010) 47 *Common Market Law Review* 405.

[118] S Peers, 'Mutual Recognition and Criminal Law in the European Union: Has the Council got it wrong?' (2004) 41 *Common Market Law Review* 5, 20.

[119] See generally V Mitsilegas, *EU Criminal Law After Lisbon: Rights, Trust and the Transformation of Justice in Europe* (Hart Publishing, 2016) 153.

areas of Member State competence (eg legal capacity). Indeed, a need for *more* EU involvement was identified in the area of legal capacity, where the EU (in principle) does not have any competence.[120]

V. THE IMPLEMENTATION OF ARTICLE 33 CRPD IN THE EU

A. The Commission as the EU's Only Focal Point and the Lack of a Coordination Mechanism

Article 33(1) CRPD envisions the implementation of the CRPD through national implementing mechanisms, consisting of 'one or more focal points within government' and, potentially, a 'coordination mechanism'. The Council's Decision on the conclusion of the CRPD[121] entrusted the Commission with the role of the EU's focal point, but is silent on the coordination mechanism. The functioning of the focal point is then set out in the Code of Conduct,[122] which, as pointed out by Reiss, is 'preoccupied foremost with management within the UN monitoring context but not truly with the division of responsibilities between the levels of governance'.[123]

According to De Beco and Hoefmans, the purpose of focal points is '[ensuring] a legitimate place for disability rights on the political agenda' and acting as an 'administrative tool meant for rationalising and centralizing all possible institutional players involved in disability rights policies'.[124] Given its role in the EU's institutional structure,[125] the choice of the Commission as a focal point seems appropriate, and, indeed, necessary. It is, however, more questionable whether the Commission *alone* can fulfil the tasks of an EU focal point, and whether it would not be, in the light of the EU's institutional structure and the division of competences between the EU and the Member States, more appropriate and more effective to add further focal points. At a horizontal level, the CRPD Committee (and indeed the European Parliament)[126] recommended that the EU consider 'the designation of focal points in each European Union institution, agency and body'.[127] While this recommendation was not heeded

[120] Commission, 'Commission Staff Working Document Evaluation of the EDS' (n 114) 26.
[121] Art 3 of the Council Decision (n 1).
[122] Code of Conduct (n 10).
[123] JW Reiss, 'The Convention on the Rights of Persons with Disabilities in the Post-Lisbon European Union' (2012) 19 *Human Rights Brief* 18, 21.
[124] G de Beco and A Hoefmans, 'National Structures for the Implementation and Monitoring of the UN Convention on the Rights of Persons with Disabilities' in G de Beco (ed), *Article 33 of the UN Convention on the Rights of Persons With Disabilities. National Structures for the Implementation and Monitoring of the Convention* (Brill, 2013) 23.
[125] See in particular Art 17 TEU.
[126] European Parliament, 'European Parliament Resolution of 7 July 2016 on the Implementation of the UN Convention on the Rights of Persons with Disabilities, with Special Regard to the Concluding Observations of the UN CRPD Committee' P8_TA(2016)0318, para 166.
[127] CRPD Committee (n 51) para 77.

by the EU,[128] the Commission in its latest Strategy 2021–2030 agreed to 'invest in strengthening coordination at EU level in line with the recommendations' by the CRPD, in particular by 'working with the European Parliament and the Council to ensure that disability matters are adequately taken into account in inter-institutional negotiations', and to 'work together to identify gaps in existing legislation'.[129] In this vein, it suggested designating disability coordinators for EU institutions, bodies, agencies and delegations; organising regular high-level meetings between the Parliament, the Council, the Commission and the European External Action Service, involving also representative organisations of persons with disabilities; and arranging an annual exchange of views with the European Economic and Social Committee and the Committee of Regions. It also encouraged the Member States to mainstream disability in the work of the Council.

Surprisingly, the CRPD Committee did not express any objection to a lack of a coordination mechanism. The Evaluation Study of the EDS mentioned that there was sufficient engagement with Member States, EU institutions and organisations representing persons with disabilities through institutional mechanisms, public events, public consultations and informal meetings.[130] In its initial report to the CRPD Committee, the Commission indicated that '[f]ormal coordination with the Member States is ensured through the human rights working group (COHOM) of the Council'.[131] However, its description – with reference to the Code of Conduct – concentrates on the coordination of international responsibility and representation.[132] Other coordinating methods mentioned by the Commission, ie the High-Level Group on Disability and the annual Work Forum on the Implementation of the CRPD, also 'hardly qualify as a proper governmental coordination mechanism'.[133]

In the EU's quasi-federal structure, in particular having regard to the cross-cutting nature of the CRPD and the array of concurrent powers shared by the EU and the Member States, omitting the creation of a coordination mechanism seems to be functional to the centralising dynamic in the implementation of the CRPD and the Europeanisation of disability rights, while potentially losing out on the benefits of learning from the experience of the Member States.

B. The EU's Multi-Prong Monitoring Mechanism

The EU's monitoring mechanism was first laid out in October 2012, when the Council confirmed a structure comprised of five actors: the European Parliament's

[128] A Hoefmans, 'The EU Framework for Monitoring the CRPD' in Ferri and Broderick (n 4) 83.
[129] Strategy 2021–2030 (n 71) 23.
[130] Commission, 'Commission Staff Working Document Evaluation of the EDS' (n 114) 42.
[131] Commission, 'Initial Report of the European Union' (2014) CRPD/C/EU/1, para 220.
[132] Ibid; see also Hoefmans (n 128) 77.
[133] Hoefmans (n 128) 77.

Petitions Committee, the European Ombudsman, the European Commission, the EU Agency for Fundamental Rights (FRA) and the European Disability Forum (EDF).[134] Following the observations by the CRPD Committee,[135] as well as concerns expressed by scholars,[136] in 2017 the Commission stepped aside.[137] The tasks of the framework – promoting, protecting and monitoring CRPD rights – are to be exercised 'primarily in relation to EU legislation and policy (areas where the Member States have transferred competences to the EU) and, secondarily, vis-à-vis the EU institutions themselves and their internal implementation of the CRPD'.[138]

While the EU's monitoring framework aims to complement national frameworks and independent mechanisms,[139] a mechanism for collaboration and coordination among the EU monitoring framework and the Member States' ones would support an effective monitoring in a quasi-federal structure such as the EU. In its 2016 report, the FRA also argued in favour of closer cooperation between the EU monitoring framework with, inter alia, national frameworks and national human rights institutions (NHRIs).[140] The European Group of NHRIs called for the recognition of the role of the Eurogroup, of Equinet members and of EDF members in relation to undertaking some of the tasks under Article 33(2).[141] In a similar vein, Birtha proposes the establishment of a 'European Platform for CRPD monitoring', including 'representative[s] of the national-level independent mechanisms' as 'the sixth element of the designated European-level framework'.[142] Such a platform could be, inter alia, a forum for 'exchange of experience between national and EU-level CRPD implementation, which might be useful considering the issue of shared competency in many areas, which also effects implementation and monitoring of the Convention in many ways'.[143]

VI. CONCLUDING REMARKS

The EU presents a unique legal nature – it is not a state and it is not a typical international organisation – a federal-like structure that encompasses features

[134] Ibid 76; M Birtha, 'A Chance to Pioneer or a Lost Opportunity? Monitoring Disability Rights Effectively and Independently in the EU in Line with Article 33 of the UN CRPD' (2014) 5 *European Yearbook of Disability Law* 43, 62.

[135] CRPD Committee (n 51) para 77.

[136] Birtha (n 134) 64–65.

[137] Hoefmans (n 128) 82–83. See also the Council, 'Revised EU-Level Framework Required by Article 33.2 of the UN Convention on the Rights of Persons with Disabilities' (2017) 6170/17.

[138] Hoefmans (n 128) 76.

[139] See Commission (n 131) paras 227–28.

[140] FRA, 'Opinion of the European Union Agency for Fundamental Rights concerning Requirements under Article 33(2) of the UN Convention on the Rights of Persons with Disabilities within the EU Context' (20 May 2016) www.fra.europa.eu.

[141] See Birtha (n 134) 71.

[142] Ibid 73.

[143] Ibid.

of a cooperative federalism. In this context, the implementation of the CRPD has rather deeply affected the balance 'between unity and diversity', provoking a centralising effect. It is undeniable that the push towards a deep integration is long-standing, and so is the harsh debate about the *longa manus* of the internal market, which certainly predates the CRPD. However, the need for ensuring some level of uniformity throughout the EU in the enshrinement of disability rights has supported the Europeanisation of disability rights, with the overall deepening of the EU influence over domestic disability law.

The Europeanisation of the concept of disability upheld by the CJEU and endorsed by political institutions and other EU bodies has gone hand in hand with the expansion of disability related legislation. Article 114 TFEU, which, as Schütze notes, is per se a 'functional competence that cuts horizontally across (almost) all other policy areas' not thematically limited, and typical of federal unions,[144] has been the gateway for the 'centralisation' of accessibility legislation. Paradoxically, the CRPD-led centralising dynamic is less pronounced in the non-discrimination field, which is the traditional remit of EU disability law, but where no new legislation was adopted. Further, in the EU's *sui generis* legal order and complex institutional structure, the implementation of Article 33 CRPD has been challenging.[145] The fundamental lack of a coordination mechanism with Member States, although being crucial both for the successful implementation of the CRPD and for a balanced power relationship between the EU and the Member States, is a notable gap. While the EU acting in isolation from its Member States is not reflective of the cooperative federalism-like nature of the EU, it is somewhat 'self-serving' and supports the progressive Europeanisation of disability rights.

On the whole, the implementation of the CRPD in the EU shows a federal centripetal dynamic, in that the EU tends to centralise powers related to disability eroding Member States' prerogatives.

[144] R Schütze, 'Limits to the Union's 'Internal Market' Competence(s)' in L Azoulai (ed), *The Question of Competence in the European Union* (Oxford University Press, 2014) 215.
[145] Birtha (n 134) 44.

2

Germany

Is Cooperative Federalism Generating Multi-Level Barriers or Facilitating Multi-Level Inclusion?

FELIX WELTI

I. INTRODUCTION

THE FEDERAL REPUBLIC of Germany (*Bundesrepublik Deutschland* – BRD) has more than 83 million inhabitants and an annual GDP of around $50,000 per capita. Germany is a member of the European Union (EU), the Council of Europe (COE) and the United Nations (UN) and is a party to nearly all international human rights treaties, including the UN Convention on the Rights of Persons with Disabilities (CRPD), which was ratified in 2008.[1] The Federal Republic of Germany has a parliamentary system of government with a proportional voting system, with the chief of government (the Chancellor) elected by the parliament (*Bundestag*). The current Federal Government consists of a coalition formed by the (progressive) Social Democratic Party of Germany (*Sozialdemokratische Partei Deutschlands* – SPD), the Green Party (*Die Grünen*) and the Free Democratic Party (*Freie Demokratische Partei* – FDP). For the purpose of this analysis, it is useful to recall that, in the last two decades, the SPD and the (conservative) Christian Democratic Union of Germany (*Christlich Demokratische Union Deutschlands /Christlich Soziale Union* – CDU/CSU) alternated in leading the government, partially in coalitions with each other or with the Green Party or the FDP.

[1] See generally M Ganner et al (eds), *The Implementation of the UN Convention on the Rights of Persons with Disabilities in Austria and Germany* (Innsbruck University Press, 2021). It had been clear from the beginning that the CRPD implementation would involve the Federation and the *Länder*. T Degener, 'Welche legislativen Herausforderungen bestehen in Bezug auf die nationale Implementierung der UN-Behindertenrechtskonvention in Bund und Ländern?' (2009) *Behindertenrecht* 34–51.

The Left Party (*Die Linke*) and the right-wing Alternative for Germany (*Alternative für Deutschland* – AfD) are established as minority opposition parties at the federal level.

The Federal Republic of Germany consists of 16 federal states (*Länder*). When it was founded in 1949, the Basic Law (*Grundgesetz* – GG)[2] aimed to establish a strong division of powers, in contrast to the centralised Nazi state of 1933 to 1945, in line with the tradition of a strong role of the sub-national entities since the founding of the German Empire (*Deutsches Reich*) in 1871 with 25 states, that had been sovereign beforehand. In East Germany, the German Democratic Republic (*Deutsche Demokratische Republik* – DDR), allied to the Soviet Union, was established in 1949 as a centralised state. In the process of the reunification of the Federal Republic of Germany and the DDR in 1990, five new *Länder* were established on the territory of the former DDR. Berlin was reunited as a single *Land* through the merging of the former eastern and western parts.

The 16 *Länder* are quite diverse in population, wealth, size, and legal structures. Each of the *Länder* has its own constitution and the power to legislate. Article 28 GG states that the *Länder* must conform to the principles of a republican, democratic and social state governed by the rule of law, and must guarantee democratic municipal self-government. The *Länder* are involved in federal legislation through the second chamber (*Bundesrat* – Federal Council). They also have a parliamentary system of government, characterised by proportional vote. The respective *Länder* governments are usually comprised of different coalition governments centred around the mentioned parties, sometimes including the Left Party or other regional parties.

Further to this brief introduction, which lays out the key features of Germany as a federal state, this contribution aims to discuss the implementation of the CRPD and to unveil whether it has affected German cooperative federalism. While it would not be possible to ascertain a 'measurable' impact of the CRPD on German federal structures, this chapter does, however, discuss the challenges related to the implementation of the CRPD in such a complex federal system. The chapter will adopt the following structure. Section II will explore the division of competences in Germany according to the GG with a distinction of exclusive federal legislative powers, unconditional and conditional concurrent legislative powers and exclusive *Länder* legislative powers. The executive powers rest regularly with the *Länder* except in some special cases. Section III discusses the CRPD implementation in four subsections: the implementation of the concept of disability, non-discrimination provisions, accessibility and participation respectively. Section IV looks at the implementation of Article 33 CRPD. The concept of disability is laid down in nearly identical definitions in federal and

[2] Grundgesetz für die Bundesrepublik Deutschland (Grundgesetz), vom 23 Mai 1949, BGBl S 1, Teil III Gliederungsnummer 100–1, zuletzt geändert durch Artikel 1 und 2 S 2 des Gesetzes vom 29 September 2020, BGBl I S 2048.

Länder laws, which, since 2016, are formulated very similarly to Article 1 CRPD. Non-discrimination based on disability has been enshrined in the GG since 1994. This was derived from the constitutional process in the new *Länder* after German reunification in 1990. Non-discrimination as a duty of authorities is regulated in Disability Equality Acts (*Behindertengleichstellungsgesetze* – BGG) of the Federation and of the *Länder* enacted between 1999 and 2008. These Acts were generally amended in light of the CRPD, in a process that started in 2014. Reasonable accommodation was incorporated in the federal Disability Equality Act in 2016. In federal civil law, non-discrimination is derived from the implementation of EU law, with the General Equal Treatment Act (*Allgemeines Gleichbehandlungsgesetz* – AGG) of 2006,[3] where reasonable accommodation is still not explicitly provided for. Accessibility has also been regulated in the BGG at federal and *Länder* level. For the private sector, in 2021, the Accessibility Strengthening Act (*Barrierefreiheitsstärkungsgesetz* – BFSG) has established, for the first time, a legislative framework to implement the European Accessibility Act (EAA).[4] When it comes to Article 33 CRPD, the chapter discusses how this provision has been implemented by means of a focal point within the Federal Ministry of Labour and Social Affairs and focal points within the *Länder* governments. A coordination mechanism has also been established within the Federal Disability Commissioner, who benefits from an advisory board of representatives of organisations of persons with disabilities. Finally, the independent monitoring task envisaged by Article 33(2) CRPD is exercised by the German Human Rights Institute. Based on the discussion conducted in sections III and IV, section V offers some concluding remarks.

II. DIVISION OF COMPETENCES

According to the GG, the authority to exercise public powers and discharge state functions remains with the *Länder* in so far as the GG does not provide or permit otherwise (Article 30 GG). Consequently, the *Länder* have the right to legislate insofar as the GG does not confer legislative power on the Federation (Article 70 GG). Not only do the *Länder* execute their own laws, but also federal laws (Articles 84–85 GG) as far as there is no special federal authority explicitly tasked to do so (Article 87 GG). The judicial power is vested in the judges; it is exercised by the Federal Constitutional Court (*Bundesverfassungsgericht* – BVerfG), by the federal courts provided for in the GG and by the courts of the *Länder* (Article 92 GG).

[3] Allgemeines Gleichbehandlungsgesetz (AGG) vom 14 August 2006, BGBl I S 1897, zuletzt geändert durch Artikel 8 des Gesetzes vom 3 April 2013, BGBl I S 610.

[4] Directive (EU) 2019/882 on the accessibility requirements for products and services [2019] OJ L151/70. See D Ferri and N Šubic, 'The European Union: Federal Trends in Disability Rights' in this volume.

Regarding legislative powers, the GG distinguishes between concurrent legislative powers (Articles 72–74 GG) and exclusive legislative powers (Article 73 GG) of the Federation. The Federation has exclusive legislative power with respect to 14 subjects, including foreign relations, citizenship and benefits for persons disabled by war (Article 73 GG). On matters coming under concurrent legislative powers the *Länder* shall have the power to legislate so long as, and to the extent that, the Federation has not exercised its legislative power (Article 72(1) GG). Federal law has precedence over *Land* law (Article 31 GG). If there is a divergence between federal law and *Land* law, where both the Federation and *Land* are entitled to legislate, federal law supersedes *Land* law. There is a long list of 31 matters of concurrent legislative power including civil law, public welfare, labour law and social security (Article 74 GG). However, disability and non-discrimination are not explicitly mentioned as areas of competence, except for disabilities that are caused by war.

Since the constitutional reform of 2006,[5] the Federation has had the right, for some of these matters, to legislate only if and to the extent that the establishment of equivalent living conditions or the maintenance of legal or economic unity renders federal legislation necessary. Federal legislation can be subject to judicial review by the BVerfG, with each of the *Länder* being empowered to bring a case. This conditional concurrent legislative power applies, eg for public welfare, whilst unconditional concurrent legislative power applies, eg for civil law and social security. Especially on these matters, the Federation tends to use the legislative power extensively. As noted above, matters not mentioned in the GG fall within the exclusive power of the *Länder* (Article 70 GG). Some examples of these matters comprise education and public security.

The governments of the *Länder* are involved in the adoption of federal legislation. The *Bundesrat* as the federal body representing the *Länder* plays a role in each act of federal legislation. Within the *Bundesrat*, depending on the size of their population, the *Länder* governments each have between three and six votes (Article 51 GG), which gives a relatively strong position to smaller *Länder*. The *Bundesrat* can comment upon, and delay, each bill and is entitled to introduce federal bills itself. The *Bundesrat* must consent to bills that regulate the execution of federal laws by the *Länder* (Article 84 GG), or if they bear financial expenditure for the *Länder* (Article 104a GG). Consequently, social welfare laws are normally dependent on *Bundesrat* consent, whilst social security in the form of social insurance is not.

The *Länder* execute federal laws, partially in their own right (Article 84 GG), and partially on federal commission (Article 85 GG). Federal administration (Articles 86–90) is foreseen for foreign service, armed forces, financial administration, some regulation authorities, and social insurance institutions, as far as

[5] Gesetz zur Änderung des Grundgesetzes vom 28 August 2006, BGBl I, 2034; A Gunlicks, 'German Federalism and Recent Reform Efforts' (2005) 6 *German Law Journal* 1283–95.

their jurisdiction extends beyond the territory of more than three *Länder*, and especially the Federal Labour Agency. Also, according to the execution of laws, *Länder* oversee social welfare, but they are not strongly involved in social insurance, which also, even if their bodies are on *Länder* level, are self-administrating with a strong input role of employers and trade unions.

This constitutional order and practice have led to a system of cooperative federalism.[6] Federation and *Länder* are intertwined in legislation and execution of laws, and the *Länder* represent the interest of public administration in the constitutional process. Consequently, formal and informal cooperative structures are vital. In several areas of competence, conferences of the *Länder* governments, partially involving the Federal Government, take place. One example is the Conference of Educational Ministers (*Kultusministerkonferenz* – KMK), where the *Länder* coordinate their educational policies. In several matters, especially in higher education and social security and welfare, the GG allows administrative cooperation of the Federation and the *Länder* (Articles 91a–91e GG). There is also a complex architecture within the federal finance system (Articles 104a–109 GG). Federation and *Länder* have, in principle, separated budgets which, however, are not independent from each other.

The *Länder* are involved in the participation of the Federation in international treaties. Both the *Bundesrat* and *Länder* take part with regard to legislative Acts of the EU (Article 23 GG) and the *Bundesrat* must participate in the conclusion of treaties and consent if they refer to their competences (Article 59 GG). International treaties, like the CRPD have the same standing as federal laws and, like them, shall take precedence over *Land* law.[7] The *Länder* are committed to federal loyalty, and consequently to compliance with international treaties including the CRPD.[8]

The BVerfG and German case law follow a dualistic approach to international law. International treaties are not fully incorporated into German legislation. However, German courts and public authorities are, according to the BVerfG, obliged to take international treaties in account for interpretation and application of federal and *Länder* law including constitutional law and, as far as possible, to prefer an interpretation in line with international law that is binding for Germany. They also shall take into account the interpretations of international courts, especially the European Court of Human Rights (ECtHR).[9] The UN Committees do not have the status of a court in the view of the BVerfG, and this para-judicial status has been made explicit with

[6] I Härtel (ed), *Handbuch Föderalismus – Föderalismus als demokratische Rechtsordnung und Rechtskultur in Deutschland, Europa und der Welt – Band 2 Probleme, Reformen, Perspektiven des deutschen Föderalismus* (Springer, 2012).

[7] M Banafsche, 'Die internationalen Menschenrechter und das deutsche Recht' in M Banafsche and H-W Platzer (eds), *Soziale Menschenrechte und Arbeit* (Nomos, 2015) 57–88.

[8] M Krajewski, 'Zur Bindung der Bundesländer an das Völkerrecht – Die innerstaatliche Wirkung der Behindertenrechtskonvention' (2010) *Sozialrecht und Praxis* 250–56.

[9] Bundesverfassungsgericht (BVerfG) ('Görgülü') 14/10/2004, 2 BvR 1481/04, BVerfGE 111, 307.

regard to the UN Committee on the Rights of Persons with Disabilities (CRPD Committee).[10] Consequently, German courts shall take the jurisprudence of the CRPD Committee into account only as a political statement, which, however, can give interpretative support. In this regard, German scholars have posited that the BVerfG works as a 'hardener of soft law', without, however, giving this process a clear dogmatic basis.[11]

III. THE ROLE OF THE NATIONAL GOVERNMENT VIS-À-VIS SUB-NATIONAL ENTITIES IN SELECTED AREAS

A. The Concept of Disability

Disability (*Behinderung*) as a term and a concept has been the subject of federal legislation, especially in the field of social security and welfare, and of *Länder* legislation, in particular regarding the field of education, since the 1950s. A legal definition, which followed the International Classification of Impairments, Disabilities and Handicaps (ICIDH), had been implemented in federal legislation in 1986.[12]

In 2001, the Social Code Book Nine – Rehabilitation and Participation of Disabled Persons (*Sozialgesetzbuch* – SGB IX)[13] – was adopted. In paragraph 2 SGB IX, a new definition of disability was enshrined:

> Persons are disabled, if their physical, mental or intellectual functions with high probability deviate more than six months from the typical conditions usual for their age and therefore their participation in society is hindered.

According to the government's legislative material,[14] this definition was meant to adopt the concept of disability encompassed by the International Classification of Functioning, Disability and Health (ICF). The same definition, aligned with the ICF, was adopted in 2002 in paragraph 3 BGG.[15] The *Länder* included similar definitions in their Disabled Equality Acts, which were adopted after the

[10] BVerfG ('Voting Rights') 29/01/2019, 2 BvC 62/14, BVerfGE 151, 1; BVerfG ('Medical Treatment') 26/07/2016, 1 BvL 8/15, BVerfGE 142, 313. For a critical account see K Schmalenbach, 'Anmerkung' (2019) *Juristenzeitung* 567–69.

[11] K Reiling, 'Die Anwendung des Grundsatzes der Völkerrechtsfreundlichkeit auf rechtsunverbindliche internationale Standards' (2018) 78 *Zeitschrift für ausländisches öffentliches Recht und Völkerrecht* 311–38.

[12] Deutscher Bundestag, BT-Drs 12/7148, 2.

[13] Sozialgesetzbuch – Neuntes Buch – Rehabilitation und Teilhabe von Menschen mit Behinderungen vom 23 Dezember 2016, BGBl I S 3234, zuletzt geändert durch Art 7c des Gesetzes vom 27 September 2021, BGBl I S 4530.

[14] Deutscher Bundestag, BT-Drs 14/5074, 98.

[15] Gesetz zur Gleichstellung von Menschen mit Behinderungen (Behindertengleichstellungsgesetz) vom 27 April 2002, BGBl I S 1467, 1468, zuletzt geändert durch Artikel 9 des Gesetzes vom 2 Juni 2021, BGBl I S 1387.

federal BGG.[16] The General Equal Treatment Act of 2006, which is meant to implement the EU Equal Treatment Directives,[17] also prohibits discrimination on the grounds of disability. While it does not define disability, preparatory material related to the AGG refers to paragraph 2 SGB IX.[18]

In the case law of the Federal Social Court (*Bundessozialgericht* – BSG), certain changes in the recognition of persons as severely disabled were based on the new concept of disability outlined in paragraph 2 SGB IX. For example, the burden of therapeutic measures was taken into account when classifying the severity of diabetes for an individual.[19] Notably, the preparation for reform of criteria for the recognition of a person as severely disabled is currently ongoing. It is a very complex process due to the fact that it must be carried out by

[16] Bayerisches Behindertengleichstellungsgesetz vom 9 Juli 2003, GVBl S 419, zuletzt geändert durch para 1 und para 2 des Gesetzes vom 24 Juli 2020, GVBl S 388; Gesetz des Landes Brandenburg zur Gleichstellung von Menschen mit Behinderungen (Brandenburgisches Behindertengleichstellungsgesetz) vom 11 Februar 2013, GVBl I Nr 5, zuletzt geändert durch Gesetz vom 18 Dezember 2018, GVBl I Nr 38; Gesetz des Landes Sachsen-Anhalt zur Gleichstellung von Menschen mit Behinderungen (Behindertengleichstellungsgesetz Sachsen-Anhalt) vom 16 Dezember 2010, GVBl LSA S 584, zuletzt geändert durch Gesetz vom 6 Mai 2019, GVBl LSA S 85; Gesetz des Landes Nordrhein-Westfalen zur Gleichstellung von Menschen mit Behinderung (Behindertengleichstellungsgesetz Nordrhein-Westfalen) vom 16 Dezember 2003, GV NRW S 766, zuletzt geändert durch Gesetz vom 11 April 2019, GV NRW S 207; Bremisches Behindertengleichstellungsgesetz vom 18 Dezember 2018, Brem GBl S 608, zuletzt geändert durch Geschäftsverteilung des Senats vom 20 Oktober 2020, BremGBl S 1172; Hessisches Gesetz zur Gleichstellung von Menschen mit Behinderungen (Hessisches Behinderten-Gleichstellungsgesetz) vom 20 Dezember 2004, GVBl I S 482, zuletzt geändert durch Gesetz vom 19 Juni 2019, GVBl S 161; Hamburgisches Gesetz zur Gleichstellung von Menschen mit Behinderungen (Hamburgisches Behindertengleichstellungsgesetz) vom 19 Dezember 2019, HmbGVBl S 13; Landesgesetz zur Gleichstellung, Inklusion und Teilhabe von Menschen mit Behinderungen [Rheinland-Pfalz] (Landesinklusionsgesetz) vom 22 Dezember 2020, GVBL RLP S 719; Gesetz über die Gleichberechtigung von Menschen mit und ohne Behinderungen [Berlin] (Landesgleichberechtigungsgesetz) vom 27 September 2021, GVBl S 1167 (Landesinklusionsgesetz) vom 17 Dezember 2020, GVBl S 719.

[17] Deutscher Bundestag, BT-Drs 16/1780, 1; Landesgesetz zur Gleichstellung von Menschen mit Behinderungen [Baden-Württemberg] (Landes-Behindertengleichstellungsgesetz) vom 17 Dezember 2014, GBl S 819, zuletzt geändert durch Gesetz vom 18 Dezember 2018, GBl S 1560; Gesetz zur Gleichstellung, gleichberechtigten Teilhabe und Integration von Menschen mit Behinderungen (Landesbehindertengleichstellungsgesetz) vom 10 Juli 2006, GVOBl M-V S 539, zuletzt geändert durch Gesetz vom 29 Mai 2021, GVOBl M-V S 838; Gesetz zur Gleichstellung von Menschen mit Behinderung in Schleswig-Holstein (Landesbehindertengleichstellungsgesetz) vom 18 November 2008, GVOBl Schl-H S 582, zuletzt geändert durch Gesetz vom 2 April 2019, GVOBl Schl-H S 76; Niedersächsisches Behindertengleichstellungsgesetz vom 25 November 2007, Nds GVBl S 661, zuletzt geändert durch Artikel 1 des Gesetzes vom 16 Dezember 2021, Nds GVBl S 921; Gesetz zur Stärkung der Inklusion von Menschen mit Behinderungen im Freistaat Sachsen (Sächsisches Inklusionsgesetz) vom 2 Juli 2019, SächsGVBl S 542; Gesetz zur Gleichstellung von Menschen mit Behinderungen im Saarland (Saarländisches Behindertengleichstellungsgesetz) vom 26 November 2003, Amtsbl I S 2987, zuletzt geändert durch Gesetz vom 8 Dezember 2021, Amtsbl I S 2629; Thüringer Gesetz zur Inklusion und Gleichstellung von Menschen mit Behinderungen vom 30 Juli 2019, GVBl S 303, zuletzt geändert durch Gesetz vom 21 Dezember 2020, GVBl S 682; See generally H Frehe and F Welti (eds), *Behindertengleichstellungsrecht, Textsammlung mit Einführungen*, 3rd edn (Nomos, 2018).

[18] Deutscher Bundestag, BT-Drs 16/1780, 31.

[19] BSG 25/10/2012, B 9 SB 2/12 R; S Knickrehm, 'Die Feststellungen nach § 69 SGB IX im Lichte des "modernen" Behinderungsbegriffs' (2008) *Die Sozialgerichtsbarkeit* 220–27.

authorities and physicians who are part of the *Länder* authorities. This means that the federal Ministry for Labour and Social Affairs has to go through a cooperative process with the *Länder* ministries and their physicians, who have administrative competence and are a prerequisite for the implementation. However, the federal Ministry also aims to involve in the process organisations of persons with disabilities, who are sceptical towards it and fear a hardening of recognition criteria.[20]

In case law related to the application of the AGG as federal labour law, the concept of disability enshrined in the CRPD was implemented via EU law. The Federal Labour Court (*Bundesarbeitsgericht* – BAG), in 2013, with reference to the Court of Justice of the European Union (CJEU) and the CRPD, ruled that a claimant with HIV but who was asymptomatic could be regarded as a person with disabilities and hence be protected against discriminatory dismissal.[21]

In 2013, the Federal Government commissioned an evaluation of the BGG, to examine whether there was a need for reform with a view of aligning with and implementing the CRPD.[22] This evaluation stated that there was not enough awareness of the new concept of disability and recommended an improved alignment with the CRPD, which had already occurred in the *Länder* BGG in Brandenburg and Saxony-Anhalt.[23] Following this evaluation, in 2016, paragraph 3 BGG was reformulated[24] as follows:

> Persons with disabilities in the sense of this act are persons who have long-term physical, mental, intellectual or sensory impairments which, in interaction with attitudinal and environmental barriers, may hinder their equal participation in society. A long-term is one with a duration of most probably more than six months.[25]

Also in 2016, the Federal Participation Act (*Bundesteilhabegesetz* – BTHG)[26] reformed the SGB IX and included in paragraph 2 SGB IX a nearly identical formulation.[27] Unlike paragraph 3 BGG, it provides that impairments typical of

[20] 'Deutscher Behindertenrat, DBR kritisiert die geplante Neufassung der VersMedV' (2019) *Sozialrecht und Praxis* 296–306.

[21] BAG 19/12/2013, 6 AZR 190/12, BAGE 147, 60; V Aichele, 'Die praktische Geltung der Menschenrechte – Zur aktuellen Diskussion über die Bedeutung und Tragweite des UN-Völkervertragsrechts für die gerichtliche Praxis am Beispiel der UN-Behindertenrechtskonvention' (2016) *Deutsche Richterzeitung* 342–47.

[22] F Welti et al, 'Evaluation des Behindertengleichstellungsgesetzes – Abschlussbericht' (BMAS-Forschungsberichte 445I, 2013); F Welti, 'Barrierefreiheit und angemessene Vorkehrungen' (2015) *Sozialer Fortschritt* 267–73.

[23] Para 2 BGG LSA (2010); para 3 BbgBGG (2013).

[24] Gesetz zur Weiterentwicklung des Behindertengleichstellungsrechts vom 19 Juli 2016, BGBl I S 1757.

[25] Deutscher Bundestag, BT-Drs 18/7824, 21.

[26] Gesetz zur Stärkung der Teilhabe und Selbstbestimmung von Menschen mit Behinderungen (Bundesteilhabegesetz) vom 23 Dezember 2016, BGBl I S 3234 zuletzt geändert durch Artikel 9 des Gesetzes vom 2 Juni 2021, BGBl I S 1387.

[27] Deutscher Bundestag, BT-Drs 18/9522, 227.

older age cannot be the basis for recognition of a disability, which is a concept related to employment. Those definitions have however been subject to criticism and scholarly discussion. Controversial points have, in particular, centred upon the relationship between age and disability, the six-month rule and the failure to use the wording of the CRPD 'full and effective participation' in paragraph 2 SGB IX and paragraph 3 BGG.[28]

The Federal Participation Act 2016 included a reform of the social welfare system for persons with disabilities (*Eingliederungshilfe*). It constitutes a part of federal legislation and is implemented and financed by *Länder* and municipalities. Persons with disabilities are entitled to benefits in the form of integration assistance when they are 'essentially disabled'. This term traditionally applies to blind and deaf persons, persons with physical impairments, and persons with an intellectual disability, having an IQ of below 70. To a certain degree, people with mental disabilities and drug-addicted persons have been included within the scope of this Act. Long and controversial discussions about this new definition of 'essentially disabled' occurred among the Federal Ministry, the *Länder* (represented by the conference of Ministries for Labour and Social Affairs (*Arbeits- und Sozialministerkonferenz* – ASMK)) and municipality representatives (represented by the organisations of towns (*Deutscher Städtetag*), counties (*Deutscher Landkreistag*), and social assistance bodies (*Bundesarbeitsgemeinschaft überörtlicher Träger der Sozialhilfe* – BAGüS)) as well as the representatives of organisations of persons with disabilities,[29] given the fear of *Länder* and municipalities that this new definition could expand the scope of the system and the financial burden upon them.[30] A first draft of the reform included the 'five of nine' formula, meaning that the essentially disabled would comprise those persons who are impaired in five of the nine ICF domains.[31] After political debates and protests by organisations of persons with disabilities, a research project was set up to ascertain whether this new concept would narrow the scope of the Act. The report was published in 2018[32] and presented the findings of this research, stating that it was likely that some persons would fall outside of the system and lose their entitlements. Moreover, the report suggested that the ICF concept was not designed to define the scope of a social welfare system. Notwithstanding the results of this research, in 2021, federal legislation still referred to 'essentially disabled' as a legally non-defined

[28] H Frehe, 'Kritik am Behinderungsbegriff des Bundesteilhabegesetzentwurfes' Beitrag D 27–2016 (18 July 2016) www.reha-recht.de; R Kessler, 'Anmerkungen zur Reform des sozialrechtlichen Behinderungsbegriffs' (2016) *Die Sozialgerichtsbarkeit* 373–378.

[29] Compare R Schmachtenberg, 'Das Bundesteilhabegesetz – Vom Koalitionsvertrag zum Gesetz' (2018) *Neue Zeitschrift für Sozialrecht* 337–350.

[30] See for critical account H Fuchs, 'Rechtsetzung, Rechtsimplementierung und Glaubwürdigkeit am Beispiel des Teilhaberechts' in M Fuchs et al (eds), *Gesundheit, Alter, Pflege, Rehabilitation – Recht und Praxis im interdisziplinären Dialog – Festschrift für Gerhard Igl* (Nomos, 2017) 351–363.

[31] Deutscher Bundestag, BT-Drs 18/9522, 275–277.

[32] Deutscher Bundestag, BT-Drs 19/4500.

term within the Participation Strengthening Act (*Teilhabestärkungsgesetz*).[33] It now will be concretised with a federal Directive and subsequently implemented by the *Länder* and municipal authorities.

In the Disabled Equality Acts of the *Länder*, reforms that have taken place since 2016, have changed the definition of disability. Five of the 16 Acts have aligned with the CRPD definition and include a reference to 'full and effective participation', two do not mention the long-term nature of the impairment, six still mention the deviation from the typical conditions usual for the age, and one uses the term 'external barriers'. This shows that there is an ongoing debate about the concept of disability at the level of *Länder* legislation. However, there is as yet no case law or other evidence showing whether or how the slightly differing legal definition of disability in the *Länder*-BGG has any influence on the application of the law. Differences between the federal and the *Länder* levels and, indeed, between the numerous *Länder*, often emerge at the political level and trickle down into legislation. However, it is unclear if they reach the level of administration and lead to notable practical differences. Further research would be needed to ascertain differences in implementation.

B. Non-Discrimination and Equality

The first discussions about an equality law for disabled persons in Germany started in the 1980s.[34] In 1990, there were some attempts to include a non-discrimination provision in a draft paper of the 'round table' for a new constitution of the German Democratic Republic. However, this new constitution never came into force, and the DDR adopted the *Grundgesetz*. Then, for the first time in German constitutional law, protection and non-discrimination of disabled persons were enshrined with different sentences in the constitutions of the new *Länder* of Brandenburg,[35] Berlin,[36] Mecklenburg-Western Pomerania,[37] Saxony-Anhalt,[38] Saxony,[39] and Thuringia.[40] Berlin and Brandenburg had used explicit non-discrimination clauses, whilst the other new *Länder* had enshrined the protection of disabled persons as a state objective.

With Article 5 of the Unification Treaty 1990, a Constitutional Commission of the Federation and the *Länder* (64 members, 32 appointed by the *Bundestag*,

[33] Deutscher Bundestag, BT-Drs 19/27400, 64; Gesetz zur Stärkung der Teilhabe von Menschen mit Behinderungen sowie zur landesrechtlichen Bestimmung der Träger von Leistungen für Bildung und Teilhabe in der Sozialhilfe, Teilhabestärkungsgesetz vom 2 Juni 2021 BGBl I S 1387.

[34] T Degener and M von Miquel (eds), *Aufbrüche und Barrieren – Behindertenpolitik und Behindertenrecht in Deutschland und Europa seit den 1970er Jahren* (Transcript, 2019).

[35] Art 12 Constitution of Brandenburg.

[36] Art 11 Constitution of Berlin.

[37] Art 17a Constitution of Mecklenburg-Vorpommern.

[38] Art 38 Constitution of Saxony-Anhalt.

[39] Art 7 Constitution of the Free State of Saxony.

[40] Art 2 Constitution of the Free State of Thuringia.

32 by the *Länder* via the *Bundesrat*) had been established. Changes in the GG need a majority of two-thirds in the *Bundestag* and in the *Bundesrat* (Article 79 GG). In 1994, the Constitutional Commission made proposals for a constitutional reform, but the inclusion of an anti-discrimination clause on the grounds of disability was deemed controversial.[41] As a result, in Article 3(3) GG, the following sentence was added: 'No person shall be disfavoured because of disability'.

After several reforms, as yet, 13 of 16 *Länder* constitutions mention disability explicitly, most of them in a non-discrimination context.[42] Schleswig-Holstein also refers to inclusion as a linkage to the CRPD.[43]

The constitutional reform was the starting point for new discussions, which led to the above-mentioned SGB IX and the Federal Disability Equality Act. In two of the *Länder*, Berlin (1999) and Saxony-Anhalt (2001), a Disability Equality Act had been approved before the Federal Act of 2002, while in the 14 remaining *Länder* similar Acts came into force between 2002 and 2008.[44] The Disability Equality Acts are binding for the public authorities of the Federation respectively and for the authorities of every single *Land*. Due to the protests of the disability movement and further to adoption of the EU Directives, the General Equal Treatment Act was adopted in 2006.

In its memorandum, before ratifying the CRPD, the Federal Government said that Article 5 CRPD is being implemented in German law via Article 3 GG, the BGG and the AGG.[45] This was the starting point for discussions on whether Article 5 CRPD, and specifically the duty to provide reasonable accommodation, could be implemented only by interpreting the existing German federal and *Länder* laws in an extensive manner, or if there was a requirement for legal reforms.[46] In that regard, the Federal Social Court stated that Article 5 CRPD, including the right to reasonable accommodation, was directly applicable and in line with Article 3(3) GG.[47]

[41] Deutscher Bundestag, BT-Drs 12/6000, 53; G Jürgens, 'Grundrecht für Behinderte' (1995) *Neue Zeitschrift für Verwaltungsrecht* 452–53.

[42] Art 2b Constitution of Baden-Württemberg; Art 118a Constitution of the Free State of Bavaria; Art 2a of the Constitution of the Free Hanseatic City of Bremen; Art 3 of the Lower Saxonian Constitution; Art 64 of the Constitution of Rhineland-Palatinate; Art 12 of the Constitution of the Saarland.

[43] Art 7 Constitution of Schleswig-Holstein has the heading '*Inklusion*', which is a reference to the CRPD-wording, see LT-Drs 18/2095, 27.

[44] Bayrisches Behindertengleichstellungsgesetz; Brandenburgisches Behindertengleichstellungsgesetz; Behindertengleichstellungsgesetz Sachsen-Anhalt; Behindertengleichstellungsgesetz Nordrhein-Westfalen; Bremisches Behindertengleichstellungsgesetz; Hessisches Behinderten-Gleichstellungsgesetz; Hamburgisches Behindertengleichstellungsgesetz; Landesgesetz zur Gleichstellung, Inklusion und Teilhabe von Menschen mit Behinderungen [Rheinland-Pfalz]; Landesgleichberechtigungsgesetz (n 16).

[45] Deutscher Bundestag, BT-Drs 16/10808, 48.

[46] T Degener (n 1) 34–51; F Welti, 'Das Diskriminierungsverbot und die „angemessenen Vorkehrungen" in der BRK – Stellenwert für die staatliche Verpflichtung zur Umsetzung der in der BRK geregelten Rechte' Forum D 9/2012 (31 May 2012) www.reha-recht.de.

[47] BSG 06/03/2012, B 1 KR 10/11 R, BSGE 110, 194.

Shortly after the ratification of the CRPD, the full applicability of the CRPD for the *Länder* and the municipal authorities was disputed in administration and case law.[48] In 2009, the Higher Administrative Court of Hesse, in a case concerning reasonable accommodation in school, held that it was uncertain whether the CRPD was fully binding on the Hessian school authorities.[49] However, in more recent years, *Länder* legislation and case law related to the application of *Länder* law started referring to the CRPD. Further, *Länder* governments adopted action plans for the implementation of the CRPD. The BVerfG also referred to the CRPD in decisions related to *Länder* laws,[50] and the Higher Administrative Courts started using the CRPD for interpreting the *Länder* laws[51] after *Länder* legislation had referred to it, especially in school law reforms.

In the evaluation of the BGG 2013/2014, federal authorities recommended a clarification outlining that reasonable accommodation is part of non-discrimination duties as already included in the BGG of Saxony-Anhalt. This was then laid down in 2016 in paragraph 7 BGG. The legislation for the rest of the *Länder* BGG followed this. As of today, in 14 of 16 *Länder* BGG reasonable accommodation is mentioned as a duty of the *Länder* authorities. However, in three of them (Bavaria, Hesse, Saxony), this is not completely binding for municipal authorities. In Federal Civil Law, reasonable accommodation as a duty of employers and companies still is not explicitly enshrined. This has been criticised with reference to EU Directives and to the CRPD.[52]

For the enforcement of the AGG, a Federal Anti-Discrimination Office (*Antidiskriminierungsstelle*) (paragraph 25 AGG) has been set up. For the enforcement of the BGG, a Federal Commissioner for Persons with Disabilities (*Beauftragter der Bundesregierung für die Belange von Menschen mit Behinderungen*) has been created (paragraph 17 BGG). Anti-discrimination offices and disability commissioners are also to be found on the *Länder* level. There are annual conferences of Disability Commissioners as well as of anti-discrimination offices of the Federation and of the *Länder* for coordinating their efforts.

[48] Krajewski (n 8) 250–56; J von Bernstorff, 'Anmerkungen zur innerstaatlichen Anwendbarkeit ratifizierter Menschenrechtsverträge' (2011) *Recht der Jugend und des Bildungswesens* 203–17. See for Bavaria: T Bernhard, *Anforderungen an ein inklusives Bildungssystem nach der UN-Behindertenrechtskonvention – Eine Untersuchung der Rechtslage im Freistaat Bayern* (Nomos, 2016).

[49] Hessischer Verwaltungsgerichtshof, 12/11/2009, 7 B 2763/09; Compare Lower Saxony: Oberverwaltungsgericht Niedersachsen 16/09/2010, 2 ME 278/10.

[50] BVerfG ('Medical Treatment in Psychiatric Prison') 23/03/2011, 2 BvR 882/09.

[51] Lower Saxony: Oberverwaltungsgericht Niedersachsen 07/08/2014, 2 ME 272/14; North Rhine-Westphalia: Oberverwaltungsgericht Nordrhein-Westfalen 29/12/2014, 19 A 285/13; Bavaria: Bayerischer Verwaltungsgerichtshof 14/12/2016, 7 CE 16.1861; Baden-Württemberg: Verwaltungsgerichtshof Baden-Württemberg 4/5/2018, 4 S 1394/17; Saxony: Sächsisches Oberverwaltungsgericht 14/02/2022, 2 B 334/21.

[52] E Eichenhofer, *Angemessene Vorkehrungen als Diskriminierungsdimension im Recht* (Nomos, 2018).

of 2021, which will be fully in force starting in 2025. The market surveillance authorities responsible for the implementation (Article 23 lit 2 EAA) are *Länder* authorities (paragraph 20 BFSG). This has been subject to criticism because they are expected to not be as effective as a federal authority could be.[59] The *Länder* Market Surveillance Authorities must cooperate with the Federal Institute for Occupational Safety and Medicine (paragraph 25 BFSG).

Accessibility of public transport is a matter that falls partially within the remit of federal competence and also under that of the *Länder*. Long-distance travel is federally regulated, and the German Railway (*Deutsche Bahn*) is still owned by the Federation. Local and regional transport is regulated by the *Länder* and their legislation, planning and tendering authorities. EU Directives for cross-border travel by railway, aircraft or ship mostly apply to the long-distance travel regulations of the Federation.

With the 2016 reform, a federal special department (*Bundesfachstelle*)[60] for accessibility was established (paragraph 13 BGG). It is one of the Federal Pension Insurance bodies[61] and constitutes the central point of contact in accessibility issues for federal authorities. It also provides advice to enterprises, organisations and civil society. To date, five *Länder* have begun to establish their own special departments. At present, however, there is no overarching strategy for achieving accessibility, even though the coalition agreement of the political parties forming the Federal Government of 2021–25 mentions accessibility several times as an important issue.

D. Participation

Commissioners are a vital instrument to support participation of persons with disabilities. In the Federal Disability Equality Act[62] and in nearly all *Länder* BGG, there is a legal basis for the appointment of such commissioners. At the federal level and in most of the *Länder*, they are part of the government and can participate in government actions. In some *Länder*, the Commissioners are working at parliamentary level.

At the federal level, until 2014, this had been the responsibility of a member of the *Bundestag* with a task force located in the Federal Ministry for Labour

[59] P Rott, 'Das Barrierefreiheitsstärkungsgesetz' E6-E8-2021 (15 September 2021) www.reha-recht.de; U Boysen and J Steinbrück, 'Vom European Accessibility Act zum Barrierefreiheitsstärkungsgesetz' E2-E5-2021 (31 August 2021) www.reha-recht.de.

[60] Bundesfachstelle Barrierefreiheit, 'Bundesfachstelle Barrierefreiheit: Wer wird sind' www.bundesfachstelle-barrierefreiheit.de.

[61] There are 16 administrative bodies carrying out the statutory pension insurance according to the Social Code Book 6 (SGB VI). Fourteen of them are at the *Länder* level and two are at the federal level. The *Bundesfachstelle* is located at one of the Federal Pension Insurance bodies, the *DRV Knappschaft-Bahn-See*, which is the former pension fund for miners, railway workers and seafarers.

[62] Paras 17, 18 BGG; Behindertenbeauftragter, 'English Information' (2022) www.behindertenbeauftragter.de.

and Social Affairs. Since 2014, there has been a *de facto* full-time Commissioner who is herself or himself disabled. Verena Bentele, a former Paralympic biathlon champion who is blind, was appointed in 2014. She had been, before her appointment, politically active at the *Land* level in Bavaria and a member of the municipal council of Munich. She changed position in 2017 to the presidency of the *Sozialverband* VdK,[63] which, with more than 2 million members, is the biggest organisation of persons with disabilities in Germany. Jürgen Dusel, the former Brandenburg *Land* Commissioner, was appointed Federal Commissioner in 2018 and was reappointed in 2022. These examples show that there is an exchange of personnel between federal and *Länder* levels, which can contribute to integration between the political spheres, and to the exchange of knowledge related to the challenges of implementing the CRPD at the federal, *Länder* and municipal levels.

The Federal Commissioner is appointed by the Federal Government and is responsible for working toward equal living conditions of persons with disabilities in all parts of society. Federal ministries must involve the Commissioner in all legislative Acts and other relevant plans as far as they affect persons with disabilities. The Commissioner and his or her task force work are inside the Federal Ministry for Labour and Social Affairs. This may lead to the (wrong) impression that they are primarily responsible for social affairs, which would not constitute a proper reflection of the CRPD approach. Consequently, the German Human Rights Institute, as the CRPD monitoring body, has proposed moving the Commissioner's place to within the office of the German Chancellor.

With regard to the implementation of the CRPD, the Commissioner works together with the Advisory Board of Inclusion (*Inklusionsbeirat*), which consists of members of organisations of persons with disabilities. Moreover, the Commissioner closely consults the organisations in everyday work. The German organisations on the federal level have an umbrella organisation, the German Disability Council (*Deutscher Behindertenrat* – DBR),[64] which consists of three pillars and several hundred organisations. One pillar is composed of the two large traditional social organisations (*Sozialverband*), which have derived from war veterans' organisations. A second one is that of the self-help organisations, centred mostly around a specific impairment. There are more than one hundred of these and they have their own umbrella organisation (*BAG Selbsthilfe*).[65] Moreover, independent organisations like Independent Living (*Selbstbestimmt Leben*) form a third pillar. The DBR does not have its own

[63] V Bentele, 'Yes to UN CRPD Means Yes to Protection Against Discrimination – The Active Role of Civil Society in Implementing the UN Convention on the Rights of Persons with Disabilities' in Ganner et al (n 1).

[64] See www.deutscher-behindertenrat.de.

[65] See www.bag-selbsthilfe.de.

structures or staff. The office rotates between several organisations. The DBR and the various organisations of persons with disabilities can participate in the legislative processes like others. They can be invited to make statements or can provide statements without being invited, which will also be used as material by the ministries and parliamentary committees.

At the *Länder* level, there are also organisations of persons with disabilities, and social organisations, as well as the self-help organisations that are represented. The organisations of persons with disabilities are not systematically involved in advisory bodies of educational policy. Sometimes, they lack the professional capacity for permanent involvement in the political process, and the processes in parliaments are not accessible enough for participation.[66]

Since the BGG reform that occurred in 2016, organisations of persons with disabilities can apply for money from a federal participation fund (paragraph 19 BGG) on a project basis. On the *Länder* level, no public funding mechanism for the political work of the organisations can be found. For projects in the field of self-help, funding is provided by public health insurances, *Länder* and municipalities. The multitude of organisations makes it difficult to organise participatory processes. This is one reason for the strong role of the Commissioners, who, in the eyes of politicians, serve as the 'face' of the movement. This sometimes puts them in an awkward role in-between government and movement.

Nearly all *Länder* now have a full-time Commissioner, and most of them are persons with disabilities, often coming from former activity inside the organisations of persons with disabilities. Some of the *Länder* had disabled and full-time Commissioners before the Federation, some followed later. The *Länder* Commissioners have their legal basis in the *Länder* BGG. In some cases, their independent positions are regulated more explicitly than in the federal law. In some *Länder*, they are appointed by the government, in others they are elected by the parliament (*Landtag*). Some *Länder* also provide an advisory board with a legal position. Some of the Commissioners have their position in the Ministry of Social Affairs, some at the Head of Government and some at the *Land* parliament. The Federal Commissioner and the *Länder* Commissioners hold an annual meeting, where they normally agree on a declaration, which is an important statement on ongoing processes in disability policy and often in CRPD implementation.[67] This is important, because the consensus of the Commissioners reflects a multi-party and multi-level consensus in disability policy.

[66] L Grigoryan, 'Representative Participation of Disabled Persons at Educational Policy-Making Processes in Germany' in Ganner et al (n 1).

[67] Sächsische Staatskanzlei, '"Dresdner Positionen" – Forderungen der Behindertenbeauftragten von Bund und Ländern an die Bundesregierung' (15 October 2021) www.sk-sachsen.de.

IV. THE IMPLEMENTATION OF ARTICLE 33 CRPD

A. Focal Points

As mentioned above, the Ministry for Labour and Social Affairs is the federal focal point according to Article 33(1) CRPD. It coordinates the National Action Plans. Up to now, two action plans have been made, which try to coordinate and bring together the activities of all ministries and authorities on the federal level. The national action plans also mention fields of action, which are the legislative responsibility of the *Länder*, such as the right to education. In this field, federal actions consist of the funding of research projects, conferences, and awards. The national action plan of the Federal Government cannot consist of actions that are in the legislative field of the *Länder*.

All *Länder* have designated focal points themselves. Some of the *Länder* have legal regulations about the focal point, for example paragraph 8 of the Inclusion Principles Act (*Inklusionsgrundsätzegesetz*) in North-Rhine Westphalia. The *Länder* have also developed their own action plans. The focal points of the Federation and those of the *Länder* coordinate and meet regularly.

B. Coordination Mechanism

The Commissioner of the Federal Government for persons with disabilities has been designated as a coordination mechanism according to Article 33(1) CRPD.[68] For this purpose, the Commissioner has the responsibility for the inclusion advisory board, which consists primarily of representatives of organisations of persons with disabilities and further represents the involvement of civil society according to Article 33(3) CRPD. It has four committees, which involve representatives of employers, trade unions, service providers, scientists, and other organisations.

C. Framework/Independent Mechanism

The Federal Government has appointed the German Institute for Human Rights (*Deutsches Institut für Menschenrechte* – DIM) as an independent mechanism according to Article 33(2) CRPD.[69] Since 2015, this position is

[68] Der Beauftragte der Bundesregierung für die Belange von Menschen mit Behinderungen, 'UN-Behindertenrechtskonvention' (2022) www.behindertenbeauftragter.de.

[69] Deutsches Institut für Menschenrechte, 'Monitoring-Stelle UN-Behindertenrechtskonvention' (2022) www.institut-fuer-menschenrechte.de; V Aichele, 'The State Review and the CRPD Committee in the Context of Current Challenges Faced by the International Human Rights Protection System – at the Same Time a Report on the Experiences Made by the Body of the UN Convention on the Rights of Persons with Disabilities at the German Institute for Human Rights' in Ganner et al (n 1).

legally regulated.[70] The Monitoring Body inside DIM regularly monitors the implementation of the CRPD at the federal level and participates in the political and scientific discussions about it.

The Monitoring Body of DIM also works for some of the *Länder*. North Rhine-Westphalia has given it a legal basis, other *Länder* use temporary projects. However, there is still a gap between the involvement of the Monitoring Body on the federal level and its presence at the *Länder* level.

V. CONCLUDING REMARKS

Federalism in Germany has a considerable influence upon the implementation of the CRPD. On the one hand, the complexity of the federal system makes it difficult to locate responsibilities for the implementation of disability rights rooted in the CRPD in only one level of government. For example, the realisation of the right to live independently and be included in the community according to Article 19 CRPD depends on the social welfare legislation on the federal level (SGB IX), as well as on its execution by the *Länder* and municipal authorities and their use of legal and financial margins. Article 19 CRPD, moreover, depends on conditions set on the municipal level which are a responsibility of the subnational level. In a similar vein, the realisation of the right to education, according to Article 24 CRPD, falls within *Länder* competence.[71] *Länder* laws on the school system differ greatly with regard to special schools and the integration of special units in the general education system. However, the social welfare system supports inclusion of school students with disabilities through financial assistance and reasonable accommodation in the general education system. This has been newly regulated by the Federal Participation Act of 2016, which established a new category of benefits for participation in education.

As shown for non-discrimination and accessibility, federal and *Länder* legislation and administration in Germany cooperate in the implementation of relevant goals and rights provided for in the CRPD. It is frequently the case that a minority of *Länder* function as the avant-garde, then the federal legislation sets a standard and most of the *Länder* follow. This has been the case for having, or including, a disability clause in the constitution since the early 1990s, for Disability Equality Acts between 1999 and 2008 and for the implementation of the CRPD (2010 onwards). This pattern provides an opportunity to find and compare legislative and administrative solutions and, in the best case, establish a

[70] Para 1(2) Gesetz über die Rechtsstellung und Aufgaben des Deutschen Instituts für Menschenrechte (DIMRG).

[71] A Frankenstein, 'Entitlement and Reality: Outlook on the Implementation of Art 24 UN CRPD in Germany' in Ganner et al (n 1).

competition for the best CRPD implementation. To achieve this ideal, however, the structures of cooperative federalism, which are typical for Germany, must unfold for disability policy more than they have done so yet. Federal conferences, like those of Disability Commissioners, can serve as driving forces for coordinated and sometimes competitive implementation. To enforce this process, it would be helpful if they had a permanent coordinating office. Currently, one of the Commissioners, along with their team, must serve as a coordinator without an additional workforce. One prerequisite for this process is the continuous monitoring and scientific data collection on all levels. There has been some improvement, but still the monitoring process according to Article 33 CRPD does not comprise complete multi-level monitoring, and the participation reports of the Federal Government, which serve as an implementation of Article 31 CRPD, are not multi-level reports.

On the whole, federalism thus influences the implementation of CRPD. However, it is not easy to assess whether federalism is a multi-level barrier or if it leads to a sustainable multi-level inclusive system. More comparative research is needed to find answers.[72] To what extent does CRPD implementation influence the federal system in Germany? Disability policy is not among the main issues that have affected German federal structures in the last two decades. Issues that, by contrast, have had a noticeable impact on German federalism have rather been unemployment, early childcare, higher education, digitalisation of public management and, due to the pandemic, public health. For these topics, the Federation and the *Länder* have developed common financially expensive programmes and cooperative laws, partially enshrined in the constitution (Articles 91–91e GG). This shows what is possible, but only for a few topics at one time and only with a constitution-changing majority of two thirds in *Bundestag* and *Bundesrat*. Normally, enhanced cooperation between the Federation and *Länder* clashes with constitutional separation of competences.[73]

Nonetheless, the implementation of the CRPD has left marks in the German federal system. Some matters acquired a place on the federal agenda for the first time, because they were included in an international treaty and, accordingly, the Federal Government must be able to make statements at the international level, even if it cannot act in the respective field. When comparing the implementation of accessibility of the built environment and website accessibility, it transpires that EU law is more effective in stimulating a comprehensive multi-level approach than an international treaty *per se*. Even considering that the CRPD has been at least partially incorporated into EU law, what makes a difference is the fact that EU Directives must be transposed into national law by fixed deadlines and,

[72] The current research project of Lilit Grigoryan (formerly University of Kassel, now University of Cologne) will be helpful.

[73] See BVerfG 20/12/2007, 2 BvR 2433/04. A constitutional amendment (Art 91e GG) was necessary to continue the cooperation.

if they are not properly implemented, the Member State is subject to infringement proceedings, under the CJEU judicial control. The CRPD obligations *per se* are broadly drafted, and, there are no judicial instruments to sanction lack of implementation beyond the CRPD committee reporting procedure.

The BVerfG had to point out, for the first time, the position of UN Human Rights Committees for the interpretation of German constitutional law, because it was confronted with the jurisprudence of the CRPD Committee concerning involuntary medical treatment and the right to vote. Even though the Court did not follow the Committee's various statements included in its general comments, guidelines and communications, it at least showed that German courts can and should take these statements into account, even if they do not have to comply with them. Thus, a multi-level search for justice includes a new element, which changes the relationship between the other levels. In all likelihood, administrative and social courts will follow the BVerfG and cite international human rights bodies.[74] This could be seen as a structural effect on the federal system in Germany which is connected to the CRPD.

The constitutional basic rights legal doctrine is a strongly unifying factor in the German legal and federative system. The rulings of the BVerfG not only determine federal, but also *Länder*, legislation and case law on all levels. Hence, the emerging influence of international human rights rulings, especially from the European Court of Human Rights, that takes the CRPD into consideration when interpreting the European Convention on Human Rights,[75] and the development of an inclusive rights doctrine,[76] have the potential to change federal and sub-national practices in Germany and to set new goals for cooperative federalism.

[74] See OVG Sachsen-Anhalt 13/05/2019, 3 L 44/19.

[75] European Court of Human Rights, ECHR 10/09/2020, 59751/15; F Welti, 'Inklusive Bildung als Menschenrecht und Staatenpflicht' (2020) 4 *Recht und Praxis der Rehabilitation* 53.

[76] T Degener, 'Disability in a Human Rights Context' (2016) 5 *Laws* 35; E Eichenhofer, 'The UN CRPD as International Social Law' in Wansing, Welti and Schäfers (n 55); T Degener, 'Die UN-Behindertenrechtskonvention – Ansatz einer inklusiven Menschenrechtstheorie' (2019) 67 *Jahrbuch des Öffentlichen Rechts* 487–508.

3

Austria

The Implementation of the CRPD in the Austrian Federal System

PETER BUẞJÄGER*

I. INTRODUCTION

THE CONVENTION ON the Rights of Persons with Disabilities (CRPD) was signed by Austria on 30 March 2007. After the approval by the National Council (*Nationalrat*), the lower house of the Austrian Parliament, in compliance with Article 50(1) No 1 of the Federal Constitution (*Bundes-Verfassungsgesetz* – B-VG)[1] and following the approval by the Federal Council (*Bundesrat*) in line with Article 50(2) No 2 B-VG,[2] the ratification documents were deposited with the Secretary-General of the United Nations. The CRPD was published in the Austrian Federal Law Gazette[3] on 23 October 2008 in the authentic English and French versions as well as in a German (non-authentic) version.[4] In compliance with Article 45(2) CRPD and Article 13(2) of the Optional Protocol to the Convention on the Rights of

* The author's sincere thanks go to Ina Kapusta and Julia Oberdanner for their editorial help.

[1] According to this provision, the National Council is responsible for approving international treaties which are 'politically relevant' or (like the CRPD) fall within the scope of general law.

[2] According to this provision, international treaties based on Article 50(2) No 2 Federal Constitution (*Bundes-Verfassungsgesetz* – B-VG) require, in addition to the approval of the National Council, the approval of the Federal Council if they affect *Land* competences.

[3] Federal Law Gazette (*Bundesgesetzblatt* – BGBl) III 155/2008 with amendment BGBl III 197/2022.

[4] Publication in these three languages was necessary because Article 49(2) No 1 B-VG provides that an international treaty, which is authentic in more than two languages, may only be published in two versions and with a German translation. In case of other authentic language versions, the National Council may decide on the form of publication of these language versions. On the occasion of the approval of the CRPD, the National Council decided that the Arabic, Chinese, Russian and Spanish versions should be added based on Article 49(2) B-VG and be published at the Federal Ministry for European and International Affairs to make them publicly accessible.

Persons with Disabilities (OP-CRPD)[5] both treaties came into force in Austria on 26 October 2008. On the occasion of the approval of the CRPD, the National Council decided that this treaty must be implemented by law and is not directly applicable.

The aim of this chapter is to discuss the extent to which the CRPD has been implemented in the Austrian federal system and whether this implementation has had an impact on the system. Following this brief introduction, section II discusses the division of responsibilities in the federal system. The section highlights that disability is a multi-layered cross-cutting challenge and concerns both federal and *Länder* competences. Section III explores the role of the Federal Government vis-à-vis the *Länder* in selected areas. It emphasises that, in the 30 years since the overall strategy paper on Austrian disability policy of 22 December 1992,[6] disability policy has evolved from a rather patronising policy, mostly focused on meeting the basic needs of persons with disabilities, to a policy based on human rights and equality.[7] The main reasons for this change were, on the one hand, the ratification of the CRPD in 2008 and, on the other hand, the approach of the EU Disability Strategy 2010–2020.[8] Section IV examines the implementation of Article 33 CRPD. Finally, some concluding remarks are provided in section V.

II. DIVISION OF POWERS IN THE FEDERAL SYSTEM

A. General Remarks on Division of Competences

Article 2 B-VG explicitly stipulates that Austria is a federal state, consisting of nine autonomous constituent units, the *Länder*, namely Burgenland, Carinthia, Lower Austria, Upper Austria, Salzburg, Styria, Tyrol, Vorarlberg and Vienna. Article 2 B-VG is usually considered a provision with solely programmatic character.[9] However, federalism is classified as one of the basic principles of the B-VG alongside the democratic, republican and liberal principles, the rule of law and the separation of powers. According to Article 44(3) B-VG, the repeal or substantial modification of one of these fundamental principles is considered a total revision of the B-VG, which needs to be approved by a referendum.[10]

[5] United Nations, 'Optional Protocol to the Convention on the Rights of Persons with Disabilities' (2006) www.ohchr.org.

[6] Strategy for People with Disabilities of the Austrian Government of 22 December 1992.

[7] Federal Ministry of Labour, Social Affairs and Consumer Protection, 'National Action Plan on Disability 2012–2020. Strategy of Austrian Federal Government for the Implementation of the UN Disability Rights Convention' (BMASK, 2012) 9.

[8] European Commission, 'European Disability Strategy 2010–2020: A Renewed Commitment to a Barrier-Free Europe' (2010) COM(2010) 636 final.

[9] P Bußjäger, C Schramek and M Johler, 'Federalism and Recent Political Dynamics in Austria' (2018) *Revista D'Estudis Autonòmics I Federals* 78.

[10] P Bußjäger, 'Between Europeanization, Unitarism and Autonomy. Remarks on the Current Situation of Federalism in Austria' (2010) *Revista D'Estudis Autonòmics I Federals* 12.

According to the case-law of the Austrian Federal Constitutional Court,[11] the federal principle encompasses four substantive elements: the distribution of legislative and administrative competences between the Federation and the *Länder*, the participation of the *Länder* in the adoption of federal legislation, the constitutional autonomy of the *Länder* and the participation of the *Länder* in the federal administration. However, federal theory suggests that an additional element needs to be taken into account, namely the budgetary and expenditure autonomy of the *Länder*.[12]

The distribution of competences is rooted in Articles 10 to 15 B-VG. These provisions differentiate between four types of legislative and executive powers: exclusive federal legislation and execution (Article 10 B-VG), federal legislation and administration by the *Länder* (Article 11 B-VG), federal framework legislation which is implemented and executed by the *Länder* (Article 12 B-VG) and exclusive *Länder* legislation and execution (Article 15(1) B-VG). The latter is conceived as a residual competence, ie the *Länder* are responsible for all matters not expressly listed in favour of the Federation. Most of the competences are enumerated in Article 10 B-VG. This provision contains, in particular, fundamental competences such as foreign affairs, civil and commercial law, along with labour law and public health (with certain exceptions). Among other things, the *Länder* are responsible for the subject areas of building regulations, environmental protection and spatial planning.

Over time, the *Länder* have lost powers in terms of financial matters. According to Article 13(1) B-VG, the competences of the Federation and the *Länder* on taxation are regulated by a separate federal Constitutional Act, namely the Financial Constitutional Act (*Finanz-Verfassungsgesetz* – F-VG). This Act defines abstract types of taxes and vests the federal legislature with the competence to enact laws on the distribution of tax-raising powers, which then are incorporated into the Financial Equalisation Act (*Finanzausgleichsgesetz*). The latter is negotiated between the Federal Government, the *Länder* and the municipalities. Against this background, the distribution of fiscal competences is eminently centralised. In fact, the *Länder* have few independent tax revenues. The legislative competences for school and education – like the financial area – are separately regulated in Articles 14 and 14a B-VG.

B. Implementation of International Law

As stated above,[13] under certain conditions, international treaties need the approval of the National Council and, if *Länder* competences are affected,

[11] See Collection of Judgments of the Constitutional Court (*Sammlung der Erkenntnisse und Beschlüsse des Verfassungsgerichtshofes* – VfSlg) 2455/1952, 11.403/1987 and 16.241/2001.

[12] Bußjäger, Schramek and Johler (n 9) 78.

[13] See n 2.

they additionally require the consent of the Federal Council according to Article 50(2) No 2 B-VG. This was the case with the CRPD which, as mentioned, is not directly applicable and needs to be implemented into national law by the legislature.

In general, the implementation of international law is a matter for the Federal Government as well as for the *Länder*, depending on whether it affects the competences of the Federal Government or the *Länder*. Article 16(4) B-VG explicitly provides that the *Länder* are obliged to take measures which, within their autonomous sphere of competence, become necessary for the implementation of international treaties; if a *Land* does not fulfil this obligation in time, in particular for the enactment of implementing legislation, it passes to the Federation. However, if the Federation has taken a measure instead of the *Länder*, it ceases to have effect under this provision as soon as the *Länder* have enacted the necessary implementing laws.[14] Article 16(5) B-VG provides that the Federation shall also have supervisory powers in the implementation of international treaties, including matters falling within the competence of the *Länder*. The powers of the Federal Government vis-à-vis the *Länder* are the same here as in the area of indirect federal administration (Article 102 B-VG). This means that the Federal Government can issue binding instructions to those *Länder* that are unwilling to fulfil their obligations as derived from the CRPD.[15] In practice, however, Articles 16(4) and (5) B-VG have never been applied. Hence, in the context of the CRPD, it is not surprising that the possibility of the Federal Government taking measures to fulfil Austria's obligations under this treaty if a *Land* fails to take the necessary implementation measures has never been discussed.

C. Distribution of Competences

Matters regarding the rights of persons with disabilities (in particular social aid, health care and education) are cross-cutting matters, which means that both the Federal Government and the *Länder* are, in principle, responsible for enacting legislation on those issues. It is, therefore, necessary to analyse each provision of the CRPD to determine whether the Federal Government or the *Länder* have the competence to pass legislation. Most of the provisions of the Convention are not restricted to the legislative power of one level or the other. For example, the general principles (Article 3 CRPD) and the obligations (Article 4 CRPD) affect both levels of government.

[14] T Weber, 'Article 16 B-VG' in B Kneihs and G Lienbacher (eds), *Rill-Schäffer-Kommentar Bundesverfassungsrecht* (Verlag Österreich, 2017) para 72.
[15] Ibid para 71.

According to Article 10 B-VG, federal laws are implemented in two different ways: direct federal administration by federal authorities (Article 102(2) B-VG) or indirect federal administration by the *Land* governors and the subordinate *Land* authorities (Article 102(1) B-VG). In these matters, the *Land* governors are bound by the instructions of the competent federal ministers.

Table 1 provides an overview of the competences of the Federal Government and the *Länder* not only in respect of legislation and administration in general, but also regarding administration in direct or indirect federal administration on matters covered by the CRPD.

Table 1 Overview of the Competences of the Federal Government and the *Länder* on Matters Covered by the CRPD

Competence	Type of federal administration		Article 11 (Federal legislative competence, administration by the *Länder*)	Article 12 Framework legislation (Federal legislative competence to establish general principles, execution of the principles and administration by the *Länder*)	Article 15 Residual clause (legislation and administration by the *Länder*)
	Direct federal administration	Indirect federal administration			
Healthcare and social security					
Healthcare except for hospitals, health resorts and natural curative resources, municipal sanitation, rescue organisations		X			
Hospitals				X	
Rescue organisations and municipal sanitation					X
Health resorts and natural curative resources					X

(continued)

Table 1 *(Continued)*

Competence	Type of federal administration		Article 11 (Federal legislative competence, administration by the *Länder*)	Article 12 Framework legislation (Federal legislative competence to establish general principles, execution of the principles and administration by the *Länder*)	Article 15 Residual clause (legislation and administration by the *Länder*)
	Direct federal administration	Indirect federal administration			
Social insurance and Care money	X				
Social aid				X	
Care for old people (organisation of care and homes for people who need care)					X
Education					
Education regarding public compulsory schools				X	
Early childcare and Kindergarten					X
Upper schools	X				
Universities	X				
Civil and penal law					
Civil law	X				
Penal procedural law	X				
Civil procedural law	X				
Penal law	X				

(continued)

Table 1 *(Continued)*

Competence	Type of federal administration		Article 11 (Federal legislative competence, administration by the *Länder*)	Article 12 Framework legislation (Federal legislative competence to establish general principles, execution of the principles and administration by the *Länder*)	Article 15 Residual clause (legislation and administration by the *Länder*)
	Direct federal administration	Indirect federal administration			
Civil status and migration law					
Matters about personal status		X			
Migration law	X	X			
Technical standards					
Telecommunication	X				
Building law (with exception of buildings of railways)					X
Transportation law		X			
Building law for railways		X			
Youth					
Youth protection					X
Children and youth welfare					X
Competences without exclusive assignment					
Federation and Länder as holders of private rights (eg giving subsidies or financing public transport)	X				X

Table 1 shows the strong fragmentation of the distribution of competences, especially concerning matters directly affecting the rights of persons with disabilities. Not only is such fragmentation in legislative competence problematic, but also, the division of administrative competence adds to the complexity of the implementation of the CRPD. For example, in relation to the labour market, the execution of the Employment of Persons with Disabilities Act (*Behinderteneinstellungsgesetz* – BEinstG) and the promotion of the employment of persons with disabilities by the Federal Ministry of Social Affairs and Social Assistance (*Sozialministeriumsservice* – for which the district authorities of the *Länder* are responsible) are the responsibility of different authorities. Various attempts to concentrate these competences in the hands of one authority have, as yet, failed.[16] On the *Land* level, the implementation of the Convention is usually a matter of the department in the office of the *Land* Government (*Amt der Landesregierung*) that is competent, inter alia, for social security.

The complexity of the system is increased by the fact that the Federal Government and the *Land*, when acting in the field of civil law, are not bound by the division of powers (so-called *Privatwirtschaftsverwaltung*) provided for in Article 17 B-VG. The acting of authorities within the framework of civil law is of great importance in the practice of Austrian federalism. Whether the Federation or the *Länder* take measures in the form of *Privatwirtschaftsverwaltung*, is rather a question of the available budget, which is a result of the Financial Equalisation Act.[17] Moreover, it should be noted that although the municipalities do not have legislative powers, they can also act as holders of private rights. This private-sector administration is significant because many support services such as care associations and assisted living for persons with disabilities are commissioned in this way. Furthermore, it is relevant to the present analysis that, according to the prevailing legal opinion, such measures also do not require a legal basis.[18]

III. THE ROLE OF THE FEDERAL GOVERNMENT VIS-À-VIS THE *LÄNDER* IN SELECTED AREAS

A. Concept of Disability

i. Are There Different Definitions of Disability at National and Subnational Levels?

In general, it can be said that both the Federation and the *Länder* are obliged to adopt and implement a definition of persons with disabilities in line with

[16] P Bußjäger, M Eller and D Starchl, 'Zentralisierungs- und Dezentralisierungstendenzen der hoheitlichen und privatwirtschaftlichen Einrichtungen des Bundes in Tirol' (*Arbeiterkammer Tirol,* 2021) 58.

[17] Bußjäger, Schramek and Johler (n 9) 81.

[18] A Kahl and K Weber, *Allgemeines Verwaltungsrecht*, 7th edn (Facultas, 2019) 111.

the CRPD and to comply with the Convention.[19] Nevertheless, there are differences due to the autonomous approach of the *Länder* in the implementation of the CRPD, and currently definitions of disability included in the legislation of the *Länder* coexist with definitions in federal laws. However, differentiation also emerges within the federal legal order and within the legal orders of the *Länder.* The BEinstG at paragraph 3[20] as well as paragraph 1(2) of the Federal Law on Persons with Disabilities (*Bundes-Behindertengesetz* – BBG)[21] still do not fully comply with the social-contextual definition provided for in Article 1 CRPD.[22] These provisions only refer to the fact that persons with disabilities include those persons whose impairments may hinder their full and effective participation in society on an equal basis with others.

Similarly, subnational laws do not fully align with Article 1 CRPD. For example, paragraph 3 of the Law on Persons with Disabilities in Salzburg[23] was found to be incompatible with the Convention.[24] This was also pointed out by the Committee on the Rights of Persons with Disabilities (CRPD Committee) in the Concluding Observations[25] on its First Report on Austria in 2013:

> The Committee noted that there are differing concepts of disability across the State party's laws and policies. The Committee is concerned that the State party misunderstands the difference between defining disability and identifying groups of persons to whom different kinds of services should be provided. The Committee is concerned that some of the definitions are based on the medical model of disability.[26]

A study of the Faculty of Law of the University of Innsbruck confirmed the findings of the CRPD Committee in 2014.[27]

In 2014–15, the Federal Ministry for Social Affairs, Health, Care and Consumer Protection (*Bundesministerium für Soziales, Gesundheit, Pflege und Konsumentenschutz* – BMSGPK) prepared a draft for a Target Agreement on Inclusive Disability Policies for a uniform implementation of the CRPD between the Federal Government and the *Länder*. However, this project did not gain the consent of the *Länder* and has not yet been completed.[28] The National

[19] Rechtswissenschaftliche Fakultät der Universität Innsbruck, 'Gutachten über die aus dem UN-Übereinkommen über die Rechte von Menschen mit Behinderungen erwachsenden Verpflichtungen Österreichs' (Universität Innsbruck, 2014) 22.

[20] BGBl 22/1970 with amendment BGBl I 82/2005.

[21] BGBl 283/1990 with amendment BGBl I 81/2010.

[22] See the introduction to this volume.

[23] In the meantime, this law has been replaced by the Salzburg Participation Act (*Salzburger Teilhabegesetz* – S. THG) *Land Law Gazette* (*Landesgesetzblatt* – LGBl) 93/1981 with amendment LGBl 64/2019.

[24] Rechtswissenschaftliche Fakultät (n 19) 125.

[25] Committee on the Rights of Persons with Disabilities (CRPD Committee), 'Concluding Observations on the Initial Report on Austria Adopted by the Committee at its Tenth Session 2–13 September 2013' (2013).

[26] Rechtswissenschaftliche Fakultät (n 19) 125.

[27] Ibid 124.

[28] M Rubisch, 'Die UN-Behindertenrechtskonvention in Österreich: Von der Staatenprüfung 2013 zum zweiten und dritten Staatenbericht 2019' in M Ganner et al (eds), *Die Umsetzung der UN-Behindertenrechtskonvention in Österreich und Deutschland* (Innsbruck University Press, 2021) 79.

Action Plan on Disability 2022–2030 (*Nationaler Aktionsplan Behinderung 2022–2030* – NAP Disability 2022–2030),[29] which is currently being developed, offers a new chance to address inconsistencies. In fact, while the first NAP Disability 2012–2020, which will be further discussed in the subsequent section, was an exclusive plan of the Federal Government without the involvement of the *Länder*, the new NAP Disability will be a joint plan of the Federal Government and the *Länder*.[30]

The 2020 evaluation report on the previous NAP Disability 2012–2020[31] suggested that the participation of the *Länder* was unsatisfactory. As the *Länder* were not involved in the preparatory phase of the NAP Disability 2012–2020, the measures were largely limited to areas that fall within the Federal Government's remit for pragmatic reasons. Most of the challenges in disability policy are due to the fact that certain thematic fields either fall under the responsibility of the *Länder* (such as de-institutionalisation) or are divided between the Federal Government and the *Länder* (eg accessibility or personal assistance). Accordingly, some of the 'big issues' remained either unsolved or insufficiently addressed. Moreover, problems in the implementation of legislative reforms at the federal level were, and continue to be, evident. For example, the Adult Protection Law[32] was repeatedly referred to as requiring the participation of the *Länder* for the provision of social work assistance for supported decision-making. Further, one of the main problems from the perspective of the *Länder* is the unresolved issue of funding.

With delay and at different times, the *Länder* have entered the process of implementation and representatives of the *Länder* have been included in the monitoring group. The exchange of information in this context has been considered a step forward. Together with the new joint NAP on Disability, it allows the Federal Government and the *Länder* to commit to common objectives and determine the measures by which these objectives are to be achieved. For example, the Federal Government and the *Länder* could agree that certain measures concerning accessibility should be taken in their respective areas (eg in the area of building laws of the *Länder*).

ii. Has a Process of 'Harmonisation' Concerning Definitions of Disability Occurred?

A process of 'harmonisation' of federal and *Land* laws regarding persons with disabilities has taken place via cooperative federalism. In the second half of

[29] Bundesministerium für Soziales, Gesundheit, Pflege und Konsumentenschutz (BMSGPK), 'Nationaler Aktionsplan Behinderung 2022–2030. Österreichische Strategie zur Umsetzung der UN-Behindertenrechtskonvention' (BMSGPK, 2022) 1.

[30] Rubisch (n 28) 79.

[31] BMSGPK, 'Evaluierung des Nationalen Aktionsplans Behinderung 2012–2020' (BMSGPK, 2020) 20.

[32] Federal Ministry of Constitutional Affairs, Reforms, Deregulation and Justice, 'The New Adult Protection Law' (BMJ, 2018) 7.

the last century, various vertical and horizontal cooperative instruments were introduced. These wide-ranging instruments of cooperative federalism led to a tendency toward unitarisation.[33] One of these instruments is the Conference of *Land* Governors (*Landeshauptleutekonferenz*). This horizontal model of cooperation works as a relatively efficient counterbalance to the weight of the federal order of government and has developed into an important platform for the *Länder*, especially in the field of financial equalisation and in negotiations concerning cost-sharing for the execution of federal law by the *Länder* and municipalities. This kind of model is also being used in relation to social welfare matters including matters related to the implementation of the CRPD.[34]

Furthermore, there are other joint Federal-*Land* platforms. In this context, the Conference of Ombudsmen for Equality Measures of the *Länder* and the Conference of Ombudsmen for Anti-Discrimination Measures should be mentioned. These conferences do not have an explicit legal basis, they are informal instruments of cooperation and coordination, but both the political (members of *Länder* governments) and the expert level (anti-discrimination ombudsmen) coordinate their efforts.

B. Non-Discrimination and Equality

i. Levels of Government Involved in Implementing the CRPD Provisions on Non-Discrimination and Equality

As mentioned above, the competences to implement the CRPD are divided between the Federal Government and the *Länder*. The Federal Government has some 'supervisory' powers, which, in practice, are exercised with restraint.

From the constitutional perspective, the Federation, as well as the *Länder*, are obliged to comply with international law. On the federal level, the competent Federal Ministry is the Federal Ministry for Social Affairs, Health, Care and Consumer Protection.[35] However, there are also other Federal Ministries concerned, for example, the Federal Ministry for Labour and Economy, competent for the employment of persons with disabilities. The Federal Chancellery is competent for family policies as it concerns aid for persons with disabilities.[36] But other Federal Ministries are also involved: the Federal Ministry of Justice, for example, is competent for civil law or civil procedural law, criminal law

[33] P Bußjäger, 'Austria's Cooperative Federalism' in G Bischof and F Karlhofer (eds), *Austrian Federalism in Comparative Perspective* (Innsbruck University Press, 2015) 32.

[34] Ibid 16.

[35] Austrian Federal Ministries Act (*Bundesministeriengesetz* – BMG) BGBl 76/1986 with amendment BGBl I 98/2022 Appendix 2 Part 2 L Federal Ministry for Social Affairs, Health, Care and Consumer Protection No 4 as it concerns care, No 9 as it concerns medical aspects of persons with disabilities.

[36] BMG Appendix 2 Part 2 A Federal Chancellery No 20 d.

and criminal procedural law.[37] When it comes to persons with disabilities in the public service, the Federal Ministry for Arts, Culture, the Civil Service and Sport is competent.[38]

The NAP Disability 2012–2020 was a strategy of the Austrian Federal Government for the implementation of the CRPD, drafted by the BMSGPK and approved by the decision of the Federal Government on 24 July 2012.[39] As the NAP Disability is a policy document and not a law, the two chambers of Parliament, ie the National and Federal Council, were not involved, even though the NAP Disability was repeatedly discussed in Parliament.[40] Furthermore, as mentioned above, the *Länder* were not involved in the elaboration of the plan. The NAP Disability formulates policy objectives and contains 250 measures with corresponding timelines and responsibilities. In line with disability mainstreaming, the measures must be implemented by the individual Federal Ministries according to their responsibilities.

In the opinion of the Austrian Federal Government, the NAP Disability was a useful and appropriate instrument for implementing the CRPD in the period of 2012–2020, especially as action plans are expressly recommended by the UN and the World Health Organization.[41] Setting longer-term disability policy goals and measures and reaching political agreement creates the conditions under which 'political participation, transparency, predictability, accountability and further development are possible' and is therefore in the interests of persons with disabilities.[42]

It should, however, be noted that all competences not expressly assigned to the Federation by the B-VG fall within the competence of the *Länder*. The NAP Disability does not go beyond the responsibility of the Federation, but the competences of the Federal Government and the *Länder* are so closely linked that some of the objectives of the NAP Disability may have an indirect effect on the *Länder*.

To achieve an efficient and transparent administration and thus guarantee easier access to services for persons with disabilities, mixed funding has to be avoided. However, it was not possible to assess the impact of such mixed funding on the *Länder* at that moment,[43] since the Federal Government has failed to carry out a financial evaluation of the measures.[44]

[37] BMG Appendix 2 Part 2 H.

[38] BMG Appendix 2 Part 2 B.

[39] BMSGPK, 'Nationaler Aktionsplan Behinderung. Strategie der österreichischen Bundesregierung zur Umsetzung der UN-Behindertenrechtskonvention' (BMSGPK, 2020) 8.

[40] See eg Parliamentary Question No 8105/J concerning the National Action Plan Persons with Disabilities 2022–2030 and Parliamentary Question No 9187/J regarding the NAP 2022–2030.

[41] World Health Organization (WHO), 'World Report on Disability' (WHO, 2011) 156.

[42] BMSGPK (n 39) 10.

[43] In particular personal assistance, covered under social insurance law and inclusive model regions in the school sector.

[44] The government pointed out that questions related to competences and the organisation of the administration are neither a preliminary issue nor the subject of the NAP on Disability. Rather, the question of how to organise (and, if necessary, reorganise) matters between the Federal Government

In 2015, it became clear that the Federal Government and the *Länder* had started negotiations on the topic of 'inclusive disability policy'. Disability organisations were excluded deliberately. The 2016 negotiations on an inclusion fund for an enhanced and coordinated implementation of the CRPD failed. At their conference in April 2018, the *Länder* repeatedly argued in favour of an inclusion fund and uniform federal standards – provided that the Federal Government would supply budgetary resources. An additional conference took place in September 2019. No agreement has been reached so far.[45]

The programme of the current Federal Government, consisting of the Austrian People's Party (*Die Österreichische Volkspartei* – ÖVP, also known as *die neue Volkspartei* – the new People's Party) and the Greens (*Die Grünen*), envisages a revised action plan. A draft of the NAP Disability 2022–2030 was formulated. It was elaborated with participation, inter alia, of representatives of the *Länder*. Moreover, other Federal Ministries and representatives of organisations for disabled persons were involved.[46] Since 6 July 2022, the NAP 2022–2030 comprises, to date (Autumn 2022), the final political decision on the adoption of the new NAP Disability 2022–2030 and was approved by the Federal Government.[47]

ii. New Legislation Enacted at the National and Subnational Levels

Several laws have been passed by both levels of government over the last years to implement the CRPD into the Austrian legal system; although they focus on specific areas, many of these laws have the overarching purpose of achieving equality.

At the federal level, the amendment of the Guardianship Law (*Sachwalterrecht*) was a very important project. Since 1 July 2018, this has been called Adult Protection Law (*Erwachsenenschutzgesetz*), in-line with international trends. For the first time, persons with disabilities were comprehensively involved in the reform. With the new adult protection law, the autonomy of persons with disabilities falling into its scope was expanded and restrictions on their ability to act were reduced. Its principles are:

- the capacity to act is no longer automatically lost during representation;
- adult representation is limited to certain matters;
- legal and judicial adult representation is limited to three years, clearing became mandatory;

and the *Länder* in the most expedient, cost-saving and people-orientated way is a matter for future general structural reform. See BMSGPK (n 39) 11.

[45] Austrian Disability Council (*Österreichischer Behindertenrat*), 'Second Alternative Report on the Implementation of the UN Convention on the Rights of Persons with Disabilities in Austria' (Austrian Disability Council, 2018) 5.

[46] See Request Response 8921/AB XXVII GP.

[47] BMSGPK, 'Nationaler Aktionsplan Behinderung 2022–2030 – Ministerratsvorlage' (BMSGPK, 2022).

– all existing guardianships will be abolished or converted into adult representations by 1 January 2024.

Training on the new legal framework is offered to legal professionals (eg lawyers), medical staff, bank employees and others. This reform is considered a major step forward by legal scholars.[48] Initial results indicate that the new law has largely proved its worth.[49] Further, it appears the number of guardianships/representations has been decreasing since 2015. However, it still seems uncertain whether this new law will actually be a success in practice. The main problems are that courts are understaffed and the *Länder* have so far created too few support structures for those affected.

In addition, measures have been taken in the field of education and employment of persons with disabilities in the public sector. For universities and higher education, it was standardised that the objectives of inclusive education must also be observed in the curricula of these institutions.[50]

The Federal Law on the Equality of Persons with Disabilities (*Bundes-Behindertengleichstellungsgesetz* – BGStG) was passed in 2005 and preceded the CRPD.[51] It has been amended several times since the CRPD was signed. The provisions of this law are relevant to the administration of the Federation including the actions of the Federation as holder of private rights (paragraph 2(1) BGStG) and in all contexts of civil law. It prohibits direct and indirect discrimination (paragraph 4(1) BGStG).

As far as the *Länder* are concerned, it seems that they have become increasingly ambitious in their efforts to implement the CRPD in recent years. Upper Austria, for example, has introduced the service of personal assistance in the client model with an amendment to the Upper Austrian Equal Opportunities Act (*Oberösterreichisches Chancengleichheitsgesetz* – Oö-ChG),[52] which provides a higher degree of self-determination for the person concerned. Notifications of benefits have to be issued in 'easy to read' and 'easy to understand' formats. The 'personal future planning' benefit is a new addition. It is a peer counselling and information service for persons with disabilities.[53]

Looking more closely at what has occurred in various *Länder*, Carinthia modified the Act of Equality of Chances (*Kärntner Chancengleichheitsgesetz* – K-ChG)[54] and established a monitoring committee according to Article 33 CRPD (paragraphs 35–40 K-ChG). In Tyrol, in 2018,[55] the regional parliament

[48] Rubisch (n 28) 81.

[49] See M Ganner, 'Das 2. ErwSchG – ist die Intention des Gesetzgebers in der Praxis angekommen?' (2020) *Hikaku kōken hōsei* 25.

[50] M Ganner, 'Einblicke in die UN-BRK und ihre Umsetzung in Österreich' in M Ganner et al (eds), *Die Umsetzung der UN-Behindertenrechtskonvention in Österreich und Deutschland* (Innsbruck University Press, 2021) 21.

[51] BGBl I 82/2005 with amendment BGBl I 32/2018.

[52] LGBl 41/2008 with amendment LGBl 10/2015 (Upper Austria).

[53] Ganner (n 50) 21.

[54] LGBl 8/2010 with amendment LGBl 70/2019 (Carinthia).

[55] LGBl 32/2018 with amendment LGBl 62/2022 (Tyrol).

(*Landtag*) passed the Tyrolean Law on Participation and Inclusion Rights (*Tiroler Teilhabegesetz* – TTHG), which provides a framework for all Tyrolean legislation concerning disabled persons with a view to fully implementing the CRPD in the legal order of the *Land* Tyrol.[56] This law aims to contribute to the realisation of an inclusive society and to enable persons with disabilities to lead a self-determined life, to enable the full, effective, equal and non-discriminatory participation of persons with disabilities in social life and to support persons with disabilities in overcoming barriers that make such participation difficult. In order to achieve these objectives, Tyrol grants subsidies which must be necessary in the individual case and suitable in their entirety for achieving the stated objectives. For example, they are intended to contribute to persons with disabilities receiving support services for independent living, but also access to training and employment.

The need to enact legislation that fully embeds the principles of the CRPD is highlighted in the Second Alternative Report of the Austrian Disability Council[57] on the implementation of the CRPD in Austria, which was released in July 2018:

> In many areas, the situation for persons with disabilities has changed only minimally or not at all compared to the last civil society report in 2013. The situation has even clearly deteriorated in some areas (e.g. education, work, accessibility) or otherwise, the government programme 'Together for Our Austria – 2017–2022' presents goals that will result in a deterioration of the situation. Financial cuts in the areas of work, education, health care, social affairs and research will affect persons with disabilities to a large extent. Due to the federal form of government, the standards and legal provisions concerning persons with disabilities still vary across Austria, resulting in great legal uncertainty and inequality. The paradigm shift away from the medical model and toward a human rights-based model of disability is, for the most part, not understood and much less implemented, either by governments or by civil society.[58]

iii. The CRPD Impact on the Division of Competences Between National and Subnational Entities

So far, the CRPD has had little impact on the division of competences between the Federal Government and the *Länder*. In 2011, the competence on the Nursing Care Allowance (*Pflegegeldwesen*) was established in Article 10(1) No 11 B-VG[59] and transferred to the legislative and administrative competence

[56] See Institut für Föderalismus, '43. Bericht über den Föderalismus in Österreich (2018)' (New Academic Press, 2019) 63.

[57] The Austrian Disability Council (*Österreichischer Behindertenrat*) is a political lobby organisation. As an umbrella organisation it represents about 80 member associations and about 1.4 million persons with disabilities. Its tasks contain the development and upkeep of various documents, collaboration in numerous panels and commissions with the aim of coordinating the various interests of the member organisations and the development of measures to implement these interests.

[58] Austrian Disability Council (n 45) 3.

[59] BGBl 1/1930 with amendment BGBl I 14/2019.

of the Federation. At the same time *Pflegegeldwesen* was added to the catalogue of Article 102(2) B-VG and can therefore be executed in direct federal administration. Until that time, matters of allowances for persons in need of long-term care were divided between the Federal Government and the *Länder*, insofar as the Federal Government was competent for nursing care allowance as part of social insurance and the *Länder* insofar as these matters were part of social welfare. The centralisation of this competence, however, did not relate to the CRPD; the Convention was not even mentioned in the legislative documents.[60] In the reasoning of the proposal of the government, the only aim was to overcome the distribution of competences concerning this matter.

In 2017, another constitutional provision, paragraph 330a General Social Insurance Act (*Allgemeines Sozialversicherungsgesetz* – ASVG),[61] interdicted the taking of property from people who lived in care homes and their relatives to finance their stay in these homes.

C. Accessibility

It is difficult to precisely identify which level of government is primarily involved in implementing accessibility provisions. Since building laws fall under the legislative and administrative competence of the *Länder*, it can be assumed that they have great responsibility. Nevertheless, it may not be overlooked that there are also important competences on the federal level in fields such as labour law, consumer law and trade law, that are relevant to the realisation of accessibility in all areas of life.

In its Concluding Observations[62] of 2013 the CRPD Committee acknowledged that there have been improvements in accessibility of buildings, public transport and information in Austria. However, there was a lack of accessibility in rural regions, public facilities and media.[63] The CRPD Committee recommended to develop an overarching and inclusive approach to accessibility, and to create standards for all public facilities, given the different responsibilities of the Federal Government and the *Länder*, to shorten the timetable for staging plans for public buildings and to expand subtitling of programmes of the Austrian Broadcasting Corporation (*Österreichischer Rundfunk* – ORF). In the meantime, the following measures have been taken:[64]

- the staging plan for barrier-free federal buildings contained in the Federal Disability Equality Act was implemented at the end of 2019;

[60] Government Bill (*Regierungsvorlage* – RV) 1208 BlgNR XXIV GP.
[61] BGBl 189/1955 with amendment BGBl I 125/2017.
[62] CRPD Committee (n 25) Ch II.
[63] Ibid Art 9; Rubisch (n 28) 80.
[64] Rubisch (n 28) 80.

- the Federal Procurement Act 2018[65] stipulates that the technical specifications must comply with the principles of accessibility. Principles of accessibility must be observed;
- the Web Accessibility Act 2019[66] stipulates that all public websites of the Federal Government and institutions acting on behalf of the Federal Government must be barrier-free (*Land* laws stipulate the same for the websites of the *Länder*);
- the Austrian Federal Railways (*Österreichische Bundesbahnen* – ÖBB) created a 'Design for all', which means barrier-free mobility for all passenger groups. By 2027, 90 per cent of the passengers should be able to use barrier-free railway stations;[67]
- in some *Länder*, public sector information resources and administrative information are also issued in easy-to-read language.

Some scholars have argued that due to short-sighted economic considerations, the building laws of some *Länder* have taken steps backwards in terms of accessibility, by lowering the structural engineering standards that should ensure accessibility of all building components for persons with disabilities.[68] The *Länder* are facing an enormous increase in housing costs and are striving to mitigate standards which make housing more expensive. However, this increase in cost does not have a significant impact on the implementation of accessibility standards in the building laws of the *Länder*.

Regarding the question whether the CRPD has had an impact on the division of competences between national and subnational entities concerning accessibility, it can be stated that the CRPD did not lead to changes in the division of competences, but it increased the awareness that the existence of different regulations within a comparatively small country is problematic due to federal differentiations. The idea that different regulations can also lead to federal competition for a better solution has unfortunately not taken hold. Of course, this is also the fault of the *Länder*, which very often only implement or undertake what is necessary for cost reasons.

D. Participation

It is difficult to identify which level of government has been more involved in ensuring the participation of persons with disabilities in social, economic and

[65] Para 2 No 37, para 107 and para 275 Federal Procurement Act (*Bundesvergabegesetz 2018 – BVergG 2018*) BGBl I 65/2018 with amendments BGBl I 100/2018 and BGBl II 91/2019.

[66] Web Accessibility Act 2019 (*Web-Zugänglichkeits-Gesetz* – WZG) BGBl I 59/2019. This law implements the Directive (EU) 2016/2102 on the accessibility of the websites and mobile applications of public sector bodies [2016] OJ L327/1.

[67] *Österreichische Bundesbahnen*, 'Future Rail, Target Network 2025+' (2018) www.infrastruktur.oebb.at/en.

[68] Rubisch (n 28) 80.

cultural life. Since these matters are also divided between the Federal Government and the *Länder*, there are different responsibilities. It should not be overlooked that in many cases, for instance, in cultural events, the Federal Government acts as a holder of private rights (eg, in giving subsidies), where the provisions on the division of competences are not applicable. In general, the competent BMSGPK endeavours to monitor the implementation of the CRPD at the subnational level and to ensure a certain degree of coordination, taking into account the current constitutional framework that limits the powers of the Federal Government. In this context, the competent Federal Ministry has commissioned a study on the implementation of the CRPD in Austria. In addition, numerous informal rounds of talks take place within the framework of cooperative federalism.

The *Länder* also play an important role when it comes to participation as they are positioned closer to the citizens. They design innovative forms of participation in the process, as the following example demonstrates:

> Legislators in the province of Tyrol have started an ambitious participatory legislative process in early 2016. The development of a new disability support system shall be preceded by an extensive consultative process which is designed as a 'Legislative Theatre'. This form of participation is based on the concept of 'Theatre of the Oppressed', developed by Brazilian theatre director, politician and activist Augusto Boal. It enables citizens to raise their voices in the setting of a stage play. The objective is to start an open dialogue between citizens and governmental and administrative institutions. Citizens can take the stage and share their opinions and lived experience with legislators, thereby helping the legislative process.[69]

In recent years, a series of events have been held in all Tyrolean counties, inviting an estimated 10,000 people who have received support as persons with disabilities. This represented an unprecedented participatory approach in Tyrol.

IV. THE IMPLEMENTATION OF ARTICLE 33 CRPD

The Federal Law on Persons with Disabilities, dating back to 1990,[70] includes Chapter IIc (paragraphs 13f–13l BBG), introduced in 2017,[71] that focuses on the CRPD – Implementation and Monitoring. It contains provisions on the focal point, the Monitoring Committee, the appointment of its members and its meetings. The BMSGPK is the federal focal point for questions concerning the implementation of the CRPD (paragraph 13f BBG). To fulfil these tasks of protection, monitoring and promotion, the above-mentioned Federal Ministry

[69] A Lamplmayr and E Nachtschatt, 'Observing Legislative Processes: Implementation of the CRPD. Research Report' (Innsbruck University Press, 2016) 60.
[70] BGBl 283/1990 with amendment BGBl I 185/2022.
[71] BGBl I 155/2017.

has set up the Monitoring Committee, which includes various experts and representatives. In addition, the *Länder* have to create or designate bodies that meet the requirements of an independent mechanism in accordance with Article 33 CRPD (paragraph 13h BBG). Meetings of the Committee shall be convened by the chairman as necessary, but not less than eight times a year, or at the request of at least one-third of its members, giving written notice of the subject matter of the negotiations.

Austria had already established a Federal Monitoring Committee (*Monitoringausschuss* – MA) immediately after the ratification of the Convention in 2008,[72] which is enshrined in paragraph 13 Federal Disability Act. The MA is embedded in the Federal Disability Council (*Bundesbehindertenbeirat* – BBB),[73] which is an advisory body to the board of the BMSGPK.

However, the CRPD Committee noted that the federal MA 'does not have its own budget and appears to lack the independence required by the principles relating to the status and functioning of national institutions for protection and promotion of human rights (the Paris Principles)'.[74] In implementing this recommendation, the amendment of the BBG 2017 organised the Monitoring Committee independently as an association and provided it with its own budget of €320,000 per year.

Despite the Austrian government's proud conviction of compliance with the requirements of the Paris Principles[75] via the setup of the MA, there were numerous critical dissenting voices, including the MA itself.[76] The main reasons for the alleged lack of independence are insufficient financial resources and the lack of a constitutional guarantee of independence.[77] With regard to the latter, the MA consists of a total of seven members: four representatives of disabled persons' organisations,[78] one representative of an NGO in the field of human rights, one representative of an NGO in the field of international development, and one representative of academia. All members as well as a substitute member for each of the seven full members are to be nominated by the Austrian

[72] See Government Bill (*Regierungsvorlage* – RV) 1208 BlgNR XXIV GP, para II.

[73] Established in 2001, the BBB's functions and composition are regulated in paras 8–12 BBG. In addition to the representatives of significant Federal Ministries, members of all political parties represented in Parliament and representatives of the *Länder*, Members of the Council also include the chairperson of the MA and eight representatives of disabled persons' organisations, self-advocacy organisations as well as war victims' organisations.

[74] CRPD Committee (n 25).

[75] European Network of National Human Rights Institutions, 'UN Paris Principles & Accreditation' (2022) www.ennhri.org.

[76] Unabhängiger Monitoringausschuss zur Umsetzung der UN-Konvention über die Rechte von Menschen mit Behinderungen (Monitoringausschuss), 'Stellungnahme. Nationale Menschenrechtsinstitutionen' (2009) www.monitoringausschuss.at.

[77] Lamplmayr and Nachtschatt (n 69) 52.

[78] The Austrian legislature has recognised the importance of Article 33(3) CRPD and has therefore included persons with disabilities directly in the monitoring mechanism. In fact, four of seven members within the Committee represent persons with disabilities.

National Council of Disabled Persons (*Österreichischer Behindertenrat*, formerly known as *Österreichische Arbeitsgemeinschaft für Rehabilitation* – ÖAR) and appointed by the Minister of Social Affairs for a period of four years with legally enshrined independence. They must then elect a chairperson for the same period. Representatives of all Austrian Federal Ministries are authorised to attend and deliberate at the meetings, but they do not have the right to vote.[79]

The MA regularly publishes critical statements on current problems and holds a series of public sessions throughout Austria, which has given it a very proactive role. By doing so, the MA hopes to ensure that civil society has a say in the monitoring process.[80] All sessions are public,[81] closed sessions and annual reports[82] to the BBB and CRPD Committee are available online. Furthermore, various comments on existing law and statements concerning drafts of law[83] are available and regularly updated on the MA's website.[84] In sum, the federal MA has not only stood up for civil society and especially persons with disabilities but also strives to make its work transparent and publicly accessible. Any kind of deficiency regarding the involvement of civil society in the mechanism of monitoring is therefore 'caused by the MA's lack of resources',[85] especially when considering that aside from the chairperson, all members exercise their position in the Committee without pay.

Regarding the subnational level, in 2015 all *Länder* finally managed to establish their own monitoring mechanisms as stipulated in Article 33 CRPD. By September 2012, only the *Länder* of Carinthia and Vienna had designated monitoring bodies. Even though all *Länder* have established monitoring mechanisms, the majority of them are not newly set up entities. The *Länder* have often decided to extend the competences of existing administrative bodies. Monitoring the CRPD's implementation was simply added to their existing portfolio. Therefore, their independence from other administrative and legislative entities was questioned. As an example of good practice, the Tyrolean Monitoring Committee (*Tiroler Monitoringausschuss*) shall be described briefly.

It is located in the Equal Treatment and Non-Discrimination Service Unit (*Servicestelle Gleichbehandlung und Antidiskriminierung*) and was established in January 2014. 'The composition of the Committee according to the rules of operation is quite similar to the federal MA's composition but has an even stronger emphasis on persons with disabilities representing the lived experience

[79] Lamplmayr and Nachtschatt (n 69) 52.
[80] Ibid 53.
[81] Monitoringausschuss, 'Protokolle des Monitoringausschusses' www.monitoringausschuss.at/protokolle.
[82] Monitoringausschuss, 'Berichte' www.monitoringausschuss.at/dokumente.
[83] Monitoringausschuss, 'Stellungnahmen' www.monitoringausschuss.at/stellungnahmen.
[84] Monitoringausschuss, 'Begutachtungen' www.monitoringausschuss.at/begutachtungen.
[85] Lamplmayr and Nachtschatt (n 69) 53.

within the Committee'.[86] The Tyrolean Law on Anti-Discrimination (*Tiroler Antidiskriminierungsgesetz* 2005 – TADG 2005) was amended in 2017,[87] and the task to evaluate the implementation of the CRPD was transferred from the anti-discrimination officer to the Monitoring Committee. In paragraph 17(1) TADG 2005 it is provided that the anti-discrimination officer and the members of the Monitoring Committee are not bound by any instructions. According to paragraph 3, all organs of the *Land*, the municipalities, the associations of municipalities and the self-governing bodies established by *Land* law shall support the anti-discrimination commissioner(s) and the Monitoring Committee in the performance of their duties and shall grant them access to files and provide information to the extent required, unless this conflicts with a legal obligation to maintain secrecy.

Currently, the Tyrolean Committee consists of nine members and nine deputy members, representing: science and teaching, human rights associations, persons with disabilities, people with sensory impairments (hearing and/or vision impairments), people with learning difficulties and people with mental illness.[88] The chair of the Committee is the Tyrolean anti-discrimination officer. The Committee can be mirrored as independent and not bound to any instructions. The Tyrolean Monitoring Committee deals with all issues of monitoring the CRPD, in particular it:

- holds non-public and public meetings;
- issues statements especially on *Land* laws and amendments that concern matters covered by the CRPD;
- determines the topics for the public meetings;
- gives advice and accompanies important projects and the development of laws;
- points out problems and deficiencies in the implementation of the CRPD and suggests changes and improvements;
- monitors legal implementations;
- obtains necessary data and information;
- prepares reports and recommendations at any time.

The chairperson sets out meetings, but the members of the Monitoring Committee can also request for a meeting to be held. Meetings, which are non-public, are held at least four times a year, but there has to be at least one public meeting within a year and the people must be informed that such a public meeting will be taking place.

[86] Lamplmayr and Nachtschatt (n 69) 54.
[87] LGBl 25/2005 with amendment LGBl 138/2019 (Tyrol).
[88] Tiroler Monitoringausschuss, 'Zusammensetzung des Ausschusses' www.tirol.gv.at.

As regards the other *Länder*, Monitoring Committees are established in Burgenland,[89] Carinthia,[90] Lower Austria,[91] Upper Austria,[92] Salzburg,[93] Styria,[94] Vienna[95] and Vorarlberg.[96] The freedom of direction and instruction seems to be expressly guaranteed, even if there are many differences in the legal framework of the individual institutions.

V. CONCLUDING REMARKS

The implementation of the CRPD is difficult in a federal state with such fragmented competences like Austria. One of the main criticisms is the lack of willingness to implement the CRPD by the *Länder*.[97] However, this is a one-sided approach. It overlooks that many measures have not been, and are not being, supported because the *Länder* were not involved sufficiently in the decision-making process at the national level. This was particularly evident in the NAP Disability 2012–2020. It is to be hoped that the mistakes of the past will not be repeated in the NAP Disability 2022–2030.

Overall, it should not be overlooked that considerable progress has also been made in Austria since the CRPD came into force. This applies in particular to monitoring, which is increasingly being carried out at the *Land* level. In the meantime, monitoring committees, which are sufficiently autonomous, have also been formed in the *Länder*.

However, it is expected that the pressure on the *Länder* to fully adopt the contents of the CRPD into national law will increase. The pressure for harmonisation in Austria, which is characterised by overall strong support for harmonisation of legislation, is also expected to increase. Representatives

[89] Para 6a Burgenland Health, Patients' and Disabled Persons' Ombudsman Act (*Burgenländisches Gesundheits-, Patienten- und Behindertenanwaltschaftsgesetz* – Bgld GPB-A-G) LGBl 51/2000 with amendment LGBl 39/2014.

[90] Para 35 Carinthian Act of Equality of Chances (*Kärntner Chancengleichheitsgesetz* – K-ChG) LGBl 8/2010 with amendment LGBl 70/2019.

[91] Para 2 Lower Austrian Monitoring Act (*Niederösterreichisches Monitoringgesetz* – Nö. MTG) LGBl 9291-0.

[92] Para 14 Upper Austrian Anti-Discrimination Act (*Oberösterreichisches Antidiskriminierungsgesetz* – Oö. ADG) LGBl 50/2005 with amendment LGBl 51/2017.

[93] Para 40a Salzburg Equal Treatment Act (*Salzburger Gleichbehandlungsgesetz* – S. GBG) LGBl 31/2006 with amendment LGBl 49/2016.

[94] Para 53 Styrian Disability Act (*Steiermärkisches Behindertengesetz* – StBHG) LGBl 26/2004 with amendment LGBl 94/2014.

[95] Para 7 Vienna Anti-Discrimination Act (*Wiener Antidiskriminierungsgesetz* – W ADG) LGBl 35/2004 with amendment LGBl 22/2017.

[96] Para 11 Vorarlberg Anti-Discrimination Act (*Vorarlberger Antidiskriminierungsgesetz* – V ADG) LGBl 17/2005 with amendment LGBl 16/2017.

[97] Rubisch (n 28) 87.

of the Federal Government and, in particular, those of the competent Federal Ministry, also contribute to this. This development is probably welcomed by the representatives of people with disabilities, but they overlook the fact that, with increasing harmonisation, federal innovations are being lost and that harmonisation is taking precedence over diversity.

4

Italy

Is the CRPD Engendering a Centripetal Dynamic in the Italian Regional State?

PAOLO ADDIS AND MATTEO MONTI

I. INTRODUCTION

THE ITALIAN LEGISLATIVE framework on disability[1] experienced a notable evolution in the last decades. As pointed out by several scholars,[2] a new approach arose since the approval of the Law No 104 of 5 February 1992,[3] which aims to guarantee the dignity and the social inclusion of persons with disabilities. In its early stages, this evolution was led by a dynamic interpretation of constitutional principles and values by the Italian constitutional court.[4] The ratification of the UN Convention on the Rights of Persons with Disabilities (CRPD) by means of Law No 18 of 3 March 2009[5] increased the complexity of the Italian system of protection of the rights of persons with disabilities. Notwithstanding the dualist approach of the Italian legal framework and the

[1] The chapter makes frequent reference to the English translation of the Italian Constitution published by the Parliamentary Information, Archives and Publications Office of the Senate Service for Official Reports and Communication, available at www.senato.it/documenti/repository/istituzione/costituzione_inglese.pdf. With regard to judicial decisions, unless otherwise specified, all translations from the original Italian legal text are ours.

[2] See C Colapietro and F Girelli, *Persone con disabilità e Costituzione* (Edizioni Scientifiche, 2020) 49–50.

[3] Law No 104, 5 February 1992, 'Legge-quadro per l'assistenza, l'integrazione sociale e i diritti delle persone handicappate'.

[4] See Italian Constitutional Court, Decision No 215 of 1987.

[5] Law No 18, 3 March 2009, 'Ratifica ed esecuzione della Convenzione delle Nazioni Unite sui diritti delle persone con disabilità, con Protocollo opzionale, fatta a New York il 13 dicembre 2006 e istituzione dell'Osservatorio nazionale sulla condizione delle persone con disabilità'.

provision of Article 117(1) of the Italian Constitution (*Costituzione Italiana* – CI),[6] the CRPD has been very influential. As noted by Ferri:

> the Italian legal framework relating particularly to disabled people … did not undergo significant changes as a result of Italy's ratification of the CRPD … By contrast, case law in Italy has been significantly influenced … Civil and administrative courts, as well as the Constitutional Court, have made reference to the CRPD in several Decisions.[7]

While the hermeneutical relevance of the CRPD is well established, this chapter interrogates whether the CRPD is slowly becoming a benchmark for lawmakers and policymakers, as well as disability rights activists. It also aims to answer key research questions, in line with the aims of this volume: Did the CRPD implementation influence Italian regionalism? If so, in what way? What impact have CRPD related policies had on the subnational entities in Italy?

Firstly, it provides an overview of the core tenets of the Italian regional state. After that, the chapter analyses the implementation of the CRPD at the regional level, focusing on specific topics, including accessibility measures, participation of persons with disabilities, and the enforcement of Article 33 CRPD. With regard to the latter, the chapter discusses the National Observatory on the Condition of Persons with Disabilities (*Osservatorio nazionale sulla condizione delle persone con disabilità Presidenza del Consiglio dei Ministri*). This Observatory was created by Law No 18/2009 and has been entrusted with the task of periodically drawing up planning and monitoring Acts relating to the legal status of people with disabilities. The National Observatory includes two representatives of the Conference of Regions and Autonomous Provinces (*Conferenza delle Regioni e delle Province autonome*). Further, regions are often mentioned in the national programmatory Acts delivered by the National Observatory, but – as pointed out by Ferri – 'the efforts at national level are not counterbalanced by identical commitments in the Regions (despite their important powers in the disability domain)'.[8]

Finally, the last section provides an overview of the application of the Convention in Italy taking into account the Next Generation EU (NGEU) and the National Recovery and Resilience Plan (*Piano Nazionale di Ripresa e Resilienza* – PNRR).[9]

[6] 'Legislative powers shall be vested in the State and the Regions in compliance with the Constitution and with the constraints deriving from EU legislation and international obligations'.

[7] D Ferri, 'Italy' in L Waddington and A Lawson (eds), *The UN Convention on the Rights of Persons with Disabilities in Practice: A Comparative Analysis of the Role of Courts* (Oxford University Press, 2018).

[8] D Ferri, 'Reshaping Disability Policy Making in Italy: The "Focal Point", the National Observatory on the Situation of Persons with Disabilities, and … the Absence of Regions?' (2012) *Perspectives on Federalism* 50.

[9] The NGEU programme, adopted on 14 December 2020 by the European Union, is a recovery plan developed for the post-Covid era. The PNRR is the Italian plan implementing the NGEU and defines a consistent package of reforms and investments for the period 2021–26. A text of the PNRR is available at www.governo.it/sites/governo.it/files/PNRR.pdf.

II. THE ITALIAN REGIONAL FORM OF STATE

The main characteristic of the Italian regional system[10] is the distinction between 'special' regions, often endowed with broader legislative competences than ordinary ones and with a particular fiscal/financial regime that permits them greater capacity to set regional policies in the welfare-state sectors, and 'ordinary' regions, which are mostly dependent on the revenues distributed by the state and with more limited legislative competences. With the reform of Title V of the Constitution, which occurred in 2001, Italy underwent a major decentralisation process that resulted in the ordinary regions being endowed with important legislative prerogatives and, in many areas, exclusive competences. In this regard, Article 117 CI, as amended by the reform of 2001, has substantially reversed the previous allocation of competences, allocating, in the name of the principle of subsidiarity, most of those competences to the regions, by means of a residual clause in their favour.[11]

The state is endowed with a legislative power on enumerated and exhaustive matters, which are listed in Article 117(2) CI. The regions, on the other hand, are now endowed with 'general' and 'residual' legislative power: it is worth noting that from this point of view ordinary and special regions have become more similar, compared to the situation before the 2001 constitutional reform. In that connection, it is also interesting to point out how the 2001 constitutional reform eliminated the so-called supplementary-implementing competence, although areas remain in which there may be concurrent competence.

Further, after the reform of 2001, Article 116(3) CI enables special conditions of autonomy to be granted to ordinary regions, through the attribution of state competences to them. Notably these new forms of autonomy and new competences were demanded by some northern Italian regions (Emilia-Romagna, Lombardy and Veneto) in 2018, and, to date, other regions are requesting new competences claiming the application of Article 116(3) CI. Although no agreement has yet been reached on the application of this constitutional provision for the three northern regions mentioned above, it is clear that in such a case the division of competences between the central state and the regions would become

[10] On the peculiar characteristics of Italian regionalism: E Arban, G Martinico and F Palermo (eds), *Federalism and Constitutional Law. The Italian Contribution to Comparative Regionalism* (Routledge, 2021).

[11] On Art 117 Italian Constitution (*Costituzione Italiana* – CI) after the 2001 Constitutional Reform, see, *ex multis*, S Ninatti and G Tiberi, 'Art. 117, I comma' in F Clementi et al (eds), *La Costituzione italiana. Commento articolo per articolo* (Il Mulino, 2021); L Cuocolo, 'Art. 117, II comma' in F Clementi et al (eds), *La Costituzione italiana. Commento articolo per articolo* (Il Mulino, 2021); D Morana, 'Art. 117, III, IV, V comma' in F Clementi et al (eds), *La Costituzione italiana. Commento articolo per articolo* (Il Mulino, 2021); M Massa, 'Art. 117, VI comma' in F Clementi et al (eds), *La Costituzione italiana. Commento articolo per articolo* (Il Mulino, 2021); M Caielli, 'Art. 117, VII comma' in F Clementi et al (eds), *La Costituzione italiana. Commento articolo per articolo* (Il Mulino, 2021); EC Raffiotta, 'Art. 117, VIII, IX comma' in F Clementi et al (eds), *La Costituzione italiana. Commento articolo per articolo* (Il Mulino, 2021).

(further) diversified across the country (far beyond the difference between ordinary and special regions).[12]

In this 'federalising' framework, the constitutional reform of 2001 introduced, in order to guarantee the uniformity of fundamental rights on the territory of the state and to protect equality of Italian citizens regardless of the region they live in, Article 117(2) letter m) CI. This provision establishes the competence of the state to determine 'the basic level of benefits relating to civil and social entitlements to be guaranteed throughout the national territory'.

This clause, read in light of the Constitutional Court's case law that prohibits the creation of regional 'fundamental' rights,[13] has not only substantially guaranteed the state primacy in the identification of fundamental rights, but has also (theoretically) provided for the possibility of setting a minimum level of social rights (in Italian, the so-called *livelli essenziali*, ie, the basic level of benefits in the enjoyment of social rights).[14] However, identification of the basic level of benefits has been implemented only belatedly and not in all sectors, even though it appears to be a central issue in the regional system with respect to the enforcement of fundamental rights, as pointed out by the Constitutional Court.[15]

Against this background, the broad competences of the regions in the field of healthcare and welfare services, as well as a lack of clarification of what is the basic level of benefits to be guaranteed by the state, have generated a system where it is quite difficult to identify, in the field of social rights, the scope of application of fundamental rights. This also renders the implementation of international commitments undertaken by the central state more difficult, including those undertaken by the ratification of the CRPD.

In such a multilevel legal system,[16] it appears that implementing the CRPD is particularly complex. Notably, some regions had enacted laws in order to protect and safeguard persons with disabilities long before the ratification of the CRPD (see for example Regional Law No 29/1997 of the Emilia Romagna region). After the adoption of the Convention other regions undertook a process of harmonisation and codification of existing sectoral legislation on disability. For example,

[12] G Delledonne, G Martinico and M Monti, 'Subnational Constitutionalism in Italy – Unfulfilled expectations?' in P Popelier, G Delledonne and N Aroney (eds), *Routledge Handbook of Subnational Constitutions and Constitutionalism* (Routledge, 2021). About the recent developments regarding Article 116 CI, see also E Gianfrancesco, 'L'attuazione dell'art. 116, comma 3, Cost. tra nodi problematici e prospettive evolutive del regionalismo italiano' (2020) *Consultaonline* 36; C Tubertini, 'La proposta di autonomia differenziata delle Regioni del Nord: una differenziazione solidale?' (2018) *Federalismi.it*.

[13] G Delledonne and G Martinico, 'Legal Conflict and Subnational Constitutionalism' (2012) *Rutgers Law Journal* 892.

[14] See M Luciani, 'Diritti sociali e livelli essenziali delle prestazioni pubbliche nei sessant'anni della Corte costituzionale' (2016) *Rivista AIC* 1.

[15] See Italian Constitutional Court, Decision No 62/2020.

[16] A Candido, *Disabilità e prospettive di riforma. Una lettura costituzionale* (Giuffrè, 2018).

Tuscany adopted a unified 'code' on disability by means of Regional Law No 60/2017.[17] Over the last few years, regional legislation on disability has increased considerably in almost all the regions, but there are still significant differences between one region and another. The regional exclusive competence in many areas relevant to the protection of persons with disabilities and the absence of a formalisation of the basic levels of benefits in the field of disability have actually resulted in an inconsistent and fragmented scenario. Despite the Constitutional Court's ruling[18] with regard to the state's contribution aimed at the realisation of adequate rights for persons with disabilities (their essential core, or minimum standard) by the regions, many regional disability policies still depend on the budgets of the regions and their spending programmes.

The framework outlined here illustrates how the territorial structure of the Italian Republic on the one hand makes it problematic to precisely identify the institutional actor competent to implement the CRPD and, on the other hand, generates fragmentation, as a result of the absence of a state regulation of the basic levels of benefits in the field of disability.

It is precisely this 'systemic confusion', due to the need to reconcile autonomy and a minimum standard of protection of fundamental rights, that has recently led the central parliament to attempt to enact a comprehensive legislation aiming, among other things, at identifying the basic level of benefits relating to civil and social entitlements of persons with disabilities;[19] after a first (unsuccessful) attempt by the Conte Government, a delegation law was approved by the Draghi Cabinet (Law No 227 of 22 December 2021).[20] The latter law entrusts the executive with the task of determining procedures for establishing the essential levels of benefits in the field of the rights of people with disabilities (Article 2(I) letter g), point No 2).

III. THE CRPD IN ITALY: A DIFFICULT MARRIAGE?

A. The Impact of the CRPD on the Italian Legal Framework Regarding Disability

As mentioned above, the Italian regional system is based on a division of competences laid out in Article 117 CI. This provision is particularly complex. As a

[17] On Tuscany's Regional Law No 60/2017, see P Addis, F Pacini and E Rossi (eds), *La legge regionale toscana sulle persone con disabilità. Uno sguardo critico* (Pisa University Press, 2020).

[18] Italian Constitutional Court, Decision No 83/2019.

[19] 'Disegno di legge: Delega al Governo in materia di disabilità' (Atto Camera (AC) 3347) (2 November 2021) www.camera.it; M Bezze and E Innocenti, 'Il disegno di legge delega in materia di disabilità: osservazioni sulla "disciplina dei benefici"' in E Vivaldi and A Blasini (eds), *Verso il 'Codice per la persona con disabilità'* (Special Issue, 2021) *Forum di Quaderni Costituzionali*.

[20] See Law No 227 of 22 December 2021; See also n 15.

consequence, the attempt to frame disability within the matters enumerated by Article 117 is fraught with difficulties.

The implementation of the CRPD in Italy proved even more difficult, given the profound economic crisis during the decade 2010–20 and the emergency related to the Covid-19 pandemic. Moreover, the Italian Constitutional Court's case law did not provide a consistent interpretation of the CRPD within the Italian hierarchy of the sources of law, using the CRPD as a hermeneutical tool but assigning it a merely programmatic value.[21]

Recently, references to the CRPD have become more frequent in both national and regional legislation. For example, a recent national law regarding assistance to persons with severe disability affirms that:

> [the mentioned law] is aimed at promoting well-being, full social inclusion and autonomy of persons with disabilities … in implementation of the principles established by Articles 2, 3, 30, 32 and 38 of the Constitution, by Articles 24 and 26 of the Charter of Fundamental Rights of the European Union and by Articles 3 and 19, with particular reference to paragraph 1, letter a), of the [CRPD].[22]

At the regional level, in a similar vein, the above-mentioned Tuscan law on disability (No 60/2017) refers to Articles 2, 3, 30, 32 and 38 CI and to the rights of persons with disabilities as set out in the Charter of Fundamental Rights of the European Union and the CRPD. Furthermore, the regional law states that '[Tuscany region] will promote and support, within the scope of its competences and with particular regard to Article 24 of the [CRPD], the right to education, training and work of persons with disabilities' (Article 1). Piemonte's Regional Law No 3/2019 states that:

> [t]he Region, in accordance with the Charter of Fundamental Rights of the European Union proclaimed in Strasbourg in 2007, the United Nations (UN) Convention on the Rights of Persons with Disabilities of 13 December 2006 ratified by law 3 March 2009, No. 18 …, the principles referred to in Articles 2, 3, 30, 32 and 38 of the Constitution, the statutory principles, as well as in compliance with the relevant state and European legislation, promotes the implementation of interventions aimed at promoting policies for people with disabilities.[23]

Whether the references to the CRPD by regional laws imply a centrifugal dynamic in the implementation of the provisions of the Convention itself, or whether the process is still firmly in the hands of the central state, remains a complex issue.

However, regarding four areas of particular relevance (legal definition of disability, accessibility, anti-discrimination framework, and mechanics of

[21] See eg Italian Constitutional Court, Decisions Nos 80/2010 and 2/2016.

[22] See Art 1 Law No 112, 'Disposizioni in materia di assistenza in favore delle persone con disabilità grave prive del sostegno familiare'; See also E Vivaldi, 'Disabilità, autonomia, diritti. Alcune riflessioni a tre anni dall'approvazione della legge n. 112/2016' (2019) *Diritti fondamentali* 1.

[23] Regional Law of Piemonte No 3/2019, 'Promozione delle politiche a favore dei diritti delle persone con disabilità'.

participation of persons with disabilities), we argue that the CRPD implementation process must be contextualised in dynamics that seem to be centripetal.

B. The Notion of Disability: New Perspectives

Before analysing the definitions of disability in the Italian legal system, two preliminary observations can be made.

First, there is a wide number of definitions regarding persons with disabilities in our legal framework. Multiple sources of law provide measures regarding disability but referring to diverse concepts such as 'inability to work' (*inabilità al lavoro*; Article 38 CI and Law No 335 of 8 August 1995), 'civil invalidity' (*invalidità civile*; Law No 118 of 30 March 1971), 'blind and deaf persons' (*persone cieche e sorde*; Law No 107 of 24 June 2010), 'handicapped persons' (*persone handicappate*; Law No 104 of 5 February 1992). Each defining formula corresponds to particular economic benefits or specific assistance measures and this fragmentation has been considered an 'Achilles' heel' of the Italian welfare system regarding persons with disabilities.[24]

Secondly, Law No 104/1992 has been considered a fundamental achievement with regard to the protection and promotion of the rights of persons with disabilities by the Italian Constitutional Court.[25] The definition of 'handicapped person' provided for in Article 3 of this law, which makes reference to social disadvantage, has influenced the notion of disability, becoming a sort of 'standard rule'. Article 3 affirms that a handicapped person is anyone who is in a particular condition of a physical, psychic or sensory nature, stabilised or progressive, 'which is the cause of learning, relationship or integration difficulties work and such as to determine a process of social disadvantage or marginalisation'. Moreover, Article 3(2) states that '[t]he handicapped person is entitled to the benefits set out in its favour in relation to the nature and consistency of the handicap, to the total residual individual capacity and to the effectiveness of rehabilitation therapies'. Despite what could be considered its outdated language, Article 3 of Law No 104/1992 had the merit of highlighting structural barriers faced by persons with disabilities, and the role of the state in dismantling these barriers. While this definition of disability, wide and encompassing a large variety of personal conditions, has become a cornerstone of the Italian legal system, it is likely to be superseded soon. The recent Law No 227/2021 states that the government will ensure the adoption of a definition of 'disability' consistent with Article 1(2) CRPD, 'including by amending Law No. 104 of 5 February 1992, and introducing measures that provide for a basic assessment

[24] Candido (n 16) 73.

[25] See Italian Constitutional Court, Decisions Nos 406/1992, 167/1999 and 325/1996; See G Arconzo, *I diritti delle persone con disabilità. Profili costituzionali* (Franco Angeli, 2020) 154–55.

of disability … based on the bio-psycho-social approach'. This law also provides for the embedding of:

> the International Classification of Functioning, Disability and Health (ICF), approved by the 54th World Health Assembly on 22 May 2001, and by related technical operational assessment tools, for the purposes of description and analysis of operation, disability and of health, together with the version adopted in Italy of the International Classification of Diseases (ICD) of the World Health Organization and any other eventual rating scale available and consolidated in the literature scientific and clinical practice.[26]

Considering the nature of such provisions, aiming at harmonising different and multiple definitions of disability, it is evident that a centripetal dynamic is taking place: a new notion of disability, adopted at the state level and consistent with the principles of the CRPD, will be a new uniform standard valid throughout the national territory. Ultimately, the centripetal standardising drive seems to have as its goal that of avoiding inequality and ineffective guarantee of rights linked to strained and heterogeneous definitions of disability.

C. Regional Anti-Discrimination Measures: An Unexplored Land?

The Italian disability anti-discrimination legal framework revolves around Legislative Decree No 216 of 9 July 2003 with regard to employment and occupation and – more generally – on the mentioned Law No 67 of 1 March 2006, also inspired by supranational institutions. Such a legal framework follows a centralised approach, firmly anchored to measures adopted by the state.

The new definition of disability when adopted will be applied *de iure* within the anti-discriminatory Italian framework, aligning also formally Italian law and CRPD, as Article 1 of Law No 67 of 1 March 2006 provides that anti-discriminatory measures:

> pursuant to Article 3 of the Constitution, promotes the full implementation of the principle of equal treatment and equal opportunities *for people with disabilities referred to in Article 3 of law No. 104*, in order to guarantee them the full enjoyment of their civil rights, political, economic and social.[27]

However, this definition has already penetrated the Italian legal framework by virtue of EU non-discrimination law.

Although anti-discrimination law is in the hands of the state, the regions have become progressively more active in the field, adopting measures to combat discrimination and to raise awareness regarding the rights of minorities. For example, Piemonte region approved measures aiming at implementing

[26] Law No 227 of 21 December 2021, 'Delega al Governo in materia di disabilità'.
[27] See Law No 67 of 1 March 2006, 'Misure per la tutela giudiziaria delle persone con disabilità vittime di discriminazioni'.

the prohibition of discrimination enshrined in Article 21 of the Charter of Fundamental Rights of the EU and by Article 3(1) CI and enacting the duty to ensure and promote the substantive equality contained in Article 3(2) CI 'as well as to implement the principles sanctioned by the regional statute' within regional competences as defined by Article 117 CI.[28] It has to be underlined that, in the past, anti-discrimination regional measures related to private law relationships were regarded with suspicion, since Article 117 CI affirms that '[t]he State shall have exclusive legislative powers [in the field inter alia of] jurisdiction and procedural rules; civil and criminal law; administrative justice'.[29] Hence, in the future, regions could approve further complementary regulations.

D. Accessibility Measures: One (Centrally Decided) Size Fits All?

In the Italian legal framework, the concept of accessibility has been addressed, mostly, with reference to architectural barriers.[30]

Since the end of the 1960s, public entities have dealt with what, in various ways, can prevent some people (those with disabilities) from accessing physical spaces in which to manifest themselves and enjoy their rights. The circular of the Ministry of Public Works No 465 of 29 January 1967, at point 6, affirms the need:

> to take into account, both in urban planning and particularly in building projects, the problem of the so-called 'architectural barriers', namely obstacles that physically disabled individuals encounter in moving around urban spaces and buildings: obstacles essentially consisting of altimetric elements that are encountered along the paths (steps, ledges, differences in height, stairs, etc.), or by scarcity of passages and narrowness of environments (bottlenecks, lift cabins, opening doors, etc.). In order to eliminate these difficulties as much as possible, it is advisable to avoid, as far as possible, paths that present such drawbacks, or specific paths should be provided, possibly alternatively, which facilitate the movement of spastic or otherwise impeded or handicapped people.

Without retracing the evolution of national law, we can limit ourselves to emphasising how the rules relating to architectural barriers are placed in sources of various rank and scope: Articles 27 and 28 of Law No 118 of 31 March 1971 (containing 'Conversion into law of D.L. 30 January 1971, No 5 and new rules in

[28] The mentioned regional law enumerates 'health, health services and social policies; housing; vocational training and education; labour policies, promotion of entrepreneurship and corporate social responsibility; cultural, tourist, sporting, recreational and commercial activities; training and organisation of regional personnel; communication; transport and mobility' (Art 3(2)).

[29] Art 117(1)(l) CI. See F Viglione, 'Il principio di non discriminazione nei rapporti tra privati: quali spazi per la legislazione regionale?' (2012) *Le Regioni* 192.

[30] See AD Marra, 'Barriere architettoniche', *Enciclopedia del diritto* (2011).

favour of the mutilated and disabled civilians'; the two Articles cited are respectively entitled, 'Architectural barriers and public transport' and 'Provisions for school attendance'), the Ministerial Decree (Lav. Pub.) No 236 of 14 June 1989 ('Technical requirements necessary to guarantee the accessibility, adaptability and visitability of private buildings and subsidised and facilitated public residential buildings, for the purpose of overcoming and eliminating architectural barriers'), Law No 104 of 5 February 1992 (in particular, Articles 8, 23 and 24, respectively entitled 'Insertion and social integration', 'Removal of obstacles for the exercise of sports, tourism and recreational activities' and 'Elimination or overcoming of architectural barriers'), the Presidential Decree No 503/1996 ('Regulation laying down rules for the elimination of architectural barriers in buildings, spaces and public services') and the Presidential Decree No 380/2001 ('Consolidated text of legislative and regulatory provisions on construction matters'). This framework is complemented by provisions of regional legislation, for the most adopted after the constitutional reform of 2001.

Article 2 of the Ministerial Decree (Lav. Pub.) No 289/1989 includes a first notion useful for framing in a more precise way the concept of accessibility: in fact, in addition to the notion of architectural barriers, the provision in question, in letter g), also offers a first definition of accessibility and states:

> Accessibility means the possibility, even for people with reduced or impaired motor or sensory ability, to reach the building and its individual real estate and environmental units, to enter it easily and use spaces and equipment in conditions of adequate safety and autonomy.

It is clear that the scope of the concept of accessibility, in this provision, is limited to the dimension, already mentioned, of the triadic relationship between persons with disabilities, legal rules and physical spaces. It is a perspective that has also been reflected in the constitutional jurisprudence, in the context of various cases regarding the links between subjects of law, rules and physical space.

Among the Decisions of the Constitutional Court, three cases are particularly interesting for our analysis. The first one (Decision No 167/1999) concerns the constitutional illegitimacy of Article 1052(2) of the Italian Civil Code as it did not provide for the establishment of transit privileges across residential buildings in order to ensure adequate access to public roads for physically disabled persons with walking difficulties. In this Decision, the Constitutional Court in accepting the position proposed by the referring court and declaring the illegitimacy of the legislation in question, resumes the letter of the aforementioned Article 2 of the Ministerial Decree No 289/1989 and affirms that accessibility constitutes:

> an essential quality of newly built private buildings for residential use, as a consequence of the affirmation, in the social conscience, of the collective duty to remove,

> in advance, any possible obstacle to the explanation of fundamental rights of people with physical disabilities.[31]

In addition to this, it should be noted that the concept of accessibility is related to the right of people with disabilities to social life: housing inaccessibility is a prelude to a situation of social isolation contrary to what derives from Articles 2 and 3 of the Constitution. More precisely, the Court affirms that hindering the accessibility of residential property and, consequently, the socialisation of people with disabilities also involves 'an infringement of [their] fundamental right … to health, understood in the meaning of Article 32 of the Constitution, also including mental health whose protection must be of a degree equal to that of physical health'.[32]

The second judgment relevant for the purposes of this analysis is Decision No 251/2008. In this Decision, after having recalled some of its previous judgments on the rights of persons with disabilities, the Court leaves to the legislator (ie to the Parliament) the task of balancing the right of persons with disabilities to accessibility with other constitutional values at stake, 'without prejudice, in any case, to respect of an indefectible core of guarantees for the interested parties'.

Highly relevant is Decision No 111/2014. In declaring the constitutional illegitimacy of a law of the Valle d'Aosta region, it points out that the regulation in question:

> derogates from the State discipline referred to in Art. 82 (1) of the Presidential Decree No. 380/2001, which establishes that all construction works concerning public buildings and private buildings open to the public, with respect to which accessibility and visitability by the handicapped [*sic*] is in fact limited, must be carried out in compliance with the law regarding the elimination and overcoming of architectural barriers.

This being so, the regional legislation violates 'the exclusive legislative power of the State in order to determine the essential levels of services, with regard to the implementation of the rights of people with disabilities'.[33] The passage just reported therefore places a clear limit on regional legislative power, since it cannot affect *in peius* the state's measures.

Accessibility – in the meaning referred to so far – has also been addressed by civil courts and administrative judges. The Court of Cassation, for example, has been able to clarify how the presence of architectural barriers in private places open to the public can constitute discrimination pursuant to Article 3 of

[31] Italian Constitutional Court, Decision No 167/1999, point 5 of the *Considerato in diritto*.

[32] Ibid point 7 of the *Considerato in diritto*.

[33] Italian Constitutional Court, Decision No 111/2014, points 7(4) and 7(5) of the *Considerato in diritto*.

Law No 67 of 1 March 2006.[34] The Court – in the wake of the aforementioned jurisprudence of the Constitutional Court – further reiterated that 'the affirmation in the social conscience of the collective duty to preventively remove any possible obstacle to the implementation of the fundamental rights of people with physical disabilities' and 'the radical change of perspective in addressing the problems of people with disabilities, now considered as problems not only [as] individual, but such as to be assumed by the whole community' imply that the measures 'aimed at the elimination of architectural barriers, regardless of the actual use of the buildings themselves by persons with disabilities' are in any case applied.[35]

With regard to administrative case law, the Council of State recently ruled in a case on the removal of architectural barriers in structures considered as cultural assets, after having emphasised that legislation 'expresses the principle according to which the issues faced by people suffering from some kind of disability must be addressed by the whole community', that 'architectural barriers [must be] eliminated regardless of the actual use of the buildings by disabled people … since it is a question of guaranteeing fundamental rights'.[36]

With Italy's ratification of the CRPD, it has become even more evident how the concept of accessibility must be addressed with a holistic approach, taking due account of its complex nature. As required by Article 9 of the Convention in question, in fact, the States Parties undertake to adopt:

> adequate measures to guarantee people with disabilities, on an equal basis with others, access to the physical environment, transport, information and communication, including information and communication systems and technologies, and other equipment and services open or provided to the public, both in urban and rural areas.

States Parties must also undertake, among other things, to 'promote access for people with disabilities to new technologies and information and communication systems, including the internet'. And all this – as stated in the opening words of the Article in question – 'in order to allow people with disabilities to live independently and to participate fully in all aspects of life'.

From the reading of the provision in question, therefore, it is clear that the concept of accessibility cannot be limited to the mere need to eliminate architectural barriers. Rather, the perspective adopted by the Constitutional Court with Decision No 167/1999, based on accessibility and the right to health, could be further expanded, reconsidering accessibility as a *sine qua non* for the enjoyment of constitutional rights and freedoms.

It has to be noted that national lawmakers adopted measures regarding the accessibility of the websites of the public administration (*Pubblica*

[34] See Civil Cassation, Section III, Judgment of 23 September 2016, No 18762; More recently, see also Civil Cassation, Section III, Judgment of 13 February 2020, No 3691.

[35] Civil Cassation, Section II, Judgment of 25 October 2012, No 18334.

[36] Council of State, Section II, Decision No 355/2020.

amministrazione), provided for by Law No 4 of 9 January 2004 (entitled 'Provisions to facilitate access for disabled people to IT tools', amended several times). Furthermore, the European Accessibility Act was implemented by Legislative Decree No 82 of 27 May 2022, regarding '[i]mplementation of Directive (EU) 2019/882 of the European Parliament and of the Council, of 17 April 2019, on the accessibility requirements of products and services'.[37]

The Italian regions approved several regulations regarding accessibility. But the regional regulations – considered in the cited Decision of the Constitutional Court No 111/2014 – seem to be aimed merely at strengthening state-level measures. This is exemplified by Article 1(3) and (4) of Friuli Venezia Giulia Regional Law No 10 of 19 March 2018, which affirms that:

> This law is adopted in compliance with Article 117(2), letter m), of the Constitution, and in compliance with the national provisions in force concerning the overcoming and elimination of architectural … barriers. This law is also adopted in adherence to the principles of the [CRPD] … and the principles of non-discrimination pursuant to law No 67 of 2006.

In conclusion, considering accessibility rules 'as an essential level of guarantees of civil and social rights' *ex* Article 117 CI it is possible, at the national level, to move the limits of the regional legislative competence in order to ensure consistence with Article 9 CRPD or to transpose the law of the European Union.

E. 'Nulla su di noi senza di noi': The Participation of Persons with Disabilities

To some extent, a first form of participation of persons with disabilities is provided for by Law No 18/2009, which transposed the Convention into Italian law and established the National Observatory on the Condition of Persons with Disabilities. The Observatory also envisages the participation of the most representative national associations of persons with disabilities. In particular, the Observatory is supposed to guarantee a forum for making proposals for participation policies. Additionally, following the European Commission's Strategy for the Rights of Persons with Disabilities 2021–2030 of 3 March 2021, a number of measures are being discussed at the national level. The policies on participation under discussion could be improved by the Italian National Recovery and Resilience Plan. At the national level, a public consultation entitled 'Towards Full Inclusion of People with Disabilities' has also been opened at the end of 2021 to implement best practices in this field.[38]

[37] See D Ferri and N Šubic, 'The European Union: Federal Trends in Disability Rights' in this volume.

[38] ParteciPa, 'Report finale della consultazione. Verso una piena inclusione delle persone con disabilità' (ParteciPa, 2021).

At the regional level, in most of the regions, there does not seem to be a comprehensive regulation, only some interventions and initiatives regarding the participation of people with disabilities in some fields. In almost all the regions, both the actions of the Regional Guarantors and those of the Ombudspersons are pushing for an adjustment of the regional regulations on the subject (architectural barriers, inclusion funds, etc). A particularly virtuous example in this framework is that of the region of Tuscany. Tuscan Regional Law No 60 of 18 October 2017 enshrined Chapter VII as specifically dedicated to the 'Participation in Culture and Sport' of people with disabilities (Article 22 and following).

Chapter VIII of the same law ('Bodies for Participation') created a series of mechanisms to represent the interests of people with disabilities. A similar piece of legislation is that of the Piemonte region, which enacted Regional Law No 3/2019. The Regional Law No 3/2019 provides in a less detailed manner than the Tuscan law a framework to implement, among other aspects, the participation of persons with disabilities at social, school, training, employment, economic, cultural, sport and political levels (Article 2), with a particular emphasis on sports (Article 12). Eventually, this law appears to be a sort of act of guidance for future regional laws and policies, and it is accompanied by the establishment of a steering committee in the regional council to monitor and propose projects also related to the participation of people with disabilities (Article 14). In addition to these measures, it is worth noting that coordination plans for the various activities concerning disability and participation policies are being developed in some regions, such as the one recently voted for by the Lombardy Regional Council.[39] Other regions have also presented coordination plans in the past or proposals to regulate in a more coordinated way the participation of persons with disabilities in economic, social, and cultural life.

IV. IMPLEMENTATION OF ARTICLE 33 CRPD

A. Focal Point and Coordination Mechanism

Having regard to the focal point as defined by Article 33(1) CRPD, Italy opted for a single national focal point. As noted by Ferri, at first the Italian government 'started the CRPD implementation process by designating the focal point and the coordination mechanism: both of them coincide with the Directorate-General for Inclusion and Social Policies'.[40] It has to be noted that since 2018 Italy has established a Minister for Disability (*Ministero per la disabilità*).

[39] Deliberation No XI/5809, Session of 29 December 2021, 'Regional Action Plan for Policies in Favour of People with Disabilities 2021/2023'.

[40] See Ferri (n 7) 60.

The Minister is supported by an administrative structure, the Office for Policies in favour of People with Disabilities (*Ufficio per le politiche in favore delle persone con disabilità*)[41] since 1 January 2020. This Office is 'the support structure for the Prime Minister' in every task regarding the promotion and coordination of policies in favour of people with disability,[42] cooperating with the National Observatory on Disability mentioned above. So, the coordination mechanism has a distinctly centralistic connotation. On the whole this seems consistent with the Italian regional approach and with the need to guarantee a single direction for disability policies.

B. Monitoring the Rights of People with Disabilities

Regarding the implementation of Article 33 CRPD, it is first of all necessary to point out that in Italy there is no national human rights institution (NHRI) compliant with the so-called Paris Principles.[43] The draft laws currently before Parliament[44] seek to remedy the absence of this institution in our country: Italy is one of the five Member States of the EU without an NHRI.[45]

In Italy,[46] a considerable number of commissions and authorities with specific competences in the field of human rights exist, for example, the National Guarantor of the Rights of Persons Detained or Deprived of their Liberty. However, on the basis of Article 2 of Resolution No 48/134, many scholars have indicated the need to establish an NHRI. Presently, two bills at the national level, which would establish an NHRI and allow the monitoring of the proper application of the CRPD, are under discussion: Bill AC 855[47] proposes the creation of an NHRI with the classic tasks of monitoring respect for human

[41] See *Decreto del Presidente del Consiglio dei Ministri* (Decree by the President of the Council of Ministers – DPCM) 21 October 2019 and Decree of the Secretary General of the Presidency of the Council of Ministers 4 March 2020.

[42] See DPCM 12 July 2022, 'Modifiche del decreto del Presidente del Consiglio dei ministri 1 ottobre 2012, recante: «Ordinamento delle strutture generali della Presidenza del Consiglio di ministri». Istituzione dell'Ufficio per le politiche spaziali e aerospaziali e modifiche relative all'Ufficio per le politiche in favore delle persone con disabilità' Art 1.

[43] United Nations General Assembly Resolution No 48/134 of 20 December 1993.

[44] Namely, Bill Proposals AC 855 and AC 1323. 'Proposta di legge: Quartapelle Procopio ed altri: "Istituzione della Commissione nazionale per la promozione e la protezione dei diritti umani fondamentali" (AC 855)' (3 July 2018) and 'Proposta di legge: Scagliusi ed altri: "Istituzione della Commissione nazionale per la promozione e la protezione dei diritti umani fondamentali" (AC 1323)' (20 October 2018) www.camera.it.

[45] European Union Agency for Fundamental Rights (FRA), 'Strong and Effective National Human Rights Institutions – Challenges, Promising Practices and Opportunities' (Publications Office of the European Union, 2020); See also F Laiolo di Cossano, 'L'Autorità indipendente per i diritti umani in Italia' (2020) *federalismi.it*; F Laiolo di Cossano, 'L'Autorità indipendente per i diritti umani in Italia: adelante con juicio?' (2022) *federalismi.it*.

[46] E Santiemma, B Terenzi and M Gressi, *The Italian National Human Rights Institution (NHRI): What It Is And Why It Is Needed* (Aracne, 2020).

[47] Bill Proposal AC 855 (n 44).

rights, verifying the effective implementation of international conventions, collaborating with the public authorities, formulating opinions, promoting awareness-raising campaigns in the society on the scope of human rights. Bill AC 1323[48] envisages among the tasks of the NHRI, alongside monitoring compliance with human rights, that of promoting human rights in civil society (including activities in schools, the establishment of a permanent forum, the relationship with professional categories for the development of deontological codes in line with human rights), that of providing recommendations and opinions, that of receiving complaints but also that of providing statements on Italy's foreign policy actions and finally that of cooperating with international organisations. The two proposals differed not only in the scope of the tasks but also in the 'composition' of the Commission. The two texts were eventually merged into one. However, despite the fact that the bills were presented in 2018, discussion in Parliament still appears to be deadlocked, as was also pointed out by the 2021 Rule of Law Report of the European Commission.[49] The setting up of an NHRI could be accelerated by the reorganisation of public policies on disability that the above-mentioned delegation law empowering the government at harmonising the actions in the field of disabilities is attempting.[50] In this regard, the reorganisation of the *basic levels of benefits* in the field of disability could actually give a new impulse to the establishment of the Italian NHRI.

Additionally, the aforementioned Law No 227/2021 provides that the government will approve a legislative Decree regarding a brand new 'National Guarantor of Disability', having the functions, inter alia, of collecting 'reports from people with disabilities who denounce discrimination or violations of their rights, through the provision of a contact centre dedicated to this' and monitoring the compliance with the rights, the rules and the principles established by the CRPD by the Constitution, by state laws and regulations. Further, the National Guarantor for the Rights of Persons Detained or Deprived of Liberty plays a relevant role in monitoring the rights of people with disabilities living in institutions.

Moreover, it is also important to highlight the role in implementing and verifying the application of the CRPD played by some regional Ombudspersons,[51] who often use the Convention as a tool to enforce certain administrative policies,[52] or by those Regional Guarantors that are charged with general anti-discrimination functions, as in the case of Friuli Venezia Giulia (Article 10(1)

[48] Bill Proposal AC 1323 (n 44).

[49] European Commission, 'Commission Staff Working Document 2020 Rule of Law Report Country Chapter on the Rule of Law Situation in Italy' SWD(2020) 311 final.

[50] See n 15.

[51] M Magri, 'Le autorità regionali di tutela dei diritti: il caso dell'Emilia-Romagna' (2017) *Istituzioni del federalismo*.

[52] Regione Emilia-Romagna Assemblea Legislativa, 'Sospensione idrokinesiterapia a persone con disabilità a Piacenza, Difensore civico ne chiede la ripresa' (22 January 2021) www.assemblea.emr.it.

Regional Law No 9/2014). In other regions, such as Puglia, a body specifically aimed to guarantee the application of the CRPD, the Regional Guarantor of the Rights of Persons with Disabilities (Puglia Regional Law No 19/2006), was established. Similar bodies (Guarantors) were also instituted in Sicily (Regional Law No 47/2012), Campania (Regional Law No 25/2017), Lombardy (Regional Law No 10/2021), and most recently Umbria (Regional Law No 1/2022). In many other regions, the establishment of a Guarantor for the protection of the rights of persons with disabilities is being discussed or has been proposed. In this perspective, it is interesting to recall how Guarantors for persons with disabilities have also been created at a municipal level.[53]

In conclusion, the impulse to implement and monitor the CRPD seems to have come more from the actions of local authorities (regions and municipalities) than from the central state.

V. CONCLUDING REMARKS

The Covid-19 pandemic seems to have led to a re-centralisation within the relations between the state and the regions. 'Unifying' and 'standardising' trends would also be attributable to the political, social and economic opportunity to use the EU funds available for the post-pandemic phase, based on the guidelines of the PNRR. As regards specifically people with disabilities, those general centralising trends tally with the ones already prompted by the CRPD. First, it should be noted that the PNRR contains several references to the CRPD and the European Disability Strategy 2021–2030.[54] Secondly, it has to be underlined that one of the immediate consequences of the PNRR was the approval of Law No 227/2021, referred to several times in this chapter and implementing one of the reforms (reform 1.1) envisaged by Mission 5 'Inclusion and Cohesion', Component 2 'Social infrastructures, families, communities and the third sector' of the PNRR.[55]

Hence, it seems plausible to state that the need to proceed with the approval of the measures envisaged by the PNRR and by Law No 227/2021 put a highly effective tool to condition regional disability policies in the hands of the state.

[53] A first, well-structured model is that of the Municipality of Pisa (CC No 24 of 19 June 2014). Other examples are those of the Municipality of Lecce (Municipal Council Resolution No 141 of 12 November 2018); Sondrio (Council Resolution No 63 of 30 November 2018) and the Municipality of Pesaro (Municipal Council Resolution No 19 of 25 February 2019); most recently another good example is the Municipality of Ferrara (Municipal Council Resolution of Ferrara No 10 – PG 53504/2021 of 18 May 2021). It is a trend that is constantly developing.

[54] European Commission, 'Union of Equality: Strategy for the Rights of Persons with Disabilities 2021–2030' (Publications Office of the European Union, 2021).

[55] See F Masci, 'P.N.R.R., delega al Governo in materia di disabilità e legge di bilancio 2022: per un paradigma di tutela costituzionale che garantisca la riduzione del "disability divide"' (2021) *Costituzionalismo* 87.

This could lead to different consequences. Firstly, regions could be pushed to adapt their legislation to the indications coming from the central level (and, presumably, consistently with the principles of the CRPD) because this compliance will be necessary to obtain the resources to finance disability policies. Thus, a sort of conditionality mechanism could be developed even at the domestic level. Secondly, it cannot be taken for granted that this dynamic will lead to a substantial standardisation of the actual living conditions of people with disabilities in the different regions, whose adaptation capacities, as well as their financing management, are not uniform throughout the national territory.

In conclusion, 'the regional surplus with respect to the protection of the rights of persons with disabilities is able to emerge, thanks to experiments and innovations, mostly on the side of the performance of administrative functions'.[56] However, centralising trends and the approval of the Decrees implementing Law No 227/2021, expected by 2024, could have a significant impact on relations between state and regions.

[56] See Arconzo (n 25) 174.

5

Spain

Alignment with the CRPD through Centralisation

MARIBEL GONZÁLEZ PASCUAL

I. INTRODUCTION

SPAIN CONSENTED TO be bound by the UN Convention on the Rights of Persons with Disabilities (CRPD) and its Optional Protocol at the time of deposit of the corresponding instruments of ratification on 3 December 2007, with the CRPD being directly applicable in Spain since 3 May 2008. According to the Spanish Constitution (*Constitución Española* – CE) international treaties validly ratified by Spain automatically form part of the domestic legal system once they have been officially published (Article 96(1) CE). There is no need for a national statute to incorporate international treaties into domestic law. In addition, Article 10(2) CE provides that constitutional provisions concerning fundamental rights and liberties shall be interpreted in accordance with the Universal Declaration of Human Rights, as well as the international treaties or conventions ratified by Spain on such matters.

The alignment of the Spanish legal order with the CRPD was initially slow,[1] but has sped up in the last four years. The central government tabled a proposal to amend Article 49 CE on 21 May 2022,[2] aligning the Constitution with the CRPD.[3] The proposal not only changed the terminology previously used in the

[1] See Committee on the Rights of Persons with Disabilities (CRPD Committee), 'Concluding observations on the combined second and third periodic reports of Spain' CRPD/C/ESP/CO/2-3, 13 May 2019.

[2] Art 49 of the Spanish Constitution (*Constitución Española* – CE): 'The public authorities shall carry out a policy of preventive care, treatment, rehabilitation and integration of the physically, sensorially and mentally handicapped who shall be given the specialised care that they require and be afforded them special protection in order that they may enjoy the rights conferred by this Title upon all citizens.'

[3] The proposal has long been waiting to be passed but the far-right political party does not want to pass anything coming from left-wing political parties. The People's Party followed this political strategy but recently changed its position, showing its support to the constitutional amendment.

CE, which was completely obsolete and inadequate, but it also moved away from a medical understanding of disability to a social and human rights approach.[4] This growing legislative concern for the rights of persons with disabilities is also visible in the Statutes of Autonomy.

Originally, the Statutes of Autonomy did not even mention the rights of persons with disabilities, but the most recent reforms have included the need to guarantee those rights in a manner consistent with the CRPD. In this regard, the last Statute of Autonomy that has been amended, from the Canary Islands, explicitly enshrines the right to an inherent dignity and individual autonomy of persons with disabilities.[5] With this goal in mind, public authorities are obliged to actively promote the rights of persons with disabilities on an equal footing with others and without discrimination, thereby ensuring their social and personal development. Public authorities must also provide public services that are suitable for persons with disabilities, eliminating physical and legal barriers. Measures will be adopted to allow communication between the deaf community and the regional administration.[6] The learning of sign language will be facilitated (Article 16 of the Statute of Autonomy of Canary Islands).

In a nutshell, the Spanish legal system is aligning with the CRPD. This process is taking place at both the national and regional levels. Still, the predominant reading of the allocation of powers has favoured the national level, the regions following the lead of central government. In the following pages the alignment of the Spanish legal system with the CRPD, along with the parallel centralisation, will be highlighted in specific and paradigmatic cases. This centralisation derives from the powers of the state on constitutional rights, in accordance with case law, and it is fostered by a weak cooperation among tiers of government. Therefore, it will also be analysed whether the ongoing reforms in the frame of Spain's National Recovery and Resilience Plan (*Plan de Recuperación, Transformación y Resiliencia* – PRTR) could change this path.

[4] In the Government's proposal the wording of Art 49 is: '1. Persons with disabilities are holders of all the rights and duties enshrined in this title, on the basis of an effective and actual freedom and equality, without discrimination. 2. Public authorities will enforce the necessary policies to guarantee personal autonomy and social inclusion of the persons with disabilities. These policies will take due account of their freedom of choice and preferences, and they will be adopted with the involvement of the most representative organisations of the persons with disabilities, in the terms established by the law. The specific needs of women and children with disabilities will be particularly attended. 4. The special protection of the people with disabilities to guarantee their full enjoyment of their rights and duties will be regulated. 5. People with disabilities will enjoy the protection envisaged by the international treaties ratified by Spain.'

[5] The Statute of Autonomy of Canary Islands was passed on 5 November 2018.

[6] I use the term 'regions' to refer to the autonomous communities, since Spain is generally considered a regional state. F Palermo and K Kössler, *Comparative Federalism. Constitutional Arrangements and Case Law* (Hart Publishing, 2017) 9–10.

II. DIVISION OF COMPETENCES: NATIONAL ENJOYMENT OF CONSTITUTIONAL RIGHTS AS A COMPETENCE CREEP

Legislative and executive powers have been distributed between the regions and the state according to different techniques, depending on the field.[7] There are, however, three main types of division of competences. A first type entails that the state is empowered to enact the laws, while the regions enforce them. This is the case, for instance, in relation to labour law. Regions cannot even issue regulations since their power is limited to administrative enforcement.[8] A second type entails that the state is empowered to enact statutes that establish the basic framework in a specific domain, while regions may enact detailed legislation and enforce it. This is the case, among others, in respect to the division of competences of the national system of public health. However, in many cases the basic legislation may extend to very detailed legislation. Finally, the competence can be exclusive for one tier of government. This is the case for immigration, a field reserved to the state, or for tourism, a domain of the regions. However, this last type is particularly problematic since it is based on a theoretically clear definition of domains, even though the overlap between fields of action of the public authorities is quite unavoidable. Moreover, the state tends to resort to the so-called horizontal clauses, such as its competence on equality among citizens regarding constitutional rights (Article 149(1)(1) CE).

In fact, Article 149(1)(1) CE is the main basis of the competence of the state regarding the rights of the persons with disabilities. This competence extends to any field in which a right might be involved. There are numerous heterogeneous sectors[9] in which the state is entitled to guarantee equality, and no matter has ever been excluded *per se* by the Constitutional Court. The Constitutional Court established that the state is empowered only if its decision is necessary to guarantee equality, but no conclusion has been drawn from this statement. Instead, the Constitutional Court has decided a standard of living, which must be preserved above the powers of the regions on a case-by-case basis. In that regard, judgment 18/2017 by the Constitutional Court on parking permits for persons with disabilities is relevant. The central government passed a Decree on the conditions of access and use of the parking permit based on Article 149(1)(1) CE. The Decree was very detailed and ruled very specific issues, such as how many parking spaces must be reserved and how to renew the parking permit. However, several regions have already ruled extensively on the matter, given that social welfare is a regional competence. The government of

[7] V Ferreres, *The Constitution of Spain. A Contextual Analysis* (Oxford University Press, 2013) 173–74.

[8] Judgment of the Spanish Constitutional Court 18/1982.

[9] In this regard, the competence of the central state to achieve equality has been projected upon rules over environment, education, civil service, cinema, social security, consumer rights, public health system, the stock market, several kinds of fines, subsidies and registers, and others.

the Basque Country challenged the Decree before the Constitutional Court. The Constitutional Court rejected all the arguments put forward by the government of the Basque Country because it considered that the parking permit is essential for the freedom of movement of persons with disabilities. Therefore, the controversial Decree was considered to be aimed at preserving equality throughout the territory in the enjoyment of a fundamental right. The Constitutional Court went even further, arguing that the link between Article 49 CE and Article 149(1)(1) CE implies that only the state is empowered to rule on the social protection of persons with disabilities in many cases.

This outcome is not surprising. The Spanish allocation of powers may be characterised as an extremely detailed list of competences contained in a constitution whose amendment is *de facto* extremely complicated. The system depends on courts and lacks flexibility. The lack of space for political arrangements and the mistrust among antagonistic actors has led to a theoretical separation of powers that relied on the legal fiction that powers can be apportioned by courts. This fiction derives from the belief that the Constitution and the Statutes of Autonomy, to begin with, could or even should, foresee each and every detail of the separation of powers and, subsequently, that the meaning of those provisions would be so plain as to leave no room for divergent or evolving interpretations. The outcome is the growing prominence of the Constitutional Court, which has tried to settle the conflict of powers between state and regions by relying on the textual interpretation. Nevertheless, since indeterminate legal concepts are likely to be ambiguous and open to dispute, this interpretive effort of the Court leads to a rather paradoxical result: while the Constitutional Court's definition of the competence norm remains open to debate due to its controversial foundations, the Constitutional Court rules out the possibility of future changes. Such a denial of boundaries to its interpretative methods impinges upon the Court's legitimacy and draws even more criticism towards its reasoning.[10]

Paradoxically, the literal interpretation has been proposed to reinforce the powers of the regions.[11] Nonetheless, the outcome is the growing irrelevance of the regional powers in fields such as social welfare because regional statutes or regulations must follow the particularly exhaustive legislation of the state on constitutional rights. This trend is particularly obvious regarding the rights of persons with disabilities. In fact, Article 149(1)(1) CE has allowed the state to rule extensively and in a very detailed manner in this field.

[10] M González Pascual, 'Methods of Interpreting Competence Norms: Judicial Allocation of Powers in a Comparative Perspective' (2013) 14 *German Law Journal* 1518–19.

[11] L López Guerra, 'El futuro del Estado de las Autonomías' (2007) *Cuadernos de Derecho Publico* 14–15.

III. THE RISE OF THE RIGHTS OF PERSONS WITH DISABILITIES AND THE DECLINE OF REGIONAL POWERS

A. The Harmonisation of the Concept of Disability Along with Key Provisions on the Rights of Persons with Disabilities

At the legislative level the transition from a medical model of disability to a social and human-rights one took place through the Equality of Opportunities, Non-Discrimination, and Universal Accessibility for Persons with Disabilities Act, which was passed on 2 December 2003. However, further reforms were needed to align with the CRPD.[12] Thus, on 1 August 2011 the Spanish Parliament passed the Legal Adaptation to the Convention on Rights of the Persons with Disabilities Act No 26/2011, in which key concepts and duties of the CRPD were introduced to the Spanish legal system. Two years later, a comprehensive and far- reaching law on the rights of persons with disabilities was passed, the Royal Legislative Decree No 1/2013. This Decree compiled and updated the national legislation on the matter. It comprises the definition of basic concepts such as disability, direct and indirect discrimination, reasonable accommodation, universal accessibility, or social inclusion, among others. However, it establishes not only the general framework, but also very specific provisions such as the number of dwellings that must be reserved for people with disabilities in housing plans approved by public authorities, or the percentage of jobs that must be reserved for persons with disabilities in any public job offer. In fact, only 11 out of 105 Articles must be implemented by the regions, whereas the rest are within the exclusive competence of the state based on Article 149(1)(1ª) CE.

Unsurprisingly, given the existence of this legal framework, only four out of 17 regions have passed general legislation on the rights of persons with disabilities, following to the letter the Spanish legislation.[13] The rest of the regions have passed sectorial legislation focused on specific domains, particularly on accessibility.[14] This harmonisation of general rules and main concepts has a positive side since it has mainstreamed a human-rights approach of disability placing emphasis on the inherent dignity and autonomy of individuals with disabilities, along with the principles of non-discrimination, equality, inclusion, participation, accessibility, and respect for diversity.[15] Before the implementation

[12] I Campoy Cervera, 'Spain' in L Waddington and A Lawson (eds), *The UN Convention on the Rights of Persons with Disabilities in Practice. A Comparative Analysis of the Role of Courts* (Oxford University Press, 2018) 390.

[13] A case in point is the Equal Opportunities for Persons with Disabilities in Castilla Leon Act No 2/2013.

[14] In fact, all the regions have passed Acts or Decrees on accessibility.

[15] A Broderick, *The Long and Winding Road to Equality and Inclusion for Persons with Disabilities* (Intersentia, 2015) 26–27.

of the CRPD through national legislation, a medical model of disability could be found in regional Acts.[16] The new concept of disability eventually permeated the whole legal system through the national legislation implementing the CRPD but at the cost of the regional powers.

B. A Recent Push Towards Non-Discrimination and Equality: Complying with the CRPD

Combating discrimination of persons with disabilities is a competence of the state, since it is intrinsically linked to the equal enjoyment of constitutional rights throughout the territory. Furthermore, key domains in which achieving equality, such as the legislation on labour law or civil law, are also reserved to the state. In fact, regarding the right to work, the competence of the regions is limited to put in place training, integration, and vocational programmes.

Regarding non-discrimination and equality three quite problematic issues in Spain have been addressed recently: the limited legal capacity of persons with disabilities, the shortcomings in the right to vote and the poor understanding of reasonable accommodation concerning the right to education.

Concerning the legal capacity framework, the Committee on the Rights of Persons with Disabilities (CRPD Committee) recommended that the Spanish government should abolish the substituted decision-making regimes, and recognise the full legal capacity of all persons with disabilities and introduce supported decision-making mechanisms, in line with Article 12 CRPD.[17] Furthermore, the Legal Adaptation to the Convention on Rights of Persons with Disabilities Act No 26/2011, had foreseen a reform of the Spanish legal capacity system (7th Additional Provision). Even so, it took 10 years to amend such a legal capacity framework.

In 2021 the Amendment of the Civil and Procedural Legislation to Support Persons with Disabilities in the Exercise of their Legal Capacity Act No 8/2021 was passed. This new statute implies the transition from a substitute decision-making regime to a supported decision-making regime.[18] In this regard, Act No 8/2021 abolishes parental authority over persons with disabilities of legal age and establishes a guardianship. However, the appointment of the guardian must consider the will of the person with disabilities. This guardian does not substitute the will of the person that they are supporting. Regarding the right to own property, the preferences of the person with disabilities must be

[16] See Art 1 Care of the Persons with Disabilities in Andalucía Act No 1/1999, which was in force until 2017.

[17] CRPD Committee (n 1).

[18] As defined by the CRPD Committee, 'General Comment No 1 (2014) Article 12: Equal recognition before the law of the Committee on the Rights of Persons with Disabilities' CRPD/C/GC/1, 19 May 2014, para 27.

respected. The mode of communication cannot be a barrier, it being mandatory, for instance, that notaries put in place any reasonable accommodation necessary to grant to persons with disabilities the right to take their decisions. Further the guardianship is subject to periodic judicial oversight.

Act No 8/2021 also governs equal access and participation of persons with disabilities in civil procedures[19] by requiring accessibility and full participation, that can be asked by either any party in the procedure or by the prosecutor, or decided by the Court through its own motion. Unsurprisingly, Act No 8/2021 has been praised by scholarship, and by organisations of persons with disabilities as a long-awaited transition to a legal capacity system in line with the CRPD.[20] In fact, before Act No 8/2021, the Spanish Civil Procedure Law provided for incapacitation that could result in the total deprivation of a person's legal capacity. Several Spanish courts tried to reconcile Spanish civil law with the CRPD by making a very strict interpretation of the provisions regarding the incapacitation,[21] but total incapacity was not completely ruled out until the 2021 amendment. This amendment had a diverse impact upon the powers of the regions, given that most of them have no powers in civil law matters. Moreover, only Aragon and Catalonia had legal provisions on the incapacitation or partial restriction of legal capacity of persons with disabilities. After the approval of Act No 8/2021 by the Spanish Parliament, Catalonia passed a Decree Law[22] adapting its legal scheme to the new national statute, but Aragon has not done so. However, in practice, legal incapacitation is no longer applicable once the Spanish civil procedure law has been amended, since the regional provisions relied on the national legal scheme. Thus, any regional or national provision in which legal capacity plays a role has been affected by the new Civil Procedure Code.

In a similar vein the reform of electoral laws in Spain has been praised for being a step forward in the safeguarding of the rights of persons with disabilities,[23] but it has not impacted much upon regional powers, since the electoral scheme is ruled by an Organic Act,[24] that is a national Act. The Organic Act No 2/2018

[19] The government tabled a bill to amend the Criminal Procedure Act aiming at reinforcing the autonomy of the persons with disabilities, but it was not passed. On this proposal, see AI Luaces Gutiérrez, 'El Estatuto de la persona encausada con discapacidad en el anteproyecto de la ley de enjuiciamiento criminal de 2020' in AI Luaces Gutiérrez and C Vázquez González (eds), *Sociedad, Justicia y Discapacidad* (Aranzadi, 2021).

[20] EW Petit de Gabriel, 'Lo prometido es deuda; la Ley 8/2021 o de cómo avanzar en la aplicación interna de las obligaciones internacionales de España conforme a la Convención de Nueva York sobre los derechos de las personas con discapacidad' in M García Mayo and G Cerdeira Bravo (eds), *Un nuevo orden jurídico para las personas con discapacidad* (Wolters Kluwer, 2021) 73.

[21] Campoy Cervera (n 12) 401–404.

[22] Adaptation of the Catalan Civil Code to the Amendment of the Legal Capacity Scheme, Decree Law No 19/2021.

[23] CRPD Committee (n 1) para 4.

[24] The electoral system must be ruled by an Organic Act, whose passing amendment or repeal requires an absolute majority of the members of Congress in a final vote (Art 81 CE).

which modifies Organic Act No 5/1985 on the general electoral system abolished the deprivation of the right to vote of persons with disabilities, lifting existing judicial limitations to the right to vote to circa 100,000 people.[25] However, the new provisions have not put in place further mechanisms to support and make fully accessible the right to vote to people with disabilities.[26]

Moreover, even though the reform of the legal capacity framework of persons with disabilities supports their right to political participation,[27] it is necessary to promote such participation in practice and to guarantee access to the rights. Further steps must be taken to make fully effective the amendments of the civil and the electoral laws. These steps must be taken also by the regions, since they are empowered to rule, safeguard, and promote the right to participation at the regional level. Still, there are no meaningful measures, either national or regional, in this regard. This is regrettable since the low participation of persons with disabilities in Spain is a constant[28] that has been worsened by the Covid-19 pandemic.[29]

Regarding the right to education, it has to be pointed out that the Spanish educational system does not comply with the CRPD, since it is based on a very poor understanding of 'reasonable accommodation'. A relevant case is the Constitutional Court's decision 10/2014, in which the Court did not recognise the right of a child with disabilities to study in the regular education system. The administration simply alleged a psycho-pedagogical report, drafted by the very same administration that stated that the child needed special support that was to be found only in a special education centre. The Constitutional Court did not ask the administration to explain why it could not provide such support within the regular education system, and if it could, why it would be a disproportionate burden for the administration. As the dissenting opinion highlighted,[30] the judgment did not even consider applying the standards of Article 24 CRPD.

Case law eventually ensured a better protection of the right to be provided with a 'reasonable accommodation' in other areas, such as access to justice,[31] but exclusion of persons with disabilities from the general system of education has not yet been tackled by the Constitutional Court. Furthermore, the harsh conflict between political parties regarding the right to education has given rise

[25] M Garrote, M Pérez Moneo and E Pano, 'Derecho de sufragio y discapacidad. Análisis e impacto de la reforma del Art. 3.1 de la Ley Orgánica de Régimen Electoral General' (Informe elaborado para el Real Patronato de la Discapacidad, December 2019).

[26] The existing regulation on the accessibility to the right to vote of people with disabilities is limited to support persons with visual impairment. Royal Decree No 1612/2007.

[27] Given that legally incapacitated persons could not be members of any association (Art 3 of the Right to Association Organic Act No 2/2002), the former legal capacity scheme was also curtailing the right to association.

[28] As highlighted by the CRPD Committee in all the periodic reports of Spain.

[29] Bizkaia, 'Plan para la participación y calidad de vida de las personas con discapacidad en Bizkaia 2021–2023'.

[30] Dissenting opinion of Judges Luis Ignacio Ortega Álvarez and Juan Antonio Xiol Ríos.

[31] See the judgment of the Spanish Constitutional Court No 77/2014.

to a long list of Framework Acts on education, impairing the implementation of successive legal schemes on the matter. This political struggle has also impinged upon the right to education of persons with disabilities. In fact, the principle of inclusion was pivotal in Organic Act No 2/2006 on education, since it obliged the education authorities to provide specialist teachers and necessary resources. Furthermore, schools had to make necessary curricular adjustments and diversifications for pupils with disabilities. However, the statute was never properly developed and implemented, reasonable accommodation being provided only at the request and expense of the parents.[32] Besides, the Organic Act No 2/2006 was profoundly amended by the Improvement of the Quality of Education Act No 8/2013, that was heavily contested by the main organisations representing persons with disabilities.[33] The most recent legislation is the Organic Act No 3/2020. This new Act is particularly relevant from the point of view of the right to education of persons with disabilities. This statute repealed the Improvement of the Quality of Education Act No 8/2013 and paid due regard to Article 24 CRPD.[34]

In fact, Act No 3/2020 establishes the need of reasonable accommodation to guarantee that children with disabilities are included within the regular education system. This involves, inter alia, that additional supporting measures and resources have to be provided (Article 74), that teachers have to be properly trained, that access to vocational training of children with disabilities must be guaranteed (Article 75), that the evaluation of the students must be apt to the specific needs of the children (Article 20) or that at each and every level personal support and alternative teaching and learning methods must be offered. In a nutshell, Act No 3/2020 aims at addressing the numerous shortcomings of an education on equal footing for children with disabilities in Spain.[35]

Still the new legislation has been heavily criticised in certain regions, whose authorities have explicitly stated that they will try to reduce the actual impact of the new Organic Act. The controversy has been spurred, among other reasons,[36] because the additional provision 4 of the Organic Act No 3/2020 foresees a sharp reduction of special education centres over a 10-year period, in parallel to an increase of resources and means to guarantee full integration and inclusion of children with disabilities within the general education system. The key issue

[32] Consideration of reports submitted by States Parties under Art 35 of the Convention. Spain CRPD/C/ESP/CO/1, 19 October 2011, para 43.

[33] See A Jiménez Lara, A Huete García and M Arias García, 'Alumnado con discapacidad y educación inclusiva en España' (Observatorio Estatal de la Discapacidad, 2019).

[34] G Cerdeira Bravo, 'La Ley Celaá y el derecho de las personas con discapacidad a una educación inclusiva' in García Mayo and Cerdeira Bravo (n 20) 332–41.

[35] On the right to education of persons with disabilities in Spain, see RM Roig Martinez, 'La educación inclusive de las personas con discapacidad en España' in Luaces Gutiérrez and Vázquez González (n 19).

[36] The most controversial issue of Act No 3/2020 is the promotion of the public education centres versus the private ones.

was whether parents have the right to decide that their children must attend a centre of special education and, if they do, whether this provision would impede such right. As generally stated, the right to choice is a cornerstone of the right to education in the liberal tradition.[37] However, Article 24 CRPD remains silent on this right and the Committee has explicitly stated that the right to inclusive education is a fundamental human right of all learners and not a right of the parents.[38] Thus, the debate concerned a fundamental trait of the right to education of children with disabilities because the core of the dispute was to what extent parents can decide on their education. Still, the Ministry of Education, after stating that children do not belong to their parents, tried to settle the controversy by emphasising that the special centres will not disappear completely.

Nonetheless, the criticism against this provision led to a huge demonstration against the new legislation on 22 November 2020, that was explicitly supported by several regional governments. Moreover, the Act has been challenged before the Constitutional Court and its development by several regions is proving extremely problematic. This trend is worrisome, because the national legislation on the right to education needs the regions to be effective. The state has the power to adopt the basic legislation on education, but regions develop and implement it. Even though, there have been an extremely generous understanding of the basic legislation on education by the Constitutional Court,[39] education is a regional domain. Regions economically support education centres, hire all the staff, decide a relevant part of the school curriculum and put in place the supporting mechanisms that the students need.

The amendment of the Organic Act was a step forward to the inclusion of children with disabilities in the regular education system, but its future development is particularly problematic. Eventually, the mistrust among territorial players is bound to impair the compliance with Article 24 CRPD. The right to an inclusive education is a battlefield between different political forces that use their regional power as leverage.

C. Accessibility: Still a Regional Task?

The Spanish regions dealt with accessibility before the Spanish state did. In fact, the first rule at national level aiming at guaranteeing accessibility was passed

[37] D Anastasiou, M Gregory and JM Kauffman, 'Art. 24 Education' in I Bantekas (ed), *The UN Convention on the Rights of Persons with Disabilities: A Commentary* (Oxford University Press, 2018) 695.

[38] CRPD Committee, 'General comment No 4 (2016) on the right to inclusive education' CRPD/C/GC/4, 25 November 2016, para 10.

[39] MI Alvárez Vélez, 'La Ley Orgánica 3/2020 del derecho a la educación y su impacto en las Comunidades Autónomas' in J García Roca (ed), *Informe Comunidades Autónomas 2020* (Instituto de Derecho Público, 2021) 62–64.

in 2003,[40] before ratification of the CRPD. The regions passed several Acts and rules before that time,[41] as accessibility was considered a regional competence.[42]

Currently, the already mentioned Royal Legislative Decree No 1/2013 governs, in general terms, the duty of public authorities to guarantee universal accessibility to buildings, facilities, information and communication technologies, public and open services (including transport). It is up to the sectorial legislation, national or regional, to develop and implement it. In fields such as transport or public buildings the state will only rule in detail on accessibility to them when it holds the property of the building[43] or if the mean of transport is considered a national one.

Spanish regions have passed abundant legislation regarding accessibility to buildings, public services, transportation, or services open to the public. They have also ruled on accessible information and communication between the public administration and persons with disabilities, emphasising the common use of sign language or Braille and the use of guide dogs.[44] Notwithstanding this, the performance of Spain regarding accessibility is quite low since the legislation has not been properly implemented in practice.[45]

However, accessibility is gaining terrain in Spain for three different reasons. First, the Supreme Court, at the request of the Spanish Committee of Representatives of People with Disabilities (*Comité Español de Representantes de Personas con Discapacidad* – CERMI), asked the central government to pass a ruling on accessibility of goods and services provided to the public establishing a national standard.[46] A Decree on this topic was expected to be passed by the end of 2022.[47] Second, there is strong social pressure to guarantee accessibility to older people in rural areas. The ageing of the population has prompted several proposals to make accessible services open to the public such as the financial ones. In that regard, the Consumer Protection against Social and Economic Vulnerabilities Act No 4/2022 has recently been adopted. This statute aims to raise the standards of consumer protection and to adapt the current legislation to the diversity of needs of consumers. The statute foresees the passing of a new ruling on labelling, to include Braille, the improvement of information of commercial offers, the duty to provide legible documents to consumers and the need to consider the digital breach.

[40] Universal Accessibility for Persons with Disabilities Act No 51/2003.

[41] The first comprehensive act on accessibility was passed by Castilla La Mancha in 1994.

[42] J Tejada Ríos, 'Accesibilidad de las personas con discapacidad en España y Portugal: perspectiva jurídica' (2021) *Revista Jurídica de Investigación e Innovación Educativa* 98.

[43] Regarding private buildings, regions hold the exclusive competence on town and country planning and housing (Art 148(1)(3) CE).

[44] All the regions have passed legislation on accessibility in transportation and edification. Furthermore, 14 out of 17 regions have passed a comprehensive Act on universal accessibility.

[45] As highlighted by the CRPD Committee in all the periodic reports of Spain.

[46] Judgment of the Supreme Court 348/2019.

[47] Gobierno de España et al, 'Proyecto de Real Decreto por el que se Regulan las Condiciones Básicas de Accesibilidad y No Discriminación de las Personas con Discapacidad para el Acceso

Moreover, the central government has stated that it will pass a new statute to put in place an independent body to safeguard financial inclusion.[48] In this framework, the association of Spanish banks has recently adopted a new protocol on accessibility of financial services. The protocol foresees the need to maintain attention in person or, at least, free telephone services for the elderly or persons with disabilities, along with making cash dispensers and websites more accessible.[49] Both proposals are a response to the increasing digitalisation, that has spurred a heated debate on the digital breach in Spain. Even though these proposals have been instigated by the ageing of the Spanish population, they are also bound to improve accessibility for persons with disabilities.

Finally, the PRTR foresees several legal reforms to improve the accessibility in different areas, such as transportation, buildings, facilities or information and communication technology.[50] Even more importantly, the PRTR has foreseen investments up to €197 million to make services, buildings, sport and culture centres, and equipment of the public administrations at all levels more accessible. The deadline to develop the reforms and investments included in the PRTR under the headline 'Spain: an accessible country' is December 2023. Accessibility is then a salient topic in Spain and the poor implementation of the Acts and rulings will be addressed. This positive trend, however, has involved a growing activity of the state which is displacing regional competences. The PRTR has brought with it a further undeniable centralisation. The development and implementation of the PRTR is being handled in the Sectorial Conferences, and the regions decide the details of the programmes that they put in place in their territory, but the PRTR was mostly drafted and designed by the central government.[51] On the whole, regional policies are developed within the very strict margins of the PRTR.

D. An Approach to Disability in Line with the CRPD

In recent years several reforms have been passed that respond to a human-rights based approach to disability, integrating human rights into policy-making and practice at all levels. The reforms of the electoral laws, of the legal capacity

y Utilización de los Bienes y Servicios a Disposición del Público' (12 May 2022) www.mdsocialesa2030.gob.es.

[48] La Moncloa, 'Referencia del Consejo de Ministros. Ley de Autoridad de Defensa del Cliente Financiero' (5 April 2022) www.lamoncloa.gob.es.

[49] Asociación Española de Banca, Confederación Española de Cajas de Ahorro and Unión Nacional de Cooperativas de Crédito, 'Documento de firma de la actualización del Protocolo Estratégico para Reforzar el Compromiso Social y Sostenible de la Banca' (21 February 2022) www.aebanca.es.

[50] In this framework, the Cognitive Accessibility Act No 6/2022, the Quality of the Architecture Act No 9/2022, emphasising the universal design principle and the Audio-Visual Communication Act No 13/2022, establishing higher standards regarding the accessibility of all audio-visual services have been passed.

[51] European Committee of the Regions, '2021 EU Regional and Local Barometer' (Directorate for Communication of the European Committee of the Regions, 2021) 39–46.

scheme, of the Right to Education Act, among others, are a leap forward for the rights of persons with disabilities.

Furthermore, the implementation of the rights is also being duly considered. This is a particularly important step since a main shortcoming of the compliance with the CRPD in Spain is the poor development and implementation of the rights of persons with disabilities already enshrined in the legislation. Acts and Decree Laws are passed, but the Regulations that make them effective fall behind[52] or the necessary resources to put new measures in place are not provided.[53] However, breaking down barriers to ensure the principle of equality and non-discrimination may require additional financial and/or human resources so that people with disabilities can take advantage of the rights that are available to others. Positive measures are essential in many cases.

Currently financial resources are being allocated. Moreover, the training of the judiciary, state officials, and teachers on the promotion of equality and non-discrimination is essential to guarantee the rights of persons with disabilities. That is a need that the 'Spanish Strategy on Disability 2022–2030' recognises, devoting a big part of the strategy to fostering the awareness and training of a wide array of social actors.[54] Unluckily enough, the right to participation seems to have been overlooked by the new measures, even though, given the cross-cutting nature of this right, the measures adopted to improve accessibility clearly assist it.

This new approach has been monopolised by the central government. Regions follow this fresh impetus to the rights of persons with disabilities, implementing the statutes and programmes that the central government designs. The more the CRPD is complied with, the lesser role the regions play. Still, this trend was to be expected since the implementation of the CRPD was always first and foremost in the hands of the state. After all, any element relatively closely to the exercise of a constitutional right is reserved to the state (Article 149(1)(1) CE).

IV. THE IMPLEMENTATION OF ARTICLE 33 CRPD

A. The Spanish Government as the Only Focal Point and the Main Driver of Coordination

The focal point is the General Directorate on the Rights of Persons with Disabilities, a directorate of the Ministry on Social Rights and Agenda 2030.[55]

[52] These shortcomings also occur at the regional level. M Lizarraga Rada, *Informe sobre la adaptación de la legislación foral de Navarra a la Convención Internacional sobre los derechos de las personas con discapacidad* (CINCA, 2021) 88–89.

[53] See CRPD Committee (n 1).

[54] The Strategy highlights that the most recent reforms, such as that of the education centres or the new procedural civil law, are bound to fail unless civil servants have a human rights approach. Therefore, it foresees an array of training programmes for employees of the state, recommending

Additionally, the Office on Human Rights, a subdivision of the General Directorate on UN and Human Rights International Organisations in the Foreign Affairs Ministry is also considered a focal point. Still, the latter oversees the direct relationship with the Committee on the Rights of Persons with Disabilities, whereas the General Directorate on the Rights of Persons with Disabilities deals with the implementation of the CRPD. At the regional level, there are no focal points.

Article 33(1) CRPD explicitly declares that states 'shall designate one or more focal points within the government', but this two-pronged approach is expected to involve a focal point located at the highest possible level while also designating focal points in other ministers. The goal of designating more than one focal point is supposed to ensure the coordination of the entire government to safeguard the effective implementation of the Convention.[56] However, at present, the General Directorate on the Rights of Persons with Disabilities alone assumes the whole coordination of all the departments. The General Directorate on the Rights of Persons with Disabilities employs 42 people. Further, the Directorate is assisted by the Royal Disability Trust, an organisation with 15 workers, whose main tasks are to foster research and raise awareness on the rights of persons with disabilities.

It is also worth mentioning that the rights of persons with disabilities is one of the main domains of the Ministry on Social Rights and Agenda 2030. In fact, this ministry does not deal with social rights in general, but with policies addressed to very specific groups (ie, persons with disabilities, children, Romani, and people at risk of social exclusion). Its main goal is to evaluate the needs of these groups, to draft laws on regulation of the field and, particularly, the mainstreaming of these groups' needs in all the branches of the government. Regarding the financial means to put in place the measures envisaged by the Ministry of Social Rights and Agenda 2030, it is responsible for the already mentioned programme, 'Spain: an accessible country', and for the development and strengthening of the Personal Autonomy Act, No 39/2006. This statute foresees allowances and different kinds of assistance, including personal assistance, to guarantee the autonomy of persons with disabilities and elderly. From 2012 onwards the financial resources for the implementation of Act No 39/2006 decreased sharply,[57] but new funds have been allocated recently.[58]

that regions and councils follow its lead in this regard. Gobierno de España et al., 'Estrategia Española Sobre Discapacidad 2022–2030. Para El Acceso, Goce y Disfrute de los Derechos Humanos de las Personas con Discapacidad' (4 May 2022) www.mdsocialesa2030.gob.es.

[55] Before July 2018 the General Directorate on the Rights of Persons with Disabilities was a subdivision of the Ministry on Public Health.

[56] V Aichele, 'Article 33 National Implementation and Monitoring' in Bantekas (n 37) 988.

[57] L Cayo Pérez Bueno and J Martín Blanco (eds), *Derechos Humanos y Discapacidad. Informe España* 2018 (CERMI, 2019) 214.

[58] The central government has recently approved the allocation of €900 million to reinvigorate the implementation of the Personal Autonomy Act. La Moncloa, 'Referencia del Consejo del Ministros' (1 August 2022) www.lamoncloa.gob.es.

This central role of the state is also found in the coordination mechanism. In this regard, the Territorial Council on Social Services must be mentioned. Its members are the regions (one ministry for each region), along with eight representatives of the central government. The president is the Ministry on Social Rights and Agenda 2030. The decisions are adopted by most of its members, necessitating a vote in favour of the central government representatives. The decisions are only compulsory for the regions that have voted in favour. The Territorial Council on Social Services was created on the basis of the Personal Autonomy Act No 39/2006, to guarantee its implementation, but the ruling of the Territorial Council on Social Services included among its tasks the cooperation and coordination among tiers of government on social services. Still, any policy that is not directly related either to social services, or to Act No 39/2006 falls outside the scope of the Territorial Council on Social Services. Thus, it does not have a comprehensive horizontal approach to the policies related to the rights of persons with disabilities. This shortcoming is in line with the malfunctioning of the intergovernmental cooperation in Spain, that has normally been strictly vertical, sectorial, and quite contested.[59]

This sectorial understanding of the relationship between the state and the regions is also clear regarding the policies on the rights of persons with disabilities. In fact, in 2004 the National Council on Disability was established,[60] whose members are representatives of each department of the central government, along with members of CERMI. Also, at the regional level there are Councils on Disability in 14 regions, but there is no relationship between the national and the regional Councils. Thus, there is a horizontal mechanism of coordination within the central government and within 14 out of 17 regions, but not between the central government and the regional governments.

However, the Covid-19 pandemic reinvigorated intergovernmental relations in Spain.[61] Bilateral and multilateral cooperation has grown not only in terms of the number of meetings but also in the relevance of their deliberations and possible outcomes. Intergovernmental relations are becoming a determinant variable in the formula for successful regional participation in central government decision-making, and now represent much more than forums for the technical coordination of the minutiae of specific policies and collaboration. The executive-based institutions are proving to be the most effective guarantee for regional interests in the state's decision-making.[62]

[59] MJ García Morales and X Arbós Marín, 'IGR in Spain: an essential but underestimated element of the State of Autonomies' in J Poirier, C Saunders and J Kincaid (eds), *Intergovernmental Relations in Federal Systems. Comparative Structures and Dynamics* (Oxford University Press, 2015) 353–55.

[60] Royal Decree 1865/2004.

[61] M González Pascual, 'The State of Autonomies in Troubled Times: The Pandemic Provides a Catalyst for Reinvigorating Inter-Governmental Relations' (2022) 54 *Diritto Pubblico Comparato ed Europeo*.

[62] F Palermo, 'Beyond Second Chambers: Alternative Representation of Territorial Interests and their Reasons' (2018) 10 *Perspectives on Federalism*.

In this regard, the Spanish PRTR includes a proposal to improve the Sectorial Conferences. In fact, a new ruling of the Conference of Presidents has been approved by the Conference of Presidents itself.[63] The amendment has turned the Conference of the Presidents into the key organ of intergovernmental relations, one disposing of a secretary and charged with specific tasks. This should institutionalise the role of the Conference of Presidents to allow it to play a relevant role in intergovernmental relations on a regular basis rather than only during critical junctures. This new role includes the impulse and coordination of the Sectorial Conferences.

The central government has not yet tabled a bill to improve intergovernmental relations, but one is in the pipeline, that foresees the need for a more horizontal understanding of cooperation, allowing for the inter-sectorial meetings (in which issues from different departments will be discussed by the governments). It also reinforces cooperation with local entities, that might attend to these meetings if the field requires it. This could provide the cooperation with a wider and better perspective on fields in which the mainstreaming is essential, as is the case of the policies regarding the rights of persons with disabilities.

B. The Independent Mechanism: The Committee of People with Disabilities Representatives and the Ombudsman

Spain has designated two independent mechanisms to monitor the implementation of the CRPD: the Spanish Ombudsman and CERMI.[64] CERMI is an organisation, officially founded in 1997, that brings together more than 8,000 associations of persons with disabilities.

CERMI makes comments on state reports during the drafting phase and coordinates so-called 'shadow reports', which are a traditional task of NGOs – a practice that has been criticised, given that CERMI has a monitoring function towards the Spanish government.[65] The independence of both the Ombudsman and CERMI is out of question. However, both are national mechanisms, even though there are regional CERMIs that are integrated in the national CERMI, because they are partners (but not members). They share goals and principles,[66] but there is no organ or mechanism in which they cooperate on a regular basis.

[63] Conferencia de Presidentes, 'Reglamento de la Conferencia de Presidentes' (13 March 2022) www.mptfp.gob.es.

[64] Royal Decree No 1276/211 on the implementation of the CRPD.

[65] G De Beco, 'Article 33 (2) of the UN Convention on the Rights of Persons with Disabilities: Another Role for National Human Rights Institutions?' (2011) 29 *Netherlands Quarterly of Human Rights* 101.

[66] Protocol of cooperation between the national CERMI and the regional CERMIS. CERMI, 'Ambito Genérico de Colaboración Conjunta Entre el Cermi Estatal y los Cermis Autonómicos' www.cermi.es.

In the reports drafted by CERMI on the compliance with the CRPD, the regional dimension is included thanks to the feedback of the regional CERMIs. However, the reports are particularly focused on the national level. In fact, information on regional initiatives regarding or affecting the rights of people with disabilities is harder to find.

CERMI is a member of the Council on Disability, which is entrusted with the task to promote the rights of persons with disabilities throughout the public policies, to make recommendations or any kind of report that they consider relevant.[67] The Council on Disability is duly informed about the proposals that might affect the rights of the persons on disabilities, being a forum for persons with disabilities to exchange their opinion on public policies and legislation with the public authorities drafting, designing and/or implementing them. At the regional level there are also Councils of Disability in 14 regions, but the regional CERMIs are not members in all cases. Given that the National Council of Disability deals only with national legislation and policies, there is no mechanism promoting the rights of persons with disabilities at the regional level in several regions. It is true, though, that the competence of the Ombudsman comprises the activities of the regional administrations, to the same extent as the national one (Article 54 CE). Still, the Ombudsman is particularly focused on the protection and safeguarding of rights but not on their promotion.

V. CONCLUDING REMARKS

The CRPD has been a trigger for the action of the state, a clear driver of centralisation. Compliance with the CRPD has been achieved through statutes, rulings and even public policies adopted at the national level, mostly by central government. This trend has been caused by the competences of the state on constitutional rights, the lack of effective intergovernmental relations mechanisms, and the passivity of the regions. In fact, scholars have put into question the expanding nature of the competence of the state on the rights of persons with disabilities, but the regions have barely challenged them before the courts.[68] In line with this, the current increasing interest in the CRPD has brought with it an intense activity of the central government but not of the regions.

Even though several reforms are to be made at the national level, such as the ones concerning Organic Acts or procedural law, the regions are the key for the actual implementation of those reforms. In fact, where regions have no genuine interest in fostering the rights of persons with disabilities, most of the

[67] Art 2 Royal Decree on the National Council on Disability No 1855/2009.

[68] In fact, the Personal Autonomy Act has been heavily contested by scholars, but it was challenged only by Navarra and, eventually, this region withdrew the challenge. I Lasagabaster, 'La ley de promoción de la autonomía personal y atención a las personas en situación de dependencia: una reflexión desde la perspectiva competencial' (2007) 4 *Revista d'Estudis Autonómics i Federals*.

reforms recently approved will fail. In a nutshell, the CRPD has impacted upon the balance of powers between the state and the regions, but the relationship between regions and the state also affects the CRPD. The struggle surrounding the right to an inclusive education is a blatant example of the negative impact that a troubled regional state may have in complying with the human rights standards.

On the 'bright side', the PRTR has implied a huge investment on disability and the strengthening of cooperation. This might be extremely helpful to put an end to some of the shortcomings in the implementation of the CRPD, such as the ones regarding the principle of accessibility, and ensure compliance with the Convention. Furthermore, it could also improve the cooperation among tiers of government in this field. Such a development would eventually lead to a more nuanced balance between human rights' protection and political autonomy in Spain.

6

Belgium

The Quest for Equal Employment and Coherence in the Social Protection and Participation of Persons with Disabilities

NAOMI GHYS, FREEK LOUCKX AND DANIEL DUMONT

I. INTRODUCTION

THE BELGIAN FEDERAL Government approved the UN Convention on the Rights of Persons with Disabilities (CRPD) on 13 May 2009, through a law declaring that this Convention will have full effect.[1] Belgium's federated entities, called 'communities' and 'regions', also agreed to this treaty.[2] However, in spite of what the cited law might suggest, its formal approval does not mean the CRPD is directly applicable in the Belgian legal order. The criteria for deciding whether or not a treaty (provision) is directly applicable

[1] Wet 13 mei 2009 houdende instemming met volgende Internationale Akten: Verdrag inzake de rechten van personen met een handicap, Facultatief Protocol bij het Verdrag inzake de rechten van personen met een handicap, aangenomen te New York op 13 december 2006. All Belgian legislation referred to in this chapter can be consulted online in Dutch or French, via www.ejustice.just.fgov.be/wet/wet.htm. Note that where the text of Belgian legislation or case law is cited in English, this is our own translation of the authentic sources in Dutch or French. In the same way, the original names of institutions and organisations have been translated from Dutch or French into English for the purpose of this chapter. This chapter was written taking into account the legislation in force on 1 May 2022 and other data available at that time.

[2] Pursuant to Art 167, para 3 of the Belgian Constitution (Const), the community and regional Governments have the power to conclude international treaties in matters falling within their substantive competence. The treaty-making power is further specified in Arts 16 and 18 of the Special Act on Institutional Reform (Bijzondere Wet 8 augustus 1980 tot hervorming der instellingen – SAIR), which stipulates that the parliaments of the federated entities must give their assent to treaties in matters for which they are competent, hence to the Convention on the Rights of Persons with Disabilities (CRPD). See generally R Smet, *Treaty-Making in Federations* (Intersentia, 2022).

are determined by case law, in particular by the jurisprudence of the highest court of the judiciary, the Court of Cassation. According to the case law of this court, to be directly applicable, a provision of an international treaty must be sufficiently precise and complete.[3] In particular, the obligations it imposes on the state must be fully and precisely expressed.[4] According to the Court, a treaty provision is not directly applicable if it leaves several possibilities for fulfilling those obligations.[5] Similarly, case law indicates that, when the obligations laid down by a treaty provision require further implementation through domestic law and the provision in question leaves a certain margin of discretion, this prevents the direct effect of those obligations in domestic law.[6] Anyone somewhat familiar with the text of the CRPD knows that many of its provisions have to be implemented in domestic legislation, and that the Convention leaves room for States Parties to achieve their obligations in different ways.[7] Hence, it is unlikely that Belgian courts will be inclined to give direct effect to CRPD provisions such as, for example, the rights to work and social protection.[8]

A lack of direct effect is, however, no obstacle to invoking treaty provisions before the Belgian courts, the Council of State or the Constitutional Court, within the framework of their power to exercise judicial review over certain legislative measures. The Belgian Constitutional Court, for example, has authority to review legislative Acts of the Federal Government and federated entities and thereby takes into account provisions of international treaties. The Court considers that, when a treaty provision binding Belgium has a scope analogous to the scope of one or more of the constitutional provisions against which it may review legislative norms, the safeguards contained in that treaty provision form an 'inseparable whole' with the safeguards contained in the constitutional provisions concerned. Thus, when a breach of the latter is alleged, the Court, in its examination, takes into account the provisions of international law which guarantee analogous rights or freedoms.[9] With regard to the effects of the

[3] Court of Cassation (Cass) 10 mei 1985, *Arresten van het Hof van Cassatie (AC)* 1984–1985, 1230; Cass 6 maart 1986, *AC* 1985–1986, 937; Cass 4 november 1999, *AC* 1999, 1378; Cass 4 november 1999, *AC* 1999, 1386; Cass 19 september 1997, *AC* 1997, 843.

[4] Cass 21 april 1983, *Rechtskundig Weekblad (RW)* 1983–1984, 2315; Cass 11 mei 2001, *AC* 2001, 872.

[5] Cass 10 mei 1985, *AC* 1984–1985, 1230; Cass 6 maart 1986, *AC* 1985–1986, 937; Cass 19 september 1997, *AC* 1997, 843; Cass 4 november 1999, *AC* 1999, 1378; Cass 4 november 1999, *AC* 1999, 1386; Cass 17 januari 2002, *AC* 2002, 179.

[6] Cass 18 december 2001, *AC* 2001, 2220; Cass 15 mei 2001, *AC* 2001, 895.

[7] This has also been affirmed by the Court of Justice of the European Union (CJEU). See CJEU, Case C-363/12 *Z v A Government Department* ECLI:EU:C:2014:159.

[8] See generally A D'Espallier et al, *De doorwerking van het VN-Verdrag inzake de rechten van personen met een handicap* (Intersentia, 2014) 46–48; D Cuypers et al, *In welke mate bevordert het Vlaamse beleid de inclusie van personen met een handicap?* (Intersentia, 2017) 61–62. According to a judgment of the Labour Tribunal of Ghent, the CRPD as a whole lacks direct effect (Arbeidsrechtbank Gent 27 mei 2015, *Sociaalrechtelijke Kronieken* 2019, 174–176).

[9] See eg Constitutional Court (CC) 22 juli 2004, n° 136/2004. From this perspective, the Court was questioned on the compatibility of a Decree of the Flemish community with Arts 10 and 11 of the Constitution, read in conjunction with Arts 19 and 26 CRPD. The Flemish Government argued

CRPD in the Belgian legal order, it is therefore noteworthy that a new provision on persons with disabilities was recently included in the Constitution.[10] Inspired in its drafting by the CRPD,[11] Article 22*ter* of the Constitution, passed in 2021, grants every person with a disability the right to full inclusion in society, including the right to reasonable accommodation.[12] It instructs the Federal Government and the federated entities to ensure the protection of that right.[13]

In sum, the CRPD must be implemented by means of legislation. However, due to the complexity of the Belgian State structure, different levels of government are involved in that implementation process. Against this background, this chapter discusses the challenges the implementation of the CRPD poses to the Belgian model of federalism. We first explain how the competences with regard to the protection of persons with disabilities are divided within the Belgian state (section II). Secondly, we illustrate how this division of competences comes to expression in the Belgian legislation with regard to the implementation of the rights to work and social protection the CRPD proclaims and the obligations on participation that it imposes (section III). Next, in section IV, we describe how Article 33 CRPD was implemented in the Belgian federal context. Section V provides some concluding remarks and critical considerations.

II. A BRIEF OVERVIEW OF THE DIVISION OF COMPETENCES

A. The Peculiar Nature of Belgian Federalism

The current division of competences in Belgium is the result of no less than six 'state reforms', which transformed the original unitary state into a federal state

that the Court could not review the Decree against the CRPD, because of the lack of direct effect of this treaty. The objection was rejected by the Court, which considered that, when questioned about a breach of Arts 10 and 11 of the Constitution read in conjunction with an international treaty, it is not required to examine whether that treaty has direct effect in the domestic legal order (CC 17 maart 2016, n° 42/2016). All case law of the Belgian Constitutional Court can be consulted online in Dutch or French, via www.const-court.be.

[10] *Parl.St.* Senaat 2019–20, n° 7-169/1. The references to the parliamentary documents of the federal Chamber of Representatives (*Kamer*) or Senate (*Senaat*) mentioned in this contribution can be consulted on the website of the Chamber (www.dekamer.be) or the Senate (www.senate.be). See generally I Hachez, 'La consécration constitutionnelle du droit à l'inclusion des personnes en situation de handicap (article 22*ter*). De la duplication du cadre juridique au dessin de politiques publiques' (2022) *Journal des tribunaux* 17–24.

[11] The preparatory works show that Art 22*ter* of the Constitution is meant to be a constitutional confirmation of Art 19 CRPD and its clarification in General Comment N° 5 of the UN Committee on the Rights of Persons with Disabilities (*Parl.St.* Senaat 2019–20, n° 7-169/2, 7–8).

[12] Unfortunately, the Constitution did not define the notion of reasonable accommodation. Nevertheless, the preparatory works clearly demonstrate a will to align the meaning of the wording used in the Constitution with the CRPD (*Parl.St.* Kamer 2020–21, n° 1445/002, 8).

[13] Other provisions in the Belgian Constitution protect the rights of persons with disabilities. This is the case in particular of Art 23 of the Constitution proclaiming the right to social security, which imposes a so-called 'standstill obligation'. The Constitutional Court for example in 2020 annulled a law introducing a residence history requirement for the eligibility of allowances to persons with

composed of communities and regions.[14] Whereas the protection of persons with disabilities originally was a national competence, today it is a shared responsibility of the Federal Government, the communities and regions.

For a clear understanding of the legislative diversity and the coordination problems to which this can lead, it should be noted that three communities as well as three regions have been set up in Belgium. Their respective competences differ and the territory on which the communities exercise their competences does not, as a rule, coincide with the territory on which the regions exercise their powers. This 'double-layering' of the Belgian federal system is one of its key characteristics.[15] The Flemish community and the Flemish region cover more or less the same territory, ie the Dutch language area. However, the French- and German-speaking communities do not coincide with any regions. The French community covers the French language area, and the German-speaking community covers the German language area. No specific community has been established for the bilingual area Brussels-Capital, so the Flemish and French communities also exercise their competences in that linguistic area, over those institutions which belong exclusively to one or the other community. To that end, a Flemish and a French Community Commission function in Brussels. Their action is complemented by the Common Community Commission, which has competence for person-related matters common to the whole of the Brussels population. This Common Community Commission shares its institutions with the Brussels region, which also covers the bilingual area Brussels-Capital. The Walloon region spans the territory of the French- and German-speaking communities.

A last feature that characterises the peculiar nature of Belgian federalism is that the Federal Government and the federated entities, as a rule, have exclusive competence over matters within their constitutional responsibility. Unlike many other federal systems, there is no priority of federal legislation over regional or community legislation. In this configuration, the central command is rather weak and policy coordination is often cumbersome.[16]

disabilities. The Court considered that this law led to a significant decrease in the level of protection, which was in no way justified by reasons of public interest, and thus concluded a breach of the standstill obligation (CC 12 maart 2020, n° 41/2020). See generally D Dumont, 'La condition de passé de résidence introduite en matière d'allocations aux personnes handicapées: un recul inconstitutionnel, sur fond de processus législatif fort peu soigneux' (2019) *Journal des tribunaux du travail* 409–412.

[14] Art 1 Const.

[15] B Cantillon, P Popelier and N Mussche (eds), *Social Federalism: The Creation of a Layered Welfare State. The Belgian Case* (Intersentia, 2011).

[16] Overall Belgian federalism is much more of a dualist than a cooperative type. See M El Berhoumi and S Van Drooghenbroeck (eds), *Principes de la répartition des compétences* (Larcier, 2022).

B. Main Competences of the Federal Government

The competences of the Federal Government with regard to the protection of persons with disabilities have been largely reduced over time.[17] Nevertheless, the Federal Government is still responsible for 'the regulation and financing … of the allowances for persons with disabilities'.[18] This specific competence is in line with the more general competence of the Federal Government on labour law, social security and (at least the basic rules on) social assistance.[19]

Nevertheless, a particular exception to the cited competence was made with regard to the 'allowance for assistance to the elderly',[20] which was originally a federally regulated allowance for persons with disabilities aged 65 years or older suffering from reduced self-reliance. Furthermore, since the last 'state reform', the Federal Government is no longer competent for family benefits,[21] which include the increased benefits allowed for parents of children with disabilities.[22]

C. Main Competences of the Communities and Regions

At present, the communities are competent to regulate the above-mentioned allowance for assistance to the elderly and child benefits.[23] They are also, more generally, competent to legislate on the so-called 'person-related matters',[24] which include key aspects of the policy on 'assistance to people'.[25] Under that banner, the communities were assigned the general competence for 'policy on persons with disabilities, including their vocational training and retraining and mobility aids'.[26] Apart from the competence of the Federal Government

[17] See generally G Loosveldt, 'Het beleid inzake personen met een handicap' in B Seutin et al (eds), *De bevoegdheden van de Gemeenschappen* (die Keure, 2017); K Reybrouck and S Sottiaux, *De federale bevoegdheden* (Intersentia, 2019) 510–514; X Delgrange and M El Berhoumi, 'La répartition belge des compétences en matière de handicap' in I Hachez and J Vrielink (eds), *Les grands arrêts en matière de handicap* (Larcier, 2020) 100–119.

[18] Art 5, para 1, II, 4°, a) SAIR.

[19] Arts 5, para 1, 2°, a)-b) and 6, para 1, VI, vijfde lid, 12° SAIR.

[20] Art 5, para 1, II, 4°, a) SAIR. Nevertheless, the Federal Government is still competent for the guaranteed income for the elderly (Art 5, para 1, II, 5° SAIR), which is a means-tested basic old age pension. Many poor persons with disability receive it as main replacement income when they reach retirement age.

[21] Art 5, para 1, IV SAIR.

[22] The transferred competence on family benefits includes the competence to regulate the supplements on those benefits, such as the supplements for children with disabilities (*Parl.St.* Senaat 2012–13, n° 5-2232/1, 68).

[23] Art 5, para 1, II, 4°, a) and IV SAIR.

[24] Arts 128 and 130 Const *juncto* Art 5, para 1 SAIR.

[25] Art 5, para 1, II SAIR.

[26] Art 5, para 1, II, 4° SAIR.

mentioned above, there is only one exception to that broad community competence, with regard to 'the financial compensation for the employment of disabled workers'.[27] The competence in that respect belongs to the regions, which are also responsible for employment policy.[28] Particularly relevant to the labour market participation of persons with disabilities is the competence the regions thus have on the so-called 'target group policy', which includes, inter alia, the reductions in the employer's social security contributions that are determined according to the employees' characteristics.[29]

This complex picture is further blurred as the result of secondary transfers of competences between the federated entities. The French community, for example, transferred most of its competences on assistance to people to the Walloon region and the French Community Commission in Brussels.[30]

III. THE IMPLEMENTATION OF THE CRPD IN SELECTED AREAS

In this section we illustrate how the described division of competences comes into play in the implementation of the CRPD. First, we focus on the legislation implementing the right to work. This allows us to give an insight, from a sufficiently specific angle, into some of the existing guarantees on equal treatment, non-discrimination and accessibility. Next, we look at the legislation implementing the right to social protection to give an idea of the approaches and concepts of disability used in Belgium. This order of discussion is consistent with the understanding that employment is the primary means of ensuring a decent standard of living, and social protection plays a complementary role in that respect,[31] as well as with the structure of the CRPD, which successively proclaims the right to work and the right to social protection of persons with disabilities. Finally, we address the implementation of the obligations on participation the CRPD imposes.

[27] Art 5, para 1, II, 4°, b) SAIR.

[28] Art 6, para 1, IX SAIR. According to the Council of State, the regions are competent under Art 6, para 1, IX SAIR for the exception to the communities' competence on disability policy, more in particular for 'the rules concerning the financial compensation for the employment of disabled workers, which is granted to the employer who employs persons with disabilities' (Adv Council of State (CS) 29 juni 1989, n° 19.193/8). The advices given by the Belgian Council of State can be consulted online in Dutch or French, via www.raadvst-consetat.be.

[29] However, the federal institutions remain the only administrative and technical operators in that area (Art 6, para 1, IX, 7°, a) SAIR).

[30] Art 3, 7° Decr Fr 3 april 2014 betreffende de bevoegdheden van de Franse Gemeenschap waarvan de uitoefening naar het Waalse Gewest en de Franse Gemeenschapscommissie wordt overgedragen. On the resulting situation in Brussels, see D Dumont, 'Vers une protection sociale bruxelloise?' (2022) *Administration publique* 467–516.

[31] See E Dermine and D Dumont, 'A Renewed Critical Perspective on Social Law: Disentangling Its Ambivalent Relationship with Productivism' (2022) 39 *International Journal of Comparative Labour Law and Industrial Relations* 237–268.

A. Equality and Accessibility in the Area of Work and Employment

The principle of and right to equality and non-discrimination, proclaimed in Articles 3 and 5 CRPD, are an interpretative instrument for all other rights in the Convention.[32] This is also apparent from the text of Article 27 CRPD, which requires the States Parties to recognise the right of persons with disabilities to work on an equal basis with others. It includes the right to the opportunity to work in the open labour market and in a work environment that is inclusive and accessible to persons with disabilities.[33] To ensure the exercise of this right, States Parties must adopt legislation to prohibit discrimination on the basis of disability, with regard to all matters and in all forms of employment. Besides that, they have to adopt legislation to employ persons with disabilities in the public sector and to promote their employment in the private sector through measures like affirmative action programmes and incentives.[34] The employment field is a particularly interesting case study to better gauge the interplay between measures taken by the Federal Government and federated entities to promote equality. At the same time, this approach allows us to address the issue of accessibility in the workplace.[35]

In addition to the provisions of the Belgian Constitution guaranteeing equality and non-discrimination,[36] both the Federal Government and the federated entities enacted legislation to combat discrimination of persons with disabilities in the field of work and employment. Federal legislation prohibits any form of discrimination, including the refusal to make reasonable accommodations to the benefit of persons with disabilities.[37] The federated entities adopted legislation that guarantees non-discrimination in the field of employment and vocational training and prescribes reasonable accommodations.[38] Notwithstanding the autonomy of each of these governments, mutual cooperation was considered necessary for the success of their policies. This resulted

[32] Art 5 CRPD; Committee on the Convention on the Rights of Persons with Disabilities, 'General Comment No. 6 on equality and non-discrimination' (2018) CRPD/C/GC/6 3.

[33] Art 27, para 1 CRPD.

[34] Art 27, para 1, a), g) and h) CRPD.

[35] Art 9, para 1, a) CRPD.

[36] Arts 10 and 11 of the Constitution provide for a general principle of equality and non-discrimination which prohibits any discrimination, regardless of its origin. The constitutional principle of non-discrimination applies to all rights and freedoms, including those arising from international treaties binding Belgium (CC 28 januari 2015, n° 11/2015).

[37] Art 14 Wet 10 mei 2007 ter bestrijding van bepaalde vormen van discriminatie.

[38] Art 3, eerste lid, 3° and Art 5, para 4 Decr Vl 8 mei 2002 houdende evenredige participatie op de arbeidsmarkt; Decr W 6 november 2008 ter bestrijding van bepaalde vormen van discriminatie, met inbegrip van de discriminatie tussen vrouwen en mannen inzake economie, tewerkstelling en beroepsopleiding; Ord Br 4 september 2008 ter bevordering van diversiteit en ter bestrijding van discriminatie in het Brussels gewestelijk openbaar ambt; Decr Fr Gem Comm 22 maart 2007 betreffende de gelijkheid van behandeling van personen in de beroepsopleiding; Decr D 19 maart 2012 ter bestrijding van bepaalde vormen van discriminatie.

in the adoption of a 'protocol' between the Federal Government, the regions and the communities that sets out common criteria for interpreting the concept of 'reasonable accommodation'.[39] According to this protocol, adaptations must meet four criteria. First, they must be effective, so that the person with a disability can actually participate. Secondly, they must allow for equal participation of the disabled person. Furthermore, they must ensure that the person with a disability can participate independently, and must guarantee the safety of the person with a disability. The protocol further provides that the reasonableness of an adaptation should be assessed in the light of various indicators, such as, among others, the financial and organisational impact of the adaptation, the expected frequency and duration of use of the adaptation by people with disabilities, the impact of the adaptation on the quality of life of users with disabilities and the impact of the adaptation on the environment and other users.[40]

Legislation to employ persons with disabilities in the public sector was also adopted at the various levels of government. The federal legislation requires private undertakings and public authorities to employ a quota of persons with disabilities, when they engage at least 20 employees.[41] Thus, each federal public service has an obligation to employ a quota of 3 per cent of persons with disabilities.[42] For the administrations of the Flemish community and the Flemish region the same target of 3 per cent is used,[43] whereas in the Walloon region and the French community, an employment quota of 2.5 per cent of persons with disabilities applies to the civil service.[44] The services and institutions of public utility of the French Community Commission in Brussels are obliged

[39] Protocol 19 juli 2007 tussen de Federale Staat, de Vlaamse Gemeenschap, de Franse Gemeenschap, de Duitstalige Gemeenschap, het Waals Gewest, het Brussels Hoofdstedelijk Gewest, de Gemeenschappelijke Gemeenschapscommissie en de Franse Gemeenschapscommissie ten gunste van de personen met een handicap (Protocol 19 juli 2007).

[40] Art 2 Protocol 19 juli 2007.

[41] Art 21 Wet 16 april 1963 betreffende de sociale reclassering van de minder-validen. As far as the private sector is concerned, this principle has never been put into practice.

[42] Art 3, para 1 Koninklijk Besluit (KB) 6 oktober 2005 houdende diverse maatregelen met betrekking tot de vergelijkende aanwervingsselectie en met betrekking tot de stage.

[43] Art 5, para 4 *bis* Decr Vl 8 mei 2002 houdende evenredige participatie op de arbeidsmarkt; Art 4, para 1 B Vl Reg 24 december 2004 houdende maatregelen ter bevordering en ondersteuning van het gelijkekansen- en diversiteitsbeleid in de Vlaamse administratie. Pursuant to Art 7, para 1 of said Decree and Art 7, paras 4–5 of said Regulation, the target numbers are included in an annual progress report and action plan, the latter being part of a five-year strategic plan. In the last five-year plan, which ended in 2020, the Flemish Government set a goal of 3 per cent (Vlaamse Overheid, 'Strategisch Gelijkekansen- en Diversiteitsplan Vlaamse overheid 2016–2020' (May 2016) www.vlaanderen.be).

[44] Art 81, para 1 B W Reg 18 december 2003 houdende de Waalse Ambtenarencode; Art 1 B Fr Reg 21 december 2000 betreffende de tewerkstelling van gehandicapten in de Diensten van de Regering en in sommige instellingen van openbaar nut die onder de Franse Gemeenschap ressorteren.

to employ 5 per cent of persons with disabilities.[45] An employment quota of 2 per cent applies to officials of the regional public services in Brussels.[46]

The federated entities also adopted other specific measures to promote the employment of persons with disabilities on an equal footing. The Flemish region, for example, provides a 'support premium',[47] ie financial support for employers recruiting people with a work disability or self-employed workers suffering from such a disability. It compensates for the costs of their integration into working life, the support they need and their reduced productivity.[48] The Walloon region in its turn provides for an 'integration premium', which amounts to 25 per cent of the gross salary of the employed person with a disability plus the compulsory employer's social security contributions.[49] In addition, this region also provides 'discovery internships' for persons with disabilities wishing to take part in a programme aimed at their integration into the labour market, premiums to compensate for the costs of reasonable accommodations and a compensation of travelling costs.[50] The French Community Commission in Brussels also provides for an 'integration premium'.[51] Furthermore, the communities facilitate the employment of persons with disabilities in sheltered workshops by means of several types of support.[52]

Although the foregoing shows that measures were taken to enhance the employment of persons with disabilities on an equal footing with others and to guarantee accessibility in the workplace, it should be emphasised that the approval of the CRPD has not led to significant changes of the legislation in

[45] Art 279/1 B Coll Fr Gem Comm van 13 april 1995 houdende het statuut van de ambtenaren van de diensten van het College van de Franse Gemeenschapscommissie, ingevoerd door Art 2 B Coll Fr Gem Comm 2010/207 van 2 februari 2013 tot wijziging van het besluit van het College van de Franse Gemeenschapscommissie van 13 april 1995 houdende het statuut van de ambtenaren van de diensten van het College van de Franse Gemeenschapscommissie.

[46] Art 332, para 1 B Br Reg 21 maart 2018 houdende het administratief statuut en de bezoldigingsregeling van de ambtenaren van de gewestelijke overheidsdiensten van Brussel.

[47] Arts 28-36 B Vl Reg 18 juli 2008 betreffende de professionele integratie van personen met een arbeidshandicap.

[48] Art 12 Decr Vl 4 maart 2016 houdende het Vlaamse doelgroepenbeleid; Art 1, 5° en 8° B Vl Reg 18 juli 2008 betreffende de professionele integratie van personen met een arbeidshandicap.

[49] Art 1107 *juncto* Art 1069, 7° Reglementair deel van het Waals Wetboek van Sociale Actie en Gezondheid van 4 juli 2013 (Executive Part of the Walloon Code on Social Action and Health – EPWCSAH).

[50] Boek V, titel IX, Hoofdstuk V EPWCSAH.

[51] Art 48 Decr Fr Gem Comm 17 januari 2014 betreffende de inclusie van personen met een handicap (Decree on the Inclusion of Persons with Disabilities – DIPD).

[52] The Flemish community provides three types of support in this area, namely employment support measures, consisting of a contribution to wage costs and compensation for guidance on the shop floor, organisational support measures and infrastructural support measures (Arts 9–21 Decr Vl 12 juli 2013 betreffende maatwerk bij collectieve inschakeling). The Walloon region provides a subsidy to cover the wage costs of persons with disabilities and the costs of assistance (Arts 1016–25 EPWCSAH). The French Community Commission in Brussels also provides a subsidy for the remuneration of persons with disabilities, the costs of assisting personnel, investment costs (for investments

this area. The legislation enacted to combat discrimination, for instance, was not intended to implement the CRPD, but to implement the European anti-discrimination Directives.[53] Those Directives remain the driving force behind numerous regulations and the protocol on reasonable accommodation. However, some policy developments suggest that the CRPD could become more influential over time. It is, for instance, noteworthy that to increase the employment opportunities of persons with disabilities in the regular labour market, the Flemish Parliament recently adopted, in implementation of Article 27 CRPD, a specific Decree on 'customised individual inclusion', which offers financial incentives to self-employed workers and employers to engage persons with disabilities.[54]

B. Concepts of Disability in the Field of Social Protection

According to Article 28 CRPD, States Parties recognise the right of persons with disabilities to social protection and need to take measures to ensure the realisation of this right.[55] To that end, they have to take measures to ensure persons with disabilities have access to appropriate and affordable services, devices and other assistance for disability-related needs. They should also take measures to ensure access for persons with disabilities to social protection programmes, as well as measures to ensure access for persons with disabilities living in poverty to assistance with disability-related expenses, including financial assistance.[56] By highlighting the Belgian legislation implementing those treaty obligations, we get a picture of the different approaches to, and concepts of, disability used at the various policy levels.

The Belgian social security system, which is organised by the Federal Government, contains various social insurance schemes that allow persons with disabilities to build up social protection on the basis of their employment as

in equipment or real estate) and operational costs (Arts 52–55 and 86 DIPD; Hoofdstuk 4, afd 1-5 B Coll Fr Gem Comm 28 november 2019 betreffende de maatwerkbedrijven dat uitvoering geeft aan afdeling 2 van hoofdstuk 5 van het decreet van de Franse Gemeenschapscommissie van 17 januari 2014 betreffende de inclusie van personen met een handicap).

[53] Council Directive 76/207/EEC of 9 February 1976 on the implementation of the principle of equal treatment for men and women as regards access to employment, vocational training and promotion and working conditions [1976] OJ 1976 L39/40; Council Directive 2000/43/EC of 29 June 2000 implementing the principle of equal treatment between persons irrespective of racial or ethnic origin [2000] OJ 2000 L80/22; Council Directive 2000/78/EC of 27 November 2000 establishing a general framework for equal treatment in employment and occupation [2000] OJ 2000 L303/16; Council Directive 2004/113/EC of 13 December 2004 implementing the principle of equal treatment between men and women in the access to and supply of goods and services [2004] OJ L373/27; Council Directive 2006/54/EC of 5 July 2006 on the implementation of the principle of equal opportunities and equal treatment of men and women in matters of employment and occupation [2006] OJ L204/23.

[54] Decr Vl 14 januari 2022 over maatwerk bij individuele inschakeling.

[55] Art 28, para 2 CRPD.

[56] Art 28, para 2, a)–c) CRPD.

employees, self-employed workers or civil servants.[57] However, the system also provides some benefits specifically aimed at the protection of persons with disabilities, without regard to any professional activity. The most important federal legislation in this respect is the Allowances Act, which provides for an income replacement allowance and an integration allowance.[58] To be entitled to these allowances, which are means-tested, an applicant must have his or her disability attested by a doctor of the Directorate-General on Persons with Disabilities of the Federal Public Service for Social Security.[59] However, the legal definition of disability differs significantly for the two benefits, which cover different social risks. To be entitled to an income replacement allowance, an evaluation is made of the impact of the disability on the applicant's earning capacity. The allowance is granted only when the physical or psychological condition of the applicant has reduced his or her earning capacity to one-third or less of what a person without a disability could earn on the general labour market.[60] This approach, which is partly medical and partly economic, is at odds with the CRPD, and it has not been revised despite the ratification of the Convention. Furthermore, the (harsh) one-third threshold is not defined more precisely by any regulation and, in practice, leads to very divergent assessments due to a lack of criteria. The integration allowance, on the other hand, is granted to a person with a disability who suffers a reduction in or lack of self-reliance.[61] Self-reliance is measured on the basis of a so-called medico-social scale that takes into account six factors: the ability to move about, to care for and dress oneself, to maintain one's home and perform household tasks, to prepare and eat food, to assess and avoid danger, and to maintain contact with others.[62] This evaluation is clearly more contextualised than the former and is based on more concrete criteria.

The evaluation of disabilities for the purposes of the Allowances Act has its implications on other aspects of the social security organised by the Federal

[57] In this context the social insurance covering incapacity to work is of particular importance, because it covers many of the persons with disabilities in the meaning of the CRPD.

[58] Wet 27 februari 1987 betreffende de tegemoetkomingen aan personen met een handicap (Allowances Act).

[59] Art 2, paras 1–2 Allowances Act *juncto* Art 10, para 2 KB 22 mei 2003 betreffende de procedure voor de behandeling van de dossiers inzake tegemoetkomingen aan personen met een handicap. Formally, the law also provides the possibility of an assessment by a multidisciplinary team, but unfortunately this remains only a theoretical possibility, as it has not been put into practice yet (D Dumont, 'Les allocations fédérales aux personnes handicapées: "dessine-moi une personne handicapée"' in Hachez and Vrielink (n 17) 489). Nevertheless, the Federal Government has expressed its intention to modernise the legislation on disability benefits and to focus on strengthening the multidisciplinary character of the assessment (FOD Sociale Zekerheid, 'Federaal Actieplan Handicap 2021–2024' (2021) www.socialsecurity.belgium.be 14).

[60] Art 2, para 1 Allowances Act. For a detailed critical analysis, see D Dumont, 'La définition et l'évaluation de la capacité de gain en matière d'allocations aux personnes handicapées: enquête sur une boîte noire' (2023) *Chroniques de droit social* (forthcoming).

[61] Art 2, paras 2 and 6 Allowances Act.

[62] Art 5 KB 6 juli 1987 betreffende de inkomensvervangende tegemoetkoming en de integratietegemoetkoming; Art 3 *juncto* de Bijlage 'Handleiding voor de evaluatie van de graad van zelfredzaamheid' Ministerieel Besluit 30 juli 1987 tot vaststelling van de categorieën en van de handleiding voor de evaluatie van de graad van zelfredzaamheid met het oog op het onderzoek naar het recht op de integratietegemoetkoming.

Government. People whose reduced earning capacity or self-reliance is attested under that law are, for example, covered on that basis by the compulsory health-insurance, which recompenses medical expenses.[63] Periods of professional inactivity covered by the income replacement allowance are also taken into account for the purpose of calculating the length of the career that determines the extent of an employee's old-age pension.[64] Anyone who has not built up sufficient pension rights through employment and reaches pensionable age can apply for an income guarantee for the elderly.[65] But one who benefits from an allowance under the Allowances Act does not have to apply for that guarantee. The Federal Pension Service will grant it on its own initiative.[66]

Remarkably, the evaluation of disability for the purposes of federal law is also still relevant in the context of the social protection schemes organised by the federated entities, although they are free to use their own concepts of disability. Thus, the federal evaluation of disability remains important in the context of the former 'allowance for assistance to the elderly'. In the Flemish community, this allowance was reformed into a 'care budget for elderly people with care needs' that can be granted to persons who are at least 65 years old and whose reduced self-reliance is attested.[67] To that end, the impact of the disability on the ability to carry out daily activities is measured and the degree of self-reliance is determined in the same way as it is done to decide on the granting of the federal integration allowance.[68] The Walloon region has also taken up its competence on the allowance for assistance to the elderly, so that henceforth Walloon sickness funds, under the supervision of the Agency for Quality of Life, are responsible for the medical evaluation of the required disability.[69] A specific scheme on allowances for assistance to the elderly was created in Brussels as well.[70] Since 1 January 2022, the evaluation of the reduction of self-reliance is carried out by a medical doctor or multidisciplinary team on the basis of a manual approved by

[63] Art 32, eerste lid, 13° Gecoördineerde wet 14 juli 1994 betreffende de verplichte verzekering voor geneeskundige verzorging en uitkeringen *juncto* Art 128*ter* KB 3 juli 1996 tot uitvoering van de wet betreffende de verplichte verzekering voor geneeskundige verzorging en uitkeringen, gecoördineerd op 14 juli 1994.

[64] Art 34, para 1, D KB 21 december 1967 tot vaststelling van het algemeen reglement betreffende het rust- en overlevingspensioen voor werknemers.

[65] Art 3 Wet 22 maart 2001 tot instelling van een inkomensgarantie voor ouderen.

[66] Art 10, para 1, eerste lid, 1° KB 23 mei 2001 tot instelling van een algemeen reglement betreffende de inkomensgarantie voor ouderen.

[67] Art 4, eerste lid, 2° and 84 Decr Vl 18 mei 2018 houdende de Vlaamse sociale bescherming (Flemish Social Protection Act – FSPA).

[68] Arts 193, 212-213 B Vl Reg 30 november 2018 houdende de uitvoering van het decreet van 18 mei 2018 houdende de Vlaamse sociale bescherming.

[69] Art 43/36 Waals Wetboek van Sociale Actie en Gezondheid van 29 september 2011 (Walloon Code on Social Action and Health – WCSAH); Art 10/20 EPWCSAH.

[70] Art 22 Ord Gem 10 december 2020 betreffende de tegemoetkoming voor hulp aan bejaarden; Art 55, para 3 B Ver Coll Gem Gem Comm 28 januari 2021 tot uitvoering van de ordonnantie van 10 december 2020 betreffende de tegemoetkoming voor hulp aan bejaarden.

the ministers of the united college of the Common Community Commission.[71] In practice, however, all federated entities rely on the federal medical-social scale, which ensures consistency of evaluation across all levels of government.

Nevertheless, there is a tendency in the legislation of federated entities towards a new approach on disability, which differs from the old and still dominant medical approach and aligns more with the approach promoted by the CRPD.

This is apparent, for example, in the policy of the Flemish community that provides for a person-to-person financing for persons with disabilities, which has two components: a basic support budget and a budget for non-directly accessible care and support.[72] The basic support budget is a fixed monthly amount granted to persons with disabilities who have a need for care and support, which can be used to fund non-medical assistance and services.[73] However, the Flemish Government recently decided to abolish this budget,[74] notwithstanding the negative advice in that regard from the Council of State.[75] The budget for non-directly accessible care and support, on the other hand, is allocated to persons with disabilities who need more frequent, intensive or specialised care. As a rule, a provincial evaluation committee assesses, on the basis of a multidisciplinary report in which the need for care and support is evaluated, whether an applicant asking for this budget can be considered a person with a disability.[76] In this context, a specific definition of disability is used, which describes a disability as 'any long-term and important participation problem of a person that is due to the interplay between functional disorders of a mental, psychological, physical or sensory nature, limitations in the performance of activities and personal and external factors'.[77]

In the Walloon region, the Agency for Quality of Life offers three-part assistance in daily life. Its first component is the individual integration assistance, which is a financial allowance to compensate the costs of adaptations and

[71] Art 55, paras 1–2 B Ver Coll Gem Gem Comm 28 januari 2021 tot uitvoering van de ordonnantie van 10 december 2020 betreffende de tegemoetkoming voor hulp aan bejaarden.

[72] Art 3 Decr Vl 25 april 2014 houdende de persoonsvolgende financiering voor personen met een handicap en tot hervorming van de wijze van financiering van de zorg en de ondersteuning voor personen met een handicap (Flemish Personal Finance Act – FPFA).

[73] Arts 91–94 FSPA; Hoofdstuk 4 FPFA.

[74] B Vl Reg 23 december 2020 tot wijziging van het besluit van de Vlaamse Regering van 30 november 2018 houdende de uitvoering van het decreet van 18 mei 2018 houdende de Vlaamse sociale bescherming, wat betreft de wijziging van het basisondersteuningsbudget.

[75] According to the Council of State, the fact that certain categories of beneficiaries lose their right to this budget, without any alternative, leads to a significant reduction in the level of protection, while there seems to be no sufficient reason in the public interest to justify this (Adv CS 22 december 2020, n° 68.343/1).

[76] Arts 12–13 and 16 B Vl Reg 27 november 2015 over de indiening en de afhandeling van de aanvraag van een budget voor niet rechtstreeks toegankelijke zorg en ondersteuning voor meerderjarige personen met een handicap en over de terbeschikkingstelling van dat budget.

[77] Art 2, 4° FPFA *juncto* Art 2, 2° Decr Vl 7 mei 2004 tot oprichting van het intern verzelfstandigd agentschap met rechtspersoonlijkheid Vlaams Agentschap voor Personen met een Handicap.

technical aids aimed to promote the integration of persons with disabilities.[78] The second component consists of services for assistance in daily life.[79] The third component is the budget for personal assistance, which allows paying for the services provided by one or more personal assistants.[80] This budget is intended for persons with disabilities with significantly limited autonomy. The degree of autonomy is determined through an evaluation of the limitations in certain activities, in particular daily life activities, mobility, behaviour, communication, mental functions, household activities, social and leisure activities.[81] For the purposes of this system, as a rule, a specific definition of persons with disabilities is used. It defines a person with a disability as 'any minor or adult whose capacities for social integration and integration into the labour process are significantly limited as a result of an impairment of his mental, sensory or physical abilities, necessitating an intervention of society'.[82] For the disability to be recognised, there must be at least a 30 per cent reduction in physical capacity or a 20 per cent reduction in mental capacity.[83] However, it is presumed that a person has a disability if a document can be presented showing that he or she is eligible for a federal integration allowance due to a very low degree of self-sufficiency.[84]

A similar arrangement was also put into place by the French Community Commission in Brussels. There, the 'Person with Disabilities Autonomy Wanted Service' provides for compensation of the costs of certain material aids.[85] To be eligible for this compensation, an applicant needs to be qualified as a person with a disability.[86] In this context, in a way that is more akin to the CRPD definition, a person with a disability is defined as 'a person with one or more incapacities resulting from a long-term physical, mental, intellectual or sensory impairment which, in interaction with various barriers, may prevent him from participating fully, effectively and on an equal basis with others in society'.[87] A multidisciplinary team, set up within the abovementioned service, decides on submitted applications. To make a decision this team can be guided by the principles defined in the International Classification on Functioning, Disability and Health endorsed by the World Health Organization.[88] Nonetheless, there is primarily a medical requirement, which presupposes at least a 30 per cent reduction in physical capacity or a 20 per cent reduction in mental capacity.[89]

[78] Art 266, 3° WCSAH; Arts 784–796 EPWCSAH.
[79] Boek V, Titel VII WCSAH.
[80] Arts 797–820 EPWCSAH.
[81] Art 802 EPWCSAH.
[82] Art 261 WCSAH.
[83] Art 408 EPWCSAH.
[84] Art 803 EPWCSAH.
[85] Art 22, 2° DIPD.
[86] Arts 5–6 and 8 DIPD.
[87] Art 2, 2° DIPD.
[88] Art 12 DIPD.
[89] Art 6 DIPD. In a somewhat ambiguous manner, the applicable legislation states that if a disability is clearly established without one of the aforementioned percentages being reached, the person

It goes without saying that the diversity of measures taken by the federated entities, given their respective territorial scopes, could jeopardise the coherence of the social protection for persons with disabilities. It is therefore noteworthy that, to reduce this risk, the Flemish community entered into a cooperation agreement with the Walloon region which specifies that persons with disabilities who have a residence in the Walloon region can get conditional access to the benefits provided by the Flemish Agency for Persons with Disabilities, and vice versa.[90]

Nevertheless, the foregoing clearly shows that the approval of the CRPD has by no means resulted in a uniform and centralised approach to the concept of disability at all levels of government. Moreover, the paradigm shift from the medical to the social approach on disability envisaged by the CRPD has occurred only to a limited extent. Whereas the Flemish legislation clearly puts forward the social approach, this is less obvious for the outdated federal Allowances Act – which is still mainly based on the medical approach – and for the legislation of the Walloon region and the theoretically CRPD-based inclusion Decree of the French Community Commission, both of which still observe medical criteria.

C. Participation in Policy and Decision-Making

The CRPD obliges States Parties to consult closely with persons with disabilities in decision-making processes on issues relating to them, and to actively involve persons with disabilities through their representative organisations.[91] In Belgium the participation and consultation of persons with disabilities in decision-making processes is pursued at the various policy levels through the establishment of advisory councils.

At the federal level, there is a National High Council for Persons with Disabilities (*Nationale Hoge Raad Personen met een Handicap* – NHRPH), which was established back in 1967. The Council's task is to investigate all problems concerning persons with disabilities that fall within the federal competences. The NHRPH can give advice or formulate proposals in that regard.[92] Advice from the NHRPH is also required with regard to all regulations issued in implementation of the federal Allowances Act.[93] The NHRPH is further involved in the implementation of the CRPD, through participation in structural consultations organised in that regard with, amongst others, the Federal Public Service for Social Security.[94]

can nevertheless be recognised, taking into account the actual impact of the established reduction (ibid).

[90] Samenwerkingsovereenkomst 5 juni 2009 tussen de Vlaamse Gemeenschap en het Waals Gewest betreffende de integratie van personen met een handicap.

[91] Art 4, para 3 CRPD.

[92] Art 1 KB van 9 juli 1981 tot oprichting van een Nationale Hoge Raad voor personen met een handicap.

[93] Art 20 Allowances Act.

[94] La Belgique, '2ème et 3ème rapports périodiques' (April 2020) www.ohchr.org 51.

Unlike the Federal Government, the communities and regions struggle to establish advisory councils that structurally guarantee the participation and consultation of persons with disabilities in decision-making processes.

In the Flemish community and region, the Flemish Advisory Council 'NOOZO' was established in 2018. Various organisations joined within the NOOZO project and worked towards the lasting recognition of the Advisory Council, which provides advice and recommendations with regard to disability-related themes in all Flemish policy areas.[95] Initially, the Flemish Government decided to extend the NOOZO project by only one year.[96] But in implementation of its Equal Opportunities Policy Plan 2020–2024, which expresses the intention to find the best way to structurally anchor the voice of persons with disabilities in policy making,[97] the Flemish Government adopted a regulation that provides for the recognition procedure of a Structural Advisory Council.[98] In accordance with this regulation, a cooperation agreement was concluded that provides for the recognition of NOOZO for another period of five years.[99]

In the French- and German-speaking communities, there are no advisory councils for people with disabilities at the moment.[100] In the Walloon region, when the Agency for Quality of Life was set up, an advisory function was created using a body of that agency. To this end, the Strategy and Foresight Council was established.[101] However, the composition of this council, which does not include a majority of representatives of people with disabilities,[102] was criticised.[103] To improve the representation and coherence of actions carried out, the Walloon Government announced that an advisory body representing persons with disabilities will be set up to replace the Council.[104]

In the Brussels-Capital region, various consultation and participation channels coexist. For example, the French Community Commission set up

[95] NOOZO, 'Rapport. Niets over ons zonder ons. Participatie door personen met een handicap in het beleid' www.noozo.be 10, 85, 92.

[96] NOOZO, 'NOOZO voor één jaar verlengd' (11 January 2021) www.noozo.be.

[97] Vlaamse Regering, 'Horizontaal integratie- en gelijke kansenbeleidsplan 2020–2024' (23 October 2020) www.beslissingenvlaamseregering.vlaanderen.be 28.

[98] B Vl Reg 17 december 2021 houdende de erkenningsvoorwaarden, de erkenningsprocedure en het toezicht op de Vlaamse advies en beleidsparticipatieraad van personen met een handicap.

[99] Art 11 B Vl Reg 17 december 2021 houdende de erkenningsvoorwaarden, de erkenningsprocedure en het toezicht op de Vlaamse advies- en beleidsparticipatieraad van personen met een handicap; Vlaamse Overheid, 'Minister ondertekent samenwerkingsovereenkomst met NOOZO' (13 May 2022) www.vlaanderen.be.

[100] Nationale Hoge Raad Personen met een Handicap (NHRPH), 'Advies n° 2020/10 betreffende het rekening houden met de adviesraden van personen met een handicap in het kader van het beheer van de gezondheidscrisis COVID-19' (17 April 2020) www.ph.belgium.be.

[101] Decr W 3 december 2015 betreffende het Waals agentschap voor gezondheid, sociale bescherming, handicap en gezinnen.

[102] Arts 5 and 5/1 WCSAH.

[103] NHRPH (n 100).

[104] La Région wallonne, 'Déclaration de politique régionale pour la Wallonie, législature 2019–2024' (9 September 2019) www.wallonie.be 93.

the French Brussels Advisory Council for Assistance to People and Health, ie an advisory board composed of four departments, one of which concerns persons with disabilities.[105] It gives advice on all matters relating to persons with disabilities.[106] The Common Community Commission also provided for an advisory function in the context of Iriscare, ie the Common Community Service for Health, Assistance to People and Family Benefits. Its technical committee on 'persons with disabilities' advises on policy with regard to persons with disabilities. It is composed of representative organisations active in the field, insurance institutions, trade unions of the staff and associations representing persons with disabilities.[107] The Brussels-Capital region in turn adopted legislation on the mainstreaming of disability issues ('handistreaming').[108] This policy, being inspired by the CRPD, aims to ensure the inclusion of persons with disabilities and to put into practice the principle of 'Nothing about us without us', through the consultation and participation of representative associations of persons with disabilities in the 'handistreaming' process.[109] To achieve this, the Brussels Council for Persons with Disabilities was created. This Council may give opinions and make recommendations on all issues relating to the inclusion of persons with disabilities in the Brussels-Capital region. The Council is composed of members of the advisory bodies of the distinct Community Commissions and further includes 'handistreaming' experts and a representative of the Interfederal Centre for Equal Opportunities and Combating Racism and Discrimination (UNIA), an independent body monitoring the implementation of the CRPD.[110]

All in all, it is obvious that at the level of the federated entities there is still work to be done to organise a proper participation of persons with disabilities in policy and decision-making. While some entities clearly made progress in that respect, or at least expressed the intention to do so, others still need to begin setting up sustainable participation channels. In Brussels, there is rather a problem of an 'excess' of participatory tools and channels. In this context, coherence seems lacking and the various advisory bodies lose visibility.

[105] Art 4, para 1, 4° Decr Fr Gem Comm 5 juni 1997 houdende oprichting van de Brusselse Franstalige Adviesraad voor Welzijnszorg en Gezondheid.

[106] Art 5, para 4 Decr Fr Gem Comm 5 juni 1997.

[107] Art 23, paras 3 and 27 Ord Gem 23 maart 2017 houdende de oprichting van de bicommunautaire Dienst voor Gezondheid, Bijstand aan Personen en Gezinsbijslag.

[108] Ord Br 8 december 2016 betreffende de integratie van de handicapdimensie in de beleidslijnen van het Brussels Hoofdstedelijk Gewest.

[109] *Parl.St.* Br Parl 2015–2016, n° A-385/1, 1, 3 www.parlement.brussels/parlementaire-stukken.

[110] Art 6 Ord Br 8 december 2016 betreffende de integratie van de handicapdimensie in de beleidslijnen van het Brussels Hoofdstedelijk Gewest; Arts 2-4 B Br Reg 23 november 2017 tot oprichting van de raad voor personen met een handicap.

IV. NATIONAL IMPLEMENTATION AND MONITORING OF THE CRPD

Article 33(1) CRPD requires that the States Parties designate one or more focal points within government for matters relating to the implementation of the Convention. It also requires due consideration to be given to the establishment or designation of a coordination mechanism within government to facilitate related action in different sectors and at different levels.[111]

In Belgium, both the Federal Government and the federated entities have designated focal points. A Directorate-General within the Federal Public Service for Social Security acts as a focal point for the federal level and as an inter-federal coordination mechanism. The various federal authorities also have a disability focal point, each of which is responsible for the implementation of the Convention in its own policy domain.[112] As a federal focal point, the Directorate-General is responsible for coordinating the actions of the federal focal points within the administrations and political support units. In its role as coordination mechanism, it coordinates the exchange of information on the implementation of the CRPD and ensures cooperation between the different focal points at each level of government, as well as with the independent mechanism and civil society.[113]

Nevertheless, there is little to no evidence that the CRPD provoked a real 'centralisation' of disability issues. The specificity of Belgian federalism, which is based on the distribution of exclusive competences and equality between the Federal Government and the federated entities, encourages idiosyncratic policies rather than central coordination. Its peculiarity did not help to advance the rights of persons with disabilities in a coordinated manner.

Article 33(2) CRPD further obliges States Parties to maintain, designate or establish a framework, including one or more independent mechanisms to promote, protect and monitor the implementation of the Convention.[114] In Belgium, this role is assigned to UNIA. UNIA was established on the basis of a cooperation agreement between the Federal Government, the communities and the regions,[115] and its financing is provided by all parties to that agreement.[116]

[111] Art 33, para 1 CRPD.

[112] Beslissing van de Ministerraad van 20 juli 2011, 'Personen met een handicap' (20 July 2011) www.news.belgium.be/nl; FOD Sociale Zekerheid, 'Handistreaming op federaal niveau. Hoe het verdrag van de verenigde naties inzake de rechten van personen met een handicap toepassen?' (December 2013) www.socialsecurity.belgium.be 3.

[113] FOD Sociale Zekerheid, 'Convention des Nations Unies relative aux droits des personnes handicapées' www.socialsecurity.belgium.be/fr.

[114] Art 33, para 2 CRPD.

[115] Samenwerkingsovereenkomst 12 juni 2013 tussen de federale overheid, de Gewesten en de Gemeenschappen voor de oprichting van het interfederaal Centrum voor gelijke kansen en bestrijding van discriminatie en racisme onder de vorm van een gemeenschappelijke instelling zoals bedoeld in artikel 92bis van de bijzondere wet van 8 augustus 1980 (Samenw 12 juni 2013).

[116] Art 16 Samenw 12 juni 2013.

UNIA carries out its mission in complete independence and in accordance with the Paris Principles, which govern the functioning of national human rights institutions and guarantee their independence and pluralism.[117] UNIA is qualified as a national human rights institution with B-status in the ranking of the Global Alliance of National Human Rights Institutions.[118]

However, at the time of writing, it is uncertain whether UNIA will remain the only independent body with the official task of promoting, protecting and monitoring the implementation of the Convention. The Flemish Government has expressed its intention to stop cooperating with UNIA and to set up its own centre, which would take over its task.[119] Various human rights organisations, however, have voiced their concern at this policy option, which could lead to fragmentation in the monitoring process.[120]

V. CONCLUSIONS AND CRITICAL CONSIDERATIONS

Although the CRPD can be invoked before the courts of the judiciary, the Council of State and the Constitutional Court within the framework of their power to judicial review, it is rather unlikely that the CRPD will be interpreted as having direct effect, at least insofar as its provisions on the rights to work and social protection are concerned.

The specific structure of the Belgian state, with its lack of hierarchy between the Federal Government and the federated entities and its complex division of exclusive competences, creates particular challenges for attaining coherent policies on persons with disabilities. The Belgian state evolved according to its own logic, which sprang from the cultural and economic preferences of the federated entities and their aspiration to ever-greater autonomy, but did not grow from the ambition to implement the CRPD in the most efficient way. While the centres of gravity for policymaking on persons with disabilities currently lie at the community level,[121] the regions nevertheless play an important role in the field of employment, and social protection largely remains the competence of

[117] Art 3, para 3 Samenw 12 juni 2013; General Assembly of the UN, 'Resolution 48/134 on national institutions for the promotion and protection of human rights' (4 March 1994) www.documents.un.org.

[118] Unia, 'Unia internationaal erkend als nationaal mensenrechteninstituut' (5 Juni 2018) www.unia.be.

[119] Vlaamse Regering, 'Regeerakkoord 2019–2024' (30 September 2019) www.vlaanderen.be 112; Vlaamse Regering, 'Ontwerp van decreet tot oprichting van een Vlaams Mensenrechteninstituut' (January 2022) www.vlaanderen.be.

[120] Unia, 'Voorlopige standpuntnota over de oprichting van een Vlaams gelijkheidsorgaan en de uitstap uit Unia' (17 December 2021) www.unia.be; F Segers, 'Vlaanderen krijgt in 2023 een Vlaams Mensenrechteninstituut' (19 December 2021) www.vrtnws/nl; NOOZO, 'Advies over het Vlaams Mensenrechteninstituut' (1 February 2022) www.noozo.be 13.

[121] At least in Flanders. In practice this is less the case in Wallonia and Brussels, due to secondary transfers of competences between federated entities in those parts of the country.

the Federal Government. The approval of the CRPD did not in itself change the balance of power between these authorities and did not lead to any greater centralisation of policy or unity of command.

Our brief analysis on the right to work indicates that measures to ensure equal treatment and non-discrimination have been taken at each of the relevant policy levels, and that legislation has been adopted to promote, inter alia, the accessibility of workplaces for persons with disabilities. However, these measures largely preceded the ratification of the CRPD, which indicates that the Convention has not had much influence in this regard. Furthermore, despite the extensive legal protection against discrimination, a recent survey showed that persons with disabilities still face discrimination.[122] It also remains relatively difficult for them to participate in the Belgian labour market. Their employment rate is 26 per cent, while for the entire population it is 65 per cent.[123] In addition, the available figures show that the employment quota set by the Federal Government and the federated entities to promote the employment of persons with disabilities in the public sector are in fact not met.[124]

Our analysis on the implementation of the right to social protection shows that a comprehensive system of social protection for persons with disabilities has been organised in Belgium, covering a wide range of needs. But it also shows that the policy autonomy of the different authorities having competences in that field has led to the use of very different approaches to, and concepts of, disability. There are still remnants of the narrow medical approach to disability, especially at the federal level, and at the same time openings toward the 'social' approach promoted by the CRPD at the level of some of the federated entities. These openings have often been explicitly inspired by the Convention. In this area, it is therefore desirable to achieve greater coherence, preferably by a more systematic substitution, on all policy levels, of the old narrow medical approach. There are other reasons to be critical. The Directorate-General of

[122] Unia, 'Bevraging van personen met een handicap over de naleving van hun rechten' (December 2020) www.unia.be.

[123] Statbel, 'Internationale Dag van Personen met een handicap' (2 December 2021) www.statbel.fgov.be.

[124] A review of the figures shows that the standard for employment of persons with disabilities in the federal public sector is not met, given the employment rate of 1.22 per cent in the federal public office in 2020 (Begeleidingscommissie voor de aanwerving van personen met een handicap in het federaal openbaar ambt, 'Evaluatieverslag 2020' (6 October 2021) www.fedweb.belgium.be 3). At the Flemish level, the target of 3 per cent was not achieved, with an employment rate of 2.3 per cent by the end of 2020 (Sociaal-Economische Raad van Vlaanderen, Commissie Diversiteit, 'Advies Strategisch Gelijkekansen- en Diversiteitsplan Vlaamse Overheid 2021–2025' (12 January 2021) www.vlaanderen.be 10). The Walloon region and the French community also do not meet the quota they imposed on themselves (Unia, 'Parallelrapport over het tweede en derde periodieke rapport van België' (3 December 2021) www.unia.be 21). A report on 'handistreaming' further shows that the quota for the administration of the French Community Commission to employ 5 per cent of persons with disabilities, is also not being met (Parlement francophone bruxellois, 'Handistreaming' (29 May 2019) www.parlementfrancophone.brussels 11). See also Committee on the Rights of Persons with Disabilities, 'Concluding Observations on the Initial Report of Belgium', CRPD/C/BEL/CO/1, 28 October 2014, paras 38–39.

the Federal Public Service responsible for granting allowances to persons with disabilities suffers considerable delays in the processing of submitted applications as well as poor accessibility for its users.[125] Moreover, the amount of the income replacement allowance is below the poverty line.[126] The Flemish system of person-following financing for adults and the Walloon and Brussels personal assistance budget systems also have long waiting lists.[127] Besides the fact that this means some social needs of the applicants are not met, such waiting lists pose a problem of accessibility. In addition, the European Committee of Social Rights condemned Belgium for the lack of places in care or accommodation centres for highly dependent persons with disabilities, and for the long waiting lists that hinder access to these social services.[128]

As far as participation is concerned, our outline shows that greater coherence can also be achieved in the way advisory councils are currently set up in Belgium. It should therefore come as no surprise that some civil society organisations note that the policy participation of persons with disabilities has not yet been sufficiently elaborated.[129]

Finally, our look at the national implementation and monitoring of the CRPD in Belgium shows that different strategies are being developed at different policy levels, with regard to the organisation of the independent monitoring of the Convention. Time will tell whether or not developments in this field will lead to an undesirable fragmentation of the monitoring process.

It goes without saying, therefore, that the implementation of the CRPD poses major challenges for Belgian federalism, which are related to the complexity of the Belgian state structure, the high degree of policy autonomy of its components and the particular way in which the competences are distributed between them. To put it another way, the quest for equality in the employment of people with disabilities and coherence in the organisation of their social protection and participation is clearly not over yet.

[125] In September 2021, 15,000 applications had been waiting for more than six months to be examined (Unia (n 124) 22). The NHRPH has repeatedly expressed its concern about the long processing times and the reduced accessibility of the service (NHRPH, 'Advies nr. 2018/29 over de algemene beleidsnota Personen met een handicap' (15 October 2018) www.ph.belgium.be.

[126] Belgian Disability Forum, 'Submission to the Committee on the Rights of Persons with Disabilities within the Framework of the 2nd and 3rd Review of Belgium (2019)' (11 February 2019) www.ohchr.org 30; FOD Sociale Zekerheid, 'Analyse van de evolutie van de sociale situatie en sociale bescherming in België' (March 2021) www.socialsecurity.belgium.be 27-28. The Federal Government has made the commitment to increase the income replacement allowance up to the poverty line, with a target increase of 10.75 per cent by 2024 as an end point (KB 6 augustus 2021 houdende verhoging van het bedrag van de inkomensvervangende tegemoetkoming met toepassing van Artikel 6, para 6 van de wet van 27 februari 1987 betreffende de tegemoetkomingen aan personen met een handicap).

[127] Unia (n 124) 13–14.

[128] European Committee of Social Rights (ECSR), Decision of 18 March 2013, *International Federation for Human Rights (FIDH) v Belgium*, complaint No 75/2011. The ECSR, in its follow-up decision of 2020, found that this is still a challenge for Belgium (Findings of the ECSR on the follow-up of Complaint No 75/2011, 2020).

[129] Grip, 'List of Issues Prior to Reporting for Belgium' (February 2019) www.ohchr.org 5.

7

The United Kingdom

Asymmetrical Challenges to Implementing the CRPD

KASEY McCALL-SMITH

I. INTRODUCTION

EQUALITY LAW IN the United Kingdom is the dominant prism through which disability is addressed. Countless examples across the United Kingdom demonstrate how disabled people's rights cannot be fully realised unless equality law is delivered in conjunction with the human rights-based approach outlined in the UN Convention on the Rights of Persons with Disabilities (CRPD).[1] Since the United Kingdom ratified the CRPD in 2009, efforts to maximise the transformative potential of the CRPD have been driven from the bottom-up through careful advocacy and political campaigns focused on securing rights for disabled people through the devolved governments in light of the central government's general apathy for human rights. Sectoral laws and policies have ensured and promoted some specific rights in different areas of disability but these are generated predominantly by the sub-national governments. The focus of this contribution is the extent to which the United Kingdom's constitutional framework has shaped implementation of the CRPD.

For clarity of terminology used in this chapter, when referring to the sub-national governments within the United Kingdom, the specific government, such as the Welsh Government or Northern Ireland Executive (NI Executive), or the term 'sub-national administration' or 'devolved nation' will be utilised in line with the United Kingdom's approach to referring to the four separate entities as 'nations'. Furthermore, reflecting the social model of disability, the

[1] This chapter was developed from a 2020 briefing paper by the author, see K McCall-Smith, 'Incorporating the United Nations Convention on the Rights of Disabled People into Scots Law' (November 2020) www.alliance-scotland.org.uk.

term 'disabled people' is used to acknowledge that 'people with an impairment are disabled by barriers in the environment and society'.[2] This choice takes into account the terminology preferred by various advocacy organisations focused on disability rights and law as well as UK law and policy.[3]

This chapter explores how ratification of the CRPD drives the asymmetric governance arrangements and developments of disabled people's rights in the United Kingdom. Section II will outline how the unique governance arrangements of each of the United Kingdom's devolved nations enable Wales, Scotland and Northern Ireland to give effect to disabled people's rights using distinct policies and programmes developed under the umbrella of equalities law and general human rights law. Section III will dive deeper into sub-national law and policy to demonstrate how the three sub-national governments aim to entrench the transformative vision of the CRPD into the devolved legal systems. This localised approach should ensure that the rights of disabled people are brought to life in those areas that matter most, particularly in the promotion of the social model of disability. However, in focusing on four areas underpinning implementation – the concept of disability, non-discrimination and equality, accessibility and participation – it becomes clear that the potential for disabled people in the United Kingdom to exercise, enjoy and claim the rights set out in the CRPD is often dependent on the constitutional capacity of the devolved government. The chapter then considers how the United Kingdom implements Article 33 CRPD and whether greater coordination could make the focal point and independent mechanism more effective tools in the United Kingdom. Section IV offers thoughts on how the varying devolution settlements in Britain create both opportunities and barriers to implementing the CRPD.

II. DISABILITY RIGHTS GOVERNANCE IN THE UNITED KINGDOM AND ITS DEVOLVED NATIONS

While the United Kingdom is 'decidedly not a federal State', it follows a 'method of dividing powers so that the general and regional governments are each, within a sphere, coordinate and independent'.[4] Unlike most federal states, the United Kingdom has no unified, written constitution and each of the devolved UK nations has a unique legal settlement with the national government that defines which areas of governance sit at the central or devolved levels. In other words, the limits on sub-national entities are not identical across the same level of

[2] UK Independent Mechanism (UKIM), 'Disability Rights in the UK. Updated Submission to the UN Committee on the Rights of Persons with Disabilities in Advance of the Public Examination of the UK's Implementation of the UN CRPD' (July 2017) www.equalityhumanrights.com 3.

[3] Eg Disability Discrimination Act 1995, s 1; Equality Act 2006, s 8(4).

[4] R Schütze, 'British "Federalism"? From England to United Kingdom: Internal Structures' in R Schütze and S Tierney (eds), *The United Kingdom and the Federal Idea* (Hart, 2018) 11.

sub-national government, though through subsequent amendments the differences are increasingly disappearing.[5] The Supreme Court is the highest court in the United Kingdom and is the final court of appeal for all civil suits. It may also decide devolution issues when there is a question about whether one of the devolved nations has infringed on reserved powers – a point that can create tension when the sub-national entities legislate to give greater force to human rights. In the context of human rights policy development there are identifiable grey areas where the competence to govern is mixed or unclear between the United Kingdom and devolved administrations. For this reason, three of the four distinct jurisdictions are presented independently, including Wales, Scotland and Northern Ireland. England is not treated separately, as general UK law is applicable as the *lex loci* and it does not have a second, concurrently governing sub-national administration.

In Wales and Scotland, all matters not expressly reserved to the United Kingdom fall under the competence of the devolved administrations. As the devolution settlements detail, however, the catalogue of matters falling in either sphere of governance are not identical between the Welsh and Scottish governments.[6] This legal reality can make cross-sub-national comparisons difficult to develop. As Tierney notes, the adaptation to the devolved settlements of the United Kingdom 'has occurred without any sense of coherent planning'.[7] To add to the complexity in comparative analysis across devolved competences, in Northern Ireland the devolution settlement is more nuanced, with distinctions being made between excepted, transferred and reserved areas of competence. Here, the 'excepted' matters align with many of the policy areas reserved to the UK Government through the Scotland Acts and Government of Wales Acts. 'Transferred' matters under the Northern Ireland Act (NI Act) are those areas expressly designated as matters of competence of the Northern Ireland Executive. 'Reserved' matters in Northern Ireland are those that are currently governed by the UK Government but could be transferred in the future. The identification of potentially transferable areas of competence is not part of the existing settlements with Wales or Scotland and recent history demonstrates that transfers of new areas of competence are relatively *ad hoc* responses to political pressure.[8]

The United Kingdom requires incorporation of international law before it becomes binding on state actors at any level. For this reason, the Human Rights Act 1998 (HRA 1998) is arguably the cornerstone of human rights protections

[5] Ibid 8.

[6] Compare new Sch 7A to the Government of Wales Act 2006, amended by Government of Wales Act 2017, Sch 1, with Scotland Act 1998, Sch 5, amended by Scotland Act 2016.

[7] S Tierney, 'Drifting Towards Federalism? Appraising the Constitution in Light of the Scotland Act 2016 and Wales Act 2017' in Schütze and Tierney (n 4) 102.

[8] See Scotland Act 2012 and 2016 and Government of Wales Act 2017, and discussion in Schütze and Tierney (n 4) 104 *et seq*.

for the British population as it directly incorporates the European Convention on Human Rights (ECHR) into UK law.[9] Common law and other legislation supplements human rights protections. However, the HRA 1998 does not specifically address the rights of the disabled community, and ongoing attempts to weaken the Act threaten to minimise its value in protecting the most marginalised members of British society.[10] As a result, disabled people in the United Kingdom still face barriers to exercising their civil and political rights and are under-represented in public office.[11]

The CRPD's breadth of coverage across civil, political, economic, social and cultural rights opens up a range of opportunities to respond to challenges faced by the disabled community using the devolved competences of the sub-national governments. The UK Government is reticent to strengthen economic, social and cultural rights in law despite these rights playing a crucial role in developing the full range of human rights for every person. The barriers preventing disabled people from accessing their rights in the United Kingdom reinforce the interrelated and indivisible nature of all human rights in that failure to secure economic, social and cultural rights directly impedes disabled peoples' abilities to exercise their civil and political rights.[12] The UN Committee on the Rights of Persons with Disabilities (CRPD Committee) has called upon the United Kingdom to bring its law and policy into conformity with the Convention. Specifically, the Committee has 'observe[d] with concern: … The insufficient incorporation and uneven implementation of the Convention across all policy areas and levels within all regions, devolved governments and territories under its jurisdiction'.[13]

The key legislation protecting disabled people in the United Kingdom is the Equality Act 2010 (EqA), though it is not applicable in Northern Ireland, as will be discussed below. The EqA exists to ensure Ministers of the Crown have regard to socio-economic inequality when making decisions and to harmonise equality law in relation to nine protected characteristics, including disability. It is common for states to rely upon non-discrimination or equality law to respect, protect and fulfil disabled people's rights, which is required by Article 5 CRPD. Discussed further in section IV, to advance equality in the United Kingdom, the Equality and Human Rights Commission (EHRC) promotes and monitors the EqA across England, Wales and Scotland and also aids in coordinating CRPD

[9] Human Rights Act 1998, s 29(2)(d).

[10] Eg J Swinney, 'Human Rights Act: Letter to the Rt Hon Dominic Raab MP, Lord Chancellor and Secretary of State for Justice' (21 December 2021) www.gov.scot.

[11] UKIM (n 2) 10.

[12] Eg R Sandland, 'Lessons for Children's Rights from Disability Rights?' in E Brems, E Desmet and W Vandenhole (eds), *Children's Rights Law in the Global Human Rights Landscape* (Routledge, 2017) 121.

[13] Eg Committee on the Rights of Persons with Disabilities (CRPD Committee), 'Concluding Observations on the Initial Report of the United Kingdom of Great Britain and Northern Ireland' CRPD/C/GBR/CO/1 (3 October 2017) para 6.

implementation.[14] The following offers a general outline of the devolution settlements for Wales, Scotland and Northern Ireland that are relevant to the CRPD.

Devolution through the Government of Wales Acts of 2006 and 2017 (collectively 'Wales Act') is not as extensive as the constitutional settlement between the United Kingdom and the other devolved nations. Sections 81 and 82 of the Wales Act prohibit Welsh Ministers (the Welsh Senedd)[15] from passing any subordinate legislation that is incompatible with the ECHR and prevents any actions that would be contrary to the United Kingdom's international obligations, including under the CRPD. The Wales Act also enables the Senedd to do anything it considers appropriate to promote economic, social and environmental well-being in Wales (section 60). The devolution settlement enables the Welsh Government and Senedd to develop disability law and policy distinct from England.

The Scotland Act 1998, and subsequent revisions in 2012 and 2016 (collectively 'Scotland Act'), enables the Scottish development of law and policy in relation to issues such as education and training, health and social services, housing, law and order, some aspects of equality, social security and taxation, among others. Even where the legal demarcation between the devolved and reserved powers is blurred, such as in the area of social security, Scotland is able to improve the rights of disabled people in distinctive ways, including directly incorporating international human rights into Scots law.[16] The Scotland Act makes clear that the Scottish Government is responsible for implementing international obligations in devolved areas of competence, including the CRPD.[17] As with the Wales Act, the Scotland Act demands that all Acts of the Scottish Parliament comply with the ECHR.

The Northern Ireland Act 1998 (NI Act) imposes general human rights obligations on the NI Executive. Section 26(2) permits the Executive to implement international obligations.[18] The NI Act also prohibits subordinate legislation that is incompatible with the ECHR.[19] The EqA is not applicable in Northern Ireland. Alternatively, the Disability Discrimination Act 1995 (DDA) is the primary disability non-discrimination legislation. The DDA applied throughout the United Kingdom prior to the adoption of the EqA. The key distinctions will be introduced in subsequent sections.

This chapter now turns to examining the approaches to CRPD implementation exercised in the United Kingdom. In particular, section III considers the

[14] In Scotland, the Equality and Human Rights Commission (EHRC) monitors implementation of the CRPD in the areas that are not devolved. See Equality Act 2006, ss 7, 10.

[15] The Welsh Parliament, Government of Wales Act 2006, s 1, amended by Senedd and Elections (Wales) Act 2020, s 42(2).

[16] Ministry of Justice, 'Rights and Responsibilities: Developing Our Constitutional Framework' Cm 7577 (23 March 2009) para 3.70.

[17] Scotland Act 1998, Sch 5, s 7(2)(a).

[18] Northern Ireland Act 1998, Sch 2, s 3(c).

[19] Ibid s 6(2)(c).

common and distinctive approaches of the UK Government in comparison to the sub-national regions in four areas: the concept of disability, non-discrimination and equality, accessibility and participation.

III. IMPLEMENTING THE CRPD

As is frequently noted, implementation of international human rights law must be flexible. At the same time, embedded rights should at all times remain tethered to the international legal frameworks from which they are derived. The CRPD framework is particularly important in this regard due to the transformative potential offered through the implementation of the full suite of rights elaborated in the Convention. The differing concepts of disability employed at various levels of government appear to underpin the asymmetry in CRPD implementation across the central and sub-national governments. As will be demonstrated, the employment of human rights in opposition to or in conjunction with equality law in the United Kingdom has yielded different results across the devolved nations.

A. The Concept of Disability

The potential for tide change in the treatment of disabled people offered by the CRPD lies in its embrace of the social model of disability, in opposition to the medical model utilised by most states. The medical model that shaped many laws relating to disabilities during the twentieth century is distinguishable as it focuses on an individual's impairment, rather than the disability, which should be understood as 'the social, material, and cultural barriers which exclude people with impairments from mainstream life'.[20] This model promotes the equal opportunity for all disabled people to engage with and activate all of their rights as part of an inclusive social and political environment that is enriched by the participation of every member of society.[21]

Section 6 of the EqA defines a disabled person as an individual who has a 'physical or mental impairment' that has a 'substantial' and 'long-term' adverse

[20] K Stalker et al., 'A Study of Disabled Children and Child Protection in Scotland – a Hidden Group?' (2015) 56 *Children and Youth Services Review* 126, 128; Relying on Union of the Physically Impaired against Segregation and the Disability Alliance discuss 'Principles of Disability' (22 November 1975) www.disabledpeoplesarchive.com.

[21] Implementing the social model is also complex and triggers many further inquiries as to how disabled people actually benefit from it. See SR Smith, 'Disability: What Rights for Disabled People in a Welfare State? Need-Fulfilment versus Identity-Assertion and the "Problem of Dependency"' in G Calder, J Gass and K Merrill-Glover (eds), *Changing Directions of the British Welfare State* (University of Wales Press, 2012).

effect on their ability to carry out normal daily activities.[22] The DDA employs the same definition. This definition relies on the medical model of disability and the associated regulations determine which conditions are protected under the Act and provide guidance to public authorities and service providers' duties under the Act.[23] Provision of social support determined by the UK Government relies explicitly on the medicalised approach to disability – for example, the use of a 'functional impact on daily life' test in the determinations of the Personal Independence Payment (PIP).[24] The 2017 PIP Regulations further distinguish between physical and mental disability, disadvantaging mentally disabled people who do not meet medically defined mobility criteria.[25] Other sectoral laws also reflect the medical model of disability and focus on needs-based assessments, which enhances discrimination against those disabled by society.[26] Recent court judgments raise concerns about the strictures employed to identify what amounts to a mental disability under section 6 of the EqA.[27] Overall, the medical model approach to disability in UK legislation departs from the approach promoted through the CRPD and, as a result, presents multiple challenges to giving effect to the CRPD.

While existing UK law strongly favours the medical model of disability, guidance developed through the UK Government's Disability Unit advocates the social model of disability.[28] However, the most recent National Disability Strategy demonstrates the UK Government's lack of clarity on its approach to disability, though the strategy is noted as complementing the CRPD.[29] The devolved governments have offered a much clearer position on their approaches to disability in terms of policy, although they are bound by the EqA or DDA medicalised approaches when it comes to enforcement.

Despite the primary legislation relating to disability being the EqA, both Wales and Scotland promote the social model of disability through their primary policy instruments directed toward empowering disabled people.[30]

[22] Equality Act 2010, s 6.

[23] Eg Equality Act 2010 (Disability) Regulations 2010. See S Bunbury, 'Unconscious Bias and the Medical Model: How the Social Model May Hold the Key to Transformative Thinking about Disability Discrimination' (2019) 19 *International Journal of Discrimination and the Law* 26, 33–37.

[24] Social Security (Personal Independence Payment) Regulations 2013; Social Security (Personal Independence Payment) (Amendment) Regulations 2017.

[25] EHRC, 'Social Security (Personal Independence Payment) (Amendment) Regulations 2017 – Motion Debate House of Commons: Advice for Parliamentarians' (16 April 2017) www.equalityhumanrights.com.

[26] Smith (n 21) 167; G de Beco, 'Intersectionality and Disability in International Human Rights Law' (2020) 24 *The International Journal of Human Rights* 593.

[27] Eg *Sullivan v Bury Street Capital Ltd* [2021] (EWCA Civ) 1694.

[28] Office for Disability Issues, 'Guidance: Portraying Disability' (15 March 2021) www.gov.uk.

[29] Eg UK Government, 'National Disability Strategy' (July 2021) www.gov.uk 14, 20.

[30] Welsh Government, 'Action on Disability: The Right to Independent Living – Framework and Action Plan' (7 October 2019) www.gov.wales 7; Welsh Government, 'Strategic Equality Plan (2020–2024)' (2 April 2020) www.gov.wales; Scottish Government, 'A Fairer Scotland for Disabled People: Delivery Plan' (2 December 2016) www.gov.scot.

As will be discussed below, these policy affirmations do not necessarily translate into a more transformational approach to ensuring the rights of disabled people. In Northern Ireland, the shared EqA/DDA definition of disability is narrowed by excluding different conditions, including certain addictions and personality disorders.[31] The narrow interpretations of the DDA are arguably responsible for a reduction to the benefits received by disabled people in Northern Ireland.[32] Interestingly, policy and strategy publications suggest the Northern Ireland approach is unsettled. The Northern Ireland Disability Strategy 2012–2015 stated that any welfare reform should reflect the social model of disability.[33] However, the Disability Action Plan 2021–2026, which sets out the most recent NI Executive plans to fulfil its obligations under the DDA, does not refer to the social model of disability at all.[34] In practice, it appears that the NI Executive continues to apply the medical model of disability in the design of policies and delivery of services.

There is no harmony across the national and devolved governments of the United Kingdom in terms of their approaches to disability. While the legal definition of disability is shared through application of the EqA or DDA, policies produced in Wales and Scotland advance a social model of disability, while Northern Ireland has narrowed its approach over that of even the central government. Stronger support for and use of the social model of disability by the central government would expand the potential to drive transformative change through the CRPD. As it stands, this leadership deficit restrains devolved implementation in the next three areas under discussion.

B. Non-Discrimination and Equality

Equality and non-discrimination laws have developed separately from human rights law in the United Kingdom.[35] This has made it difficult to navigate claims based on discrimination in many circumstances and caused particular difficulty

[31] Disability Discrimination Act 1995, s 49A; Disability Discrimination (Meaning of Disability) Regulations (NI) 1996, explanatory note.

[32] Bunbury (n 23); Equality Commission for Northern Ireland (ECNI) and Northern Ireland Human Rights Commission (NIHRC), 'Jurisdictional "Parallel" Report on Implementation in Northern Ireland' (August 2017) www.equalityni.org 73; Personal Independence Payment Regulations (Northern Ireland) 2016, Pt 2; W Rader, 'Personal Independence Payment (PIP) – An Independent Review of the Assessment Process' (20 November 2018) www.communities-ni.gov.uk 37.

[33] NI Executive, 'A Strategy to Improve the Lives of People with Disabilities 2012–2015' (2013) 18, 22.

[34] NI Executive, 'Disability Action Plan 2021–26' (30 April 2021) www.executiveoffice-ni.gov.uk.

[35] N Crowther and L Sayce, 'Was Ratification of the CRPD the High Watermark for United Kingdom Disability Rights? Ten Years of Monitoring Implementation of the CRPD' in EJ Kakoullis and K Johnson (eds), *Recognising Human Rights in Different Cultural Contexts* (Palgrave Macmillan, 2020) 303.

in promoting a human rights-based approach to disability rights using the social model of disability. With the departure of the United Kingdom from the EU, the EU Charter on Fundamental Rights Articles 21 (non-discrimination), 26 (integration of persons with disabilities) and 35 (preventative health care) no longer apply in the United Kingdom. Thus, the valuable prism offered through the combination of the Charter and CRPD interpretations no longer influence the UK approach to disabled people's rights.[36]

The primary responsibility for ensuring the rights of disabled people is through the EqA Public Sector Equality Duty (PSED), which requires certain public authorities in England, Wales and Scotland to carry out their functions with due regard to eliminating discrimination, harassment, victimisation and other prohibited conduct. The PSED further requires public authorities to advance equality of opportunity for those with a protected characteristic, including disability, and to publish information demonstrating how they comply with the PSED. While the PSED provides some protection, the due regard obligation does not offer much by way of effectiveness in securing rights for the often complicated, intersectional human rights interferences experienced by many disabled people. Nonetheless, there are a variety of sectoral laws and policies focusing on disability discrimination and inequality in different areas, such as employment and education, that offer additional protections.[37]

The UK National Disability Strategy aims to increase equality of opportunity and protection from discrimination for disabled persons by increasing accessible products and services, tackling crime against disabled people and increasing social participation. This strategy voices the government's public commitment to take action against employment discrimination and social stigma yet there is no strength behind the policy. Instead, a range of further policies that include specific attention to disabled people reinforce the Strategy, including the Hate Crime Action Plan 2016–2020.[38] However, two years into the Action Plan, little concrete evidence of 'action' is evident.[39] Inequalities suffered by disabled people following the policies adopted in response to the 2007 financial crisis and throughout the Coronavirus pandemic have only grown since the United Kingdom ratified the CRPD.

The EqA is enhanced in Wales through the Equality Act 2010 (Statutory Duties) (Wales) Regulations 2011 which implements the Welsh PSED. This requires the Welsh Government to publish the steps it has taken to fulfil its equality objectives, publish the timeline for fulfilment and monitor the extent to which its aims have been achieved.[40] The Welsh Government considers the

[36] UKIM (n 2) 6–7.

[37] Eg Public Contracts Regulations 2015, reg 20.

[38] UK Government, 'Action Against Hate: The UK Government's Plan for Tackling Hate Crime' (July 2016) www.gov.uk.

[39] UK Government, 'Action Against Hate – The UK Government's Plan for Tackling Hate Crime – "two years on"' (October 2018) www.gov.uk 6, 17.

[40] Equality Act 2010 (Statutory Duties) (Wales) Regulations 2011, ss 3(2)–(3).

CRPD a reference point for the development of many of its laws and policies.[41] Aside from the EqA, the most recent potentially enforceable law that could advance equality for disabled people is the Well-being of Future Generations (Wales) Act 2015, though it does not refer expressly to the CRPD.[42] Statutory instruments on disabled children's education[43] offer potential pathways to justice for children's disability discrimination claims in educational settings and are reinforced by the Welsh Measure on children's rights, which indirectly incorporates the UN Convention on the Rights of the Child and its provisions for disabled children.[44] The instruments that do exist to drive non-discrimination and equality in Wales respond to the EqA, rather than the CRPD. Welsh policy has definitive long-term objectives to eliminate discrimination against disabled people, but without more comprehensive binding legislation, equality for disabled people in Wales will be difficult to achieve.[45]

While Scotland has a range of laws, policies and national strategies specific to promoting non-discrimination and equality for disabled people,[46] implementation has failed to enable people with disabilities to exercise some of their most fundamental human rights and fully participate in their communities.[47] The Scotland Act permits Scottish Parliament to impose duties to encourage equal opportunities on cross-border public bodies operating in Scotland but the 2021 *UNCRC Reference* case complicates this possibility in the overlapping areas of competence.[48] In that case, the Supreme Court held that different aspects of the Scottish Bill incorporating the UN Convention of the Rights of the Child (UNCRC) could be interpreted as modifying the UK Parliament's power to make laws for Scotland and, as such, were not permissible under the Scotland Act. The UK Government rebuffed subsequent attempts by the Scottish Government to work together to ensure that revisions to the Bill would both give greatest effect to the UNCRC and comply with the devolution settlement.[49] Going forward, the judgment and lack of engagement by the UK Government suggests that devolved nations will need to be extremely specific when legislating

[41] Welsh Government (n 30) 5.

[42] See EHRC, 'Disability Rights in Wales: Supplementary Submission to Inform the CRPD List of Issues on the UK' (2017) www.equalityhumanrights.com 9.

[43] The Right of a Child to Make a Disability Discrimination Claim (Schools) (Wales) Order 2011; See also The Special Educational Needs and Disability Act 2001(Commencement No 2) (Wales) Order 2003.

[44] Rights of Children and Young Persons (Wales) Measure 2011.

[45] Eg Framework for Action on Independent Living (2019); Strategic Equality Plan (2020–2024); The Diversity and Inclusion Action Plan 2017–2020.

[46] Eg Social Care (Self-directed Support) Act 2013 and A Fairer Scotland for Disabled People 2016–2021 Delivery Plan.

[47] Inclusion Scotland, 'Alternative Report from Civil Society' (October 2019) www.ohchr.org 4.

[48] Scotland Act, ss 53, 88; *Reference by the Attorney General and the Advocate General for Scotland – United Nations Convention on the Rights of the Child (Incorporation) (Scotland) Bill* [2021] UKSC 42.

[49] J Swinney, 'Statement to Scottish Parliament' (24 May 2022) www.parliament.scot beginning at 14:26.

in areas of overlapping or more recently devolved areas of competence. The case demonstrates how the United Kingdom's asymmetric governance framework and reticence to legislate in favour of human rights in Westminster hinders the realisation of international human rights obligation exceeding the most basic civil and political rights. Notably, the Scottish Government remains committed to incorporating the CRPD into Scots law,[50] and work on new, comprehensive human rights legislation is presently underway.[51]

Section 75(1)(c) of the NI Act obliges public authorities to have due regard to the need to promote equality of opportunity, inter alia, between persons with disabilities and persons without.[52] Here, the Equality Commission for Northern Ireland (ECNI) plays an important role in ensuring equality and non-discrimination. The Commission monitors the equality schemes produced by public authorities in line with the section 75 duty. The ECNI may also receive complaints by individuals who assert that a public authority has failed to comply with an equality scheme approved by the Commission.[53] Complaints, however, trigger only investigations into the alleged failure with the outcome being a report to the Secretary of State who may choose to give direction to the errant public authority correcting the failure. The ECNI also 'may lay' an investigation report before the NI Assembly. As the DDA is the specific disability discrimination legislation applied in Northern Ireland, the approach to disability is narrower and applies only to the provision of goods, facilities, services and premises. Section 49(a) of the Act places on specified public authorities a due regard duty to promote positive attitudes toward disabled people and encourage participation by disabled people in public life. The DDA does not prohibit indirect discrimination. Instead, it prohibits direct discrimination and the failure to make reasonable adjustments, in line with the 2008 *London Borough of Lewisham v Malcolm* case in the context of employment and higher education, though other sectoral laws further support equality for disabled people.[54] CRPD ratification has had limited effect on changes to law in Northern Ireland and there have been no proposals by the NI Executive to reform disability discrimination law or bring it level with the rest of the United Kingdom.[55] Nevertheless, the

[50] Scottish Government, 'A Fairer, Greener Scotland: Programme for Government 2021–22' (7 September 2021) www.gov.scot 35, 49; Scottish Government, 'Protecting Scotland, Renewing Scotland: The Government's Programme for Scotland 2020–2021' (1 September 2020) www.gov.scot 107.

[51] Scottish Government, 'Human Rights Bill Governance and Engagement Advisory Board' (9 September 2021) www.gov.scot.

[52] Sch 9 sets out the specific requirements concerning the publication of 'Equality Schemes' that show how a particular public authority proposes to fulfil its duties under s 75, including the duty to perform impact assessments (s 4(2)(b)). See Equality (Disability) (NI) Order 2000 and Disability Discrimination (NI) Order 2006.

[53] Eg ECNI, 'Annual Report and Accounts 2020–2021' HC 446 (15 July 2021) www.equalityni.org.

[54] *London Borough of Lewisham v Malcolm* [2008] UKHL 43. See eg Autism (NI) Act 2011; Special Educational Needs and Disability (NI) Act 2016.

[55] CRPD Committee (n 13) para 17; B Byrne et al., 'Disability Policies and Programmes: How does Northern Ireland Measure Up? An Update for ECNI' (21 February 2014) www.equalityni.org 4–5.

most recent Disability Action Plan identifies tackling disadvantage and promoting equality of opportunity for disabled persons as one of the NI Executive's main objectives.[56]

Non-discrimination and equality in the United Kingdom are dominated by equality law and not generally linked to the CRPD. In NI, the CRPD has had less influence on non-discrimination and equality than anywhere else in the United Kingdom. Furthermore, as a result of the *Lewisham* case, the previously accepted more expansive approach to disability-related discrimination was replaced by a narrower view of what amounts to direct discrimination. The implications of this case were obviated in the rest of the United Kingdom by the passing of the EqA and its subsequent interpretations. Difficulty in navigating the relationship between human rights and equality law in the United Kingdom is evident from the disjointed ways in which the distinct laws operate. Recent laws and policies suggest some proactive progress on the rights of disabled people in the context of non-discrimination and equality, however, Northern Ireland continues to lag behind compared to the rest of the United Kingdom due to the lack of harmonisation across equality law.[57] The United Kingdom's asymmetric approach to non-discrimination and equality for disabled people undermines the principle of non-discrimination in human rights law and presents multiple challenges to disabled people attempting to engage their rights.

C. Accessibility

The absence of a comprehensive UK-wide accessibility plan is a key concern of the CRPD Committee.[58] The EqA includes a 'duty to make reasonable adjustments' for employers and service providers to remove disadvantages faced by disabled people in order to ensure that they can access jobs, education and services on an equal footing with non-disabled persons, but there are no harmonised minimum standards.[59] Sectoral laws deliver further specifications to assure accessibility but their application varies across the country. In England and Wales, for example, the Autism Act 2009 requires the development of an Autism Strategy to enhance service provisions to persons with autistic spectrum conditions. Meanwhile, the Public Sector Bodies (Websites and Mobile Applications) (No 2) Accessibility Regulations 2018 requires public sector bodies in England, Wales and Scotland to ensure their websites, documents and mobile applications are accessible to disabled people as a 'reasonable adjustment' pursuant to the EqA. The lack of coordination across the devolved nations means the benefits of accessibility regulation varies depending on the particular sub-national system.

[56] NI Executive (n 34) 9, 16.
[57] UKIM (n 2) 8.
[58] CRPD Committee (n 13) paras 24–25.
[59] Equality Act 2010, ss 20–22, 98.

Accessibility to products and services is one of the UK Government's three current priority areas of action under its National Disability Strategy. This includes action on law reform, funding allocation and service improvement for equal access to: justice, courts and legal support; housing; transport; work and employment services; schools and education; goods and services (including innovative technology); arts/culture/sports facilities; and public services. Additional soft guidance addresses autism,[60] inclusive transport,[61] accessibility to information and access to public bus services[62] and online information and services regarding government policy and programmes.[63] None of the most recent accessibility strategies connect the UK objectives explicitly with its obligations under the CRPD.

The Welsh Government is working to embed accessibility in line with the social model of disability and key post-2009 legislation is designed to achieve this, including: the Social Services and Well-being (Wales) Act 2014; the Well-being of Future Generations (Wales) Act 2015; and the Public Contracts Regulations 2015.[64] The 2014 Act, in particular, aims to increase access to services and benefits for disabled people to be able to live independently and participate equally in social life. Additional accessibility-focused legislation passed by the Senedd includes the Housing (Wales) Act 2014 and the Renting Homes (Wales) Act 2016, both of which contain provisions to improve accessible housing and service provision by housing authorities. These legislative efforts align directly with powers devolved through the Wales Act. Welsh policy expands on these laws and commits to increasing accessibility to public transport, information on tourism and public appointments, apprenticeship programmes and training, and technology.[65]

Similar to Wales, above the obligation of the EqA there are a range of Scots laws that promote and ensure greater accessibility to different services and opportunities, including the Social Care (Self-directed Support) Act 2013; the Disabled Persons' Parking Badges (Scotland) Act 2014; Children and Young People (Scotland) Act 2014; among others. '[R]ooted firmly in the CRPD', the Fairer Scotland Delivery Plan seeks to ensure that all places in Scotland are accessible to all people.[66] For example, the government has worked to reform

[60] UK Government, 'National Strategy for Autistic Children, Young People and Adults: 2021 to 2026' (22 July 2021) www.gov.uk.

[61] UK Government, 'Inclusive Transport Strategy: Achieving Equal Access for Disabled People' (3 November 2020) www.gov.uk.

[62] UK Government, 'The Bus Services Act 2017: New Powers and Opportunities' (27 November 2017) www.gov.uk.

[63] UK Government, 'Government Digital Inclusion Strategy' (4 December 2014) www.gov.uk.

[64] Welsh Government (n 30) 15.

[65] Welsh Government (n 30) 49 *et seq*; NHS Wales, 'All Wales Standards for Accessible Communication and Information with Sensory Loss' (July 2013) www.gov.wales; Welsh Government, 'Voluntary Welsh Bus Quality Standard' (2017) www.gov.wales.

[66] Scottish Government (n 30) 4 and part 3.

the Local Housing Strategy and arrange subsidies through Affordable Housing Schemes to facilitate adjustments.

No specific accessibility legislation has been passed in Northern Ireland since the United Kingdom's ratification of the CRPD, thus accessibility requirements are outlined through the DDA and, in the context of children's education, the Special Educational Needs and Disability (NI) Order 2005. In the Disability Action Plan 2021–2026, the NI Executive commits to enhancing access to buildings, information and employment programmes. This demonstrates a positive step toward addressing older findings that people with sensory disabilities struggle to access even their GP surgeries, due to the lack of reasonable adjustments.[67] Further soft instruments have focused on accessibility for individuals with learning disabilities[68] and disabled people's access to arts and culture venues across Northern Ireland.[69]

Approaches to accessibility across the United Kingdom are sector-dependent and primarily hinge on the EqA or DDA. While soft instruments offer some recognition of accessibility in line with the CRPD, most of the identified aims and objectives are not enforceable. Ultimately, without a comprehensive, UK-wide accessibility plan, disabled people will 'continue to face difficulties in accessing appropriate housing, the built environment, transport, information and insurance'.[70]

D. Participation

A crucial component of the social model of disability is the way in which it reinforces the disability rights movement's adopted tagline – 'Nothing About Us Without Us' – by capitalising on disabled people's views and lived experiences and actively integrating them into law, policy and action plan decision-making.[71] Participation is a multifaceted concept and in a democratic society includes participation in government and community. As noted in Articles 4(3) and 33(3) CRPD, disabled people and their representative organisations should be consulted and actively involved in decision-making and monitoring processes. Presently, there are multiple barriers to disabled people's voting rights and they are under-represented in UK public and political office.[72] The 2022 decision

[67] Eg NI Health and Social Care Board, 'Best Practice Guide: Creating Accessible Primary Care Services for People with Sensory Loss' 5. See NI Department of Health, 'Physical and Sensory Disability Strategy and Action Plan: 2012–2015' (February 2012) www.dhsspsni.gov.uk.

[68] NI Department of Health, 'Learning Disability Service Framework' (2012) www.dhsspsni.gov.uk.

[69] NI Department for Communities, 'DfC Access and Inclusion Programme 2021/22 – Screening' (21 July 2020) www.communities-ni.gov.uk.

[70] UKIM (n 2) 8.

[71] See eg Welsh Government, 'Report of the Disability Equality Forum Steering Group. Locked out: Liberating Disabled People's Lives and Rights in Wales beyond COVID-19' (2 July 2021) www.gov.wales Methodology.

[72] UKIM (n 2) 10.

in *Binder v Secretary of State* demonstrates how disabled people are often under-represented or excluded from decision-making processes. This exclusion reinforces barriers to engaging disabled people's rights due to the limited, proactive impact of the EqA in this area. The *Binder* decision held that the PSED does not require that disabled people be consulted absent a statutory or common law obligation to the contrary and expressly noted that as an unincorporated treaty, the CRPD obligation to consult was not binding on UK public authorities.[73] The case demonstrates the weak approach to participation in terms of law and policy development at the core of UK governance.

The UK National Disability Strategy's second priority action area is improving participation in public and social life. This includes action on law reform, funding allocation and service improvement for equal representation in public appointments/judicial and political leadership roles as well as participation in civic duties and privileges such as jury duty and voting.[74] Following through on these commitments, proposals in the Police, Crime, Sentencing and Courts Bill (2021), for example, provide for British Sign Language interpreters in an effort to increase the participation of deaf people on juries in response to CRPD Committee criticism.[75] Proposed section 9 of the Elections Bill (2021) addresses some of the accessibility barriers for disabled people in exercising their right to vote in England, Wales and Scotland, including relaxing the information requirements for companion voters. However, without clear guidance on the interpretation of 'reasonableness' in terms of providing enabling equipment or which disabilities are covered by 'another disability', the law, if passed, is unlikely to engender change on its own.[76] Furthermore, the Ministry of Justice is investing £1 million to recruit more disabled magistrates in England and Wales and is supporting new schemes from April 2022 to support disabled people seeking to become candidates for public office.[77] While some positive movement appears on the horizon, these disjointed efforts make it difficult to secure consistent or effective participation opportunities or progress for the disabled community throughout the United Kingdom.

In the devolved nations, attention to disabled people's participation over and above the EqA is similarly sectoral and addressed primarily through policy. However, public authorities in Wales are required by law to involve disabled persons in their activities to fulfil the PSED, whereas in England there is no such obligation.[78] The Welsh Government has also committed to a 'co-production'

[73] *Binder et al v Secretary of State for Work and Pensions* [2022] EWC 105 (Admin) paras 44, 51, 52.

[74] UK Government, 'National Disability Strategy' (28 July 2021) www.gov.uk 20, 21, 26.

[75] Police, Crime, Sentencing and Courts Bill, HL Bill 95, s 194; CRPD Committee (n 13) para 32(d).

[76] HL Bill 141 (as of 28 March 2022) s 9.

[77] UK Government (n 74) 27.

[78] Disability Rights UK and Disability Wales, 'Implementation of the United Nations Convention on the Rights of Persons with Disabilities in England and Wales: Shadow Report' (January 2017) www.disabilityrightsuk.org 9.

approach to developing policies and services in conjunction with disabled people.[79] It also is working to increase disabled people's participation in political and public life, including representation in public office.[80] Similarly, the Access to Elected Office Fund Scotland supports disabled people running for public office in Scotland.[81] Scottish legislation and policy also supports distinct aspects of participation of disabled people in public life and decision-making in relation to their lives in the areas of devolved competence. The Education (Additional Support for Learning) (Scotland) Act 2004, for example, requires that a child for whom additional support needs have been identified should be consulted if the decision-making agency deems the child to have capacity to understand the issues that feed into the decision-making process.

Northern Ireland has two strategies directed toward increasing public participation of disabled people. First, the NI Disability Action Plan (2021–2026) aims to diminish a range of barriers by: enhancing access to consultations; increasing the use of technology; and improving the accessibility of and access to information about positions and the recruitment process for public appointment.[82] These measures are, however, very limited. The Physical and Sensory Disability Strategy was developed to promote positive attitudes towards disabled people and encourage their participation in public life in line with DDA equality duties.[83] However, there is little information on the Strategy or its achievements since it ended.

Altogether, it does not appear that ratification of the CRPD has had any conclusive impact on implementing disabled people's participation rights in the United Kingdom in any broad sense. Duties arising from the EqA are limited by the interpretations of the Act in the sub-national systems and the extent to which relevant policy areas are devolved. Incremental steps are being made in both law and policy but the transformative impact envisioned in the CRPD is limited in the United Kingdom.

IV. IMPLEMENTING ARTICLE 33

Prior to the United Kingdom's ratification of the CRPD there was relatively little consideration of the practical implications of Article 33. This provision requires (1) the establishment of one or more government-based focal points to

[79] Welsh Government (n 30) 6, 11.

[80] Welsh Government (n 30) 5; Welsh Government, 'Diversity and Inclusion Strategy for Public Appointments in Wales (2020–2023): Reflecting Wales by Running Wales' (2021) www.gov.wales.

[81] The Access fund is financed by the government and administered by a local civil society organisation. See Inclusion Scotland, 'Access to Politics' (2022) www.inclusionscotland.org.

[82] NI Executive (n 34) 31.

[83] NI Department of Health, '2012 Physical and Sensory Disability Strategy and Action Plan' (20 February 2012) www.dhsspsni.gov.uk.

coordinate implementation across different sectors and levels of government; (2) a framework which includes an independent mechanism to promote, protect and monitor the CRPD implementation; and (3) the participation of disabled people and representative civil society organisations in monitoring processes. In their early examination of Article 33 in the United Kingdom, Murray and Johnson pointed out the difficulties raised by the distinct devolution settlements and the lack of attention to these mechanisms prior to the Convention entering into force.[84] Ten years on from their examination, this section considers whether the UK focal point and independent mechanism have evolved to deliver more streamlined monitoring of the CRPD.

A. The UK Focal Point and Coordination Mechanism

The focal point and coordination mechanism outlined in Article 33(1) CRPD is crucial to realising the international obligations of the CRPD in a way that enriches the lived experiences of people with disabilities.[85] Following CRPD ratification, the Office for Disability Issues was designated as the combined focal point and coordinating mechanism responsible for giving effect to Article 33(1) CRPD. The Disability Unit, which replaced the Office for Disability Issues in 2019, is part of the Equalities Hub in the UK Cabinet Office and is now responsible for co-ordinating implementation of the CRPD across government, including in reserved policy areas across the United Kingdom.[86] In Scotland, the Equality and Rights Unit works with the Minister for Equalities and Older People to develop the implementation plan for the CRPD in devolved areas of competence through the Fairer Scotland for Disabled People Delivery Plan. In Northern Ireland, the Department for Communities acts as the devolved focal point and is responsible for disability policy.

The UK focal point has been criticised for its focus on developing the UK report to the CRPD rather than actually engaging in dialogue designed to better understand how to further implement the Convention.[87] There is also a lack of transparency in terms of how the focal point engages with the disabled community, which detours from the spirit of the Convention.[88] In highlighting the different initiatives by devolved governments, the UK focal point's own

[84] R Murray and K Johnson, 'Implementation of Article 33 CRPD in the United Kingdom: the Need to Consolidate Civil Society Engagement' in G de Beco (ed), *Article 33 of the UN Convention on the Rights of Persons with Disabilities: National Structures for the Implementation and Monitoring of the Convention* (Martinus Nijhoff, 2013) 98.

[85] See eg G de Beco and A Hoefmans, 'National Structures for the Implementation and Monitoring of the UN Convention on the Rights of Persons with Disabilities' in de Beco (n 84) 11.

[86] Disability Unit, 'What We Do' www.gov.uk.

[87] Murray and Johnson (n 84) 115–16.

[88] Ibid 116, 118.

publications demonstrate the lack of coordinated policy across the United Kingdom.[89] However, in reviewing the National Disability Strategy, and the devolved administrations' different policies, the UK and devolved focal points' imprints and coordination roles are evident.[90] To deliver the vision of the CRPD, greater efforts must be made to coordinate across the central and devolved governments and entrench their policies across all areas.

B. The UK Independent Mechanism

The UK Independent Mechanism (UKIM) established to implement Article 33(2) CRPD is comprised of the various independent statutory national equality and human rights institutions operating in the national and sub-national spheres. These include the EHRC, the Scottish Human Rights Commission (SHRC), the ECNI and the Northern Ireland Human Rights Commission (NIHRC). The NI Act created the NIHRC and the ECNI and the two operate together as the Independent Mechanism for Northern Ireland (IMNI) promoting and monitoring implementation of the CRPD.[91] The EHRC Wales Committee focuses on human rights, including disabled people's rights, as Wales does not have an independent human rights body.

As part of their remits, the four entities each handle complaints individually. The EHRC, for example, handles complaints in England and Wales in relation to both equality and human rights law while in Northern Ireland, the NIHRC addresses disabled people's complaints under human rights law and the ECNI addresses those raised under equality legislation.[92] The SHRC has no powers to receive complaints but may conduct inquiries into the policies and practices of different public authorities in Scotland regarding whether they are respecting the international human rights obligations of the United Kingdom, including the CRPD.[93] The individual mechanisms also each draft their own compliance reports to complement the reports and submissions to the CRPD Committee drafted under the framework of UKIM.

Each commission plays a significant role in driving law and policy that supports realisation of the CRPD in their different areas of competence, but there are limits to what each commission can do in the context of both their mandates and their resourcing. The 2017 UKIM's submission to the CRPD Committee reported dwindling funding and noted that the different commissions 'have all had to manage significant budget reductions since being designated as the

[89] Disability Unit, 'UN Committee on the Rights of Persons with Disabilities 2016 Inquiry – UK 2021 Follow-up Report' (14 December 2021) www.gov.uk.

[90] UK Government (n 74) 26, 29, 34.

[91] Northern Ireland Act 1998, part 7.

[92] ECNI, 'Promoting Equality Challenging Discrimination' (March 2019) www.equalityni.org 3.

[93] The Scottish Commission for Human Rights (Specification) Order 2008, s 2.

Independent Mechanism'.[94] Notably, the EHRC has had a budget reduction of over 70 per cent since 2010. Reduced funding of these human rights institutions underscores the UK Government's apathy toward progressing human rights, including disabled people's rights under the CRPD, and aligns with the slow uptick in comprehensive, coordinated action through general UK law and policy.

While the CRPD does not explicitly require coordination with civil society organisations or disabled people's organisations, the reference to the Paris Principles in Article 33(2) CRPD implies such engagement.[95] The Paris Principles include developing good working relationships with civil society and in particular with organisations focused on the promotion and protection of the rights of vulnerable groups, including disabled people.[96] The 'A' status of the EHRC, SHRC and NIHRC dictates that the independent mechanism, both collectively and each devolved human rights mechanism, is compliant with the Paris Principles.[97] To that end, there is a statutory requirement that at least one member of the EHRC must be or have been disabled.[98] The SHRC has no such requirement.[99] Regardless of such requirements, most of the progress on UK disability rights over the past decade was driven by the UKIM and civil society rather than by government. As Murray and Johnson foreshadowed, 'without this strong steer from independent institutions, the CRPD loses the potential it so clearly has to influence government initiatives that may make a difference for disabled people'.[100] Despite criticism on approaches to engagement and the ongoing learning curve in terms of how to implement the CRPD effectively, the distinctive commissions have engaged their roles to promote, protect and monitor CRPD implementation to different extents and these efforts run through the efforts to implement the CRPD outlined in section III.[101]

V. CONCLUDING REMARKS

Localised advocacy and implementation of disabled people's rights in the devolved nations of the United Kingdom was stimulated by ratification of the CRPD. Though research and evidence-based arguments promoting the social model of disability increasingly underpin the growing range of applicable policies, the law has not caught up, particularly in England and Northern Ireland.

[94] UKIM (n 2) 89.
[95] Murray and Johnson (n 84) 110.
[96] Ibid. See in particular Paris Principles, Methods of Operations, para (g).
[97] Global Alliance of National Human Rights Institutions, 'Paris Principles' UN General Assembly Resolution 48/134 (20 December 1993).
[98] Equality Act 2006, sch 1, s 2(3)(a).
[99] Scottish Commission for Human Rights Act (2006), s 2.
[100] Murray and Johnson (n 84) 106.
[101] Eg EHRC and Disability Advisory Committee, 'Final Report' www.equalityhumanrights.com.

The UK Government's failure to take a CRPD-based approach toward developing law and policy continue to inhibit implementation of disabled people's fundamental rights. While the devolved nations have the capacity to fill some of the gaps in promoting and protecting disabled people's lives, these efforts only reinforce the disparate support available to disabled people across the different layers of government. For example, the UK Government's 'Bedroom Tax' and 'Benefit Cap' reforms rendered a high proportion of disabled households far worse off in England than in Scotland, where the Scottish Government channels over £100 million into mitigation programmes.[102] The most recent refresh of the Welsh Programme for Government notes that there are plans to incorporate the CRPD into Welsh law.[103] If both Scotland and Wales manage to take greater steps toward legalising the CRPD and fulfilling disabled people's rights in law than the central government there will undoubtedly be pressure to harmonise access to the CRPD across the United Kingdom.

It is undeniable that implementing the CRPD is complicated where the devolved nations aspire to deliver stronger human rights protections than the UK Government. Recent cases demonstrate a growing antipathy for international law and its standards as a means of interpreting different rights in the United Kingdom. The *UNCRC Reference* case on Scottish legislation incorporating the UNCRC recognised the possibility of strengthening human rights in the devolved jurisdictions through incorporation of international treaties yet offered an overly narrow way forward for devolved governments in terms of navigating areas of overlapping legislative competence.[104] In other cases where the CRPD has been argued to be necessary to interpreting the EqA, British tribunals have refused to recognise any direct effect of the treaty in UK law where not explicitly incorporated.[105] The barrier to relying upon the CRPD or any other international human rights treaty without incorporation is an issue that can only be resolved through revisions or clarifications to the constitutional settlement in the United Kingdom. Until the CRPD is incorporated and ongoing uncertainties about HRA 1998 are resolved, significant gaps will remain in protections for the disabled community. As noted by the UKIM, '[c]lear action plans are needed by the UK and devolved governments to meet CRPD requirements'.[106] Since CRPD ratification, the United Kingdom has undoubtedly made progress in securing disabled people's rights.[107] However, the widespread breaches of disabled

[102] Inclusion Scotland (n 47) 13–14.

[103] Welsh Government, 'Programme for Government: Update' (7 December 2021) www.gov.wales 14.

[104] *Reference by the Attorney General and the Advocate General for Scotland – United Nations Convention on the Rights of the Child (Incorporation) (Scotland) Bill* [2021] UKSC 42.

[105] Eg *Binder* (n 73); *Britliff v Birmingham City Council* [2019] UKEAT 0291/18; *R (Davey) v Oxfordshire County Council* [2017] EWHC 354.

[106] UKIM (n 2) 8, 12.

[107] Eg UK Government, 'National Disability Strategy' (28 July 2021) www.gov.uk 28.

peoples' rights during the Coronavirus pandemic motivates the calls for quicker progress to deliver equality.[108]

Ratification of the CRPD has not centralised implementation of disabled people's rights in the United Kingdom. Despite the potential to secure greater CRPD implementation through the current devolution arrangements, realisation of disabled people's rights will remain patchy as long as the different spheres of law and policy are left uncoordinated. While this challenge could be addressed through a written constitution, or more effective engagement by the UK Government, entrenchment of the CRPD in areas of overlapping competence remains unresolved and at the mercy of the central government's views as to what amounts to interference in reserved areas of governance. The ongoing animosity to human rights demonstrated by successive Conservative governments and continued attempts to rollback protections for the most marginalised members of British society must be monitored in order to have a chance to deliver the promise of human rights, including the transformative potential of the CRPD.[109]

[108] Eg Welsh Government (n 71) 33.

[109] Eg J Hutt and M Antoniw, 'Concerns Raised about Human Rights Act Reform' Press Release (12 January 2022) www.gov.wales.

8

Canada

A Federal Perspective on the Implementation of the CRPD

JONAS-SÉBASTIEN BEAUDRY*

I. INTRODUCTION

CANADA SIGNED THE Convention on the Rights of Persons with Disabilities (CRPD) on 30 March 2007 and ratified it on 11 March 2010. It acceded the CRPD Optional Protocol in December 2018.

Although Canada's Constitution does not devolve the authority to make treaties to either level of government; the power to negotiate, sign, and ratify treaties has long been recognised to belong to the executive branch of the Federal Government.[1] Canada follows a dualist model of the implementation of treaties, according to which treaties signed by the country's representative do not have direct application in domestic law. As the Supreme Court of Canada stated in *Baker v Canada (Minister of Citizenship and Immigration)*, '[i]nternational treaties and conventions are not part of Canadian law unless they have been implemented by statute'.[2] Although the Federal Government can sign treaties,

* I thank my research assistant, Katrina Bland, for her excellent editorial work.

[1] See PW Hogg, 'Chapter 11. Treaties' in PW Hogg (ed), *Constitutional Law of Canada* (Thomson Reuters, 2007); L Barnett, 'Canada's Approach to the Treaty Making Process' (Parliament of Canada, 1 April 2021).

[2] *Baker v Canada (Minister of Citizenship and Immigration)* [1999] 2 SCR 817; See *Nevsun Resources Ltd v Araya*, 2020 SCC 5, 85: 'Some areas of international law, like treaties, require legislative action to become part of domestic law'. There are some obligations and interpretative norms that mitigate the dualist model. First, the *pacta sun servanda* ('agreements must be complied with') rule, reflected in Arts 12, 13 and 26 of the United Nations, Vienna Convention on the Law of Treaties, 23 May 1969, makes treaties binding upon consenting parties and establishes an expectation that they will perform their obligations in good faith. Second, 'Canada has long followed the conventional path of automatically incorporating customary international law into domestic law via the doctrine of adoption, making it part of the common law of Canada in the absence of conflicting legislation' (*Nevsun* (above) 90). Customary international law includes, for instance,

it must obtain the support and cooperation of provinces and territories before it commits Canada to perform obligations that fall under provincial/territorial heads of power.[3] To do so in practice, the Federal Government will table a treaty it is considering signing, alongside an explanatory memorandum, before the House of Commons and consider opposition before deciding to ratify it or not.[4] Implementing treaties domestically is therefore no small feat, especially given Canada's history as a decentralised federation.

As Valentine and Cameron explain, in addition to provincial and federal governments sharing powers over important areas of public life, Canada is also a multinational state that must negotiate the coexistence of Anglophones, Francophones, and Aboriginal peoples. Nation-building and province-building also imply disparities between provinces and intergovernmental conflict and competition. Federal encroachments into areas falling under provincial jurisdiction are politically conflictual, and governments may fail to achieve uniformity across the country on important issues.[5]

This chapter discusses the implementation of the CRPD in Canada's legal system in light of Canadian federalism. After these introductory remarks, section II describes Canadian federalism and the division of powers. Section III surveys constitutional grounds for potentially more robust federal interventions; and section IV highlights the importance of coordinated efforts between provincial and federal governments to implement the CRPD. Section V examines the limited power that the Federal Government has over provinces and territories to enforce a unified compliance with the CRPD in domains such as accessibility and human rights. Section VI examines the 'focal points' or 'coordination mechanisms' that Canada has proposed to use to meet its monitoring and enforcement obligation under the CRPD and surveys key criticisms from civil society.

II. THE DIVISION OF COMPETENCES: A BRIEF OVERVIEW

Canada is a constitutional monarchy and a parliamentary democracy with a federal system of governance. The Constitution of Canada is 'the supreme

jus cogens (peremptory norms of general international law 'accepted and recognized by the international community … as a norm for which no derogation is permitted', such as crimes against humanity (Vienna Convention (above) Art 53)). Finally, domestic statutes will be interpreted, '[i]n so far as possible [in ways] that reflect [the] values and principles [of customary and conventional international law]'. R Sullivan, *Driedger on the Construction of Statutes*, 3rd edn (Butterworths, 1994) 330; endorsed by the Supreme Court in *Baker* (above) 70.

[3] Established by Lord Atkin for the Privy Council in the 1937 *Labour Conventions Reference*: 'the Dominion, cannot, merely by making promises to foreign countries, clothe itself with legislative authority inconsistent with the constitution that gave it birth'. *Canada (Attorney General) v Ontario (Attorney General)* [1937] AC 326 [352].

[4] Government of Canada, 'Policy on Tabling of Treaties in Parliament' www.treaty-accord.gc.ca.

[5] D Cameron and F Valentine, 'Comparing Policy Making in Federal Systems: The Case of Disability Policy and Programs' in D Cameron and F Valentine (eds), *Disability and Federalism: Comparing Different Approaches to Full Participation* (McGill-Queen's University Press, 2001) 16.

law of Canada' and trumps any law that is inconsistent with it.[6] It includes the British North America Act 1867 (renamed the Constitution Act 1867 in 1982) and the Constitution Act 1982.[7] The Constitution divides executive and legislative powers between a national authority and subnational authorities, which are coordinated rather than hierarchical.[8] The central authority is the Federal Government and the regional ones are provincial and territorial governments. The Constitution Act 1982 includes the Canadian Charter of Rights and Freedoms, which applies to both provincial and federal governmental actions.

Sections 91 to 95 of the Constitution Act 1867 specify the distribution of governmental powers between the federal and provincial governments. For instance, the Parliament of Canada has legislative power over international trade, unemployment insurance, the military, and Aboriginal peoples. Section 92 confers power over the 'management of hospitals, asylums, charities', 'matters of a merely local or private nature', and 'property and civil rights' (which includes health insurance) to the provincial legislatures. Control over 'property and civil rights' is a particularly broad head of power 'apt to include most of the private law of property, contracts and torts'.[9] Control over communication and transportation is shared between the provincial and federal governments, depending on whether the communication and transportation issue is intra-provincial, or inter-provincial or international.[10] Both the federal and provincial governments can set up disability benefits.[11]

As a result of this division of powers, persons with disabilities are a 'shared client group' between two levels of government, and both 'disentangled' and 'collaborative' forms of federalism have shaped the evolution of disability-related policies since the 1950s.[12]

III. CENTRALISING DISABILITY ISSUES?

A. The Hope for More Robust Federal Interventions

The topic of how the constitutional division of powers affects disability-related policies has long been a central concern of the disability community in Canada. Disability organisations, such as the Council of Canadians with Disabilities and the Canadian Association for Community Living (now named Inclusion

[6] Constitution Act 1982, s 35, being Sch B to the Canada Act 1982 (UK), c 11, s 52(1).
[7] Ibid s 52(2).
[8] Hogg (n 1) 5-2.
[9] Ibid 17-2.
[10] As per s 92.10(a) and the two other sections mentioned in the following paragraph.
[11] Constitution Act 1867 (UK), 30 and 31 Vict, c 3, s 91, reprinted in RSC 1985, Appendix II, No 5, s 94A.
[12] M Prince, 'Designing Disability Policy in Canada: The Nature and Impact of Federalism on Policy Development' in AH Puttee (ed), *Federalism, Democracy, and Disability Policy in Canada* (McGill-Queen's University Press, 2002) 29–30, 72.

Canada), have made 'a national strategy on disability-related supports [their] top priorit[y]'.[13] As Sherri Torjman puts it, the disability community 'has pinned its hopes on the federal government' to protect persons with disabilities and champion their interests.[14] There are two well-known reasons for this.

One is the historical intervention of the Federal Government in provincial matters to provide support during crises when provinces struggled to meet Canadians' needs, such as during the Great Depression. As Peter Hogg explains, the post-war political climate encompassed 'humanitarian and egalitarian ideals which emphasized governmental responsibility for the provision of minimum standards of income, health, education and welfare to all Canadians [that] could only be fulfilled by action at the national level'.[15] The other, connected, reason is the rise of a human rights culture in the 1980s, as egalitarian ideals became constitutionally entrenched in the Canadian Charter of Rights and Freedoms (hereafter 'Charter').[16] This allowed disability politics to be cast as a matter of equality rights, discrimination, dignity, and citizenship, protected by the Constitution, rather than a matter of social support alone. Conceiving of disability as a fundamental democratic matter renders the plea for Parliament to ensure equal treatment of all persons with disabilities uniformly across Canada more compelling.

At the same time, the influence and role of the provinces in the field of human rights should not be dismissed. Provinces '[took] the lead in developing human rights codes and commissions' from the 1940s to the 1970s and 'by the 1980s all codes listed disability as one of the prohibited grounds of discrimination'.[17] Unlike the Charter, these codes apply to private relationships, thereby protecting against discrimination from which persons with disabilities suffer outside of interactions with the state – successfully bringing about accommodations in the workplace, housing, and commerce. Provincial human rights codes are discussed in greater detail in section V of this chapter.

The disability community's longstanding hope for stronger federal oversight is offset by its equally longstanding disappointment in the Federal Government's failure to take on this role and invest sufficiently in disability services and supports.[18] Claims based on Charter rights have been most successful in court when aimed at obtaining access to a good (eg health care or education) that non-disabled citizens could access.[19] However, persons with disabilities often need social supports and goods that non-disabled persons do not and that are

[13] Ibid 100.

[14] S Torjman, 'Canada's Federal Regime and Persons with Disabilities' in Cameron and Valentine (n 5) 152.

[15] Hogg (n 1) 6-24.

[16] Torjman (n 14) 151–52.

[17] Prince (n 12) 57.

[18] See eg M Prince, 'A National Strategy for Disability Supports: Where Is the Government of Canada in This Social Project?' in MA McColl and L Jongbloed (eds), *Disability and Social Policy in Canada* (Captus University Publications, 2006) 99.

[19] See eg *Nova Scotia v Martin*; *Nova Scotia v Laseur* [2003] 2 SCR 504.

not already offered by existing legislative measures. Judicial bodies have been reluctant to use the Charter to creatively reimagine the constitutional division of powers or to encroach upon legislative prerogatives to design social support.

In the remainder of this section, I will survey potential constitutional grounds that could justify more robust federal control over disability issues. Since federalism is always 'in a process of contested development',[20] these justifications may be more theoretical than politically realistic. Still, they invite readers to think of the concept of 'disability' and of constitutional norms in radical ways that may destabilise traditional assumptions about where responsibility for 'disability' fits in Canada's constitutional order.

B. A Survey of Available Constitutional Grounds

The Federal Government can derive power over areas falling under provincial jurisdiction from sources outside the federal heads of power listed in section 91 of the Constitution Act 1867. One is section 92(10)(c), which confers a 'declaratory power' to Parliament, that is, the power to declare that certain intra-provincial works 'although wholly situate within the Province … are for the general advantage of Canada'. The declaratory power has been applied to 'works' such as nuclear power plants or infrastructure connected to the grain trade, and was once used frequently to control local railways.[21] This power is now seldom used – probably because it met political resistance from the provinces, given its seemingly anti-federalist nature, since it enables the Federal Government to stipulate unilaterally (by parliamentary fiat not subject to judicial review) what 'works' it deems to be 'for the general advantage of Canada'.[22]

Neglect of disability issues across the provinces may have such grave effects that they could be understood as threats to the rights or citizenship of persons with disabilities, meriting state-wide regulation under Parliament's declaratory power. Consider, for instance, how physically disabled individuals must plan carefully where to work and live, given the disparity of accessibility between cities. Such constraints may violate the constitutional rights to equality and mobility, as well as other rights, the object of which (eg voting) might not be accessible.[23]

Still, it remains unlikely that such use of Parliament's declaratory power would withstand political challenges. To fit within the declaratory power, the

[20] Prince (n 12) 72.

[21] See eg *The King v Eastern Terminal Elevator Co* [1925] SCR 434; *Jorgensen v AG Can* [1971] SCR 725; *Ontario Hydro v Ontario* [1993] 3 SCR 327; and discussion in Hogg (n 1) s 22.8.

[22] Hogg (n 1) 5-22, 22-18.

[23] All such issues may, of course, be dealt with as discrete Charter rights violations, but (i) judicial interpretation of rights violations and possible remedies are limited in ways that governmental interventions are not and (ii) a finding that rights were violated would still leave it to provinces to correct the problem in a potentially disparate manner.

government would have to narrow down the broad area of disability to specific disability-related infrastructure (somehow akin to physical mills and nuclear plants). In doing so, it would probably refer to areas of disability-related needs, such as transportation, health care, education, communication, or economic support for subsistence. Provinces would be reluctant to accept encroachments upon these areas at the heart of their jurisdiction, especially when more cooperative strategies are available such as bilateral agreements or conditional gifts under the federal 'spending power'.

Before considering cooperative options, however, let me contemplate another radical route of transferring governance over disability-related issues to the Federal Government: the possibility of a constitutional amendment. Consider the historical precedents of the constitutional amendments placing unemployment insurance,[24] old age pensions,[25] and survivor and disability benefits[26] under federal jurisdiction. The framers of the 1867 Constitution did not contemplate 'social security' as a particularly salient head of constitutional power because at the time, poverty relief was left to families, the church, and municipalities.[27] Canada's transition into an industrial economy amid post-war reconstruction required contributions from the Federal Government, which began with grants to provinces and eventually took the more robust form of a national social insurance programme, Canada's New Deal.[28] These legislative measures were found to be unconstitutional for infringing provincial jurisdiction.[29] This prompted the constitutional amendment giving Parliament authority over 'unemployment insurance'.[30] Similar constitutional obstacles stood in the way of the provincial and federal governments contributing jointly to old age pensions, and led to constitutional amendments conferring concurrent power over old age pensions and supplementary benefits to Parliament.[31]

While it could be argued that disability demands a similar response, any amendment would face the same difficulty as the use of declaratory power: disability means many things. The alternative of targeting 'people with disabilities' would not resolve the ambiguity and would resemble the jurisdiction that the Federal Government has over Aboriginal peoples or veterans – the raison d'être of which would not apply to persons with disabilities, whose identity as 'disabled' may change during a lifetime. To focus on disability-related *needs*

[24] British North America Act 1940, 3-4 Geo VI, c 36 (UK).

[25] British North America Act 1951, 14-15 Geo VI, c 32 (UK).

[26] British North America Act 1964, 12-13 Eliz II, c 73 (UK).

[27] KG Banting, *The Welfare State and Canadian Federalism*, 2nd edn (McGill-Queen's University Press, 1987) 47–48.

[28] Ibid 48.

[29] Ibid; Hogg (n 1) 33-2. The relevant heads of power are: ss 92(7): 'Hospitals, Asylums, Charities, and Eleemosynary Institutions'; 92(8): 'Municipal Institutions in the Province'; 92(13): 'Property and Civil Rights in the Province'; 92(16): 'all Matters of a merely local or private Nature in the Province'.

[30] Constitution Act, 1867 (n 11) s 91(2A).

[31] Ibid s 94A; Hogg (n 1) 33-9.

would be more plausible. To some extent, this is what the Federal Government already does, for instance, through Canada Pension Plan benefits for persons with disabilities. However, just as the unemployment insurance amendment led to constitutional challenges decrying the federal encroachment upon provincial matters,[32] any constitutional amendment responding to specific disability-related needs would likely inspire similar provincial challenges.

Finally, it is worth commenting on the potential of the first clause of section 91, which authorises Parliament to 'make Laws for the Peace, Order, and Good Government of Canada'. The Federal Government has used this residuary power to fill gaps in the distribution of powers, manage matters of national concern, and respond to emergencies; however, it is only available for issues that do not already fall under provincial control.[33] The broad nature of provincial power over 'property and civil rights' explains why the Federal Government would have difficulty invoking its power to 'make Laws for the Peace, Order, and Good Government of Canada' to govern disability issues.

This exploration of possible justifications for increased federal power over disability issues may give us pause when considering calls for constitutional reform and urgent intervention to respond to disability issues. 'Disability' is a too broad concept, encompassing too many problems, needs, rights, and goods, to be appropriated by one level of government in a federal system like Canada's.

IV. COLLABORATIVE FEDERALISM: SPENDING POWER AND FEDERAL TRANSFERS

Federal 'transfers' to provinces and territories are the most likely and efficient means of improving the disparity of disability supports and services across the country. The Federal Government has a 'solid history'[34] of providing disability support to achieve economic inclusion and employment through intergovernmental transfers since the 1950s. Disability policy expert Michael Prince says this ongoing policy choice is not mere historical happenstance, but an indicator of what Canadians value and the role they expect the Federal Government to play. Specifically, Prince connects the Federal Government's rationale for continuing to operate such transfers to the following policy goals:

- to support the portability of services and the mobility rights of Canadians with disabilities within and across jurisdictions and life situations;
- to encourage the further development and enhancement of the current patchwork of disability-related supports across the country;

[32] Hogg (n 1) 33-6.
[33] Hogg (n 1) 'Chapter 17. Peace, Order, and Good Government'.
[34] Prince (n 18) 104.

— to assist provinces and territories, with their varying degrees of fiscal capacity, to undertake the provision of a range of accessible and responsive supports;

— to advance equality rights under the Charter by sponsoring programmes and activities that aim to ameliorate conditions of disadvantaged individuals because of mental or physical disability.[35]

In the remainder of this section, I will briefly present the constitutional grounds for such transfers, as well as how they have been operationalised and how they could be used in the context of disability support.

The Federal Government can influence provincial policy by exercising its 'spending power'. Parliament has used its spending power to make conditional federal grants, which transfer funds to provinces on the condition that they are invested in specific social programmes or that the use of the funds meet certain criteria. The constitutional basis of this power is inferred from the federal authority to appropriate federal funds (section 106), to legislate over property (section 91.1A) and to levy taxes (section 91.3).[36] It can also be justified by Parliament and the legislatures' commitment to 'promoting equal opportunities for the well-being of Canadians', 'furthering economic development to reduce disparity in opportunities', and 'providing essential public services of reasonable quality to all Canadians'. This commitment is listed in section 36 of the Constitution Act 1982. Section 36 refers to equalisation payments, which ensures a uniform access to 'comparable levels of public services' across richer and poorer provinces. When it exercises its spending power, the Federal Government may seek to achieve 'implicit equalization'.[37]

Attaching conditions to monetary contributions could be seen as usurping provincial legislative power, insofar as this intervenes in areas of provincial authority and requires provinces to act in a particular way in order to obtain the funds. However, both federal and provincial levels of government accept this practice and the Supreme Court of Canada has recognised its validity.[38] By contrast, federal equalisation payments correcting fiscal disparities among provinces are unconditional.

In addition to the Equalization and Territorial Formula Financing programmes, the two main federal transfer payments are the 'Canada Health Transfer' (CHT)

[35] Ibid 105; M Prince, 'Inclusive Employment for Canadians with Disabilities: Toward a New Policy Framework and Agenda' (*IRPP Study*, 11 August 2016). Prince has nonetheless long been theorising the shortcomings of these transfers. For instance, commenting on the 'Labour Market Agreements for Persons with Disabilities' (LMAPDs) to improve access to employment, he noted in 2016 that these programmes were: 'a legacy commitment and for some time now have been a low priority' and that federal contributions had diminished. As noted by the OECD, these policies have been too piecemeal and their impact has not been sufficiently monitored. Prince (above) 11.

[36] Hogg (n 1) 6-17.

[37] Ibid 6-18.

[38] Ibid 6-20.

and the 'Canada Social Transfer' (CST).[39] CHT and CST find their origins in the 'Established Programs Financing' and the 'Canada Assistance Plan', which were the federal transfers in support of post-secondary education, social welfare, and health between 1977 and 1995. The Canada Assistance Plan originated in 1957, and co-existed with other health programmes, together constituting the earliest national programmes of social assistance.[40]

CHT is the largest block transfer to provinces. CHT 'payments are made on an equal per capita basis to provide comparable treatment for all Canadians, regardless of where they live' and aim at providing 'long-term predictable funding for health care'.[41] The contributions are conditional on provinces upholding the principles set out in the Canada Health Act, which are: '(a) public administration; (b) comprehensiveness; (c) universality; (d) portability; and (e) accessibility'.[42] The criteria of comprehensiveness[43] and universality[44] could be interpreted as requiring substantial and meaningful access to health-related care and support for persons with disabilities. However, Canada Health Act annual reports[45] do not specifically consider the difficulties some persons with disabilities face in accessing health care, either because of the built environment or because of financial constraints.[46] Moreover, while equality rights have been successfully deployed by persons with disabilities to claim access to medical resources available to non-disabled persons,[47] demands for funding for disability-specific programmes not already covered by Medicare have not been as successful.[48]

CST payments are also calculated on an equal per capita basis and aim to support 'post-secondary education, social assistance and social services, and

[39] Government of Canada, 'Federal Transfers to Provinces and Territories: Major Federal Transfers' (29 August 2019) www.canada.ca.

[40] Government of Canada, 'History of Health and Social Transfers' (15 December 2014) www.canada.ca; D Béland et al, 'Equalization and the Federal Transfer System' in D Béland et al (eds), *Fiscal Federalism and Equalization Policy in Canada: Political and Economic Dimensions* (University of Toronto Press, 2017).

[41] Department of Finance Canada, 'Canada Health Transfer: What is the Canada Health Transfer (CHT)?' (19 December 2011) www.canada.ca.

[42] Canada Health Act, RSC 1985, c C-6, s 7.

[43] Ibid s 9: 'In order to satisfy the criterion respecting comprehensiveness, the health care insurance plan of a province must insure all insured health services provided by hospitals, medical practitioners or dentists, and where the law of the province so permits, similar or additional services rendered by other health care practitioners.'

[44] Ibid s 10: 'In order to satisfy the criterion respecting universality, the health care insurance plan of a province must entitle one hundred per cent of the insured persons of the province to the insured health services provided for by the plan on uniform terms and conditions.'

[45] See eg Health Canada, 'Canada Health Act: Annual Report 2020–2021' (February 2022) www.canada.ca.

[46] Note that each province may offer a variety of disability supports to cover such needs. Consider for instance Government of Ontario, 'Assistive Devices Program' (9 March 2022) www.ontario.ca; and Gouvernement du Québec, 'Assistive Devices Programs for Persons with a Physical or Intellectual Disability or an Autism Spectrum Disorder (ASD)' (2022) www.quebec.ca.

[47] *Eldridge v British Columbia (Attorney General)* [1997] 3 SCR 624.

[48] *Auton (Guardian ad litem of) v British Columbia (Attorney General)* 2004 SCC 78.

early childhood development and early learning and childcare'.[49] CST payments approximate a third of CHT payments.[50] Whereas CHT aims at ensuring national minimum health care standards, CST aims at ensuring a minimum standard of social services across the country. Nonetheless, without clearly earmarked portions for disability-related needs, both programmes fall short of providing reliable disability support nationally.

A final illustration of intergovernmental cooperation closely connected to disability would be the 'Labour Market Transfer Agreements', which include two kinds of agreements: first, the 'Labour Market Development Agreements' (LMDAs), which 'provide Employment Insurance-funded skills training and employment supports to eligible individuals', and, secondly, the 'Workforce Development Agreements' (WDAs), which 'support provinces and territories in their delivery of employment and skills training programming' and consolidate former labour agreements, including the 'Labour Market Agreements for Persons with Disabilities' (LMAPDs).[51]

Commenting on the LMAPDs, Michael Prince noted that federal contributions had declined in the 2010s, that these agreements were 'renewed one year at a time, which undercuts planning for the longer term', and that they lacked 'evaluations and information dissemination'.[52] This lack of investment, reliability and transparency drew criticisms from the OECD, which found such disability reform to be 'piecemeal and with seemingly modest impact on employment outcomes'.[53] WDAs partly respond to some of these criticisms. Each of the individual agreements between Canada and the provinces provided that one of the areas of spending will be dedicated to 'support persons with disabilities to enter and stay in the labour market',[54] and each agreement stipulated specific amounts, or formulas to determine amounts, that must be allocated toward persons with disabilities, for a period ranging from 2017 to 2023.[55]

The specific shape of disability support transfers will surely keep evolving alongside more or less collaborative kinds of federalism and more or less austere political budgets.[56] Incidentally, NGOs and international bodies could

[49] Department of Finance Canada, 'Canada Social Transfer: What is the Canada Social Transfer (CST)?' (19 December 2011) www.canada.ca.

[50] Canada's Health Transfers amounted to 15.938 million dollars in 2022–2023 whereas the Social Transfers amounted to 45.208 million dollars. Department of Finance Canada, 'Federal Transfers to Provinces and Territories' (2 February 2017) www.canada.ca.

[51] Employment and Social Development Canada, 'Labour Market Transfer Agreements' (26 April 2022) www.canada.ca.

[52] Prince (n 35) 13.

[53] Ibid.

[54] See section 6.2(b) of each individual agreement, listed Employment and Social Development Canada, 'About the Workforce Development Agreement Program' (26 April 2022) www.canada.ca. See eg Employment and Social Development Canada, 'Canada – Newfoundland and Labrador Workforce Development Agreement' (8 January 2020) www.canada.ca.

[55] Ibid ss 12–13 of each individual agreement.

[56] Prince (n 18) 105–106.

strategically pressure the Federal Government to respond to disability funding needs by using its spending powers.[57]

V. THE LIMITED IMPACT OF THE CRPD ON THE DIVISION OF COMPETENCES BETWEEN FEDERAL AND REGIONAL GOVERNMENTS

As discussed above, the Federal Government has limited power to affect decision-making in disability-related areas falling under provincial and territorial jurisdiction. The CRPD has not changed this structural reality, and disability-related laws and programmes remain uneven throughout Canada. Still, many legal frameworks across Canada mirror each other, and the Charter ensures a certain uniformity, since all laws and programmes in Canada must be compatible with it. In this section, I briefly comment on certain areas of *de facto* harmonisation, albeit enduring divergences across levels of government and between regions remain.

A. Defining Disability

The Federal Government has stated that '[b]ecause of its complexity, there is no single, harmonized "operational" definition of disability across federal programs'.[58] That different public policies may focus on specific *dimensions* of disability does not prevent Canadian national and subnational governments from embracing a broad definition of disability and endorsing the World Health Organisation's and the CRPD's definitions. Thus, the Federal Government has stated that:

> Disability is a complex phenomenon, reflecting an interaction between features of a person's body and mind and features of the society in which they live. A disability can occur at any time in a person's life; some people are born with a disability, while others develop a disability later in life. It can be permanent, temporary or episodic. Disability can steadily worsen, remain the same, or improve. It can be very mild to very severe. It can be the cause, as well as the result, of disease, illness, injury, or substance abuse.[59]

[57] Women's civil society organisations recommended to the CRPD Committee that it 'urge Canada to use its funding power and other arrangements with the provinces and territories to set standards for social programs and services that will foster compliance with the provisions of the Convention on the Rights of Persons with Disabilities'. See Canadian Feminist Alliance for International Action (FAFIA) and the DisAbled Women's Action Network (DAWN Canada), 'Women with Disabilities in Canada: Report to the Committee on the Rights of Persons with Disabilities on the Occasion of the Committee's Initial Review of Canada' (February 2017) www.fafia-afai.org 5.

[58] Human Resources and Skills Development Canada, 'Federal Disability Reference Guide' (2013) www.canada.ca 2.

[59] Ibid.

Some legal definitions can be very broad, such as the definition found in the Accessible Canada Act,[60] while other definitions target specific groups within persons with disabilities, such as people with severe disabilities.[61] There is no legislative synchronisation of disability definitions across Canada, but the definition of disability within the context of anti-discrimination laws, to which I turn next, is relatively harmonious.

B. Non-Discrimination and Equality

Anti-discrimination legislation exists at both the federal and provincial levels and applies to private and public actors unduly discriminating against persons with disabilities. As listed in Table 1, each province or territory has a human rights code, and the Federal Government has its own human rights legislation, which encompass robust provisions on equality. Human rights legislation often creates a commission or tribunal to which individuals can bring a complaint of discrimination.

Table 1 Human Rights Legislation and Human Rights Tribunals and Commissions in Canada

Jurisdiction	Human Rights Legislation	Human Rights Tribunals and Commissions
Canada (federal)	Canadian Bill of Rights 1960	Canadian Human Rights Commission, Canadian Human Rights Tribunal
	Canadian Human Rights Act 1977	
	Canadian Charter of Rights and Freedoms 1982	
Newfoundland and Labrador	An Act Respecting Human Rights 2010	Newfoundland and Labrador Human Rights Commission, Human Rights Commission Panel of Adjudicators
	An Act Respecting Accessibility in the Province 2021	
Prince Edward Island	Prince Edward Island Human Rights Act 1968	Prince Edward Island Human Rights Commission
Nova Scotia	Human Rights Act 1989	Nova Scotia Human Rights Commission, Board of Inquiry

(continued)

[60] Accessible Canada Act, SC 2019, c 10, s 2.

[61] Consider eg Canada Pension Plan, RSC, 1985, c C-8, s 42(2) for its definition of disability as 'severe and prolonged' for purposes of eligibility under the Plan.

Table 1 *(Continued)*

Jurisdiction	Human Rights Legislation	Human Rights Tribunals and Commissions
	An Act Respecting Accessibility in Nova Scotia 2017	
New Brunswick	Human Rights Act 2011	New Brunswick Human Rights Commission
Quebec	Charte des droits et libertés de la personne 1975	Commission des droits de la personne et des droits de la jeunesse, Tribunal des droits de la personne
Ontario	Ontario Human Rights Code 1962	Ontario Human Rights Commission, Ontario Human Rights Tribunal
		Human Rights Legal Support Centre
Manitoba	Human Rights Code 1987	Manitoba Human Rights Commission
Saskatchewan	Saskatchewan Human Rights Code 2018	Saskatchewan Human Rights Commission
Alberta	Alberta Human Rights Act 2000	Alberta Human Rights Commission, Alberta Human Rights Tribunal
British Columbia	Human Rights Code 1996	British Columbia Office of the Human Rights Commissioner, British Columbia Human Rights Tribunal
Yukon	Human Rights Act 2002	Yukon Human Rights Commission, Human Rights Panel of Adjudicators
Northwest Territories	Human Rights Act 2002	Northwest Territories Human Rights Commission, Human Rights Adjudication Panel
Nunavut	Consolidation of Human Rights Act 2003	Nunavut Human Rights Tribunal

Each of these statutes protects persons with disabilities against discrimination. For instance, Quebec's Charter of Human Rights and Freedoms defines discrimination as the violation of the 'right to full and equal recognition and exercise of [one's] human rights and freedoms, without distinction, exclusion or preference based on … a handicap or the use of any means to palliate a handicap'.[62] Each provincial and territorial human rights statute, as well as the federal Canadian Human Rights Act, includes a similar right to equality.

The content of these protections is relatively uniform. Human rights statutes must protect equality rights in a way that is compatible with the Charter. With regard to this protection, the Supreme Court adopted a broad notion of disability, and held that people could qualify as having a 'disability', and therefore benefit from the protection of human rights legislation, even in the absence of a functional limitation.[63] The Court also held that even an erroneous perception of disability or impairment could be the cause of discrimination. However, complainants with disabilities still face obstacles before human rights tribunals, including denial that their condition qualifies as a 'disability' (e.g. a temporary illness with residual or sporadic effects), that it is causally linked to their accommodation needs, or that the service provider or employer is under an obligation to provide it. The CRPD has not had a major impact on these obstacles.

A federal or provincial human rights code would not be constitutional if the protection it afforded to persons with disabilities was less robust than the protection required by the Charter, opening the impugned statute to a declaration of invalidity from a court.[64] Hence the Charter or human rights codes[65] can be invoked to invalidate specific disability-related norms that contravene them. For instance, in *Ontario (Disability Support Program) v Tranchemontagne*,[66] the Ontario Court of Appeal held that the Ontario Disability Support Programs Act was discriminatory under the Ontario Human Rights Code for rendering people whose disability is due to a dependence on alcohol or drugs ineligible for income benefits.

C. Accessibility and Participation

As noted above, federal and provincial governments have a large degree of discretion in managing shared resources and in making social institutions and opportunities accessible to everyone.

Not all provinces have implemented legislation specifically addressing disability accessibility, although they may have several laws or programmes related to accessibility (see Table 2).

[62] Charter of Human Rights and Freedoms, CQLR c C-12, s 10.

[63] *Quebec (Commission des droits de la personne et des droits de la jeunesse) v Montréal (City); Quebec (Commission des droits de la personne et des droits de la jeunesse) v Boisbriand (City)* 2000 SCC 27.

[64] *Vriend v Alberta* [1998] 1 SCR 493.

[65] Such codes have a 'quasi-constitutional' status and will prevail over ordinary laws issued by the same government. For instance, s 47(2) of Ontario Human Rights Code, RSO 1990, c H19, stipulates that '[w]here a provision in an Act or regulation purports to require or authorize conduct that is a contravention of [the Human Rights Act], this [Human Rights] Act applies and prevails unless the Act or regulation specifically provides that it is to apply despite this Act'.

[66] *Ontario (Disability Support Program) v Tranchemontagne* 2010 ONCA 593.

Table 2 Accessibility Laws in Canada

Jurisdiction	**Legislation Title**
Canada (federal)	Accessible Canada Act 2019
Newfoundland and Labrador	An Act Respecting Accessibility in the Province 2021
Prince Edward Island	None
Nova Scotia	An Act Respecting Accessibility in Nova Scotia 2017
New Brunswick	None
Quebec	Act to Secure Handicapped Persons in the Exercise of Their Rights With a View to Achieving Social, School and Workplace Integration 2004
Ontario	The Accessibility for Ontarians with Disabilities Act 2005
	Ontarians with Disabilities Act 2001
Manitoba	The Accessibility for Manitobans Act 2013
Saskatchewan	In development
Alberta	In development
British Columbia	Accessible British Columbia 2021
Yukon	None
Northwest Territories	None
Nunavut	None

Among the provinces that have recently enacted disability accessibility statutes, one can note a great number of similarities. No province proceeds in isolation: each government benefits from the insights that other legislatures have developed when structuring disability-related norms. The disability community, made of both local and pan-Canadian NGOs, contribute to ensuring that the best of these insights are shared between legislatures, thus advancing a more inclusive legal culture across Canada. This 'cultural' uniformisation is not the result of specific constitutional obligations, but rather, of informal cooperative federalism.

Governments within Canada can also decide to collaborate with each other toward achieving the CRPD's ideals most effectively. The 2019 Accessible Canada Act would foster such collaboration, because it stipulates that the federal minister responsible for disability matters (currently the Minister of Employment, Workforce Development and Disability Inclusion) 'must make every reasonable effort to collaborate with provincial or territorial authorities with a view to coordinating efforts in relation to matters relating to accessibility'.[67]

[67] Accessible Canada Act (n 60) s 15.

In a general fashion, disability laws concerning accessibility, participation and welfare are more likely to become more uniform across Canada because of an increasingly disability-sensitive legal culture and in relation to constitutional or statutory human rights. This is because, as mentioned above, national and subnational governments have discretion in deciding how to best meet the needs of their constituencies. They cannot violate the Charter while doing so, but simply not providing the disability benefits, accessibility measures, or participatory programmes that another province is providing would probably not amount to a violation of Charter rights.

VI. THE IMPLEMENTATION OF ARTICLE 33 CRPD

In this section, I will present a brief critical assessment of Canada's undertaking to meet its obligations under Article 33 CRPD. At the outset, it is worth noting that Canada entered an interpretative declaration on Article 33(2) CRPD. According it, Canada interprets Article 33(2) 'as accommodating the situation of federal states where the implementation of the Convention will occur at more than one level of government and through a variety of mechanisms, including existing ones'.[68] This stipulation suggests that Canada will consider itself as having fulfilled its monitoring obligations under Article 33(2) CRPD even if it did not create new mechanisms or unify mechanisms across provincial and federal governments.

A. Canada's Initial Designation of Focal Points and Coordination Mechanisms

In its explanatory memorandum on the CRPD, tabled before the House of Commons in 2009,[69] the Federal Government explained that the ministerial responsibility for implementing the Convention would be devolved to:

1. the Minister of Foreign Affairs, insofar as international work is concerned;
2. the Minister of Human Resources and Skills Development, who would provide a *'focal point' of the Convention at the federal level*, through its Office for Disability Issues (ODI). The ODI would 'promot[e] coordination across government on disability policy and developing a strategy, in

[68] Canada, 'Declaration and Reservation to the Convention on the Rights of Persons with Disabilities' (19 May 2022) www.treaties.un.org.

[69] House of Commons, 'Explanatory Memorandum on the United Nations Convention on the Rights of Persons with Disabilities' (*Parliament of Canada*, December 2009). Notably, the explanatory memorandum also announced that '[n]o changes to federal legislation or policy were identified as required for ratification', but important federal and provincial disability and accessibility legislation have been introduced since 2009.

consultation with persons with disabilities and disability organizations, to ensure ongoing compliance with the Convention';[70]

3. the Minister of Justice, who would develop policies in relation to the Convention and 'provid[e] legal advice to all federal government departments and agencies';[71]
4. the Minister of Canadian Heritage, who would be 'responsible for promoting awareness, understanding and respect for the rights entrenched in the Convention … and for *coordinating work across jurisdictions on the preparation of Canada's periodic reports to the UN Committee*'. The Department of Canadian Heritage would also chair the Federal-Provincial-Territorial Continuing Committee of Officials on Human Rights (CCOHR), which would act as '*the focal point for discussions related to the Convention across jurisdictions*'.[72]

While the ODI would constitute the federal focal point, Canada was therefore proposing that various federal departments be involved in efforts towards implementing the CRPD while the provinces and territories would remain responsible for enforcing the Convention within their constitutional jurisdiction. The memorandum emphasised that this framework was the result of negotiation and that the '[p]rovinces and territories were consulted through the CCOHR during the negotiation, signature and ratification of the Convention'. The memorandum also somewhat alluded to the role of the Minister of Canadian Heritage as coordination mechanism.

It is worth noting that the UN High Commissioner for Human Rights had recommended that a human rights body be designated as focal point under Article 33(1) CRPD. This is because the Convention endorses a 'paradigm shift … on the understanding of disability away from the medical and social understanding to one of human rights'.[73] As a result, the High Commissioner recommended that the focal point reside within ministries responsible for justice and human rights, rather than the ministry of health or 'ministries of welfare and labour as is the practice in the majority of States parties'.[74] However, as discussed, Canada has not followed this suggestion as the Canadian ODI is situated within the Ministry of Human Resources and Skills Development.[75]

[70] Ibid. Emphasis added.

[71] Ibid.

[72] Ibid. Emphasis added.

[73] UN General Assembly, 'Thematic Study by the Office of the United Nations High Commissioner for Human Rights on the Structure and Role of National Mechanisms for the Implementation and Monitoring of the Convention on the Rights of Persons with Disabilities' A/HRC/13/29 para 27.

[74] Ibid.

[75] House of Commons (n 69). Office for Disability Issues (ODI) is currently one of the external programmes within Employment and Social Development Canada (ESDC), the federal department responsible for social programmes and the labour market. ESDC includes the Minister of Employment, Workforce Development and Disability Inclusion, the Minister of Families, Children and Social Development, as well as the Minister of Labour and the Minister of Seniors. Employment and Social Development Canada, 'Organizational Structure' (14 January 2022) www.canada.ca.

Moreover, as Table 3 shows, each province and territory has an office responsible for disability issues, which can be seen as acting as regional focal points. Taken together, these provincial and federal entities were intended to meet Canada's obligation to designate focal points under Article 33(1) CRPD.

Table 3 Main Offices Responsible for Disability Issues in Canada

Jurisdiction	Office	Responsible Ministry
Canada (federal)	Canadian Human Rights Commission	Department of Justice and Attorney General of Canada
	Accessibility Standards Canada	Ministry of Employment, Workforce Development and Disability Inclusion
Newfoundland and Labrador	Disability Policy Office	Department of Children, Seniors and Social Development
Prince Edward Island	AccessAbility Supports (formerly the Disability Support Program)	Department of Social Development and Housing
Nova Scotia	Disability Support Program	Department of Community Services
New Brunswick	Disability Support Program	Ministry of Social Development
	Premier's Council on Disabilities	Office of the Premier
Quebec	Office des personnes handicapées du Québec	Ministère de la Santé et des Services Sociaux
Ontario	Disability Support Program	Ministry of Children, Community and Social Services
	Accessibility Standards Advisory Council	Ministry for Seniors and Accessibility
Manitoba	Community Living disABILITY Services	Department of Families
	Manitoba Accessibility Office	Department of Families
Saskatchewan	Office of Disability Issues	Ministry of Social Services
Alberta	Advocate for Persons with Disabilities	Ministry of Community and Social Services
	Disability Advisory Forum	Ministry of Community and Social Services
	Premier's Council on the Status of Persons with Disabilities	Office of the Premier
British Columbia	Accessibility Directorate	Ministry of Social Development and Poverty Reduction
Yukon	Disability Services	Department of Health and Social Services

(continued)

Table 3 *(Continued)*

Jurisdiction	Office	Responsible Ministry
Northwest Territories	Services for Persons with Disabilities	Department of Health and Social Services
Nunavut	Not available	Not available

While I cannot carry out an examination of each regional focal point and implementation mechanism throughout Canada in this chapter, I can note the following institutional strengths and shortcomings. First, not all provinces have enacted a statute to address disability issues specifically, and those who have, have not all created a body to function as a focal point in a detailed manner. Secondly, many federal and provincial statutes give ministers or the Governor in Council the power or obligation to appoint persons and committees to propose accessibility standards, report on systemic issues, or act as inspectors to verify conformity with disability statutes.[76] This entails on the one hand territorial disparities, on the other, the coexistence of several bodies at federal and provincial levels with an array of tasks. Finally, many regional bodies, though not uniformly across Canada, have added the specific mandate of consulting with representatives of persons with disabilities to disability legislation, which corresponds to Canada's obligation under Article 33(3) CRPD.[77]

B. Monitoring Implementation in a Canadian Context

The above-mentioned explanatory memorandum also announced how Canada intended to meet its obligations, under Article 33(2) CRPD, of maintaining a framework of independent mechanisms that would effectively protect the rights covered by the CRPD. At the federal level, it proposed relying on the combination of existing 'elements, including government reporting and promotional activities' and on the 'human rights commissions and tribunals, the courts, public guardians and ombudspersons and civil society organizations across Canada'.[78] It would also rely on existing laws, policies and practices,

[76] Eg Accessible Canada Act (n 60) ss 17, 18, 111; Accessible British Columbia Act [SBC 2021] ch 19, ss 6-7; Accessibility for Manitobans Act, CCSM c A1 7, ss 13–14, 23–24, 39; Accessibility for Ontarians with Disabilities Act 2005 SO 2005 c 11, ss 14, 16, 18, 29-31; Nova Scotia's Accessibility Act, SNS 2017 ch 2, ss 45–46.

[77] Eg Accessible Canada Act (n 60) ss 23, 42; Accessible British Columbia Act (n 76) ss 7(2), 9(2), 16; Accessibility for Manitobans Act (n 76) ss 9(3), 15(2), 39(3); Accessibility for Ontarians with Disabilities Act (n 76) ss 4(1), 8(1), 14(1), 15(1), 29(1), 31(2); Act to Secure Handicapped Persons in the Exercise of Their Rights with a View to Achieving Social, School and Workplace Integration CQLR 2004 c 31, ss 1, 6; Nova Scotia's Accessibility Act (n 76) ss 7(1), 13(3), 19.

[78] Committee on the Rights of Persons with Disabilities (CRPD Committee), 'Consideration of reports submitted by States parties under article 35 of the Convention. Initial reports of States parties due in 2012 Canada' CRPD/C/CAN/1, 7 July 2015.

including, inter alia: constitutional and statutory protections of rights to equality and non-discrimination; awareness-raising measures; accessibility guidelines and standards; income support and tax measures; the Canada Social Transfer; and the Employment Equity Act.

This choice was stigmatised by the CRPD Committee, which expressed concern that the State Party had not designated an independent mechanism in its Concluding Observations.[79] It was further concerned about the absence of mechanisms to ensure the participation of persons with disabilities, through their representative organisations, in monitoring processes. Early on, Canada was also criticised for not having established a national mechanism to monitor and enforce international norms relating to human rights. A joint submission to the Human Rights Council for the 2013 Universal Periodic Review of Canada, entitled 'Empty Words and Double Standards: Canada's Failure to Respect and Uphold International Human Rights' demanded greater transparency and accountability in Canada's implementation of its international human rights obligations. They recommended the creation of a formal mechanism that would systematically review Canada's progress and shortcomings, and that Canada regularly submit plans to meet its obligations to the UN. They equally recommended that these mechanisms and processes be developed in consultation with, and continue involving, civil society and Aboriginal peoples, in addition to provincial/territorial governments.

One key issue of contention has been the proposed nomination of the Canadian Human Rights Commission (CHRC) as an independent national monitoring mechanism to meet Article 33(2) CRPD. The CHRC itself expressed that it was disposed to do so to the CRPD Committee on a few occasions.[80] The CHRC also produced a report monitoring the implementation of the CRPD in Canada in 2015, independently taking on the role that it wished the Federal Government to officially grant it.[81] It also gathered support from some disability NGOs and the Canadian Association of Statutory Human Rights Agencies to be designated as an independent mechanism to protect and promote the implementation of the CRPD.[82] However, Canada declined the CHRC's offer in 2015[83] and again in 2017.[84]

[79] CRPD Committee, 'Concluding observations on the initial report of Canada' CRPD/C/CAN/CO/1, 8 May 2017.

[80] CHRC, 'Submission to the Committee on the Rights of Persons with Disabilities in Advance of its Consideration of Canada's 1st Periodic Report' (July 2016) www.ohchr.org; CHRC, 'The Rights of Persons with Disabilities to Equality and Non-Discrimination: Monitoring the Implementation of the UN Convention of the Rights of Persons with Disabilities in Canada' (2015) www.chrc-ccdp.gc.ca.

[81] CHRC, 'Monitoring the Implementation' (n 80) 3.

[82] Ibid.

[83] CRPD Committee (n 78) para 44: 'After giving careful consideration to the offer by the Canadian Human Rights Commission to be designated to carry out monitoring functions in respect of the Convention, Canada determined that it could maintain and rely on existing mechanisms to fulfill its obligations under Article 33(2)'.

[84] 'Replies of Canada to the List of Issues' CRPD/C/CAN/Q/1/Add 1, 20 March 2017 para 85.

Further to the criticism from the CRPD Committee, which recommended that Canada 'formally appoint the CHRC as the independent monitoring mechanism under Article 33 of the Convention',[85] in 2019, the Federal Government eventually agreed to designate the CHRC as Canada's 'National Monitoring Mechanism'.[86] Disability NGOs have noted that the CHRC's success in this role will be assessed in light of how effectively it 'collaborate[s] with provincial and territorial statutory human rights institutions and consult[s] with disability communities', because 'the Commission cannot effectively fulfill this function … on a narrowly federal mandate'.[87]

C. Input from Civil Society and the CRPD Committee

Canada's performance under Article 33 received much criticism from civil society regarding a perceived failure to establish an independent domestic mechanism to monitor and oversee the implementation of the CRPD throughout Canada. Some NGOs expressed the view that 'assign[ing] responsibility for the CRPD to existing units in government that already have some responsibility for persons with disabilities' would not 'achieve the coordinated, independent oversight of implementation' required by Article 33 CRPD.[88] A parallel criticism is that Canada had 'not enacted legislation to implement the CRPD into Canadian domestic law', which means that Canadian courts cannot adjudicate the CRPD and apply it directly to cases.[89] Other criticisms related to the vagueness or inefficiency of certain measures Canada proposed. Imprecise declarations, achievements, or initiatives make it difficult for civil society, domestic governments, and the UN to monitor progress or violations effectively. For instance, Canada states that it supported projects 'to increase knowledge of the accessibility issues' without providing specific information 'as to *what* specific financial support has been allocated; whether the amount has increased or decreased over time; what specific types of projects have been undertaken; and what the actual impact has been'.[90]

Similarly, the Canadian Civil Society Report Group challenged Canada's broad claim that the disability community could 'take part in monitoring government initiatives'[91] by noting that the Federal Government only sought

[85] CRPD Committee (n 79).

[86] CHRC, 'Monitoring the Rights of Persons with Disabilities' (14 December 2021) www.chrc-ccdp.gc.ca.

[87] Canadian Civil Society Report Group, 'Parallel Report for Canada' (27 February 2017) www.cad.ca 32.

[88] FAFIA and DAWN Canada (n 57) 3, 5. See Canadian Civil Society Parallel Report Group, 'Suggested Questions for the List of Issues for Canada' (2016) www.ohchr.org 24; DAWN, 'Submission of CRPD Shadow Report' (28 February 2017) www.fafia-afai.org 45.

[89] Canadian Civil Society Parallel Report Group (n 88) 3.

[90] Ibid 3–4. Emphasis added.

[91] 'Replies of Canada to the List of Issues' CRPD/C/CAN/Q/1/Add 1, 20 March 2017 para 86.

comments on one draft of its report to the CRPD Committee.[92] A single consultation with stakeholders on any draft policy does not suffice to meet Article 33(3)'s obligation to involve civil society 'fully in the monitoring process'. The point of ongoing participation is to verify that proposed changes effectively resolve concerns expressed by persons with disabilities and their representatives.

VII. CONCLUDING REMARKS

Disability-related laws and programmes in Canada have not only evolved alongside historical contingencies and emancipatory models of disability permeating legal and political cultures. Since the early days of welfarist interventions after the Great Depression, the evolution of disability public policies in Canada has also been shaped by more or less collaborative forms of federalism and by constitutional challenges of federal and provincial/territorial exercises of power. This is because the needs, rights, and social and political statuses of persons with disabilities are situated at the intersection of provincial and federal legislative domains. Criticisms of disability policies –including weak enforcement, lack of consultation, and insufficient funding – make it clear why it was necessary to include a duty to concretely implement and monitor in the CRPD. Efficacious monitoring and consultation mechanisms will greatly contribute to ensuring that political good intentions translate from rhetoric to action.

This chapter reviewed areas of legislative authority, different modes of collaboration, and noted that both the federal and provincial/territorial governments have an important role to play in implementing the ideals and rights set out in the CRPD. Although new configurations of collaboration between levels of government may emerge in relation to disability, a realistic hope for the time being is that the Federal Government will lead by example, by collaborating with each province and territory to create uniform human rights and accessibility legislations throughout Canada – and provide incentives to do so. While pursuing longer-term goals of universal inclusion, the Federal Government can also play a key role in ensuring an immediate income floor to all persons with disabilities, thereby responding to the mutually supportive relationship between disability and poverty that inhibits equality and accessibility every day.

[92] Canadian Civil Society Parallel Report Group (n 88) 25.

9

India

Disability Rights in a 'Quasi' Federal Country

AMITA DHANDA

I. INTRODUCTION

THE ARCHAIC PERSPECTIVE on persons with disabilities and their rights in the Indian Constitution was displaced, or at least challenged, when India ratified the UN Convention on the Rights of Persons with Disabilities (CRPD) in October 2007. With this ratification, India made a commitment to adopt a more progressive approach towards the realisation of disability rights. Even though the constitutional text on disability remained unchanged, with the assumption of the CRPD obligations India set out to re-examine its statutory regime on disability and bring it into harmony with the CRPD.

Since India follows the dualist approach, international law becomes applicable in the country only after it has been expressly incorporated into municipal legislation. However, when it comes to human rights law, the Supreme Court of India has allowed for unmediated implementation. The fundamental rights guaranteed by the Indian Constitution and the human rights enshrined in the human rights conventions are considered in harmony with each other. Since these conventions were enriching rather than impoverishing the lives of the people, they could be drawn upon by courts even without express legislative incorporation.

Against this background, this chapter examines the nature of the changes and the influence of the ratification of the CRPD on India's federal structure. Since it is difficult to appreciate the change without knowing what existed before the CRPD prompted reform, after a short overview of India's constitutional structure, this recount of the India law reform story begins with a short narrative of the state of disability law and policy in India before the CRPD. This is followed by looking at the design and implementation of the post CRPD law.

The next section discusses how the CRPD paradigm has impacted on the concept of disability, non-discrimination and equality, accessibility and participation. This section also evaluates the Indian implementation design from the lens of Article 33 CRPD. The last section examines the role performed by courts in the realisation of the CRPD. I close the chapter with some reflections on the inter-relationship between India's federal structure and the CRPD.

II. INDIA AS A 'QUASI' FEDERAL COUNTRY

The Union and the states have been allocated dedicated parts in the text of the Indian Constitution. Part V of the Constitution spells out the powers and responsibilities of the Union executive, legislature and judiciary. The same is done in relation to the states in Part VI. Part XI of the Constitution addresses the relations between the Union and the states. This part addresses both legislative and administrative relations. In dividing the legislative powers, the Constitution exclusively allocates the subjects specified in the Union List to the Union[1] and the subjects included in the State List are within the jurisdiction of the states.[2] In the Concurrent List are subjects on which both the Union and the states can legislate.[3] Whilst the exclusivity of the Union is sacrosanct, there are circumstances in the Constitution when the Union can make laws for the states.[4] Even for matters specified in the State List, the law-making powers of the states are subject to the approval of their Governors. The Governor can provide or withhold consent, or even refer the matter for the consideration of the President.[5] The Governor is appointed at the pleasure of the President,[6] and is a representative of the Union government in the states. The fact that state governments must operate under the oversight of a Governor shows the limited autonomy available to the states. The Concurrent List signifies shared space with assured primacy to the Union, as it has been provided that a Union law would prevail over a state law.[7] State legislations can depart from Union legislation, but only with permission of the President.[8]

In detailing the administrative relations between the Union and the states, the states are required to employ their executive power to ensure compliance

[1] Art 246(1) of the Constitution of India states that Parliament has exclusive power to make laws with respect to any of the matters specified in List I or the Union List.

[2] Art 246(3) of the Constitution of India confers law-making powers on the states in relation to List II.

[3] Art 246(2) of the Constitution of India.

[4] Art 249 of the Constitution of India allows Parliament to legislate with respect to a matter in the State List in the national interest and Art 250 permits it in an emergency.

[5] Art 200 of the Constitution of India. Without the assent of the Governor, a state legislation cannot become law.

[6] Arts 155 and 156 of the Constitution of India state that a Governor shall be appointed by the President and hold office during their pleasure.

[7] Art 254(1) of the Constitution of India.

[8] Ibid Art 254(2).

with the laws made by Parliament and any other laws which apply to the state.[9] The executive power of the Union extends to issuing any directions to the state as the Union deems necessary.[10]

As already mentioned, there are separate law-making bodies in the Union and the states. The power to enforce these laws are also possessed by both the Union and the states. Whilst each state creates its own subordinate judiciary, the appellate court system is controlled by the central government. Each state has a High Court which is the topmost judicial body in the state.[11] The Supreme Court of India is the apex court for the entire country. Other than the original jurisdiction it possesses,[12] there is an option to seek special leave to appeal to the Supreme Court from any court or tribunal in the country.[13] There is a single system of courts for the laws made by both the Union and the states, and an option to move the Supreme Court whenever any fundamental right is breached. The High Court can be approached when a fundamental right or any other right has been denied. The High Court lays down the law for the state, whereas the judgments of the Supreme Court are the law of the land and binding on all courts in the country.[14]

The above description shows that states in India operate under the oversight of the Union. While the Union can step in the space of the states, a reciprocal prerogative is not available to the states. Rather, there is a supervisory gaze of the Union on the functioning of the states even when they are operating within their own territorial and subject space. Moreover, there are several procedures by which the government of a state can be disciplined and even unseated[15] by the Union. Due to the unceasing supervision of the Union, and the ever-present possibility of central rule replacing the government of a state, the Indian Constitution has commonly been described as a 'quasi' federal political system which is unitary in substance if not in form.

In the division of subject-matters between the Union and the states, disability finds mention in the State List. Entry 9 of List II allocates to the states the power of making laws and policies for 'the relief of the disabled and the unemployable'. Article 13 of the Constitution of India requires all law-making bodies, be it the Union or the states, to make laws in harmony with the Bill of Rights which stands incorporated in Part III of the Constitution. Any law made in breach of these rights is to the extent of contravention void. The Indian Constitution recognises that all persons are equal before the law and have equal protection of the law. In amplification of this right to equality, it also prohibits the state from discriminating against any citizen on grounds *only* of religion, race, caste,

[9] Ibid Art 256.
[10] Ibid Art 257.
[11] Ibid Art 214.
[12] Ibid Art 131.
[13] Ibid Art 136.
[14] Ibid Art 141.
[15] Ibid Art 356.

sex, place of birth or any of them. There is no mention of disabled people or of disability rights in the Union List.

III. LAW-MAKING ON DISABILITY BEFORE AND AFTER THE CRPD

The Constitution empowered the states to make laws for the relief of the disabled, but until 1995 when the first Union legislation on persons with disabilities was enacted, not a single state in the country had enacted a law providing for persons with disabilities. All of them chose to provide relief to disabled people through schemes and programmes which largely provided financial relief to persons with disabilities. The policy of providing financial relief was common across states even as the amounts granted as relief varied from state to state.

Relief provided by schemes, unlike statutory relief, does not create an entitlement: a scheme can be withdrawn or altered, depending upon the political preferences of the ruling government. In the early 1990s, in order to ensure a certitude to their claims, some disability groups started to agitate for a central statute on the rights of persons with disabilities. For a fair amount of time the demand was repelled by the Union government on the reasoning that disability was a subject in the State List and the jurisdiction to enact suitable law lay with the states. The disability community felt that to lobby for a law with different states was cumbersome, and hence they kept pushing for a central law.

Article 253 of the Constitution of India permits Parliament to override the division of powers between the states and the Union, and make law for the entire country in order to implement 'any treaty, agreement or convention with any other country or countries or any decision made at any international conference, association or other body'. Parliament relied upon this provision to implement the Proclamation on the Full Participation and Equality of Persons with Disabilities in the Asia Pacific Region adopted in Beijing in 1992 to enact the Persons with Disabilities (Equal Opportunity, Protection of Rights and Full Participation) Act in 1995 (PWDA).

Even as the statute was enacted by the Parliament of India, there were several provisions which placed the duties on the state governments to implement the central statute. Thus, the PWDA in acknowledgment of the cross-cutting dimension of disability required state governments to establish state coordination committees[16] and to appoint Commissioners who were to both oversee implementation and provide locally accessible grievance redress to persons with disabilities.[17] In order to adapt PWDA to its local situation, the statute also conferred rule-making powers on state governments.[18] The demand for the

[16] Persons with Disabilities (Equal Opportunity, Protection of Rights and Full Participation) Act (PWDA), s 13.

[17] PWDA, s 57.

[18] PWDA, s 73.

statute arose in order to strengthen the legal entitlements of persons with disabilities, but the PWDA primarily promised to make suitable schemes to realise the various rights recognised by the Act. The schemes did not have to be enacted by the Union government alone. PWDA allowed for the schemes to be made by the Union, state and local governments. The schematic option could have made the PWDA only a rosy promise. However, some powerful judicial interpretations and some alert advocacy rendered many aspirational promises of PWDA into non-negotiable obligations of the Government.[19]

The PWDA provided an exhaustive impairment-grounded definition of disability.[20] Persons with disabilities whose impairments were not incorporated in the statute were thereby ousted, a consequence which caused early agitation to amend the PWDA. The Union government set up a committee with members from major disability organisations to advise it on the matter.

The Report of the Amendment Committee, along with other memorandums of various disability groups, were still under consideration of the Union government when India signed and ratified the CRPD. After an unsuccessful effort to harmonise PWDA with the CRPD, the then government decided to enact a new law on the Rights of Persons with Disabilities. Yet again the law-making process was started by setting up a committee with dominant membership of disabled people and their organisations but also some representation from Union ministries and state governments. The Committee primarily operated as a civil society venture which after widespread consultation with the disabled people in the length and breadth of the country, submitted its report in 2011. This civil society report became the base document to which the government responded with multiple drafts and after a final scrutiny by a Parliamentary Committee a new law on the Rights of Persons with Disabilities was enacted in 2016 (Rights of Persons with Disabilities Act – RPDA).

In this round, the matter of jurisdiction did not figure in any discussion. It was taken for granted that since the law had to be made to fulfil the country's international obligations, the new law would be made by the Union Parliament. Even as opinions were sought from the state governments before the legislation was enacted, the states had no major role to play in the preparation of the text of the RPDA. Yet as with the PWDA, realisation of the mandate of the statute primarily resides with the states. The Coordination Committees have been replaced by Central and State Advisory Bodies and the office of Commissioners of Disabilities with powers of administrative oversight and grievance redress has been continued in the new legislation. In order to enable easier access to justice

[19] Thus, for example *National Federation of Blind v State of UP* WP No 361 of 2000 decided on 28 January 2000, where the Allahabad High Court insisted that if the statute mandated a scheme for concessional housing to be made, then the UP Government could not escape its statutory obligation by contending that no such scheme had been floated. The Government was directed to formulate a scheme and then provide concessional housing to the petitioners.

[20] PWDA, s 2(i) stated that disability means blindness, low-vision, leprosy-cured, hearing impairment, mental retardation, locomotor disability and mental illness.

for persons with disabilities the new statute also speaks of special courts, and a few states have obtained the approval of the High Courts to establish such special courts locally.

All laws for persons with disabilities in India have been made by Parliament, but responsibility for their implementation largely resides with the states. The normative content of the law is uniform in the country but the realisation of the norm varies from state to state. This variation reflects the varying commitment of the state governments to disability rights, and also the vibrancy of disabled people's organisations in a state. For example, Tamil Nadu has shown a higher commitment to disability rights both before and after the RPDA. The state has a strident disabled people's movement which has required the state government not only to honour its RPDA obligations, but also to take disabled people into account in formulating and implementing general policies. Thus, for example faced with massive floods in the city of Chennai, the civil society groups ensured that the state had to plan its rescue operations in an inclusive manner so that persons with disabilities were not left behind.[21]

IV. IMPLEMENTATION OF THE RPDA

A. The RPDA Implementation Design

Implementation of the RPDA is the joint responsibility of the Union and the states. The Union has a direct role to play in relation to territories which are not states but are termed Union territories. With regard to the states, the Union can ask, exhort, persuade and threaten, but the effectiveness of implementation in the states remains a matter of state choice. The manner in which the choice is exercised is greatly dependent on the relationship between the political parties governing at the centre and in the states. If both governments belong to the same political party, there is greater convergence. In recent times this reality is openly admitted by political leaders. In earlier times, governance obligations were at least spoken of as being above party politics. The fact that the Union provides funds for its own schemes and programmes is the proverbial carrot offered by the Union to obtain state compliance. A study of the law-making activities of the states shows that in situations of soured political relations even the funds are an insufficient incentive. Illustratively, the state of West Bengal has floated state welfare schemes which run parallel to Union schemes and the state has issued a circular which obligates civil servants to refer only to the state schemes.[22]

[21] N Sampath, 'How can Chennai make flood planning disability inclusive' (*The News Minute*, 19 November 2021).

[22] A Chakraborty, 'West Bengal' in A Dhanda and F Mustafa (eds), *Annual Survey of State Laws in India* (NALSAR University of Law, 2022) 214.

Since welfare schemes earn credit for the party in power, such directives are political efforts aimed at guarding goodwill.

Politics aside, it can be said that the implementation design of RPDA consists of the following components:

(i) The preamble to the statute explicitly states that the statute has been enacted in order to implement the obligations India undertook by ratifying the CRPD. The general principles of the CRPD have been expressly incorporated in the preamble. Rules of statutory interpretation provide that whenever the text is not clear, the preamble may be consulted in order to determine the intention of the legislature. The preamble makes the CRPD the decider of normative controversies. Whenever courts may need to choose between alternative courses of action, it would be expected that the preamble would compel them to make a CRPD consonant choice.[23]

(ii) Except for statutory provisions expressly conferring obligations on either the central[24] or state government,[25] the statute has placed the obligation of implementing the statute on 'the appropriate government'. Section 3(b)(i) defines appropriate government to mean the central government or any establishment wholly or substantially financed by that government and the cantonment board.[26] Section 3(b)(ii) states that appropriate government also means the state government or any establishment wholly or substantially financed by that government and any local authority other than the cantonment board. This manner of defining appropriate government makes it clear that the implementation of the RPDA – a legislation outlining the civil-political, socio-economic and cultural rights of persons with disabilities – is the joint responsibility of the Union, states and local authorities.[27]

(iii) Even as the appropriate governments are the prime duty bearers for enforcing the duties placed on them by the statute, the statute also requires

[23] The post-CRPD case law examined in the next section confirms this expectation.

[24] Central government is required to specify: the format in which equal opportunity policies have to be maintained under s 21(1); the manner in which a grievance redressal officer is meant to maintain the register of complaints under s 23(3); the composition of the High Support Assessment Board under s 38(2); the standards of accessibility for physical environment, transportation, information and communication and other facilities and services in urban and rural areas under s 40. Central government is also required to: grant extension of time to states for conforming with access norms under s 45; notify the guidelines for the purposes of assessing the degree of specified disability under s 56; constitute the Central Advisory Board under s 60; appoint the chief disability commissioner and two additional commissioners under s 74; in s 87, to maintain accounts of the National Fund for Disabilities established under s 86 and amend the schedule listing specified disabilities under s 99 of the Rights of Persons with Disabilities Act (RPDA).

[25] State governments are required to address the matter of limited guardianship in s 14 RPDA and to set up the District Level Committee on Disability and the State Fund for Disabilities.

[26] Cantonment boards are local authorities administering defence areas.

[27] Municipalities and panchayats are local authorities recognised by the Constitution of India in urban and rural areas respectively.

specialised institutions to concern themselves with disability.[28] Illustratively, section 8 places obligations on the national, state disaster management authorities to ensure inclusion of persons with disabilities in their disaster management activities and district disaster management authorities are required to maintain a record of all persons with disabilities residing in their district as well as inform them of any impending situations of risk. A similar design has been employed for access to justice, with national and state legal service authorities required to ensure that persons with disabilities are an integral part of all their schemes and programmes.[29]

(iv) Establishing specialised authorities and tasking them both with implementation and grievance redressal duties is the third strategy employed by the statute. The Chief Commissioner of Disability and the State Commissioner for disability are evident functionaries performing this role. In addition, executive magistrates have been expressly enjoined to act to provide protection upon coming to know that a person with disability was being subjected to abuse, violence or exploitation,[30] and to initiate criminal proceedings if the act complained of constitutes an offence.[31] Section 23 requires the appointment of a grievance redressal officer in every government establishment to address problems of discrimination in employment. Such officers have been designated as internal mechanisms to resolve disputes in an establishment. Persons aggrieved by these decisions have been provided the option to appeal to the District Level Committee on Disability. Article 6 provides that no person with disability shall be a subject of research except with their consent and the prior permission of the Committee for Research on Disability.

(v) The statute has made consultation and advice an integral part of its operation. These advisory operations have happened in two ways: one, by creating dedicated advisory bodies such as the Central[32] and State Advisory Boards[33] which are to be established to advise the Union and the states respectively. Provision has also been made for the creation of an advisory group to help the Chief Commissioner of Disability to undertake their duties.[34] Secondly, advice and consultation have been made integral to the performance of certain tasks. Thus, in several provisions[35]

[28] The duty of ensuring accessibility in voting has been placed on the Election Commission of India and State Election Commissions in RPDA, s 11. RPDA, s 30(2) places obligations of inclusion on sporting authorities.

[29] RPDA, s 12(3).

[30] RPDA, s 7(2) and (3).

[31] RPDA, s 7(5).

[32] RPDA, s 60.

[33] RPDA, s 66.

[34] RPDA, s 74(8).

[35] RPDA, s 27 requires the appropriate government and local authorities to consult with non-governmental organisations working for the cause of persons with disabilities before formulating rehabilitation policies.

the appropriate government is required to consult with civil society or the Chief Commissioner and State Commissioners of Disability[36] before performing the particular function. For example, the central government is obligated to consult with the Chief Commissioner of Disability before notifying the access standards under section 40 RPDA.

The above narrative drawn from the RPDA shows that the duty to implement the statute has been allocated to a range of entities from local to national level. The description also shows that provision for grievance redress has been made with near and distant officers. Whilst a grievance redressal officer is within an establishment the District Level Committee is territorially proximate. The Chief Commissioner and Commissioner for Disability have the power to act *suo motu* if they find a breach of the Act and authorities to whom they make recommendations are expected to either follow the recommendations or explain within a period of three months why they are unable to accept their recommendations.[37] In addition to these quasi-judicial authorities, the statute also envisages the creation of special public prosecutors[38] and special courts[39] to prosecute and adjudicate upon any offences committed against persons with disabilities.

In addition to the entities created under the RPDA, the various commissions for particular vulnerable groups, such as commissions for women and children and also the national and state human rights commissions, perceive protecting the human rights of persons with disabilities as an integral part of their mandate. However, as with the RPDA grievance redress bodies, the orders of these entities are persuasive rather than binding.

Even for the persuasive impact to take effect, it is necessary that the various entities, authorities, or bodies envisaged by the statute to perform a range of tasks should have been established. For state governments to perform their obligations under the RPDA, they need to have formulated the rules prescribing the procedures by which they aim to undertake their duties.

B. States' Implementation of the RPDA

India has 28 states. The minutes of the meeting of the Central Advisory Board on 24 June 2022 provided the following latest official information on the implementation of the RPDA. Except for the states of Andhra Pradesh and Maharashtra, all other states have notified the rules through which the state would implement the Act and constitute the State Advisory Board. Even as the majority of the states have notified the rules, the further initiatives required under the Act

[36] Exempting an establishment from the purview of reservation under the 2nd proviso of s 34 RPDA; planning awareness campaigns under RPDA, s 39.
[37] RPDA, ss 76 and 81.
[38] RPDA, s 85.
[39] RPDA, s 84.

are desultory and uneven. A State Fund for Persons with Disabilities has been constituted in only one state, Madhya Pradesh, and the process has been started in Assam and Telangana. In all other states, no move has been made. Special courts have been constituted in 24 states. Except for the state of Andhra Pradesh, all other states have Disability Commissioners in position but only 12 states have independent commissioners.[40] Provisioning of facilities for persons with disabilities with high support needs are not in place in any state and only the state of Assam has initiated the process. Except for the three states of Jharkhand, Madhya Pradesh and Telangana, no other state has established a Committee for Research on Disability. However, 22 states have a District Level Coordination Committee.

The RPDA requires states to undertake a range of programmatic initiatives to realise the civil-political, socio-economic and cultural rights of persons with disabilities. The statute is normatively ambitious and has envisaged a range of entities to help it realise its goals. The above paragraph shows that except for the Advisory Board and State Commissioner, states have only notified the compositions or qualifications of other bodies required to assist implementation. The creation of these bodies does not, without more, result in the realisation of the rights of persons with disabilities. The efforts of the Union in obtaining accountability have not been very successful, partly because the normative directives have not been accompanied with financial resources. Thus, for example, the RPDA requires states to establish a State Disability Fund for persons with disabilities. The provision establishing the National Fund clearly states where the money for the fund will come from, but the provision for the State Disability Fund leaves it to the states to establish the fund and to find resources for it. Consequently, except for one state, no other state has moved to establish a dedicated fund for persons with disabilities. The minutes of the 24 June 2022 Meeting of the Central Advisory Board record the exhortation of the Union Minister on enhancing disability pensions, sharing best practices and filing reports on rehabilitation programmes as required by the Supreme Court. Even as the CRPD prompted the enactment of RPDA, this section has described the general scheme of the statute and the manner in which its implementation has proceeded. The next section examines the effect of the CRPD in select key areas.

V. THE EFFECT OF THE CRPD IN SELECTED KEY AREAS

A. The Concept of Disability

Section 2(s) RPDA defines a person with disability as 'a person with long term physical, mental, intellectual or sensory impairment which, in interaction with

[40] The fact that this office also existed in the earlier statute, PWDA, may partly explain the high compliance with this provision.

barriers, hinders his full and effective participation in society equally with others'.[41] Section 2(c) RPDA defines 'barriers' to mean and include 'any factor including communicational, cultural, economic, environmental, institutional, political, social, attitudinal or structural factors which hampers the full and effective participation of persons with disabilities in society'.[42]

The RPDA, unlike the PWDA, has opted for a more expansive definition of disability. The schedule specifies five broad categories of disabilities and mentions as many as 21 impairments. Section 99 RPDA allows the central government to add to this list. The statute has viewed a person with a disability as being constructed by an interplay between impairments and barriers, however, the disability descriptions in the schedule of the RPDA are primarily medical. The connection between impairment and barriers is again made in section 2(l), which defines 'high support' and recognises that physical, psychological and other support may be needed by a person with a benchmark disability to participate in all areas of life.

The long list of disabilities which could keep growing has caused for the construction of the concept of benchmark disability. According to section 2(r) RPDA, a person with 40 per cent or more impairment for measurable impairments has been categorised as a person with a benchmark disability.[43] Affirmative action measures such as quotas in jobs and educational institutions are only available to persons with benchmark disabilities. However, the obligation of non-discrimination and the right to reasonable accommodation has been extended to all persons with disabilities. In its Concluding Observations on the Initial Report of India the Committee on the Rights of Persons with Disabilities (CRPD Committee) is concerned about the continuance of the medical model of disability and the requirements of multiple assessments and certification.[44] Whilst the requirement of certification has not been dropped, provision for an all-purpose[45] permanent disability card has been made.[46] In its 24 June 2022 meeting the Central Advisory Board notes that as many as 7.5 million all-purpose cards have been generated in 716 districts in the country. While the Committee's criticism of the pejorative language in both law and policy is undeniable, it may be pertinent to point out that in every major consultation with disability groups on the definition of disability, both before[47] and after the CRPD,[48] the use of a generic human rights definition of disability has been overwhelmingly rejected. Disability groups feel more secure in their entitlements if their condition is

[41] RPDA, s 2(s).
[42] RPDA, s 2(c).
[43] RPDA, s 2(r).
[44] Committee on the Rights of Persons with Disabilities (CRPD Committee), 'Concluding Observations on the Initial Report of India' (2019) www.ohchr.org 2.
[45] Rule 19 of the Rights of Persons with Disabilities Rules 2017.
[46] Ibid r 18(3).
[47] Report of the Amendment Committee on the PWDA (1999).
[48] Report on the Persons with Disabilities Bill 2011 (June 2011).

expressly named in the statute. A law, they opine, operates in a particular socio-cultural clime and rules need to be formulated in such a way that the rights recognised by the law can in fact be realised. Without a process of naming, all persons with invisible disabilities will be left to fend for themselves.

B. Non-Discrimination and Equality

The Indian Constitution recognises that all persons are equal before the law and have equal protection of the law. In amplification of this right to equality, the state is prohibited from discriminating against any citizen on grounds only of religion, race, caste, sex, place of birth or any of them. It may be noted that while all persons have the right to equality, the right to non-discrimination has only been conferred on citizens. In the long list of grounds on the basis of which differentiation is prohibited, disability does not find mention. Thus, discrimination on grounds of disability is not expressly prohibited by the Indian Constitution. Further, the subject heading on disability, as indicated above, primarily views disabled people as objects of welfare who are unemployable.

The RPDA goes further and formally proclaims that discrimination in relation to disability means:

> any distinction, exclusion, restriction on the basis of disability which is the purpose or effect of impairing or nullifying the recognition, enjoyment or exercise on an equal basis with others of all human rights and fundamental freedoms in the political, economic, social, cultural, civil or any other field and includes all forms of discrimination and denial of reasonable accommodation.[49]

This promise of equal enjoyment of human rights and freedom of the main provision is then qualified by a proviso which allows for departures by stating 'unless it is shown that the impugned act or omission is a proportionate means of achieving a legitimate aim'.[50] The CRPD Committee expressed its misgiving about this differentiation, particularly in light of the Indian Constitution's silence on discrimination on the ground of disability,[51] and further notes that intersectional discrimination is not addressed in the legislation.[52] In its recommendations the CRPD Committee asks India to draw from General Comment No 6 and so modify the existing law as to align it with the Convention and to ensure the elimination of direct and indirect discrimination on the ground of disability.[53]

The recommendations of the CRPD Committee are in order if only the text of the RPDA and the Indian Constitution are perused. It is important to

[49] RPDA, s 2(h).
[50] RPDA, s 3(3).
[51] CRPD Committee (n 44) 3.
[52] Ibid.
[53] Ibid.

note that the RPDA, unlike the PWDA, has explicitly recognised the civil and political rights of persons with disabilities. This inclusion has enhanced the non-negotiable content of the statute. Further, as the analysis in section VI of this chapter will more clearly show, the High Courts and Supreme Court in the country have interpreted the equality and non-discrimination rights of persons with disabilities by extrapolating from the constitutional jurisprudence of the right to equality. The proviso to section 3(3) RPDA has not impacted on judicial interpretation of the right to equality.

National Association of Blind v Bombay Municipal Corporation[54] related to a public interest litigation filed against a circular issued by the Municipal Corporation whereby it withdrew an earlier work from home directive and required its employees with disabilities to physically attend work. On their failure to do so, they would be treated as being on leave without pay. The petitioner informed the Bombay High Court that as a result of the directive a large number of blind employees were being driven to destitution as they could not reach work without assistance and the employer was not allowing them to work from home. The primary argument of the employer corporation was that public interest petitions could not be entertained in relation to service matters. The Bombay High Court found that the petition was not a camouflage to foster personal dispute. It then drew on the preamble of the RPDA to rule that the employees were being discriminated against, and allowed them to work from home.

C. Accessibility

The RPDA makes provision for accessibility measures in both chapters II and VIII. In chapter II, access to political participation[55] and access to justice[56] find mention. Here the statute has made accessibility of persons with disabilities to the electoral process an obligation of both the Election Commission of India and the respective state election commissions.[57] Since responsibility for administration of justice is shared between the central and the state governments, the responsibility has been placed on the appropriate government.[58] However, as in the case of elections, the obligation to provide legal aid has been placed on the authorities exclusively dealing with the matter, that is the national and state legal services authorities.[59]

Section 40 RPDA confers on the central government the power of laying down normative standards of accessibility of the physical environment,

[54] *National Association of Blind v Bombay Municipal Corporation* 2020 SCC Online Bom 2032.
[55] RPDA, s 11.
[56] Ibid s 12.
[57] Ibid s 11.
[58] Ibid s 12(1) and (2).
[59] Ibid s 12(3).

transportation, information and communications as well as appropriate systems and technologies, facilities and services in urban and rural areas.[60] The obligation to implement these normative standards by establishing suitable services or formulating appropriate schemes has been placed on the appropriate government.[61] Section 43 RPDA requires appropriate governments to make all print and electronic content accessible; electronic media is to provide for audio description, close captioning and sign language interpretation. India's ratification of the Marrakesh Treaty to Facilitate Access to Published Works for Persons who are Blind, Visually Impaired, or Otherwise Print Disabled in 2014[62] has also helped enhance accessibility of information, communications and cultural products.

Other than provisions which place duties on governments to render accessibility real, there are statutory provisions which direct all establishments to produce goods and provide services in accordance with the accessibility standards formulated by the central government. Section 44 prohibits the grant of a completion certificate to any structure if the building plan is not in accord with the accessibility standards laid by the central government. Rule 15 places a similar obligation on all establishments in relation to other accessibility norms[63] formulated by the central government.[64]

Normatively, the RPDA has made a decided move forward compared to its predecessor, the PWDA. The RPDA has expanded the areas in which accessibility must be ensured (while the PWDA only provided for accessibility in relation to education, transportation and access to records).[65]

On the whole, the RPDA has conferred the power of laying standards of accessibility on the central government; the implementation of these norms is shared between the central and state governments. In addition compliance obligations have been placed on establishments which according to section 2(i) includes all government and private establishments.

D. Participation

In responding to India's initial report, the CRPD Committee voiced its concern about the actual participation of disabled people and their organisations in decision-making processes and the ultimate effect of such participation.[66] The above examination of the provisions of the RPDA would show that the statute

[60] Ibid s 40.

[61] For the significance of this formulation, see section V above.

[62] CRPD Committee (n 44) 1.

[63] A rule has lower visibility than a statute. The fact that this directive is contained in the rules and not in the statute reduces its force and effectiveness.

[64] RPDA, ss 41–44 and 47–48.

[65] PWDA, ss 26, 35, 44 and 45.

[66] CRPD Committee (n 44) 2.

has accorded consultative status or membership rights to disabled people and their organisations. This induction seems to be fulfilling the formal requirement of the CRPD, as there is no obligation on the governments to defer to the views emanating from the disability community. The community has been able to have its voice heard not so much within the formal systems as outside them.

The Union government had started the law reform process in 2010 with the active involvement of civil society. Consultation on the draft made by that Committee was undertaken in the length and breadth of the country. The draft law was translated into every language of the Union and made available as audio cassettes and in Braille. The Committee submitted its Bill in 2011 duly acknowledging every suggestion it had incorporated in the final draft. In 2014, the Union government tried to rush through a greatly diluted disability rights legislation. The unrelenting protests of the sector caused the government to send the proposed law for further examination to a parliamentary committee. This committee had to do a fresh round of consultations, and only after substantial refurbishing the RPDA was enacted in 2016.

The CRPD Committee has asked the government to strengthen the participation of organisations of disabled people, including children with disabilities. It has however been found that participation has happened less by the initiative of the government and more by the assertion of the sector. An analysis of the civil society membership of the Central Advisory Committee as reconstituted on 12 October 2022 shows that whilst the body was geographically more representative, the presence of representatives of disabled people's organisations had reduced, with as many as five members being nominated from the same organisation. There is an obligation to consult with persons with disabilities in several governance institutions as well as in policy-making impacting on persons with disabilities. Courts have also, as the next section will show, insisted on the participation of persons with disabilities. Many a time, the persons nominated are only individuals with disabilities with little understanding of their larger political function. The individual participating may gain exposure but the representational objectives of the provision are defeated.

E. Article 33 CRPD

The previous section outlined the large number of entities engaged in the process of implementing the RPDA. Chapter XI RPDA establishes the Central and State Advisory Boards on Disability while Chapter XII RPDA provides for the establishment of Chief and State Commissioners for Persons with Disabilities.[67] The Central Advisory Board on Disability is tasked with consulting and advising the central government on policies, programmes and

[67] RPDA, ss 60–73 and 74–83.

legislation on disability.[68] Yet, it shall also review and coordinate the activities of Government Departments,[69] monitor and evaluate the impact of policies and legislation on persons with disabilities. Serving as a focal point,[70] State Advisory Boards are supposed to mirror this portfolio at the state level.[71]

Similarly, chapter XII designates the Chief Commissioner to identify and review provisions that are inconsistent with the RPDA or else factors that prevent the full enjoyment of rights by persons with disabilities.[72] Moreover, the Chief Commissioner must study treaties and international instruments to make recommendations on their most effective implementation at Union level.[73] The powers of the Chief Commissioner are set to be the same as those of a civil court.[74] Again, the State Commissioners mirror the tasks and powers at the state level.

Despite the promising sound of the Advisory Boards and Commissioners, the CRPD Committee in its Concluding Observations highlighted the lack of executive power of the Boards across departments and different sectors and its subsequent inability to ensure compliance with the CRPD.[75] In addition, the CRPD Committee point out that an independent monitoring mechanism in accordance with Article 33 CRPD seems to be missing.[76] The Committee recommends to strengthen the Advisory Boards, the coordination of focal points and to involve national and state human rights institutions in the independent monitoring mechanism.[77] The Committee found national monitoring weak because despite a plethora of authorities being charged with duties, none of them can demand enforcement. That role as of now is largely being performed by the Indian appellate judiciary, that is the state High Courts and the Supreme Court of India. The next section looks at how the unified judiciary of India has propelled the implementation of the CRPD-driven disability rights.

VI. ADJUDICATIVE REALISATION OF DISABILITY RIGHTS

In order to appreciate the role of courts in the realisation of disability rights, it is important to understand that the right to move the Supreme Court of India upon a fundamental right being deprived is itself a fundamental right.[78] High Courts also have powers to issue remedies in the form of writs to remedy any breach

[68] Ibid ss 65(1) and (2).
[69] Ibid s 65(2)(a).
[70] Ibid s 65(2)(f).
[71] Ibid s 75.
[72] Ibid.
[73] Ibid s 75(e).
[74] Ibid s 77(1).
[75] CRPD Committee (n 44) 16.
[76] Ibid.
[77] Ibid.
[78] Art 32 of the Constitution of India.

of fundamental or other rights.[79] In a landmark ruling on access to justice, the Supreme Court of India recognised how in the face of social-economic and educational disadvantage, the legal entitlement to move the Court was insufficient to ensure access to justice. Consequently, it permitted a public spirited individual or organisation to move the Court for redress when the fundamental rights of a socially and economically disadvantaged individual or group were infringed or denied.[80] This liberalisation of *locus standi* allowed the Court to take up the cause of the most marginalised individuals and groups. Applying this ruling to disability rights has meant that the deprivations of persons with disabilities were examined by courts even when the aggrieved persons were unable to move the courts themselves. The abysmal conditions of institutions housing persons with disabilities and the wrongful detention of persons with disabilities in prisons and mental hospitals gained the attention of the courts due to this liberalised process.

The dualist approach to international law and the Supreme Court's endorsement of unmediated implementation of human rights law enables courts to make more extensive use of conventions that India is party to. On the strength of this reasoning the Supreme Court, relying on the Convention for Elimination of Discrimination Against Women (CEDAW), formulated an elaborate set of guidelines to address the problem of sexual harassment in the workplace.[81] The Guidelines continued to occupy the field until they were replaced by legislation on the issue.

Both these developments have had an impact on disability rights. Disability rights jurisprudence emerges from both individual and public interest cases. In *Municipal Corporation of Mumbai v Shrirang*[82] Justice Chandrachud as judge of the Bombay High Court referred to a classification devised in *Entertainment Network v Super Cassette Industries Limited*[83] in order to elaborate on how international conventions influence domestic adjudication. According to the Supreme Court in *Super Cassettes*, courts have made use of international law:

> (i) as a means of interpretation; (ii) justification or fortification of a stance taken; (iii) to fulfil spirit of international obligation which India has entered into, when they are not in conflict with the existing domestic law; (iv) to reflect international changes and reflect the wider civilization; (v) to provide relief contained in a covenant but not in a national law; (vi) to fill gaps in law.[84]

The above classification, though not on all fours, has considerably assisted me in examining how the CRPD has been referred to in judicial decisions of Indian

[79] Art 226 of the Constitution of India.

[80] *SP Gupta v Union of India* AIR 1982 SC 149.

[81] *Vishakha v State of Rajasthan* AIR 1997 SC 3011. See also *Githa Hariharan v Reserve Bank of India* (1999) 2 SCC 228 for relying upon Convention for Elimination of Discrimination Against Women (CEDAW) to bring gender parity with regard to the law of guardianship.

[82] *Municipal Corporation of Mumbai v Shrirang* 2009 SCC Online Bom 1739.

[83] *Entertainment Network v Super Cassette Industries Limited* (2008) 9 SCALE 69.

[84] Ibid.

appellate courts. I am therefore using it with the caveat that judicial decisions could have been included in more than one category and some may be interpreted differently. I shall first examine those decisions which are covered by the above classification and then make some additional observations.

A. As a Means of Interpretation

This category contains those decisions where the courts have drawn upon the CRPD to add the pro-disability gloss and to amplify the spirit in the text of the law.

In *Vikas Kumar v UPSC*[85] the Supreme Court was required to pronounce upon an examinee's entitlement to a scribe while appearing for a civil services exam. The point of controversy was whether the facility was available to all persons with disabilities, or only to persons with benchmark disabilities. The Union Public Service Commission (UPSC), the authority in charge of conducting the exam, formulated very rigorous guidelines in order to ensure that an undeserving claimant should not access the support, and hence restricted access to a scribe to persons with benchmark disabilities.

The Supreme Court pointed to the fact that the RPDA was enacted to fulfil India's international obligations, and how reasonable accommodation had become a fundamental component of the right to equality and non-discrimination. The provision of a scribe was not largesse but a right, and the procedures for providing it had to be devised accordingly. Reasonable accommodation, the Supreme Court pointed out, is a departure from status quo so some avoidable complications were inevitable. However, to limit a right which should be available to all persons with disabilities to persons with benchmark disabilities was doing a disservice to the salutary purpose of the Act.[86]

Since reasonable accommodation is a right, its provision should not disadvantage a person with a disability. Thus, in a case involving the transfer request of a person with a disability, who lost seniority, as a departmental circular provided that transfers made at the request of the employee would result in loss of seniority, the Supreme Court quashed the decision of the state, ruling that 'all statutes, rules, regulations, byelaws, orders and circulars for the benefit of the physically disabled have to be given a purposive interpretation in harmony with the UNCRPD'.[87]

[85] *Vikas Kumar v UPSC* (2021) 5 SCC 370.

[86] On similar reasoning a person with dysgraphia was held entitled to the reasonable accommodation of extra time for appearing in a competitive exam in *Avni Prakash v National Testing Agency* 2021 SCC Online SC 1112. Since a retest was not possible, the Supreme Court suggested extrapolation of marks.

[87] *Net Ram Yadav v State of Rajasthan* 2022 SCC Online SC 1022. A similar exhortation to read the operative disability law in the light of the Convention was issued in *Deaf Employees Welfare Association v Union of India* (2014) 3 SCC 173 and the government asked to provide similar travel support to all its employees with disabilities.

And yet there were cases where subordinate legislation was at odds with the parent legislation and concomitantly with the CRPD. Both the RPDA and the PWDA protected the livelihood of a person who becomes disabled during the course of employment. Yet the notifications and circulars of organisations allowed for the automatic discharge of such employees. In a number of judicial decisions the Court had to step in to protect the rights of persons with acquired disabilities, be it colour blindness[88] or a psychosocial disability.[89]

Affirmative action programmes such as quotas have been read liberally, the reasoning being that the provisions have been included in the statute in order to promote inclusion of persons with disabilities. Hence the RPDA which has been enacted to further India's international obligations must be so read that the objective of the statute is advanced. Since the RPDA provides quotas for persons with benchmark psychosocial disabilities, the court must uphold the right[90] and reservation in jobs must also extend to positions which have the trappings of an appointment, such as a notary, even if it is not strictly a post.[91]

In *Jeeja Ghosh v Union of India*[92] the Supreme Court found that the CRPD obligations were not limited to governments but also applied to private entities. When a private airline wrongfully deboarded a person with cerebral palsy, the Court required the airline to monetarily compensate that person.

B. Buttressing and Fortification

I found around 50-odd appellate court decisions since India ratified the CRPD. Many of these were under the PWDA, as the new law came into force only in 2017. Even so, courts made ritualistic, ceremonial and persuasive references to the CRPD. This was done even when no logical connection was drawn between the CRPD and the final decision of the court. Thus, in *Suchita Srivastava v Chandigarh Administration*[93] the Supreme Court allowed a woman with intellectual disability to retain her foetus even when medical boards were opining otherwise, primarily on the reasoning that the Medical Termination of Pregnancy Act 1971 did not require a guardian's consent for persons with intellectual disability. For good measure, the Court also mentioned that India had ratified the CRPD.

If the judicial decisions under this head are further segregated, I find there is one batch of decisions where the High Court or Supreme Court are required

[88] *Vikas v State of Maharashtra* 2020 SCC Online Bom 801. See also *Bijoy Kumar v Tripura State Electricity Corporation* MANU/TR/0296/2022.

[89] *Ravinder K Dhariwal v Union of India* 2021 SCC Online SC 1293.

[90] *State of West Bengal v Tathagatha Ghosh* 2019 SCC Online Cal 3482.

[91] *R Ravi Kumar v Union of India* 2019 SCC Online Mad 9103.

[92] *Jeeja Ghosh v Union of India* (2016) 7 SCC 761.

[93] *Suchita Srivastava v Chandigarh Administration* (2009) II SCALE 813.

to interpret the structural provisions in relation to reservation in higher education institutions,[94] or quotas in jobs[95] or health care facilities for persons with thalassemia,[96] where the Patna High Court is primarily liberally reading the provisions of RPDA and reference is made to the CRPD to lend weight to the decision.

The other body of decisions relate to individuals with disabilities who need accommodation, be it failing to board a train because the compartments were locked[97] or unable to obtain a medical certificate because the hospital environment was hostile[98] or failing to obtain an essential educational qualification within the time limit fixed for non-disabled people.[99]

Whilst courts effectively used the CRPD and the preamble of the Act to buttress their decision, a similar consequence did not arise for the petitioners. Thus, the effort to obtain travel concessions for the speaking deaf[100] or the plea for increasing the age of retirement for disabled employees in Uttar Pradesh at par with employees of other states[101] were seen as policy questions and not a matter of discrimination which could be addressed by the courts. A decision which showed that courts were re-examining preconceptions related to driving licences for deaf persons,[102] where the Delhi High Court required the authorities to look at each applicant and not enforce a blanket disqualification.

C. To Provide Relief Contained in a Covenant but not in National Law

The legal capacity of persons with disabilities still represents an imbroglio in the special legislation of India. General laws routinely exclude persons with intellectual and psychosocial disability. Even for persons with sensory disabilities, their testimonial capacities are often suspect. In *Patan Jamal Vali v State of AP*[103] the Supreme Court addressed the scepticism surrounding the testimony of a blind victim of rape. The Court disagreed with the opinion expressed in

[94] *Court on its own motion v State of Himachal Pradesh* 2018 SCC Online HP 2897; *Sambhavana v University of Delhi* (2013) 14 SCC 781.

[95] *Pranay Kr Podder v State of Tripura* (2017) 13 SCC 351; *National Federation of Blind v High Court of Bombay* 2018 SCC Online Bom 931; *Sajin Balu v State of Kerala* Writ Petition No 34578 of 2017 decided on 18 February 2019; *State of Manipur v Yaiphaba* 2019 SCC Online Mani 162; *Purswami Ashutosh v Union of India* (2019) 14 SCC 422; *Anu Jaypal v State of Kerala* MANU/KE/1463/2022; *Volga v State of Kerala* MANU/KE/1822/2022.

[96] *Amit K Aggarwal v Union of India* 2021 SCC Online Pat 2777.

[97] *Court on its own motion v Union of India* 2017 SCC Online Del 9968.

[98] *TR Ramanathan v State of Tamilnadu* 2022 SCC Online Mad 3032.

[99] *Bank of Baroda v Susmita Saha* 2019 SCC Online 7846.

[100] *DS Chauhan v PIL Railway Board* (2012) 132 DRJ 905.

[101] *Smt Ramkali v Union of India* 2022 SCC Online All 565.

[102] *National Association for Deaf v Union of India* 2011 SCC Online Del 801.

[103] *Patan Jamal Vali v State of AP* 2021 SCC Online SC 343.

Mange v State of Haryana[104] on the usefulness of the testimony of a child deaf and dumb witness and said:

> [w]e are of the considered view that presumptions of such nature which construe disability as an incapacity to participate in the legal process reflect not only an inadequate understanding of how disability operates but may also result in miscarriage of justice. The legal personhood of persons with disability cannot be premised on societal stereotypes of their supposed inferiority which is an affront to their dignity and a negation of the principle of equality.[105]

D. Fill Gaps in Law

Here, I refer to two decisions which have drawn upon the CRPD to draw up a set of guidelines on the education rights of children with disabilities.[106] Interestingly, *Social Jurist v NCT Delhi*[107] concerned itself with education of persons with disabilities by just incorporating their concerns in the Right to Education Act. The two decisions make an interesting contrast, as the Delhi High Court decision adopts a very unproblematic line in relation to special educators and special education. A third decision which needs to be mentioned here is *M Sameeha Barvin v Joint Secretary Ministry of Youth*[108] which, relying on the CRPD, drew up an elaborate set of guidelines to protect and advance the participation in sports rights of women with disabilities.

E. Peeping Ableism

The above description does show that the courts have largely decided for persons with disabilities and in many decisions have walked the extra mile. Yet, barring a few judges who have been sensitive to the finer nuances of rights language and ideology, in most judgments, even the pro-disability ones, ableism keeps surfacing. Except for Justice Chandrachud who has openly questioned its use, the term 'suffering from disability' has been routinely employed. Neither the CRPD nor the RPDA have restricted their coverage to physical disability, but innumerable judgments have restricted the provisions of the statute and the Convention to persons with physical disability. It is this perspective which explains why the Calcutta High Court is unable to understand how there can be job reservation for persons with benchmark mental disability.[109] And Justice Hari Shankar of the

[104] *Mange v State of Haryana* (1979) 4 SCC 349.
[105] *Patan Jamal Vali v State of AP* 2021 SCC Online SC 343, Note 129.
[106] *Kamal Gupta v State of Uttarakhand* 2018 SCC Online Utt 677 and *Social Jurist v NCT of Delhi* ILR 2016 6 Del 308.
[107] *Social Jurist v NCT Delhi* ILR 2012 6 Del 308.
[108] *M Sameeha Barvin v Joint Secretary Ministry of Youth* 2021 SCC Online Mad 6456.
[109] *State of West Bengal v Tathagatha Ghosh* 2019 SCC Online Cal 3482.

Delhi High Court combines sexism with ableism when he routinely opines that the Court 'cannot allow its decision to be permeated by the warmth of Ms .... arguments' as 'cerebral palsy significantly affects quality of life of sufferer'.[110]

In *Jeeja Ghosh* the Supreme Court objected to her deboarding and the inhuman way in which the airline's staff behaved with her. Yet the patronising tone cannot be missed when they speak of the petitioner being a living example of what a person suffering from cerebral palsy can achieve: 'She has overcome her disability and become a responsible and valuable citizen of the country'.[111]

F. Seeking Accountability

After describing the norm-heavy law and the various implementation entities I also mentioned the travails of accountability and how it was difficult to find out how things are working on the ground. The Supreme Court of India has attempted to be a catalyst on this count. In *Sunanda Bhandare Foundation v Union of India*[112] the Court attempted to push for full implementation of the PWDA by asking the governments of states and Union territories to file compliance reports according to a standard template. These compliance reports were examined by the Court in *Justice Sunanda Bhandare Foundation v Union of India*,[113] where the Court made the reports a part of its judgment and commented that the chart filed pursuant to the directions shows that states failed in many respects to comply with the provisions of PWDA.

The Court also extracted the preamble of the RPDA in its judgment to acknowledge how the Act and the Convention had brought a sea change to the way in which they perceive disability rights. The Court did not desist from its duty of seeking accountability and in this judgment asked states and Union territories to now file compliance reports on their implementation of the RPDA. The Covid-19 pandemic and the consequent lockdown have perhaps slowed down this information-seeking exercise. Union legislation like the RPDA creates the same norms for the entire country. Since the states are duty-bound to implement the law made by the centre, possibilities of customisation of the law only arise in the manner in which the law is implemented. States have the opportunity to address the particular needs of their region and people by the schemes and programmes they devise. Once Union legislation has occupied a field the states cannot depart from that normative structure without the express approval of the Union. The cumbersomeness of that process thwarts any state efforts for innovation. What cannot be obtained by legislation is sometimes attempted through litigation. The *National Association of Blind v Bombay Municipal*

[110] *Akshansh Gupta v Department of Science and Technology* 2019 SCC Online Del 8034.

[111] *Jeeja Ghosh v Union of India* (2016) 7 SCC 761, Q at para 118.

[112] *Sunanda Bhandare Foundation v Union of India* (2014) 14 SCC 383.

[113] *Justice Sunanda Bhandare Foundation v Union of India* (2017) 14 SCC 1.

Corporation[114] case discussed earlier in the chapter shows how the High Court did not allow a local authority to deny people their just due.

VII. CONCLUSION

The above description of the making of law, its implementation and adjudication shows that whilst norm laying largely happens from the Union Parliament, implementation of those norms is the responsibility of several players. In order to evaluate the performance of these players, information has to be collected from each of them. The case law shows that many of the implementation bodies seem to be acting at cross-purposes and even if the superior norm is progressive and inclusive, the subordinate norms incorporated in lesser legal artefacts like notifications and circulars continue to adopt an excluding approach towards disability.

Similarly, the decisions of the appellate courts do correct the decisions of government establishments, local bodies and private players. Since not every person with a disability can move the apex courts to realise their rights, the Supreme Court seems to be symbolically upholding disability rights. I say symbolically because except for the petitioner whose case is in fact before the Court, the impact of the decisions of the courts in changing the everyday lives of persons with disabilities is uncertain.

Federalism is a preferred form of government if the principle of subsidiarity is inextricably woven in the functioning of the federation. To make the person closest to the issue responsible for its resolution requires trust in governance. The Indian system of governance being heavily centralised is hierarchical. A hierarchical system operates on command and control, the players higher in the hierarchy seeking reports from those lower in the pecking order. Ableist prejudices subsist both at the top and the bottom. Disabled people and their organisations have been involved in the various advisory bodies, be it with the central and state governments or the Chief Commissioner of Disability. Individual and representative actions have been filed with favourable results before courts. And courts have required various norm-making bodies to involve persons with disabilities in the rule-making and standard-setting exercise.[115] It is however a reactive system: nothing happens if no one is protesting.

As noted in the Introduction to this volume,[116] Article 4(5) CRPD requires that the provisions of the CRPD shall extend to all parts of federal states without

[114] *National Association of Blind v Bombay Municipal Corporation* 2020 SCC Online Bom 2032, Note 54.

[115] In *Jeeja Ghosh v Union of India* (2022) 1 SCC 202 the Supreme Court asked the aviation regulatory authorities to seek suggestions from disabled people while formulating the Regulations Carriage by Air of Persons with Disability and Persons with Reduced Mobility.

[116] See D Ferri, F Palermo and G Martinico, 'Introduction: Conceptual and Methodological Approaches' in this volume.

any limitations or exceptions. The above narrative shows that RPDA extends to all parts of India and there are no normative exceptions. It can therefore be asserted that India has met the CRPD mandate in form. The analysis also shows that the factual realisation of the CRPD could vary from state to state, as the states are not in the same place in relation to financial or social capital. Both the courts and the Union executive and the Central Advisory Board are attempting to remedy this situation by making exhortations at meetings, issuing directives and seeking reports. The substantive initiatives which could usher change in fact are largely absent. The present structure of the Indian Constitution only allows for the initiative to come from the Union, as self-driven initiatives from the states are difficult to both start and execute. The CRPD cannot alter this situation, as the formal requirement of Article 4(5) has been complied with. This chapter also shows the partial manner in which the task of national monitoring has been addressed, be it in creating focal points or involvement of civil society. The bodies are in place but they cannot be considered independent, and except to a minimal extent in relation to the Chief and State Commissioner,[117] there is no obligation on the part of the appropriate governments to respect the recommendations of the monitoring mechanisms. By an insistence on independent monitoring and government responsiveness to the monitoring bodies, the CRPD could enhance the accountability and collaboration quotient of Indian federalism.

[117] See RPDA, ss 76 and 81.

10

South Africa

Centralised Federalism and the Implementation of the CRPD

TINASHE C CHIGWATA AND ROBERT D NANIMA

I. INTRODUCTION

APPROXIMATELY 15 PER cent of the world's population, or over 1 billion people, have some form of disability,[1] with close to 80 per cent of this population from the Global South.[2] Statistics before the outbreak of the Covid-19 pandemic showed that 2.8 million of South Africa's population were persons with disabilities, accounting for about 7.4 per cent of the entire population.[3] While the figures are high, they do not include persons who are in institutional care or the affected children who are below the age of five. These numbers show the need to further investigate and address the rights of persons with disabilities in South Africa, considering international universal and regional law.[4] South Africa ratified the United Nations (UN) Convention on the Rights of Persons with Disabilities (CRPD) and its Optional Protocol in 2007, paving the way for its implementation. Since then, there have been only incremental legislative changes aimed at protecting and promoting the rights of people with disabilities. There is still no specific disability legislation that

[1] The World Bank, 'Disability Inclusion Overview' (14 April 2022) www.worldbank.org; N Kostanjsek et al, 'Counting Disability: Global and National Estimation' (2013) 35 *Disability and Rehabilitation* 1065, 1069.

[2] UN Department of Economic and Social Affairs – Disability, 'Factsheet on Persons with Disabilities' www.un.org; S Grech, 'Disability and Development: Critical Connections, Gaps and Contradictions' in S Grech and K Soldatic (eds), *Disability in the Global South* (Springer, 2016) 3–19.

[3] Department of Women, Youth and Persons with Disabilities (DWYPD), 'Disability Statistics' www.women.gov.za.

[4] This includes the African Charter on the Rights and Welfare of the Child, the African Commission on Human and Peoples Rights, among others.

domesticates the CRPD. This has, thus far, undermined the full realisation of rights of people with disabilities.

It is worth recalling that, as will be discussed further in the subsequent parts of the chapter, South Africa adopts a dualist approach to the application of international law. While the executive may sign, accede to or ratify an international instrument, this action has to be confirmed by the National Assembly (NA) and the National Council of Provinces (NCoP), the two chambers of South Africa's Parliament.[5] South Africa's multilevel system of government, based at national, provincial and local levels, is anchored on the principle of cooperative governance which emphasises integrated and collaborative rather than independent governance. Under this system, provinces enjoy limited legislative, financial and administrative autonomy to the extent that they mostly implement national laws and policies in practice. While local governments have significant autonomy relative to provinces, the autonomy is exercised within a framework determined by the national government, and is often not fully exploited.

Against this background, this chapter addresses the following questions: What is the meaning of the concept of disability in South Africa? How has the CRPD been implemented in South Africa's centralised federal state? What has been the role of the three spheres of government in its implementation? This chapter attempts to answer these questions relating to the rights of people with disabilities in South Africa, with a particular attention on the implementation of the CRPD and its impact on the relations between the centre, provinces and municipalities. All in all, the chapter argues that the implementation of the CRPD has thus far brought to the fore the centralised nature of South Africa's federal system. As in other areas of governance, the national government has defined the implementation framework for the realisation of rights of people with disabilities through legislation and policies, with provincial and local governments merely acting as implementing agencies. There have been no significant independent initiatives from provinces and municipalities aimed at implementing the CRPD, even though they have the room to do so, particularly the latter.

The contribution adopts the following structure. Section II discusses the division of competences among the three spheres of government in South Africa's centralised federal system. Section III examines the role of national vis-à-vis subnational entities in implementing provisions of the CRPD relating to non-discrimination, accessibility and participation. Section IV assesses the implementation of Article 33 CRPD, evaluating the role of the focal point, coordination mechanism and monitoring framework. Some concluding remarks will follow.

[5] See D Tladi, 'Interpretation and International Law in South African Courts: The Supreme Court of Appeal and the Al Bashir Saga' (2016) 16 *African Human Rights Law Journal* 310.

II. DIVISION OF COMPETENCES

A. South African Hybrid Federal State: An Overview

The 1996 Constitution does not state whether South Africa is a unitary or federal state. Scholars have classified South Africa variously as quasi-federal, hybrid federal, or centralised federal, because it has a system of government with both federal and unitary components.[6] The Constitution organises government at national, provincial and local levels, creating a multilevel system of government. The three spheres of government are bound together by the principle of cooperative governance, which is entrenched in Chapter 3 of the Constitution. The Constitution states that these spheres are 'distinctive, interdependent and interrelated'.[7] According to the Constitutional Court, this means that while each sphere of government is autonomous over its powers and functions:

> the functional areas allocated to each sphere cannot be seen in isolation of each other. They are all interrelated. None of these spheres of government nor any of the governments within each sphere have any independence from each other. Their interrelatedness and interdependence is such that they must ensure that while they do not tread on each other's toes, they understand that all of them perform governmental functions for the benefit of the people of the country as a whole.[8]

While cooperative governance denotes a relationship of equality among the three spheres, in practice the relationship is centrally dominated.

The hybrid federal state is a design that was negotiated between the 'centralists' and 'federalists' parties in South Africa's transition to democratic rule. The African National Congress (ANC) and broader anti-apartheid movement advocated for a unitary form of government to effect the much-needed socio-economic transformation and promote unity, among other reasons. On the other hand, the 'federalists', such as the National Party, pushed for federalism to accommodate ethnic diversity and contribute to limited government.[9] The national sphere of government consists of Parliament and the national executive. Parliament consists of two houses, the NA and the NCoP, which represents provinces. The provincial sphere of government is constituted of nine provincial governments, each with a provincial parliament and executive. Municipalities, currently 257 and each governed by an elected council, make up the local sphere of government. The national and provincial governments are democratically

[6] See eg N Steytler, 'South Africa: The Reluctant Hybrid Federal State' in J Loughlin, J Kincaid and W Swenden (eds), *Routledge Handbook of Regionalism and Federalism* (Routledge, 2013) 442; R Simeon and C Murray, 'Reforming Multi-level Government in South Africa' (2009) 43 *Canadian Journal of African Studies* 539.

[7] Constitution of the Republic of South Africa 1996 (Constitution) Section 40(1).

[8] *Independent Electoral Commission v Langeberg Municipality* 2001 (3) SA 925 (CC), 2001 (9) BCLR 883 (CC), para 26.

[9] Simeon and Murray (n 6) 539.

elected in a single election following the proportional representation (PR) system, while municipal councils are elected in a separate election under a mixed electoral system combining the majoritarian and the PR systems.

The ANC, which follows largely a centralist tradition of organisation and governance, has dominated the political landscape at all levels of government since 1994 when the first democratic elections were held. It has majorities in both houses of Parliament, eight of the nine provincial legislatures and most municipalities. This dominance has significantly shaped how institutions of multi-level government such as provinces and NCoP function. For instance, provinces are much more comfortable with adopting and implementing central government's decisions and initiatives rather than their own independent decisions, while the NCoP has largely been a rubberstamping body with decisions taken by the NA.[10] The political dominance of the ANC has progressively been eroded by opposition parties such as the Democratic Alliance (DA) and the Economic Freedom Fighters (EFF) eating into its political support. After garnering 69 per cent and 62.5 per cent of the national vote in the 1999 and 2014 national elections, respectively, the ANC only secured 57.5 per cent in the 2019 national elections and 47.9 per cent in the 2021 local government elections. Since 2009, the DA has made the second most prosperous province economically, the Western Cape, its political home.

B. Provinces

South Africa has nine provinces, namely Gauteng, Western Cape, Free State, North West, Limpopo, Mpumalanga, Eastern Cape, KwaZulu Natal and Northern Cape. While they are a separate sphere of government, provinces function under the national government's control, mainly because of the way in which the Constitution shares powers and functions among the three spheres of government, as well as due to the political dominance of the ANC.[11] Their functional areas, together with those of the national and local sphere of government are listed in Schedules 4 and 5 of the Constitution.[12] The functional areas that are not listed in any of these two Schedules, such as defence, customs, international relations and security services – the so-called residual functions – are a preserve for the national government. Most of the functions of provinces, as well as the most significant ones, are listed in Schedule 4A which provides functional areas of concurrent national and provincial legislative competence. The functions include: education at all levels, excluding tertiary education; welfare services; cultural matters; health services; housing; and disaster management. When there is a conflict between national and provincial legislation on any area

[10] Ibid 548.
[11] Steytler (n 6) 442.
[12] These Schedules follow the main text and contain supplementary information.

of concurrent competence, the national legislation that applies uniformly across the country prevails over a provincial law if it is necessary to promote national unity, for example, or if the national law is necessary to prevent unreasonable action by a province.[13]

On the other hand, Schedule 5A lists fewer functional areas of exclusive provincial legislative competence such as ambulance services, liquor licences, provincial cultural matters, provincial sport and provincial roads and traffic. However, the national Parliament may legislate on any of the exclusive functions of provinces if this is necessary to maintain economic unity or essential national standards, for example. The national government's override powers have however seldom been exercised, 'due to the dominance of the ANC in most provinces and limited provincial legislation'.[14] It is thus clear that the national government legislatively 'dominates' provinces.

The political aspects of federalism are 'effectively undercut by the fiscal provisions' which 'reflects the most centralised elements of the hybrid state'.[15] Provinces are not allowed to impose income tax, value added tax, general sales taxes, rates on property, customs duties or to impose a surcharge on any of these taxes. Importantly, the exercise of any provincial taxing authority is regulated by the national government.[16] This means that provinces do not have any direct constitutional power to tax. However, provinces, like national and local governments, are entitled to an equitable share of revenue raised nationally in each financial year.[17] The equitable share, which funds social services such as health and education, makes up most of the transfers to provinces. Overall, about 95 per cent of provincial budgets is funded through transfers, most of which are conditional.[18]

The autonomy of provinces is further weakened by the absence of significant administrative autonomy. Their employees as well as those of the national government are part of the single public service – which is subject to national wage-bargaining agreements. In *Premier, Western Cape v President of the Republic of South Africa and Another*, the Constitutional Court ruled that provinces can only exercise administrative powers within the scope determined by the Constitution and national legislation.[19] The national government is also empowered to supervise provinces by, among other ways, intervening to address any failures.[20] Given this political, legal and financial context, provinces have

[13] Constitution Section 146(2)(3).
[14] Steytler (n 6) 448.
[15] Ibid.
[16] Constitution Section 228.
[17] Constitution Section 214.
[18] National Treasury, 'Division of Revenue and Spending by Provinces and Municipalities. 2022 Budget Review' www.treasury.gov.za 72.
[19] See *Premier, Western Cape v President of the Republic of South Africa and Another* [1999] ZACC 2.
[20] Constitution Section 100.

been willing implementors of national policy. However, the Western Cape (the only province not governed by the ANC) has in limited circumstances opposed the national government, for example, with regards to the national HIV/AIDS policy.[21] In practice, the delivery of public services by most provinces in areas such as education and health is poor due to incapacity, mismanagement and corruption, among other ills. The frequent calls for review of the role of provinces should, therefore, be understood against this background.

C. Local Government

The local sphere of government, which is constituted by metropolitan, district and local municipalities of different sizes, is more autonomous than provinces. Metropolitan municipalities are the largest and govern South Africa's biggest cities such as Johannesburg, Cape Town and Durban. The city of Johannesburg has a budget bigger than that of the Northern Cape Province, for example. Local government's functional areas are listed in Part B of both Schedules. Schedule 4B lists building regulations, childcare facilities, local tourism, municipal health services and municipal public transport, while Schedule 5B lists local amenities, local sport facilities, markets, municipal roads, and traffic and parking, among others. The national and provincial governments are required to supervise the undertaking of local functions through regulation, monitoring and support. In exceptional circumstances, provinces can intervene to address municipal failures regarding the delivery of these functions. The national government can also intervene legislatively on local matters if it is necessary to maintain economic unity, for example. Thus, in this regard the powers of municipalities are even more qualified than the power of provinces.[22]

The Constitution requires the national and provincial governments to assign the administration of a matter listed in Schedule 4A or Schedule 5A 'which necessarily relates to local government if that matter would most effectively be administered locally; and the municipality has the capacity to administer it'.[23] Municipalities also have a right to exercise incidental functions – which are 'any power concerning a matter reasonably necessary for, or incidental to, the effective performance of its functions'.[24] This means that municipalities may exercise powers outside of Schedule 4B and Schedule 5B if such powers are necessary for the effective performance of local government's functions. These powers should not, however, be interpreted as giving a local government a new set of responsibilities but enabling municipalities to perform their existing functions.

[21] Steytler (n 6) 449.
[22] Simeon and Murray (n 6) 544.
[23] Constitution Section 156(4).
[24] Constitution Section 156(5).

Municipalities adopt bylaws. A bylaw that conflicts with national or provincial legislation is invalid. However, the national or provincial governments, through legislation or other means, may not 'compromise or impede a municipality's ability or right to exercise its powers or perform its functions'.[25]

Unlike provinces, municipalities have significant fiscal and administrative autonomy. The Constitution directly assigns them resource-raising powers such as property rates and surcharges on fees for services municipalities provide.[26] This has enabled bigger cities to raise around 81 per cent of their budgets from their own sources. In contrast, small, poor and often rural municipalities are only able to raise about 28 per cent.[27] As a result, they rely on transfers, mainly the equitable share, designed to subsidise the delivery of services to poor households, to fund their operations.[28] Municipalities have the autonomy to appoint staff and determine their internal organisation and procedures.[29] Fiscal and administrative powers are both exercised within a framework determined by national legislation to the extent permitted by the Constitution. Despite having strong political, financial and administrative autonomy, municipalities are in the 'main still implementers of national priorities' in areas such as the delivery of free basic services to the poor.[30] Only a few of them are functional, with a majority struggling to keep afloat or being dysfunctional. The National Treasury attributes the failure of municipalities to deliver public service to poor governance, financial mismanagement and insufficient capacity.[31]

In conclusion, whereas provinces and municipalities 'are intended to play some autonomous role in development, the broader model is one of national legislative leadership and direction, with lower levels chiefly focused on implementation and delivery of nationally mandated programs'.[32] The national government has the legislative, financial and administrative instruments to limit policy innovation and experimentation particularly by provinces. The dominance of the centralised ANC has also undercut the federal elements. Hence, provinces cannot effectively check the national government, raising questions whether they are really a level of government or mere level of administration. On the other hand, municipalities are yet to fully exploit their legislative powers due to many reasons such as incapacity. In addition, municipalities are also preoccupied with implementing national laws and decisions.

[25] Constitution Section 151(4).
[26] Constitution Section 229(1).
[27] Department of Statistics South Africa, 'Municipal dependence on national government financing' (29 July 2021) www.statssa.gov.za.
[28] National Treasury (n 18) 74.
[29] Constitution Section 160.
[30] Steytler (n 6) 450.
[31] National Treasury (n 18) 76.
[32] Simeon and Murray (n 6) 543.

III. THE ROLE OF THE NATIONAL GOVERNMENT VIS-À-VIS SUBNATIONAL ENTITIES IN SELECTED AREAS

A. The Concept of Disability in the South African Context

The concept of disability is defined in various national laws and policies. The Employment Equity Act states that 'people with disabilities are people who have a long-term or recurring physical, including sensory, or mental impairment which substantially limits their prospect of entry into or advancement in employment'.[33] As is discernible from the scope of the Act, this definition is limited to the employment sphere. With regard to transportation and accessibility of vehicles, the National Land Transport Act defines a person with disabilities as 'one whose mobility is restricted by temporary or permanent physical or mental disability, and includes the very young, the blind or partially-sighted and the deaf or hard of hearing'.[34] This definition limits its application to physical or mental disability to the exclusion of other forms like intellectual disability.

The national Department of Social Development produced and adopted a Policy Paper on Disability in 2009.[35] The Policy Paper does not give a prescriptive definition of disability but adopts a social-contextual understanding.[36] According to the Policy Paper, disability occurs due to interactions between individuals and the environment that hamper fair participation, aligning the Policy Paper with Article 1(2) CRPD.[37] This creates a problem in the contextual application of the policy because of this wide understanding. The Policy Paper also applies a spectrum to determine disability – from moderate to severe limitation to a person 'with physical, sensory, communication, intellectual or mental impairment, to function or to perform daily activities as a result of limitations/barriers which may be due to economic, physical, social, attitudinal and/or cultural factors'.[38] This conceptualisation in the Policy Paper is more comprehensive than the definition in the Employment Equity Act.

A different tone that is even more aligned to the CRPD is evident in the White Paper on the Rights of Persons with Disabilities of 2015 (WPRPD), which defines disability as a societal imposition of a status on a person with physical, psychosocial, intellectual, neurological and/or sensory impairment.[39] As a consequence of such status, the person is denied access to full participation in

[33] Employment Equity Act 55 of 1998, s 1.

[34] National Transport Act 5 of 2009, s 1.

[35] Department of Social Development, 'Social development to launch policy' (17 March 2009) www.gov.za.

[36] See the Introduction to this volume.

[37] Department of Social Development, 'Policy on Disability' (4 September 2013) www.western-cape.gov.za.

[38] Ibid 47.

[39] Department of Social Development, 'White Paper on the Rights of Persons with Disabilities' (WPRPD) Government Gazette No 39792, 9 March 2016, 4.

all aspects of life where society is unable to uphold his or her rights and specific needs and faces three interrelated social, psychological and structural barriers.

Further, South Africa recognises the application of both international law and foreign law.[40] South African courts are mandated and empowered to consider these two sources when interpreting the Bill of Rights. This adds credibility to the application of international, regional and foreign law concerning matters of persons with disabilities.[41] For instance, in *Damons v City of Cape Town*, the court recognised the critical role of international law in interpreting South Africa's legislation.[42] It also drew persuasion from the Canadian jurisprudence on reasonable accommodation in *County of Brant v OPSEU*,[43] to the effect that an employer is not entitled to require or expect a disabled employee to perform all the normal functions of the regular job, and where necessary, a disabled employee must even be excused from jobs that require hardship.

Developments at the UN level have embraced a broad concept of disability including a range of impairments (intellectual, physical, and medical conditions or illness, among others) in interaction with external barriers.[44] In particular, while the CRPD does not include a definition of disability in its Article 2,[45] it encompassed a contextual-based approach to disability.[46]

Regional human rights instruments adopt varying approaches to disability. The most recent Protocol to the African Charter on the Rights of Persons

[40] According to the Constitution 1998, Section 39(1)(b), the courts are mandated and empowered, when interpreting the Bill of Rights to consider international law. The application of foreign law is provided for in Section 39(1)(c).

[41] *Damons v City of Cape Town* [2022] ZACC 13.

[42] Ibid para 47. It stated that since the CRPD may require domestication, it guides the interpretation of the Employment Equity Act 55 of 1998.

[43] *County of Brant v OPSEU* (2013) ONSC 1955.

[44] See the definition in the UN General Assembly, 'Standard Rules on the Equalisation of Opportunities for Persons with Disabilities' (1993) A/RES/48/96, para 17. See also UN Committee on Economic, Social and Cultural Rights, 'General Comment 5: Persons with Disabilities' (1994) E/1995/22, para 3.

[45] A look at the drafting history of the CRPD shows that the drafters intended not to include a definition to avoid a situation that would stifle the jurisprudential development of the understanding of the term 'disability'. Ad Hoc Committee, 'Report of the third session of the Ad Hoc Committee on a Comprehensive and Integral International Convention on Protection and Promotion of the Rights and Dignity of Persons with Disabilities' A/AC.265/2004/5, 9 June 2004, Item 12. MK Ande, 'The Right to Alternative Care of Children with Disabilities in Ethiopia and South Africa' (Unpublished doctoral thesis, University of the Western Cape, 2020) 21. See also V Della Fina, 'Article 1 [Purpose]' in V Della Fina, R Cera and G Palmisano (eds), *The United Nations Convention on the Rights of Persons with Disabilities: A Commentary* (Springer, 2017) 95; Ad Hoc Committee, 'Report of the Ad Hoc Committee on a Comprehensive and Integral International Convention on the Protection and Promotion of the Rights and Dignity of Persons with Disabilities on its sixth session' A/60/266, 17 August 2005, 24.

[46] The CRPD's use of a descriptive approach regarding persons with disabilities in an open-ended fashion can accommodate differing perceptions of disability, subject to evolution and different sociocultural contexts. To this end, the preamble to the CRPD recognises disability as 'an evolving concept' that predominantly obtains constructions from the interaction between persons with impairments, and attitudinal and environmental barriers that affect their full and effective participation in society on an equal basis with others.

with Disabilities (African Disabilities Protocol), which was ratified by the South African Parliament in May 2022 but has yet to enter into force, aligns with the CRPD since it states that persons with disabilities include those with physical, mental, psycho-social, intellectual, neurological, developmental or other sensory impairments which in interaction with environmental, attitudinal or other barriers hinder their full and effective participation in society on an equal basis with others.[47] The Protocol hence suggests that disability should encompass a non-closed list of impairments that include the five mentioned above, and that disability derives from the interaction with various barriers which arise in different areas of life. The yardstick for measuring the existence of these barriers is inclusive equality.[48]

From the above, it emerges that there are various definitions of disability in various national laws and policies which are utilised across the three spheres of government. As such, there have not been attempts to harmonise the definitions of 'disability' given the absence of the alternative definitions at subnational level. However, there have been attempts to harmonise national and international definitions of disability through the WPRPD.

B. Non-Discrimination and Equality

Regarding non-discrimination, the Constitution has a Bill of Rights that encompasses specific rights that are instructive in the promotion and protection of the rights of persons with disabilities. These include equality before the law,[49] human dignity,[50] life,[51] privacy,[52] and healthcare.[53] The Bill of Rights offers normative guidance on the promotion and protection of the rights of persons with disabilities, by embracing the non-discrimination principle and providing for the right to equality before the law and everyone's equal protection under the law.[54]

In compliance with the provisions included in the Bill of Rights, South Africa should take a non-closed list of measures that include both legislative and other measures to protect, and advance persons who are disadvantaged by unfair discrimination on various grounds including disability.[55] Further, the Constitution makes the state a duty bearer and prohibits it from violating the

[47] African Union, 'Protocol to the African Charter on Human and Peoples' Rights on the Rights of Persons with Disabilities in Africa' (2018) (African Disability Protocol), Art 1.

[48] CRPD Committee, 'General Comment No. 6 on equality and non-discrimination' (2018) CRPD/C/GC/6.

[49] Constitution Section 9.

[50] Constitution Section 10.

[51] Constitution Section 11.

[52] Constitution Section 14.

[53] Constitution Section 27.

[54] Constitution Section 9.

[55] Constitution Section 9(2).

rights of an individual through discrimination.[56] The Constitution also makes everyone a duty bearer concerning the prohibition of both direct and indirect discrimination.[57] In this respect, it is argued that the Constitution envisages substantive equality that seeks to correct both social and economic disparities on account of historical reasons.[58] The only exception to the application of non-discrimination is where a differential treatment is proven to be fair.[59] From a legislative perspective, South Africa has the Promotion of Equality and Prevention of Unfair Discrimination Act which is a national law enacted according to Section 9(4) of the Constitution to deal with elements that stifle the impediment that affects persons with disabilities.[60]

In addition, the CRPD recognises the principle of non-discrimination as a cornerstone in the promotion and protection of the rights of persons with disabilities. It provides that discrimination occurs where there is 'distinction, exclusion or restriction based on a disability', that consequently impairs 'the recognition, enjoyment or exercise, on an equal basis with others, of all human rights and fundamental freedoms in the political, economic, social, cultural, civil or any other field'.[61] Reasonable accommodation is essential to counteract possible discriminatory practices against persons with disabilities as far as it calls for refashioning the world such that persons with disabilities have the same rights as everyone. Closely related to the above is the use of the principle of accessibility to ensure that persons with disabilities live independently and participate fully and equally in society.[62] This principle goes beyond the notion of physical accessibility to the nature and proximity of services.[63]

A look at the wording of the Constitution is suggestive of the fact that the three spheres of government have responsibilities to ensure equality. Section 9(3) of the Constitution states:

> [t]he state may not unfairly discriminate directly or indirectly against anyone on one or more grounds, including race, gender, sex, pregnancy, marital status, ethnic or social origin, colour, sexual orientation, age, disability, religion, conscience, belief, culture, language and birth.

Thus, all three spheres of government as well as the judiciary have a role to play in this regard. The national government is mandated to give policy direction to

[56] Constitution Section 9(4).

[57] Ibid.

[58] A Catherine, 'Substantive Equality and Transformation in South Africa' (2007) 23 *South African Journal on Human Rights* 254–58.

[59] This is subject to the limitation test. See *Harksen v Lane NO and Others* 1998 (1) SA 300 (CC), para 53.

[60] Section 9(c) Promotion of Equality and Prevention of Unfair Discrimination Act of 2000 (PEPUDA or the Equality Act, Act No 4 of 2000).

[61] Art 2 CRPD.

[62] Constitution Section 9. See also CRPD Committee, 'General Comment No. 2 on accessibility' (2014) CRPD/C/GC/2, para 1.

[63] Constitution Section 9.

its departments and to provincial and local governments on specified issues.[64] Various national policies that have been adopted to promote equality include the National Gender Policy Framework for various departments.[65] In addition, there are various laws that speak to equality. These include the Promotion of Equality and Prevention of Unfair Discrimination Act,[66] and the Employment Equity Act.[67] A couple of shortfalls are available on this front. However, these Acts were enacted before the ratification of the CRPD in 2007. Thus, they do not operationalise the CRPD fully. Some legislation has been enacted at the national level with patches of aspects of equality and non-discrimination. The Prevention and Combating of Trafficking in Persons Act, for example, is thin on aspects on equality and non-discrimination.[68] However, from a protectional perspective, it prohibits the abuse on any individual based on their disability.[69] This protection also extends to aspects of sentencing of persons who have been convicted where the consideration of the sentence should take into consideration the physical disability of an individual.[70] The shortfall remains evident in the normative limitation of equality to only persons with physical disabilities to the exclusion of mental, intellectual and other disabilities. In addition, the Child Justice Act recognises the constitutional virtues of building a society based on equality and fundamental human rights as a precursor to the improvement of the quality of life.[71] It prohibits the sexual exploitation of children who are mentally disabled.[72] Without prejudice, it should be recalled that these are national laws that have been promulgated by the national Parliament. Provinces and municipalities have, within the national legislative and policy framework, adopted policies or strategies aimed at promoting equality and equity particularly around employment matters. For example, Swellendam Municipality's Policy on People with Disabilities seeks to equalise employment opportunities for people with and without disabilities within the framework of the Employment Equity Act.[73]

The Constitution mandates the state, including provinces and municipalities, to implement laws and policies on non-discrimination and equality. The national government has taken a leading role in establishing anti-discrimination laws and policies which are then implemented by provinces and municipalities.

National legislation on equality and non-discrimination enacted after the ratification of the CRPD follows a piecemeal or rather thematic approach in

[64] Parliament of the Republic of South Africa, 'How a law is made' www.parliament.gov.za.

[65] Department of Forestry, Fisheries and the Environment, 'National Gender Policy Framework' www.dffe.gov.za.

[66] PEPUDA (n 60).

[67] Employment Equity Act 55 of 1998.

[68] Prevention and Combating of Trafficking in Persons Act 7 of 2013.

[69] Section 1(c) and 4(1) Prevention and Combating of Trafficking in Persons Act 7 of 2013.

[70] Section 14(l) Prevention and Combating of Trafficking in Persons Act 7of 2013.

[71] Preamble of The Child Justice Act 75 of 2008.

[72] Item 12, Schedule 3 Child Justice Act 75 of 2008.

[73] Swellendam Municipality, 'Policy on People with Disabilities', approved per item C73 on 9 December 2014, Implementation Date 1 January 2015.

dealing with persons with disabilities and this thematic approach is informed by the subjective context of the specific laws. The WPRPD is the latest national initiative aimed at ensuring that people with disabilities are treated equally and equitably. It defines equality,[74] and commits to the acceleration of implementation of existing legislation that advocates equality for persons with disabilities.[75] Thus, in as far as equality and non-discrimination is concerned the implementation of the CRPD has not provoked a centralisation of legislative competences.

C. The Role of Reasonable Accommodation in Enhancing Non-Discrimination

South Africa has adopted a Policy on the Provision of Reasonable Accommodation and Assistive Devices with the objective of assisting government departments in planning for and implementing reasonable accommodation measures for employees with disabilities.[76] While the Policy is limited to the employment sphere, it deals with various issues of accessibility. The Policy adopts the definition of the 2011 World Disability Report of accessibility as the extent to which aspects of society can be equally, easily, safely, and appropriately used or reached by people with special needs or impairments.[77] By extension, the Policy envisions accessibility as the extent to which an environment, service or product allows access, especially to people with disabilities,[78] and equal participation in available opportunities.[79] In a similar vein, an employer is obliged to ensure accessibility to the work environment with due regard to the nature and type of disability.[80] In addition, all forms of communication, including communication in different formats, should be accessible to persons with different types of disabilities.[81] In addition, the National Strategic Framework on Reasonable Accommodation for Persons with Disabilities embraces normative guidance from the CRPD. It recognises the international legal context of persons with disabilities by making reference to various Articles in the CRPD such as Articles 4, 5, 9, 14 and 19.[82] This policy has to be granulated from the theoretical to the practical contexts in provincial

[74] WPRPD (n 39) 6.

[75] Ibid 9.

[76] Department of Public Service and Administration, 'Policy on Reasonable Accommodation and Assistive Devices for Employees with Disabilities in the Public Service' (3 December 2014) www.dpsa.gov.za.

[77] Access includes buildings, facilities, constructed spaces, transport, information, equipment, services, activities, resources, utilities, language, communication and technology.

[78] Department of Public Service and Administration (n 76) 3.

[79] Ibid 5.

[80] Ibid Item 14.1.

[81] Ibid.

[82] DWYPD, 'National Strategic Framework on Reasonable Accommodation for Persons With Disabilities' Government Gazette No 45328, 15 October 2021, Section 1.4.3.

and municipal settings. In *MEC for Education, Kwazulu-Natal v Pillay*, the Constitutional Court stated that:

> 'reasonable accommodation' connotes that sometimes the community, whether it is the state, an employer or a school, must take positive measures and possibly incur additional hardship or expense in order to allow all people to participate and enjoy all their rights equally. It ensures that we do not relegate people to the margins of society because they do not or cannot conform to certain social norms.[83]

Provinces mainly implement the national laws and policies on reasonable accommodation measures and those provinces that have adopted their own policies, such as the Western Cape Province, do so within the scope of the national framework with backing from international instruments. The province's Transversal Human Resource Management Policy of 2004 seeks to 'reduce the impact of the impairment on the person's capacity to fulfil the essential functions of a job, through providing assistive devices and resources and where applicable, adjusting working times and leave, and changing training and assessment materials and systems'.[84] In addition to other applicable laws and frameworks, the national government's Disability Framework for Local Government guides provincial departments of local government, municipalities and the South African Local Government Association regarding the mainstreaming of disability rights, including reasonable accommodation.[85] The challenge in practice is that there is often a lack of resources or capacity to provide reasonable accommodation to people with disabilities.

D. Accessibility

As a concept, accessibility informs the extent to which persons with disabilities may live independently and participate fully and equally in society.[86] If persons with disabilities do not have accessibility, they are *de facto* prevented from participating in society.[87] For instance, restricted access to buildings[88] and services[89] for persons with disabilities may show a denial of accessibility

[83] *MEC for Education, Kwazulu-Natal v Pillay* 2008 (1) SA 474 (CC), paras 71–78.

[84] Provincial Government Western Cape, 'Transversal Human Resource Management Policy Document' (30 September 2004) www.westerncape.gov.za 7.

[85] Department of Provincial and Local Government, 'Disability Framework for Local Government 2009–2014' (7 April 2009) www.gov.za 27.

[86] Art 9 CRPD; See also CRPD Committee (n 62).

[87] CRPD Committee (n 62). The right to accessibility is underscored in Art 25(c) of the International Covenant on Civil and Political Rights that accords the right to access to public services.

[88] UN Committee on Economic, Social and Cultural Rights (CESCR), 'General Comment No. 14: The Right to the Highest Attainable Standard of Health (Art. 12 of the Covenant)', 11 August 2000, E/C.12/2000/4, para 12(b).

[89] Arts 3(f), 9 CRPD.

and above all, a violation of the right to the inherent dignity of persons with disabilities.[90]

The national government has adopted various laws and policies which impact on accessibility. The 2015 WPRPD lays out the obligations of the state under the CRPD and proposes ways of implementation.[91] It seeks to accelerate the implementation of policies and programmes to ensure the provision of equal access to persons with disabilities, and to address barriers to participation.[92] Three interrelated social, psychological and structural barriers that are faced by people with disabilities are addressed by national policies. At provincial level, some of the provinces have enacted their own policies on persons with disabilities. For instance, the policy of the Gauteng Provincial Government identifies some of the battlements to the enjoyment of rights by persons with disabilities. These include social exclusions, the treatment of disability rights as a peripheral aspect and continued lack of access to buildings by persons with disabilities.[93] Municipalities have also adopted bylaws and policies relating to accessibility within the framework of national legislation.

i. Access to Public Buildings

Prior to 1985, there was a fragmented legislative regime at provincial and municipal levels on the erection of buildings and access to public buildings.[94] The National Building Regulations and Building Standards Act of 1977 (NARBSA)[95] replaced this regime. The Act established a uniform framework across the country which regulates the erection of buildings and prescribes building standards. It imposes obligations on local authorities, for instance, to approve building plans and to inspect buildings,[96] and empowers the national Minister to issue regulations and directives to ensure the fulfilment of the Act's objectives.[97] Enactment of the law has enabled the erection of structures that accommodate the needs of persons with disabilities. This includes safe entry into buildings and use of facilities, such as lifts, ramps for wheelchairs and other assistive devices. The 'SANS 10400-S document', which originated from the Act, has various guidelines on

[90] Art 1 Universal Declaration of Human Rights, General Assembly Resolution 217 A(III), 10 December 1948; Preambular para 2 and Art 5 African Charter on Human and Peoples Rights, CAB/LEG/67/3 rev 5, 27 June 1981; Arts 11(5), 13(1), 17(1), 20(1)(c), 21(1) African Charter on the Rights and Welfare of the Child.

[91] WPRPD (n 39) part 2.

[92] Ibid 21.

[93] Gauteng Provincial Government, 'The Disability Rights Policy of the Gauteng Provincial Government' (13 July 2010) www.yumpu.com 20–21.

[94] 'Construction Laws & SANS 10400' (2 December 2014) www.sans10400.co.za.

[95] National Building Regulations and Building Standards Act 103 of 1977. The Act is currently under review. It came into force in 1985.

[96] Sections 4(1), 6(1) National Building Regulations and Building Standards Act of 1985 (NARBSA).

[97] Section 17 NARBSA.

the provision of facilities to persons with disabilities. These include lifts, handrails, ramps, controls, switches and power points, gadgets in auditoriums.[98] Following the Constitution, which assigns the competence of 'building regulations' to municipalities, as mentioned above, and the NARBSA, municipalities have adopted bylaws that regulate various aspects related to the erection of buildings. Some of the bylaws show the will on the part of municipalities to advance accessibility opportunities for persons with disabilities. The Municipal Planning Bylaw of the City of Cape, for instance, obliges owners of land units to provide for parking bays for persons with disabilities. However, this law only refers to physical disability.[99]

ii. Access to Transport

The National Land and Transport Act (NLTA) empowers the national Minister to make regulations for the requirements and time-frames regarding the accessibility of vehicles and facilities to persons with disabilities.[100] The Minister is empowered to make regulations in consultations with the provincial members of the Executive Council (MEC) responsible for transport regarding the provision of vehicles and facilities within specific timeframes for persons with disabilities in the public transport system.[101] The spaces for consultation show the possible engagement of the laws that have been enacted to protect the rights of persons with disabilities at both the national and provincial levels. A closer look at the regulations indicates that the regulations under the Act allow for the regulation of public transport at the national, provincial and municipal levels.[102] However, the regulations are silent on their practical application regarding persons with disabilities.[103] Across the transport sector, some developments occurred. For instance, the Passenger Rail Agency of South Africa (PRASA) has been using standard design guidelines (Universal Accessibility Standards) to deal with questions of accessibility since 2005. This led to the adoption of the universal guidelines in March 2008 to aid universal access to trains and stations.[104] These included the engagement of a deliberate programme across the major cities of Johannesburg, Cape Town, Port Elizabeth, Durban and Mbombela,

[98] South African Bureau of Standards, 'SANS 10400-S: The Application of the National Building Regulations Part S: Facilities for Persons with Disabilities' (2011) www.archive.org.

[99] Sections 142 and 143 City of Cape Town Municipal Planning Bylaw, 2015 (as amended).

[100] National Land and Transport Act 5 of 2009.

[101] Section 8(1)(y) National Land and Transport Act 5 of 2009.

[102] Department of Transport, 'National Land Road Transport Regulations' R1208 Government Gazette No 32821, 17 December 2009, Chapters 1, 2 and 3; Department of Transport, 'Amendment of the National Land Transport Regulations, 2009' R399 Government Gazette No 33185, 14 May 2010.

[103] There is no mention of the term disability/disabilities in the regulations passed under Section 8 of the National Road Transport Act.

[104] K Adeyeye, J Gibberd and J Chakwizira, 'Water Marginality in Rural and Peri-Urban Communities' (2020) 273 *Journal of Cleaner Production* 988.

that identified life cycle, impairment, and signage groups as special needs passengers.[105] This shows that implementation is largely on the part of the municipalities, other than the provincial governments. Municipalities have embraced the call for the transport infrastructure and services to be accessible and inclusive of persons with disabilities. For example, the City of Cape Town adopted its Universal Access Policy for Transport in 2014 which gives effect to the NLTA and its Constitution of Transport for Cape Town Bylaws of 2013. The Policy seeks to ensure the elimination and reduction of physical barriers for persons with disabilities in the area of transport. However, despite the investment towards making roads, parks and beach walks among others accessible, many persons with disabilities, particularly in rural areas, continue to struggle to move from one point to another due to various barriers.[106]

iii. Access to Social Security

The Social Assistance Act was enacted to provide for the rendering of social assistance to persons, to provide for the mechanism for the rendering of such assistance and to provide for the establishment of an inspectorate for social assistance.[107] At its core, the Act provides for the provision of social grants such as the child support grant, the care dependency grant, the foster child grant and the disability grant, among others.[108] It is interesting that the Act constructs eligibility for grants to include care-dependent children who require and receive permanent care on account of severe mental or physical disability.[109] The Act also places an obligation on the designated agency to accord reasonable assistance to an individual who on account of various reasons including a disability is unable to understand, appreciate or exercise his or her rights, duties or obligations under the Act.[110] The shortfall, however, is in the limited meaning accorded to a disability on account of prescription of age, physical or mental disability.[111] Other forms of disability on account of intellectual, psychological impairments are not expressly included. The provision of social security is in line with Article 28 CRPD that calls for the provision of the adequate standard of living and social protection for persons with disabilities.

Prior to 2006, provinces used to administer social grants before the function was taken over by the national government, citing maladministration and abuse of funds, among other reasons. Thus, the recentralisation of the administration

[105] AE Gibberd, 'Universally Accessible Public Transport Systems: Experiences with Implementation in the Thirteen Integrated Public Transport Network Municipalities' (Doctoral Dissertation, University of Pretoria, 2021) 33.

[106] Ibid.

[107] The Social Assistance Act 13 of 2004. See the long title thereto.

[108] Sections 1–4 Social Assistance Act 13 of 2004.

[109] Section 1 Social Assistance Act 13 of 2004.

[110] Section 2(3) Social Assistance Act 13 of 2004.

[111] Section 9 Social Assistance Act 13 of 2004.

of social grants cannot be linked to the implementation of the CRPD since South Africa had not ratified the treaty at that time.

iv. Accessibility as National Remit

With regard to accessibility, it is evident that the national government has been more involved in the implementation of the CRPD, through the development of national strategies, policies, and laws. From a thematic perspective such as access to buildings and transport, subnational governments have played a critical role in implementation of legislation and policy direction from the national level. In terms of the division of competences among spheres of government, despite the existence of the hybrid federal system, the formulation of the laws and policies relating to accessibility remains largely at the national level with a more 'implementational' approach at the provincial and municipal levels.

E. Participation

As noted in the Introduction to this volume, one of the general principles of the CRPD is the 'full and effective participation and inclusion in society' of people with disabilities.[112] The 2015 WPRPD has given meaning to this principle. First, it is about ensuring that persons with disabilities are consulted and meaningfully involved in activities that affect their lives. The emphasis is also on supported decision-making processes. Second, it is about 'creating opportunities to voice opinions, influence and complain when participation is denied'. Last, it is about 'providing an accessible, barrier-free physical and social environment, as well as access to information and communication'.[113] The WPRPD also intends to accelerate the implementation of policies and programmes to ensure the provision of equal access to persons with disabilities, and to address barriers to participation.[114]

From a national perspective, some regulations such as the national revised Draft Code of Good Practice on the Employment of Persons with Disabilities, show that participation (or the lack thereof) of persons with disabilities should be the central focus that informs initiatives that lead to or improve participation.[115] For instance, the Draft Code defines persons with disabilities in the context of participation as a barrier. It states that persons with disabilities include those who have long-term physical, mental, intellectual or sensory impairment which in interaction with various barriers may hinder their full and effective

[112] Art 3 CRPD.
[113] WPRPD (n 39) 39.
[114] WPRPD (n 39) 21.
[115] Department of Labour, 'Employment Equity Act, 1998 (Act 55 of 1998 as amended). Revised Draft Code of Good Practice on the Employment of Persons with Disabilities' Government Gazette No 38872, 12 June 2015.

participation in society on equal basis with others.[116] This position is also reflected in the guidance concerning persons with disabilities in the Employment Equity Act, which emphasises equity and the right to equal protection and benefit of the law including persons with disabilities as a designated group.[117] It is argued that the application of this Act in a bid to achieve equality or equity would require the participation of persons with disabilities.

The national government has taken the lead in ensuring the participation of people with disabilities in social, economic and cultural activities. It has defined the framework for the realisation of these rights through legislation and policies. There are several national laws that seek to promote the participation of persons with disabilities in the political, social, economic and cultural sectors. These include the Broad-Based Black Economic Empowerment Act[118] and the Municipal Systems Act.[119] The latter requires municipalities to consult and facilitate the participation of local communities, including persons with disabilities, in identification of priorities for the integrated development plans as well as in the review of the municipalities' performance. The WPRPD, mentioned above, also provides various measures aimed at ensuring the full participation of people with disabilities in the economy as well as in social and cultural lives.

As with equality, non-discrimination and accessibility, there is no evidence to suggest that the CRPD has had a significant impact on the division of competences between the national, provincial and local governments when it comes to participation. Provincial and local governments remain largely implementors of national laws and policies, even though there is scope for them to do more independent initiatives. The Expanded Public Works Programme and the Community Work Programme, which provides opportunities for persons with disabilities to earn income, are some of the common initiatives administered by subnational governments. In addition, there are special programmes (sports events, entrepreneurships and others) administered for persons with disabilities whose potential to enhance their full participation is minimal.

IV. THE IMPLEMENTATION OF ARTICLE 33 CRPD

A. Focal Points and the Coordination Mechanism

The adoption of a progressive Bill of Rights as part of the 1996 Constitution imposed obligations on the state to promote and protect human rights. The state had to identify the rights of people with disabilities, and the government initially set up the National Office on the Status of Disabled People (OSDP)

[116] Ibid Item 5.2.
[117] Section 1 Employment Equity Act 55 of 1998.
[118] Broad-Based Black Economic Empowerment Act 53 of 2003.
[119] Local Government: Municipal Systems Act 32 of 2000.

in the Presidency. The Office was cascaded down to the Premier's Office, at provincial level, and to municipalities, at local government level. This Office assumed the role of focal points for coordinating measures aiming at protecting and promoting disability rights.[120] At national level, the OSDP was tasked with mainstreaming disability rights in national policies. Its work culminated in the adoption of the White Paper on an Integrated National Disability Strategy in 1997, which among other things, requires different spheres of government to integrate disabilities issues in their activities. This marked the evolution of coordination mechanisms for disability rights in the country.

Following South Africa's ratification of the CRPD and its Protocol in 2007, disability rights were allocated to the newly created national Department of Women, Youth and Persons with Disabilities (DWYPD) in 2009, which has been designated as the national focal point for coordination purposes.[121] The DWYPD strives to ensure that persons with disabilities are not marginalised, are included in the community and have the same rights as those without disabilities. Like its predecessor, the DWYPD is based in the Presidency and monitors, evaluates, coordinates and mainstreams disability rights into national priorities.[122] Two years later, the government set up the Parliamentary Portfolio Committee on Women, Children and Persons with Disability so that the rights of women, children and persons with disabilities could receive dedicated attention through Parliament's legislative and oversight processes. The latest framework for coordinating the mainstreaming of disability rights and the implementation of the CRPD is provided for under the 2015 WPRPD which makes provision for coordination mechanisms at national, provincial and local levels of government.

When it comes to the national level, the WPRPD states that the 'President, upon taking office, decides on the macro-organisation of the state, including designation of the national disability rights co-ordination mechanism'.[123] The national disability rights coordinating mechanism is tasked with, among other functions the:

- coordination and technical support of the implementation of the WPRPD;
- development and coordination of the five-year national disability rights programme of action, aligned with the Medium Term Strategic Framework;[124]

[120] S Matsebula, M Schneider and B Watermeyer, 'Integrating Disability within Government: The Office on the Status of the Disabled Persons' in B Watermeyer et al (eds), *Disability and Social Change. A South African Agenda* (HSRC Press, 2006) 85.

[121] I Grobbelaar-du Plessis and C Grobler, 'South Africa' in C Ngwena et al (eds), *African Disability Rights Yearbook Volume 1* (Pretoria University Law Press, 2013) 334.

[122] See the website of the Department of Women, Youth and Persons with Disabilities at www.dwypd.za.

[123] WPRPD (n 39) 126.

[124] The Framework is the government's strategic plan for an election term.

- monitoring of and reporting on compliance with the CRPD and other international disability-related treaties;
- coordination and management of government-wide disability rights cooperative governance forums at national level.[125]

The WPRPD also establishes the National Disability Rights Machinery, constituted by accounting officers and/or designated disability rights coordinators of/from various national departments, Statistics South Africa, and national disability organisations as well as technical experts from research institutions, institutions of higher learning, organised business, international development partners and human rights agencies.[126] This is the platform where the government engages the civil society and other stakeholders on disability rights. The WPRPD requires the establishment of a disability rights forum for each of the government clusters[127] to enable the mainstreaming of disability into issues pertaining to these clusters.[128]

At provincial level, premiers, upon taking office, decide on the designation of the provincial disability rights coordinating mechanisms.[129] The role of the provincial disability rights coordinating mechanisms more or less mirrors that of national mechanisms. The WPRPD requires the establishment of a Provincial Disability Rights Machinery in each province, which reports to the provincial executive and the Premier's Coordination Forums, established in terms of the Intergovernmental Framework Act of 2005. The Provincial Disability Rights Machinery is composed of:

- provincial disability rights coordinating mechanisms;
- disability rights managers from each provincial government department and public entities;
- regional offices of national government departments;
- South African Local Government Association;
- municipalities;
- provincial disability rights organisations; and
- provincial offices of institutions promoting democracy.[130]

Like the National Machinery, the Provincial Disability Rights Machinery is allowed to source additional technical experts from research institutions and

[125] WPRPD (n 39) 127.
[126] Ibid.
[127] The clusters are: Economic Sectors, Investment, Employment and Infrastructure Development; Social Protection, Community and Human Development; Governance, State Capacity and Institutional Development; Justice, Crime Prevention and Security; and International Cooperation, Trade and Security.
[128] WPRPD (n 39) 127.
[129] Ibid.
[130] Ibid 128.

institutions of higher learning, among other relevant organisations. In addition, the WPRPD requires intra-institutional coordination within public institutions such as provinces to ensure the fulfilment of obligations it imposes on public institutions and the relevant office bearers. The intra-institutional coordination mechanism may involve the appointment of disability rights coordinators and intra-departmental committees. These structures, among other things, coordinate the alignment of legislation, policies, plans, programmes and services of government institutions to ensure effective mainstreaming of disability. They also serve as consultative platforms with civil society and advise the provincial executive regarding the acceleration of disability rights mainstreaming across all programmes.[131]

At local level, metropolitan and local municipalities are required to establish disability rights consultative forums. These forums are constituted by, among others, all disability organisations operating within the municipal area, the disability representatives of every ward committee, and senior management of all municipal departments.[132] They serve as the 'clearing house for disability priorities for inclusion in municipal integrated development plans and budgets'.[133] They also monitor the implementation of the WPRPD at local level. Lastly, they advise local councils and development planning committees (eg the integrated development plan steering committee) regarding the promotion and protection of disability rights. The work of the forum is supported by the designated disability rights coordination mechanism within the municipality.

Some reflections from a federal perspective can be drawn from the foregoing. First, the implementation of the coordination mechanism mostly occurs at the national level, with minimal work at the provincial level and the municipalities. In addition, the DWYPD is a creation of the executive power and as such any change of government may negatively affect the efficiency at the national level, and continue the perpetration of the non-engagement of provincial and municipal governments.[134]

Secondly, in principle, the focal points are expected to function at all levels of government – national, provincial and local. This is expected to translate from the National Disability Machinery, to the Inter-Departmental Coordinating Unit, provincial and then municipal focal points. It is argued, however, that none of the plans would succeed because of the lack of laws at the provincial and municipal levels to implement the CRPD in its own right in light of the context.[135] Various laws give insights into the probable application of accessibility for persons with disabilities.

[131] Ibid.
[132] Ibid 129.
[133] Ibid.
[134] S Djoyou Kamga, 'The National Implementation and Monitoring of the Convention of the Rights of Persons with Disabilities: South Africa's Experience' in Centre for Human Rights (eds), *South Africa Disability Legislation and Policy Gap Analysis* (University of Pretoria, 2021) 141.
[135] Grobbelaar-du Plessis and Grobler (n 121) 334.

Thirdly, the government recognises that there remains a disjuncture between the theoretical and the normative framework, on one hand, and the lack of effective implementation of the rights of persons with disabilities, on the other hand.[136] So while persons with disabilities are, in principle, able to harness the law to protect and pursue interests on an equal basis with others, several obstacles on the one hand, and the interrelatedness of disability and poverty on the other, detract from the equality provided for in law.[137]

B. Independent Mechanism of Monitoring the Implementation of the CRPD

Article 33(2) CRPD requires States Parties to 'maintain, strengthen, designate or establish … a framework, including one or more independent mechanisms, as appropriate, to promote, protect and monitor implementation of the … Convention'. When designating or establishing such a mechanism, the CRPD further mandates States Parties to 'take into account the principles relating to the status and functioning of national institutions for protection and promotion of human rights'. South Africa has six state institutions established by the Constitution to support constitutional democracy, the so called 'Chapter Nine Institutions'. These are: the Public Protector; the South African Human Rights Commission (SAHRC); the Commission for the Promotion and Protection of the Rights of Cultural, Religious and Linguistic Communities; the Commission for Gender Equality; the Auditor General and the Electoral Commission. These institutions are independent, and subject only to the Constitution and the law. The Constitution requires them to perform their functions impartially and without fear or favour.[138] They are accountable directly to Parliament, which also approves their respective budgets. Of the six, the SAHRC acts as the independent mechanism envisaged in Article 33(2) CRPD. The Commission has a duty to promote respect for human rights and a culture of human rights, to promote the protection, development and attainment of human rights as well as to monitor and assess the observance of human rights in the Republic.[139]

The South African Human Rights Commission Act of 2013 gives the SAHRC additional powers. The Act, for instance, empowers the Commission

[136] CRPD Committee, 'South Africa's Initial Report on the Implementation of the Convention of the Rights of Persons with Disabilities' CRPD/C/ZAF/1, 24 November 2015, para 51.

[137] See South African Human Rights Commission, 'Human Rights and Persons with Disabilities' www.sahrc.org.za 10; Department of Provincial and Local Government (n 85) 13; E Durojaye and R Nanima, 'Realisation of the Right to Health of Persons with Disabilities in the COVID-19 Era' (2021) 9 *African Disability Rights Yearbook* 66. The several obstacles include persistent harmful traditional beliefs, ingrained stigmatisation and consequent discrimination. The interrelatedness of disability and poverty is evident in aspects like the inability to afford legal fees, lack of information in the use of equality courts, accessibility of equality courts, communication barriers, and the lack of a disability-sensitive judiciary and court staff, inaccessible buildings and transport.

[138] Constitution Section 181(2).

[139] Constitution Section 184(1).

to 'monitor the implementation of, and compliance with, international and regional conventions and treaties, international and regional covenants and international and regional charters relating to the objects of the Commission'. The Act also mandates the Commission to report to the National Assembly on the implementation of these human rights instruments in South Africa.[140] Thus, disability rights, including the implementation of the CRPD, falls within the scope of the Commission's mandate. The SAHRC has far-reaching powers. It has the power to investigate and to report on the observance of human rights, take steps to secure appropriate redress where human rights have been violated, carry out research, and educate.[141]

The Commission has institutionalised its work on disability rights by establishing a Committee on Disability and Older Persons, in line with Section 5 of the South African Human Rights Act. The Committee has a sub-committee which meets once or twice a year with various government departments and monitors and observes the implementation of the CRPD.[142] The Commission has conducted many investigations into allegations of human rights violations involving people with disabilities.[143] It monitors the implementation of its recommendations aimed at redress, prevention of the recurrence of the violations or the improvement of conditions to ensure full realisation of human rights by people with disabilities.[144]

Besides the Commission, the rights of persons with disabilities also falls within the mandate of the Public Protector who has the power to investigate any conduct in state affairs, or in the public administration in any sphere of government, that is alleged or suspected to be improper or to result in any impropriety or prejudice, to report on that conduct and to take appropriate remedial action.[145]

The Constitution requires that the Public Protector be accessible to all persons and communities, and this includes persons with disabilities.[146] In *South African Broadcasting Corporation v Democratic Alliance*,[147] the Supreme Court ruled that the remedial action of the Public Protector is binding. This means that an organ of state cannot ignore the remedial action. The Commission for the Promotion and Protection of the Rights of Cultural, Religious and Linguistic Communities plays an important role in promoting and advancing the cultural rights of persons with disabilities, particularly of the deaf community.[148] To sum up, South Africa has set up independent mechanisms to oversee the protection

[140] Section 13(1)(b) South African Human Rights Commission Act 40 of 2013.
[141] Section 184(2) South African Human Rights Commission Act 40 of 2013.
[142] Grobbelaar-du Plessis and Grobler (n 121) 334.
[143] See South African Human Rights Commission (n 137).
[144] Section 11 South African Human Rights Commission Act 40 of 2013.
[145] Constitution Section 182(1).
[146] Constitution Section 182(4).
[147] *South African Broadcasting Corporation v Democratic Alliance* 2016 2 SA 522 (SCA).
[148] WPRPD (n 39) 130.

of disability rights, including the implementation of the CRPD, at all levels. However, the independent institutions require strengthening so that they can fully safeguard disability rights.

V. CONCLUDING REMARKS

South Africa has a progressive Constitution with an expansive Bill of Rights which entrenches comprehensive provisions on human rights. The Constitution guarantees the equality of everyone and prohibits unfair discrimination on the basis of disability, among other grounds. Human dignity as well as political, social and economic rights are also constitutionally guaranteed. The national Parliament has enacted several pieces of legislation to give effect to the constitutional framework on human rights. However, some of the Acts still define disability in traditional terms, medically and welfare-oriented, which undermines the realisation of rights of people with disabilities as enshrined in the CRPD.

As noted above, South Africa ratified the CRPD and its Optional Protocol in 2007 but there is still no specific disability legislation to domesticate the CRPD. The WPRPD of 2015 is the closest that South Africa has come to a Disability Act. The absence of a specific disability law, coupled with the lack of sufficient resources and inadequate coordination mechanisms, continue to undermine the full realisation of human rights of people with disabilities. The DWYPD is spearheading the adoption of the National Strategic Framework on Reasonable Accommodation, the Universal Access and Design Framework and Self-Representation and Awareness Raising Campaign to support the implementation of the WPRPD. In addition, the Department is coordinating efforts to consolidate the existing policies, frameworks, guidelines and directives on people with disabilities. It is anticipated that this consolidation will culminate in the adoption of the much-needed disability specific legislation.

As in many other areas, the national government has so far been the dominant actor when it comes to the formulation of disability policies. Provinces and municipalities have largely been 'happy' implementors of these policies. This is due to three main factors. First, the constitutional scheme of sharing powers and functions among spheres of government which gives provinces a few and less important areas of exclusive competence, which the national government can override under certain circumstances. Second, provinces lack financial autonomy and rely on national grants (which are conditional). This means that they lack the purse to fully exploit their legislative and policy-making powers. Lastly, the political dominance of the ANC across all levels of government has meant that most of the policy issues are dealt with by the party rather than formally in government. Once the party or the centre take a decision, provincial and local governments largely implement them without resistance. This has been evident not only in the disability sector but also in areas such as disaster management and education. However, in isolated cases, the Western Cape Province and the city of Cape Town, which are run by the opposition DA, have opposed the national government with limited success. The province and the city have also been the most active in adopting and implementing disability policies.

On the whole, in conclusion, the implementation of the CRPD has followed the 'usual' policy- and law-making and implementation dynamics that characterise the centralised federal system of South Africa.

11

Ethiopia

The Missing Relationship between Federalism and Disability

YONATAN T FESSHA AND BEZA DESSALEGN

I. INTRODUCTION

AT THE TIME of writing this chapter, the story of a disabled medical student was dominating the media. Biniyam Isayas, whose left hand had been physically impaired since childhood, had completed four years in the medical school of Addis Ababa University and was starting his fifth year when he received the news that he could not continue to study medicine. The university, that had allowed him to progress from year to year, suddenly claimed that Isayas, due to his disability, would have encountered difficulty in pursuing some of the programmes, including intravenous fluid management, cardiopulmonary resuscitation, delivery, ability to provide oxygen to patients and suture cuts. Members of the public were outraged by the decision of the university and turned to social media to express their outrage. The Federation of Ethiopian Associations of Persons with Disabilities (FEAPD) also strongly condemned the decision adopted by the medical school and referred to the obligations Ethiopia has undertaken by ratifying the UN Convention on the Rights of Persons with Disabilities (CRPD).[1] In the face of mounting public outcry, Addis Ababa University was forced to reverse its decision and allow Isayas to continue with his studies, and commit to create a conducive environment to ensure that he could successfully complete the rest of the programme.

This recent episode, in spite of what can be called 'a happy ending', reveals that persons with disabilities still face stigma and discrimination. Further, in Ethiopia, disability is often understood as a phenomenon which concerns only a

[1] 'Ethiopia: Outcry as Medicine school tells a disabled student to discontinue study' *Borkena Ethiopian News* (12 July 2022).

small segment of a nation's population. However, this is rather a misperception.[2] Based on the World Report on Disability, jointly issued by the World Bank and World Health Organization in 2011, in Ethiopia, there are an estimated 15 million children, adults and elderly persons with disabilities, representing 17.6 per cent of the population.[3] It is also estimated that 95 per cent of persons with disabilities live below the poverty line.[4]

The rights of persons with disabilities in Ethiopia have long been ignored, or, if not ignored, considered unimportant. It was only in 2010 that Ethiopia ratified the CRPD, having signed it on 30 March 2007.[5] Ratified international treaties, according to the Constitution, form an integral part of the law of the land.[6] What is not clear, and continues to be a subject of fierce academic debate, is whether Ethiopia follows the monist, dualist or intermediate approach in incorporating international treaties in its domestic legal system.[7]

Exactly a decade before it ratified the CRPD, Ethiopia had formally moved from a unitary state to a federal system of state governance. In 1995, Ethiopia became one of only two African countries that had adopted a constitution that explicitly embraces federalism as a form of government. It is also known for marrying federalism with ethnicity, evident in its decision to create sub-national units that are by and large based on ethnicity. At the same time, this is a federation that is operating under a dominant party state.[8]

The interplay between the federal arrangement and the protections offered to persons with disabilities is yet to be examined. This chapter assesses the implications of federalism on the protection and promotion of disability rights. The chapter analyses, in particular, the role of the federal and state governments in the fight for inclusion and non-discrimination of persons with disabilities in Ethiopia. The chapter is organised in the following interrelated parts. The following section examines the federal arrangement and its (in)ability to accommodate persons with disabilities as a collective identity. The focus then shifts to the distribution of power between the federal and state governments. The aim is to identify and determine the policy and law-making powers and responsibilities of federal and state governments with respect to persons with disabilities.

[2] SA Iyassu and F McKinnon, 'Disability Rights Are Human Rights: Pushing Ethiopia towards a Rights-Based Movement' (2021) 19 *Northwestern Journal of Human Rights* 51.

[3] International Labor Organization (ILO), 'Inclusion of People with Disabilities in Ethiopia' (January 2013) www.ilo.org.

[4] ILO, 'Moving Towards Disability Inclusion: Stories of Change' (2015) www.ilo.org.

[5] CRPD Ratification Proclamation No 676/2010, Convention on the Rights of Persons with Disability.

[6] Art 9(4) of the Constitution.

[7] TS Bulto, 'The Monist-Dualist Divide and the Supremacy Clause: Revisiting the Status of Human Rights Treaties in Ethiopia' (2009) 23 *Journal of Ethiopian Law* 132.

[8] Between 1991 and 2020, Ethiopia was ruled by the Ethiopian People's Revolutionary Democratic Front (EPRDF), a coalition of ethnically based parties that controlled both federal and all state governments. In 2020, the coalition transformed itself into a single national party, namely the Prosperity Party. Following the 2022 election, the Prosperity Party controls federal and all state governments except the State of Tigray.

This is then followed by a more specific examination of the role of the federal and state governments in ensuring non-discrimination and equality, accessibility and participation. The chapter then explores the mechanism created for the purposes of implementing Article 33 CRPD before it completes the discussion by offering brief concluding remarks.

II. ETHIOPIAN FEDERALISM: ANY SPACE FOR PEOPLE WITH DISABILITIES?

Ethiopia is considered a unique experiment in federalism, in particular because it represents a very extreme case of institutionalising identity politics. Its recognition of identity focuses primarily, if not solely, on cultural and, more particularly, ethnic identity.[9] For this reason, the Constitution, which formalised ethnic federalism, gives a highly disproportionate place to the country's ethnic communities (to which it refers as the 'nations, nationalities and peoples'). In several places, the Constitution has made ethnic communities the sole beneficiaries of the federal dispensation.[10]

While the tight focus on the protection of ethnic identity elevated the Ethiopian Constitution to a 'minority-friendly' document, its focus on ethnic communities is deemed problematic, begging the question as to why other identities are not explicitly protected or why the Constitution, at least implicitly, failed to recognise other identities that also continue to characterise Ethiopian society. Given the strong argument that disability constitutes a distinct group that is worthy of protection[11] and the fact that Ethiopia is a country in which a significant portion of the population lives with a disability,[12] the Constitution's failure to explicitly recognise and protect disability as one form of group identity raises questions.

Some scholars, however, claim that Ethiopia's legal regime in fact recognises disability, albeit indirectly. They base this argument on the fact that Article 9(4) of the Constitution automatically makes ratified international treaties an integral part of the law of the land. This means that Article 30(4) CRPD, which recognises disability as a particular form of identity[13] that is worthy of protection, is part of the law of the land. The CRPD recognition of disability not as a medical fact, but as an identity that deserves protection in its own right, can pave the way for disabled people to have similar protection to that of the

[9] YT Fessha, 'The Original Sin of Ethiopian Federalism' (2017) 16 *The Ethnopolitics of Ethnofederalism in Ethiopia* 232–45.

[10] See the Preamble, Arts 8, 39 and 47 of the Constitution, respectively.

[11] See eg EC Wertlieb, 'Minority Group Status of the Disabled' (1985) 38 *Human Relations* 1047–63.

[12] ILO (n 3).

[13] Art 30(4) CRPD requires States Parties to entitle persons with disabilities, on an equal basis with others, to recognition and support of their specific cultural and linguistic identity, including sign languages and deaf culture.

multiple communal identities that exist in Ethiopia.[14] It is important to highlight that the CRPD recognises a distinct culture and language for persons with disabilities, which is crucial for the existence of a particular form of identity. The Ethiopian Constitution, however, goes beyond distinct culture and language. It also includes two additional requirements that are necessary to be covered by identitarian protection and are, instead, not mentioned in the CRPD, namely a common psychological make-up and the need to occupy a contiguous territory. Seen in such light, it might not be an easy task to regard persons with disabilities as members of 'nations, nationalities and peoples' of Ethiopia.[15]

In spite of the lack of identitarian protection, nevertheless, the Constitution, through its extensive list of individual human rights, including an equality guarantee clause and a specific provision on people with disabilities, coupled with the law that ratified international treaties form part of the law of the land, provides ample protection for persons with disabilities. Yet, this will only be in the form of individual rights, and not as group entitlements. Before exhaustively dealing with these individual protections provided by the Constitution and federal laws, the next section sets the scene by outlining the division of responsibilities between the federal and state governments with respect to matters pertaining to the protection of the rights of persons with disabilities.

III. THE FRAMEWORK ON DISABILITY: ANALYSING FEDERAL AND STATE COMPETENCES

Articles 51 and 52 of the Constitution outline the division of powers between the federal and state governments. Powers that belong to the Federal Government are explicitly provided, while powers not explicitly reserved to the Federal Government are left to the states.[16] The powers of the Federal Government are not, however, limited to those listed in Article 52 of the Constitution. Other Articles of the Constitution also include powers given to the Federal Government.[17]

[14] Iyassu and McKinnon (n 2) 57.

[15] For dilemmas regarding the formation and recognition of new identities, see B Dessalegn and C Van der Beken, 'The Struggle for Recognition and the Fault Lines of Ethnic Identity Determination in Ethiopia' in C Van der Beken and WT Goshu (eds), *Constitutionalism, Constitutional Adjudication and Human Rights in Ethiopia* (Center for Human Rights, 2020).

[16] Of course, in the strictest sense, under Art 52, the Constitution also has a brief list of exclusive powers of the regions, although it eventually leaves the big chunk of the powers to the regions as reserved residual powers.

[17] See Art 51, which from the outset seems to list all the competences of the Federal Government, and Art 52(2), which declares that all powers not expressly given to the Federal Government are reserved for the regions. However, Art 55(6), which is found under the powers and functions of the House of Peoples Representatives (HoPR), expands the powers of the Federal Government by declaring that the HoPR shall enact laws, which the House of Federation (HoF) deems necessary to establish and sustain one economic community. See also Arts 55(3), 55(4), 55(5), and 55(13).

Like many other constitutions, the list of exclusive powers of the federal or state governments does not include disability as a distinct functional area or competence. It is therefore important to identify a broader category of functional area that would allow either or both levels of government to enact laws and policies that regulate matters related to disability. In this respect, it is worth noting that Article 51(2) of the Constitution gives the Federal Government the power to 'formulate and implement the country's policies, strategies, and plans in respect of the overall economic, social and development matters'. In addition, Article 51(3) entrusts the Federal Government with the power to 'establish and implement national standards and basic policy criteria for public health, education, science and technology as well as for the protection and preservation of cultural and historical legacies'. However, the Constitution also seems to give similar and overlapping powers to the states. Article 52(2)(c) authorises the states 'to formulate and execute economic, social and development policies, strategies and plans'. Although this Article does not include public health, arguably, 'public health is a social matter with respect to which the state could formulate its own policies'.[18]

From the foregoing, concurrent powers cover the bulk of social, health and economic matters of which disability is an important component. The power of the Federal Government 'to establish and implement national standards and basic policy criteria for public health' gives it broad powers in the areas of public health, including disability. At the same time, this power of the Federal Government is limited to setting 'national standards and basic policy criteria'. The Federal Government is only expected to develop a framework law and policy, the details of which need to be filled in by state legislation and policy. The Federal Government is 'expected to restrict itself to setting the standards and defining the minimum requirement to which states have to adhere'.[19] This leads to the unavoidable conclusion that states have competences over matters related to disability.

However, as we will see below, the policy and legislative field related to disability is dominated by the Federal Government. In fact, the Federal Government has taken a disproportionate, if not the entire, role of making laws and policies that relate to persons with disabilities. The three most relevant disability laws (ie, the Right to Employment of Persons with Disabilities,[20] Ethiopian Building Proclamation[21] and the Higher Education Proclamation)[22] are federal laws. A quick look at the preambles of the three laws reveals that the Federal

[18] ZA Ayele and YT Fessha, 'Controlling Public Health Emergencies in Federal Systems: The Case of Ethiopia' in N Steytler (ed), *Comparative Federalism and Covid-19* (Routledge, 2022) 322.

[19] Ibid 321.

[20] The Right to Employment of Persons with Disabilities Proclamation, Proc No 568/2008, Fed Neg Gaz, Year 14, No 20.

[21] Ethiopian Building Proclamation, Proc No 624/2009, Fed Neg Gaz, Year 15, No 31.

[22] Higher Education Proclamation, Proc No 1152/2019, Fed Neg Gaz, Year 25, No 78.

Parliament promulgated the laws using its framework powers provided under Articles 51(3) and 55(1) and (3) of the Constitution. A similar approach is visible in relation to policy documents. For instance, documents such as the 1996 Developmental Social Welfare Policy of Ethiopia, the 1999 National Program of Action of Ethiopia, Growth and Transformation Plan (GTP) I[23] and II,[24] as well as the 2012 National Plan of Action of Persons with Disabilities (NPA),[25] which directly and indirectly provide a policy framework for persons with disabilities, were all prepared and adopted by the Federal Government.

Although in relation to disability, legislative powers could in principle be exercised concurrently by the state governments, states are yet to use their own powers and issue laws and policies that directly or indirectly relate to persons with disabilities. There is no single state that has adopted a policy or legislation focusing on persons with disabilities, in spite of needing to take into account context-specific regional variations.

The fact that state governments have not been active in policymaking and legislation drafting is not unique to the area of disability. State governments have not made use of their constitutional powers to initiate and adopt legislation in general. The state governments have not exploited their legislative competences. To date, only a handful of legislation has been adopted and state law-making is practically non-existent. Such inactivity on the part of states can be explained partly by the dominant party state system under which the Federation operated for more than two decades.[26] Democratic centralism, which has been the hallmark or governing norm of the ruling political party, the Ethiopian People Revolutionary Democratic Front (EPRDF), dictates that important policy and legal considerations emanate from the party leadership, and are eventually approved in party meetings before their release as official documents. Federal and state officials are simply expected to implement the decisions of the party. This dominant party state paradigm has crippled the autonomy of states, making it impossible for them to exercise their constitutionally mandated framework powers.

In addition to the dominant party system, there are other factors that might also explain the negligible appetite for law-making on the part of state governments. First, the states receive a significant part of their budget in the form of federal subsidies, making them dependent on the wishes of the Federal Government. This has hardly made it possible for them to fully exploit their law- and policy-making space. Second, and more importantly, many states suffer from an acute shortage of skilled manpower, which means they just

[23] Ministry of Finance and Economic Development, 'Federal Democratic Republic of Ethiopia Growth and Transformation Plan I 2010/11- 2014/15' (November 2010) www.rise.esmap.org.

[24] National Planning Commission, 'Federal Democratic Republic of Ethiopia Growth and Transformation Plan II 2015/16- 2019/20' (May 2016) www.ethiopia.un.org.

[25] Ministry of Labour and Social Affairs, 'National Plan of Action on Persons With Disabilities (2012-2021)' (April 2012) www.ilo.org.

[26] A Fiseha and ZA Ayele, 'Concurrent Powers in the Ethiopian Federal System' in N Steytler (ed), *Concurrent Powers in Federal Systems: Meaning, Making, and Managing* (Brill, 2017) 250–51.

do not have the necessary human resources to formulate laws and policies of their own.

IV. THE ROLE OF THE FEDERAL GOVERNMENT VIS-À-VIS THE SUB-NATIONAL UNITS CONCERNING DISABILITY IN ETHIOPIA

A. The Concept of Disability

Disability as a concept is not normatively defined at either the federal or sub-national levels. Even though the concept is not defined, from the limited use of the term in both the federal and sub-national constitutions, it is possible to discern which model of disability the Ethiopian legal framework has embraced.

Article 41(5) of the Constitution provides that 'the State shall, within available means, allocate resources to provide rehabilitation and assistance to the physically and mentally disabled'. In this provision, despite the explicit mention of disability, it is clear that the government's responsibility is limited to allocating some resources, if and when available, to provide 'rehabilitation and assistance' to persons with disabilities. It appears that this provision adheres to the medical or charity model, as it clearly refers to rehabilitation, thereby understanding disability as a health problem. A similar, if not identical, provision is found across the sub-national constitutions of the states, which adhere to the medical model of disability. In that regard, the sub-national constitutions simply reproduce the provision on disability found in the Federal Constitution.[27]

A federal law, the Proclamation on the Right to Employment of Persons with Disabilities, enacted in 2008,[28] gives a very general definition of disability which is geared toward the social-contextual model of disability.[29] According to the proclamation, a 'person with a disability' means an individual whose equal employment opportunity is reduced as a result of his physical, mental or sensory impairments in relation with social, economic and cultural discrimination.[30] Clearly, this federal law departs from the model that is adopted by the Constitution. As a federal law, the Proclamation on the Right to Employment of Persons with Disabilities is applicable throughout the country. In this respect,

[27] See Art 41(5) of the Southern Nations Nationalities and Peoples Constitution; Art 39(5) of the Afar Constitution; Art 40(5) of the Sidama Constitution; Art 41(5) of the Harari Constitution; Art 41(5) of the Benishangul Gumuz Constitution; Art 41(5) of the Gambella Constitution; Art 41(5) of the Amhara Constitution; Art 41(5) of the Tigray Constitution; Art 41(5) of the South Western Region Constitution; Art 41(5) of the Oromia Constitution; Art 41(6) of the Somali Constitution, which deal with the rights of people with disabilities in identical ways to the Constitution.

[28] Right to Employment of Persons with Disabilities Proclamation 568/2008 (n 20).

[29] The term social-contextual model is used here in line with the understanding proffered in the Introduction to this volume.

[30] Ibid Art 2(1).

it has an important leverage in the protection of people with disabilities, but only when it comes to employment matters. However, the effectiveness of this federal law in providing protection can be questioned, considering that the Constitution, which is the highest legal source, adheres to the medical model of disability. The Constitution, as the supreme law of the land, trumps all other laws, as a result of which an amendment of its Article 41(5) is inevitably necessary to create harmony with federal laws that adhere to the social model. This will also allow changes to disability-specific laws, which for the most part seem to have adopted the charity and medical models of disability rights protection, disregarding the fact that contemporary jurisprudence on disability rights has transitioned into the social model.[31]

There is a strong need to recognise and enforce disability rights within the Ethiopian legal system. This is especially necessary in a country where disability is dogmatically considered as a punishment from God for our sins. This sentiment is also shared by the Committee on the Rights of Persons with Disabilities (CRPD Committee). In the 2016 Concluding Observations issued on the Initial Report of Ethiopia, the CRPD Committee expressed its concern that 'legislation and policies continue to employ derogatory terms to refer to persons with disabilities such as "insane", "infirm" and "deaf-mute"'.[32] The CRPD Committee advised the government to:

> eliminate the use of all derogatory language to refer to persons with disabilities and ensure that all existing and new laws and regulations, and definitions used therein, comply with the human rights-based model of disability in accordance with the Convention.[33]

B. Non-Discrimination and Equality

With regard to ensuring non-discrimination and equality, chapter three of the Constitution provides a catalogue of rights that offer protection to persons with disabilities, albeit indirectly. In addition to the general provisions of chapter three, there is only one other specific provision that, albeit insufficiently, addresses the rights of persons with disabilities. This is Article 41(5), which, as noted above, requires the Federal Government only to address the rights and needs of persons with disabilities to the extent that resources permit and in the form of charity rather than as an obligation.

Article 25 of the Constitution, otherwise known as the equality clause, provides that 'all persons are equal before the law and are entitled without any discrimination to the equal protection of the law'. Further, it states that 'the law

[31] See Michigan Disability Rights Coalition, 'Models of Disability' (2021) www.copower.org.

[32] Committee on the Rights of Persons with Disabilities (CRPD Committee), 'Concluding Observations on the Initial Report of Ethiopia' (4 November 2016) www.ohchr.org.

[33] Ibid.

shall guarantee to all persons equal and effective protection without discrimination on grounds of race, nation, nationality, or other social origin, colour, sex, language, religion, political or other opinion, property, birth or other status'. While this provision is important in fending off any discriminatory action, the explicit absence of disability as one of the prohibited grounds of discrimination is unfortunate. Of course, it could be argued that the term 'other status' encompasses disability. Yet, in a country where persons with disabilities are often the target of discriminatory actions, the fact that disability is not mentioned as one of the grounds of prohibited discrimination suggests that disability did not receive much attention during the drafting process of the Constitution and persons with disabilities are effectively side-lined from receiving any form of collective protection of their rights.[34]

Following the adoption of the Constitution, however, Ethiopia has taken several steps to ensure the inclusion and non-discrimination of persons with disabilities. In this regard, as already mentioned, the primary step was ratification of the CRPD, making it an integral part of the Ethiopian legal order. Some scholars argue that the ratification has the effect of automatically making the international Convention directly applicable and enforceable in the national system, including courts.[35] Although the monist/dualist controversy is not solved, the direct applicability of the CRPD and, more generally, of international treaties, is endorsed by the highest court of the country, the Cassation Division of the Federal Supreme Court, which in recent years started to directly apply ratified international treaties in resolving cases brought before it.

Other federal legislative acts that protect persons with disabilities from discrimination include the above mentioned Proclamation on the Employment of Persons with Disabilities. Notable for being heavily influenced by the core values of the CRPD,[36] it adopts, as discussed in the previous subsection, the social model of disability. Further, the Proclamation explicitly prohibits discrimination on the basis of disability.[37] Article 5 of the Proclamation specifically targets discrimination in the workplace. It encourages persons with disabilities to judicially enforce their rights when they are discriminated against by their employers. According to Article 7:

> any person with [a] disability who alleges that discrimination on the ground of his disability existed with respect to recruitment, promotion, placement, transfer or other conditions of employment may institute a suit to the competent court on the issue without the requirement of the burden of proof.

[34] See also the discussion above under section II.

[35] GA Woldemariam, 'The Place of International Law in the Ethiopian Legal System' in Z Yihdego et al (eds), *Ethiopian Yearbook of International Law* (Springer, 2016).

[36] See S Yohannes, 'Towards Inclusive Employment: The Conceptual Basis and Features of Proclamation 568/2008 on the Employment of Persons with Disabilities' (2010) 24 *Journal of Ethiopian Law*.

[37] M Abdo, 'Disability and the Criminal Justice System in Ethiopia' in P Toggia, TF Geraghty and K Wolde (eds), *Access to Justice in Ethiopia: Towards Inventory of Issues* (Center for Human Rights, 2014) 407.

However, as will be discussed in the subsequent sections, the litigation of this proclamation, especially in courts of law has been limited.[38]

At the sub-national level, state constitutions provide protection against discrimination and rights of persons with disabilities in an identical way to that of the Federal Constitution. In particular, all sub-national constitutions of Ethiopia simply reproduce chapter three of the Constitution and Articles 25 and 41(5), without expanding or widening the protections they can offer.[39] As Fessha argues elsewhere,[40] one is faced with a constitutional *déjà vu* while revisiting sub-national constitutions of Ethiopia. Thus, the fact that the above-mentioned rights are addressed similarly at sub-national levels is not surprising. However, this is regrettable because, while the Constitution has given wide sub-national constitutional space for the sub-national units to adopt their own constitutions, the units have not made adequate use of this autonomy in either providing for additional rights or supplementing the deficiencies of the Constitution. This in turn has led sub-national units to neglecting or maybe under-utilising their powers.

The practice of state authorities may also not live up to the expectation of their Constitution that preaches equality and prohibits discrimination. In the state of Amhara, for example, customary practice prohibited visually impaired people from becoming judges. This discriminatory practice was the object of a petition that was brought before the House of Federation (HoF), the second chamber of the Federal Parliament, the body that deals with constitutional disputes.[41] In that case, two applicants (Wossen Alemu and Dawit Oticho) challenged the constitutionality of the decision of the Amhara Justice Professionals Training and Legal Research Institute (AJPTLRI) that barred them from becoming judges.[42] Both applicants were informed that they could not be recruited as judges because they were blind. The applicants argued that they had attended the same practical short-term legal training that was attended by other able-bodied trainees, thereby fulfilling the requirements for appointment. The decision to

[38] *Mekonnen Teklu v Addis Ababa City Administration Justice Bureau*, Federal Supreme Court Cassation Division Decision Volume 13 Cassation File No 75034, 11 November 2013.

[39] See Arts 25, 41(5) of the Southern Nations, Nationalities and Peoples Constitution; Arts 25, 39(5) of the Afar Constitution; Arts 25, 40(5) of the Sidama Constitution; Arts 25, 41(5) of the Harari Constitution; Arts 26, 41(5) of the Benishangul Gumuz Constitution; Arts 26, 41(5) of the Gambella Constitution; Arts 25, 41(5) of the Amhara Constitution; Arts 25, 41(5) of the Tigray Constitution; Arts 25, 41(5) of the South Western Region Constitution; Arts 25, 41(5) of the Oromia Constitution; Arts 26, 41(6) of the Somali Constitution, which respectively deal with the right to equality and the rights of persons with disabilities.

[40] YT Fessha, 'Subnational Constitutionalism in Ethiopia: Constitutional Déjà Vu' in P Popelier, G Delledonne and N Aroney (eds), *The Routledge Handbook of Subnational Constitutions and Constitutionalism* (Routledge, 2021).

[41] See Council of Constitutional Inquiry Journal, Volume 1, 145–48.

[42] Before submitting their case to the Council of Constitutional Inquiry and House of Federation, they petitioned the Amhara Justice Professionals Training and Legal Research Institute (AJPTLRI), which was not successful. They then took the matter to the Judicial Administration Council of the regional state. That Council also rejected their application. The AJPTLRI has a customary norm of not electing visually impaired people to the position of judgeship.

bar them from judgeship, they argued, contravenes their constitutional right to choose their own profession.[43] Further, it constitutes a discriminatory act that should not be tolerated. The HoF ruled that the practice of barring visually impaired individuals from being appointed as judges not only violates the right to work, enshrined in the Constitution, but also other guarantees provided in the CRPD, to which Ethiopia is a party. It further stated that the ban on blind people becoming judges violates the rights provided by the Proclamation on the Right to Employment of Persons with Disabilities.[44]

The HoF has not always taken the opportunity to rectify the discriminatory policies and acts of state governments and their institutions. In a case that was brought by the Ethiopian National Association for the Blind,[45] the HoF was asked to rule on the constitutionality of a directive[46] of the Education Bureau of the state of Oromia that denied blind individuals admission to a teachers' training college. The association sought for the directive to be declared unconstitutional on the ground that it denied admission to two blind applicants (despite both fulfilling admission requirements). The state based its defence on the best interest of the child, arguing that children have the right to be taught by fully able teachers. The disability of the applicants was said to be against the best interest of the child. The Council of Constitutional Inquiry (CCI), the body that is tasked with assisting the HoF by examining the constitutional issue, and which can either remand the case to the competent court after it has found no need for constitutional interpretation, or submit its finding on constitutional interpretation to the HoF, resolved the matter on procedural grounds and did not deal with the substantive issues. In particular, the CCI, citing Article 84(2) of the Constitution, declared that it has no jurisdiction to rule on the matter and would only have jurisdiction when a particular law (promulgated by the federal or state parliaments) is being challenged as unconstitutional.

The Constitution only refers to the power of the HoF, assisted by the CCI, to deal with the constitutionality of federal and state laws. It makes no reference to directives. This suggests that courts are not excluded from adjudicating the constitutionality of directives. However, judges are often reluctant to resolve disputes by engaging in the interpretation of the Constitution. They argue that the courts are excluded from dealing with constitutional disputes and tend to refer matters to the CCI. Ultimately, this back and forth prolongs the process for claimants who require an immediate solution to their issue. In the case mentioned above, it is very unfortunate that neither the court that first saw the

[43] They relied on Art 41(2) of the Constitution, which states: 'every Ethiopian has the right to choose his or her means of livelihood, occupation and profession'.

[44] Right to Employment of Persons with Disabilities Proclamation 568/2008 (n 20).

[45] *Ethiopian National Association for the Blind v Oromia Region Education Bureau and Jimma Teachers Training College.*

[46] Under Ethiopia's legal system a directive is a law that is passed by the Executive to implement a law (proclamation) passed by the National Parliament or regional legislatures. Directives have binding effect like ordinary laws.

matter nor the CCI that received the matter by referral seized the opportunity to promote the rights of persons with disabilities by making it clear that respecting equality and non-discrimination does not undermine the best interest of children, especially with respect to the right to education as guaranteed under the Constitution.

Traces of sub-national activism have been witnessed in some instances. For instance, in its Initial Report to the CRPD Committee, Ethiopia stated that the state government of Amhara, one of the member states of the Federation, has introduced a compulsory placement system for those graduates who are visually impaired. Apparently, the administrative measure was taken by the state government with a view of alleviating the difficulty faced by this disability group in competing in the labour market.[47] In another instance, the Addis Ababa city administration[48] issued a directive on the prohibition against leasing government houses for commercial purposes, stating 'it was specially provided that persons with disabilities who may have rented the government house for some commercial purpose will not lose the benefit and maintain the house and use it as a means of income'.[49]

C. Accessibility

In the context of ensuring accessibility, one important federal law, although not directly framed as a disability law but with significant impact on accessibility rights of persons with disabilities, is the Ethiopian Building Proclamation.[50] Enacted in 2009, the Proclamation is designed to set a minimum national standard for the construction or modification of buildings or alteration of their use in order to ensure public health and safety.[51]

The law, among others, provides that 'any public building shall have a means of access suitable for use by physically impaired persons, including those who are obliged to use wheelchairs and those who are able to walk but unable to negotiate steps'.[52] While this provision affords the much-needed protection for the rights of persons with disabilities, particularly in the context of making buildings accessible, the expression 'public building' seems to apply only to buildings that are government-owned, and is not applicable to other types of buildings that offer public services. However, the Amharic version, which is the

[47] CRPD Committee, 'Consideration of Reports Submitted by States Parties under Art 35 of the Convention, Initial Reports of States Parties due in 2012, Ethiopia' (19 March 2015) www.un.org 7–8.

[48] Although Addis Ababa is not one of the member units of the Federation, as the capital city of the Federation it is entitled to its own measure of self-government.

[49] CRPD Committee (n 48) 11.

[50] Ethiopian Building Proclamation 624/2009 (n 21).

[51] See the Preamble of the Ethiopian Building Proclamation 624/2009 (n 21).

[52] Ethiopian Building Proclamation 624/2009 (n 21) Art 36(1).

official and binding version, seems to cover all buildings which are destined for public use. Nevertheless, in both cases, it is clear that the law does not apply to all types of buildings, and hence the duty of providing access is not applicable to buildings that are not designated for 'public use'.

In the Initial Report of Ethiopia to the CRPD Committee, it was mentioned that the state of Southern Nations, Nationalities and Peoples has taken a step in its plan to build a barrier-free environment for persons with disabilities.[53] The report, however, does not mention the legal basis for doing so and to what extent this is based on its sub-national autonomy.

Another law, also passed by the Federal Parliament, more specifically by the House of Peoples Representatives (HoPR) in 2019, relating to higher education in general, contains a specific provision regarding the right of students with disabilities to inclusive education. Article 41(1) states that 'higher education institutions shall make, to the extent possible, their facilities and programs amicable to use with relative ease by students with physical disabilities'. Additionally, Article 41(2) requires higher education institutions to 'relocate classes, develop alternative testing procedures and provide educational auxiliary aids in the interest of students with disabilities and learning disabilities'. Article 41(3) of the Proclamation mandates higher education institutions to make sure that building designs, physical landscapes of campuses, computers and other infrastructure take into account the interests of persons with disabilities. Article 41(4) obliges higher education institutions 'to ensure that students with physical challenges get academic assistance including tutorial sessions, exam time and submission deadline extensions'.

Despite the fact that these provisions represent steps in the right direction, the way in which some of these rights are framed suggests an understanding of disability rights that is shaped by the medical model. For instance, Article 41(3) by using the wording 'to the extent that situations and resources permit', seems to regard disability rights as charities that the government is at liberty to offer or deny.[54]

The federal policy documents, such as GTP I and II,[55] seem to be based on the belief that disability should no longer be regarded solely as a medical condition.[56] Yet, the manner in which these policies are sought to be implemented appears to deviate from the social model. For instance, GTP II proposes that more special schools for disabled children should be built. While the desire

[53] CRPD Committee (n 48) 17.

[54] There are also other non-disability-specific laws that address the rights of persons with disabilities. For instance, the Ethiopian Electoral Law that deals with the special needs of persons with disabilities in their capacity as voters or candidates in elections. See eg the Ethiopian Electoral, Political Parties Registration and Election's Code of Conduct Proclamation No 1162/2019, Fed Neg Gaz, Year 25, No 97, Arts 22(7), 32(2) and 52.

[55] These two policy documents were issued by the government with the aim of meeting the Sustainable Development Goals that were aimed toward fulfilling the national vision of becoming a low middle-income country by 2025.

[56] Iyassu and McKinnon (n 2) 56.

to address education-related needs of persons with disabilities is commendable, special schools are at odds with Article 24 CRPD and risk segregating disabled students from the rest of the student population. What Article 24 CRPD would instead require is putting in place mechanisms to accommodate disabled students within regular schools.[57]

D. Participation

In the context of participation, two policy documents are particularly notable. These are the Developmental Social Welfare Policy of Ethiopia (adopted by the Federal Government in 1996) and the already mentioned GTP (adopted by the Federal Government in 1999). Although neither document deals exclusively with disability, they both include relevant policies on the provision of appropriate health care, social services, assistive devices, other rehabilitation services, education, skills training, and other support services for persons with disabilities.[58]

Currently, the above mentioned NPA,[59] a policy document issued by the Federal Ministry of Labour and Social Affairs (MOLSA) in 2012, is the guiding document regarding persons with disabilities in Ethiopia. Under this document, the primary objective is enabling Ethiopia to become a more inclusive society.[60] In doing so, it aims at addressing the needs of persons with disabilities for a comprehensive rehabilitation service, equal opportunity for education, skills training and work, and full participation in the life of their families, communities and the nation.[61] In particular, it is stated in the policy document that:

> The NPA is based on a vision of fully inclusive Ethiopian society, where children, youth and adults with disabilities, regardless of gender or kind of disability, as well as their parents and families enjoy the same rights to participate in the same civil, political, economic, social and cultural spheres and to access the same medical, educational, social services, training, work and leisure opportunities enjoyed by other citizens.[62]

The policy further states that the ultimate vision to achieve 'an inclusive society, [where] people with disabilities are accepted, their abilities are valued, their diversity and independence are recognized, their human rights are protected, and they participate actively in the life and development of their communities and the nation'.[63]

[57] Ibid 60.
[58] Abdo (n 38) 235–236.
[59] This document issued in 2012 is designed to serve as a policy document until 2021.
[60] Ministry of Labour and Social Affairs, 'The National Plan of Action of Persons with Disabilities (2012–2021)' (April 2012) www.ilo.org iv.
[61] Ibid.
[62] Ibid.
[63] Ibid.

From the foregoing, it is clear that the Federal Government has dominated the legislative and policy field pertaining to the rights of persons with disabilities. Even the ratification of the CRPD has not changed that. State governments remained inactive actors in the areas of disability. This, as indicated earlier, is not for the lack of constitutional powers. As in many functional areas, the state governments have simply limited their role to that of implementing agents of the Federal Government.

V. THE IMPLEMENTATION OF ARTICLE 33 CRPD

The implementation of Article 33 CRPD is provided for, albeit not explicitly, under the NPA. According to the NPA, the planning and realisation of the NPA will be coordinated by the National Implementation and Monitoring Coordinating Committee (NIMCC). Chaired by MOLSA,[64] the Committee is composed of representatives from key federal ministries, organisations of persons with disabilities, relevant NGOs working on disability and religious organisations.[65] At the sub-national level, a similar committee is founded by a Labour and Social Affairs Bureau of a given state government. The implementation and monitoring coordinating committees, at both the federal and state levels, are expected to establish NPA technical committees, which will report to the respective coordinating committees.[66]

The National Coordinating Committee receives reports from the state coordinating committees and prepares periodic reports on the implementation of the NPA.[67] The reports from both the national and state committees are directed to MOLSA, who will, in turn, report to the national parliament annually on progress achieved in the implementation of the NPA.[68] MOLSA is expected to undertake a full review of the progress of implementation and impact of the NPA at the end of the first five years of the implementation and make necessary amendments thereafter.[69]

The NPA requires almost all federal ministries to submit annual progress reports on the implementation of the NPA to the NIMCC.[70] At the sub-national level, the NPA mandates state bureaus (without naming them) and local governments to coordinate activities regarding the implementation of the NPA. However, unlike the federal ministries, state bureaus and local governments are not required to submit annual reports.[71] The NPA also mandates organisations

[64] Ibid.
[65] Ibid 59.
[66] Ibid.
[67] Ibid.
[68] Ibid 60.
[69] Ibid.
[70] Ibid 60–62.
[71] Ibid 63.

of persons with disabilities and NGOs to actively participate in the work of national and sub-national implementation and monitoring coordinating committees.[72] However, it is not clear from the NPA to what extent these bodies can support a meaningful participation of persons with disabilities and offer an independent mechanism of coordination and, more importantly, monitoring.

Both the federal and state governments have taken some measures to implement the CRPD. To begin with, the Convention is now translated into the working languages of the state of Oromia and Tigray (Oromifa and Tigregna, respectively) as well as Amharic, the working language of the Federal Government and two other state governments.[73] At the sub-national level, the state of Southern Nations, Nationalities and Peoples has set up a task force on the implementation of the Convention.[74] While other states are also mandated to set up the same task force, that has not happened yet. There is, however, a practice of state governments submitting annual reports to the Ministry of Women and Social Affairs. A quick look at the reports submitted by the states of Tigray, Oromia, Somali and the two city administrations (Addis Ababa and Dire Dawa) reveals that the reports, except that of Oromia, are not made pursuant to Article 33 CRPD.

At the federal level, a piece of national legislation mandates each ministry to oversee the wellbeing of persons with disabilities.[75] Articles 19(11) and 36(1)(d) of the same Proclamation oblige each ministry to ensure that the policies, strategies, laws, development programmes and projects it formulates benefit, among others, persons with disabilities. Every ministry is responsible with implementing disability-related affairs and submitting periodic reports to the Prime Minister, Council of Ministers and other concerned bodies. Moreover, the Ministry of Women and Social Affairs (the Ministry which succeeded MOLSA) is particularly mandated to devise strategic plans to ensure that opportunities are facilitated to persons with disabilities in the realm of the country's political, economic and social activities.

VI. CONCLUDING REMARKS

The chapter has shown that, as yet, Ethiopia has paid very little attention to protecting the rights of persons with disabilities as an expression of a collective identity. This is despite the fact that the Ethiopian system generally gives a disproportionate consideration to group identities. However, the Constitution provides a long list of general human rights provisions, including an equality

[72] Ibid 64.
[73] CRPD Committee (n 48) 10.
[74] Ibid 40.
[75] The Definition of Powers and Duties of the Executive Organs of the Federal Democratic Republic of Ethiopia, Proclamation No 1263/2021, Fed Neg Gaz, Year 28, No 4.

guarantee clause, and a specific provision on the rights of persons with disabilities. Protection of disability rights has been further enhanced by ratification of the CRPD and the adoption of a number of laws that either directly or indirectly apply to persons with disabilities. In the context of the federal structure, these laws are entirely promulgated by the Federal Government, in spite of the fact that state governments have the power to enact laws using their significant constitutional (concurrent) framework powers.

A lot remains to be done by state governments, and they should use their law- and policy-making powers to protect and promote the rights of persons with disabilities. In fact, state governments could have already used their competences to provide for better protection of disability rights by taking the federal laws as bare minimum standards. For example, they could have issued their own building proclamations requiring all constructions within the state to be accessible to persons with disabilities. Further, they could have enacted laws in the areas of civil service, health and education. On the whole, states can and should use their policy-making powers to come up with more robust frameworks that advance the social model of disability, rather than limiting themselves to 'implementers' of federal policies and laws that still adhere to the charity and medical model.

12

Argentina

Ensuring Disability Rights in the Context of an Anachronistic Federal System

FRANCISCO J BARIFFI

I. INTRODUCTION

AFTER RETURNING TO democracy in 1983, Argentina initiated a process to ratify the core human rights treaties from both regional (Organization of American States – OAS) and universal (United Nations – UN) systems. A milestone in this process was the comprehensive reform of the National Constitution (*Constitución de la Nación Argentina* – CN) in 1994.[1] This reform not only included recognition of new rights, but also introduced profound changes to the constitutional model of hierarchy of human rights treaties. According to Article 75(22) CN, it is within the powers of the National Congress:

> [t]o approve or repeal treaties concluded with other nations and international organizations, and concordats with the Holy See. Treaties and concordats have a higher hierarchy than laws. The American Declaration of the Rights and Duties of Man; the Universal Declaration of Human Rights; the American Convention on Human Rights; the International Covenant on Economic, Social and Cultural Rights; the International Covenant on Civil and Political Rights and its empowering Protocol; the Convention on the Prevention and Punishment of Genocide; the International Convention on the Elimination of all Forms of Racial Discrimination; the Convention on the Elimination of all Forms of Discrimination against Women; the Convention against Torture and other Cruel, Inhuman or Degrading Treatments or Punishments; the Convention on the Rights of the Child; in the full force of their provisions, have constitutional hierarchy, do not repeal any section of the First Part of

[1] G Bidart Campos, *Manual de la Constitución Reformada* (EDIAR, 2001).

> this Constitution and are to be understood as complementing the rights and guarantees recognized herein. They shall only be denounced, in such event, by the National Executive Power after the approval of two-thirds of all the members of each House. In order to attain constitutional hierarchy, the other treaties and conventions on human rights shall require the vote of two-thirds of all the members of each House, after their approval by Congress.

While this provision has been interpreted in different ways by courts and academics alike,[2] the majority of scholars tend to agree on a twofold classification of international treaties within the Argentine constitutional system. On the one hand, human rights treaties listed in Article 75(22) CN have constitutional status, and, on the other hand, the rest of the international treaties have precedence over laws, but are below the hierarchy of the CN. Other human rights treaties not listed in that provision may be granted constitutional status, provided they are approved by the Congress with a qualified majority.

Since the reform of the Constitution in 1994, three additional human rights treaties have been granted with constitutional status. Among those is the UN Convention on the Rights of Persons with Disabilities (CRPD), which was ratified in 2008 and granted with constitutional status in 2011 respectively.[3] This means that the CRPD is an integral part of the Constitution, and therefore federal or provincial laws can be subject to constitutional review vis-à-vis the CRPD by all lower courts. This constitutional arrangement allowed the proliferation of several court cases challenging lower rank laws and regulations under the rationale of constitutional (conventional to be more precise) incompatibility.[4]

For example, in a recent case brought to the Supreme Court of Justice of the Nation (*Corte Suprema de Justicia de la Nación* – CSJN) pursuant to judicial review (*recurso extraordinario*), the majority of the body acknowledged that with the incorporation of the CRPD within the constitutional framework:

> there was a substantial change in the regime regarding the legal capacity of people with mental disabilities. The system of substitution and subrogation of the will was abandoned, and it was replaced by a social model of disability with the aim of promoting the person and guaranteeing the enjoyment of their rights.[5]

To sum up, Argentina incorporated into the legal systems as federal laws both the Inter-American Convention on the Elimination of All Forms of Discrimination against Persons with Disabilities (*Convención Interamericana para la Eliminación de todas las Formas de Discriminación contra las Personas*

[2] M Pinto, *Temas de Derechos Humanos* (Editores del Puerto, 2009); JC Hitters and O Fappiano, *Derecho Internacional de los Derechos Humanos, Tomo I* (EDIAR, 2007); J Barboza, *Derecho Internacional Público* (Zavalia, 2008).

[3] Act No 27,044 19-nov-2014 Boletín Oficial del 22-dic-2014, Número: 33035, Página 3.

[4] F Bariffi and E Jiménez, 'Capítulo XXVII Derechos de la Discapacidad' in JA Amaya (ed), *Tratado de Control de Constitucionalidad y Convencionalidad, Tomo IV* (Astrea, 2017).

[5] Corte Suprema de Justicia de la Nación (CSJN), Fallos: 341:745.

con Discapacidad – CIADDIS)[6] and the CRPD, the latter having constitutional status.[7]

In relation to this issue, during the first country review in 2012, the UN Committee on the Rights of Persons with Disabilities (CRPD Committee) requested Argentina to specify whether or not Act No 26,378 was a federal law or a general law that is applicable in all the provinces.[8] In its response to this question, the State Party declared that Act No 26,378 (CRPD) is a:

> Federal Law, of automatic and operative force throughout the country since its approval by the National Congress and promulgation by the Executive Branch (June 2008). It does not need to be approved or recognized by the provinces. This is due to the fact that the Supreme Court of Justice of the Nation (*Corte Suprema de Justicia de la Nación* – CSJN) has a consolidated jurisprudence that maintains that '[i]t is the obligation of local courts to apply international standards and the decisions of international protection bodies (Courts and Committees)'.[9]

Against this background, this chapter aims to investigate how the CRPD is implemented by the different components of the Argentine federal system. Section II discusses the division of competences starting with a brief description of the constitutional federal system and a short introduction to the domestic legal framework on disability. Section III identifies four selected areas of competences in order to assess the role of the national government vis-à-vis sub-national entities, ie concept of disability, equality and non-discrimination, accessibility and participation. Section IV addresses the implementation of Article 33 CRPD with a detailed analysis of all of its components – focal point, coordination mechanism and national monitoring. Finally, section V outlines some concluding remarks.

II. DIVISION OF COMPETENCES

A. Constitutional Federal System

Under Article 1 CN, the Argentine Nation adopts the representative, republican and federal form of government.[10] The Argentine federal system is a hybrid

[6] Act No 25,280 06-jul-2000 Boletín Oficial del 04-ago-2000, Número: 29455, Página 1.

[7] Act No 26,378 21-may-2008 Boletín Oficial del 09-jun-2008, Número: 31422, Página 1.

[8] Committee on the Rights of Persons with Disabilities (CRPD Committee), 'List of issues to be taken up in connection with the consideration of the initial report of Argentina (CRPD/C/ARG/1) concerning articles 1 to 33 of the Convention' CRPD/C/ARG/Q/1, 16 May 2012, para 2.

[9] CRPD Committee, 'Lista de cuestiones que deben abordarse al examinar el informe inicial de Argentina (CRPD/C/ARG/1) en relación con los artículos 1 a 33 de la Convención Adición Respuestas del Gobierno de la Argentina a la lista de cuestiones (CRPD/C/ARG/Q/1) que deben abordarse al examinar el informe inicial de la Argentina (CRPD/C/ARG/1)' CRPD/C/ARG/Q/1/Add 1, 5 September 2012, para 8.

[10] Constitución de la Nación Argentina (CN), Act No 24,430 (1994).

model, based on the constitutional model of the United States but with its own features. Currently, the Argentine decentralisation model comprises a sovereign federal or national state, 24 provinces that enjoy autonomy, the Autonomous City of Buenos Aires, and the different municipalities within the provincial units that enjoy autarchy.[11]

When the federal form of government is analysed, the distinction between sovereignty, autonomy and autarchy, which refer to how the exercise of power is carried out, becomes relevant. The federal state is the only sovereign. The provinces are political entities with their own individuality which are not sovereign according to Articles 5 and 31 CN, yet are autonomous according to Articles 5, 122 and 123 CN. Finally, the municipalities have autarchy.

Simply put, sovereignty and autonomy are expressions of political decentralisation while autarchy is an expression of administrative decentralisation. The sovereignty of the federal state implies that it exercises power supremely and independently, that it represents exclusively the nation before the international community, and that it dictates its own legal system without depending on anyone. The autonomy of the provinces implies that they have the power to dictate their own laws of a general nature, and that these are mandatory in their jurisdictional scope, although with limitations established by some norm or superior status. Finally, the autarchy of the municipalities implies powers to administer themself, but within the framework of the rules imposed by the provincial autonomy, whereas, they can choose their own government.[12]

The Argentine federal system relies on two fundamental principles that allow the articulation of the different competences between the Federation and the provinces. On the one hand, the principle of federal supremacy (Articles 5 and 31 CN) allows the federal state to control constitutionality over the entire lower legal system, on the other hand, pursuant to the principle of non-delegated power (Article 121 CN) the provinces keep all power not expressly or implicitly delegated to the Federation.[13]

The division of competences between the federal state and the provinces is based on the normative criteria included in the CN, which are divided in relation to the subject (*ratione materiae*), the territory (*ratione loci*), or the persons involved (*ratione personae*). This also has a direct impact on the division of powers between the federal jurisdiction and the different provincial jurisdictions. In short, the different components of the federal model include: a) exclusive competences of the Federation, for example, international relations or administration of customs; b) exclusive competences of the provinces, for example indirect taxation or primary education; c) concurrent competences, for example, internal indirect taxation or environmental protection; d) exceptional

[11] R Zuccherino and MJ Moreno Rithner, *Tratado de derecho federal, estadual y municipal, Volumen 1* (Lexis Nexis, 2007).

[12] N Sagües, *Elementos de Derecho Constitucional, Tomo I* (Astrea, 1993).

[13] S Linares Quintana, *Teoría e historia constitucional* (Alfa, 1958).

competences of both the Federation – indirect taxation – and the provinces – provisional codes; and e) shared competences, for example the creation of new provinces or the declaration of federal intervention by express request of the province.[14] In relation to adoption of public policies and legislations on human rights, the division of competences is complex and not without controversy.

Both scholars and case law concur in affirming that, with regard to human rights issues, the CN sets a threshold, ie a minimum standard of protection, which can be expanded (and in fact has been) in their respective provincial jurisdictional frameworks. However, the implementation of the so-called 'federal clause' included in Article 28 of the American Convention on Human Rights, or in Article 4(5) CRPD has been inconsistent.[15] For example, in the case of *Garrido and Baigorria v Argentina*,[16] the Federal Government alleged difficulties in adopting measures due to the federal structure. The Inter-American Court of Human Rights ruled that:

> When a federal state's constituent units have jurisdiction over human rights matters, Article 28 of the Convention makes provision for said federal state becoming a party to the Convention. However, from the time of its approval and ratification of the Convention, Argentina has conducted itself as if the federal state had jurisdiction over human rights matters. Hence, it can hardly argue the contrary now, as this would imply a breach of the principle of estoppel. As for the 'difficulties' invoked by the State at the 20 January 1998 hearing, the Court should note that the case law, which has stood unchanged for more than a century, holds that a state cannot plead its federal structure to avoid complying with an international obligation.

The federal structure is challenging in relation to public policies for two main reasons. On the one hand, because Argentina is a politically and administratively decentralised federation with a high geographic concentration of resource-production and wide interprovincial inequalities. On the other hand, because the Argentine provincial governments are, in general, weak and dependent from a financial point of view, yet strong and autonomous from a political point of view. Likewise, provincial governments have a crucial role in the implementation of public policies, as well as in the provision of public goods and services. Provinces are strongly influential in the provision of goods with high public visibility, given that they expend almost all of the budget on items of social public spending, such as education, culture, science and technology, followed by health, social security, promotion and social assistance, and housing.[17]

The CN does not include specific acknowledgment of the rights of persons with disabilities. Conversely, some provincial constitutions enshrine specific

[14] G Bidart Campos, *Compendio de Derecho Constitucional* (EDIAR, 2004).

[15] V Bazan, 'El Federalismo Argentino: Situación actual, cuestiones conflictivas y perspectivas' (2013) 11 *Estudios Constitucionales* 37–88.

[16] Inter-American Court of Human Rights, *Case of Garrido and Baigorria v Argentina*, Judgment of 27 August 1998, Series C No 26, para 46.

[17] L Granato, 'Federalismo Argentino y Descentralización: Sus implicancias para la formulación de políticas públicas' (2015) 18 *Prolegómenos*.

provisions on disability, yet they do not always align with the CRPD, eg Article 36 of the Constitution of Buenos Aires, Article 42 of the Constitution of the Autonomous City of Buenos Aires, or Article 27 of the Constitution of Córdoba.

Article 43 CN establishes a guarantee (*amparo*) to grant direct and summary judicial remedies against any form of discrimination. Further, Article 75(23) CN, established that the National Congress shall have the power:

> [t]o legislate and promote positive measures guaranteeing true equal opportunities and treatment, the full benefit and exercise of the rights recognised by this Constitution and by the international treaties on human rights in force, particularly referring to children, women, the elderly, and persons with disabilities.

Consequently, the CN falls into a 'trap' created by its own territorial structure. On the one hand, the federal legislative body has the power and responsibility to ensure equal opportunities with special attention to groups in situations of vulnerability and with specific reference to persons with disabilities by means of debating and adopting federal legislation, and, on the other hand, such legislation must be accepted or harmonised by each territorial entity in order to be enforceable at provincial level. This was observed already during the first country review (which occurred in 2012), when the CRPD Committee noted:

> with concern that, because not all of the State party's provincial legislation is aligned with the Convention, disparities arise in the approach taken at the local level to the rights of persons with disabilities and to the effective exercise of those rights.[18]

It is worth mentioning that this shortcoming is also present in relation to the rights of other groups in a situation of vulnerability such as the protection of children and adolescents[19] or the protection of women against violence.[20]

B. Disability Law Framework

The Argentine legal framework dealing with disability rights encompasses various sources, such as the CN, national laws and regulations, provincial constitutions, provincial laws and regulations, and international treaties.

Originally the disability legal framework revolved around Act No 22,431 on the Comprehensive Protection System for the Disabled (1981);[21] Act No 24,901 on the System of Basic Benefits in Habilitation and Comprehensive Rehabilitation in Favour of Persons with Disabilities (1997);[22] and Act No 25,504 on the Single

[18] CRPD Committee, 'Concluding observations on the initial report of Argentina as approved by the Committee at its eighth session' CRPD/C/ARG/CO/1, 8 October 2012, para 5.

[19] Act No 26,061 28-sep-2005 Boletín Oficial del 26-oct-2005, Número: 30767, Página 1.

[20] Act No 26,485 11-mar-2009 Boletín Oficial del 14-abr-2009, Número: 31632, Página 1.

[21] Sistema de Protección Integral de los Discapacitados 16-mar-1981 Boletín Oficial del 20-mar-1981, Número: 24632, Página 6.

[22] Sistema de Prestaciones Básicas por Discapacidad 05-nov-1997 Boletín Oficial del 05-dic-1997, Número: 28789, Página 1.

Disability Certificate (2001).[23] These were complemented by specific regulations, all of which supported a notion of disability essentially based on the medical model and far from the acknowledgement of persons with disabilities as social actors.[24] Act No 22,431 is still the main legislation on disability rights in Argentina. The Act was amended in 1994 by Act No 24,314[25] on Accessibility for Persons with Limited Mobility, and the relevant regulations were issued by Decree No 914/97.[26] Further, Act No 24,901 of 1996 establishes the single system of basic benefits for persons with disabilities. This statute includes multiple aspects, for example benefits in: rehabilitation (specific rehabilitation and technical aids), educational therapeutics (therapeutic educational centres, day centres, early stimulation), educational (schools, school integration support services, job training), welfare (homes, small homes, residences), complementary and special transport.

Given the federal character of the Argentine system, the express adherence of each jurisdiction is required so that the benefits established by Law No 24,901 apply in each territory. At the federal level, this generates an unacceptable inequality that results in the lack of protection of many persons with disabilities who live on the other side of a provincial border.

The ratification by Argentina of the OAS treaty on disability in 2000 and the CRPD in 2008, triggered a law reform process in order to align the domestic legislation to the regional and universal human rights obligations.[27]

On 3 December 2010, Argentina enacted the National Mental Health Act No 26,657.[28] Whereas this law was adopted in order to adjust the domestic legislation to international and regional human rights obligations, it does not seriously question the legitimacy of involuntary psychiatric commitments per se, but only purports to impose additional procedural safeguards that limit their application. Nor does the Act seriously undermine the legitimacy of legal capacity restrictions: it merely modifies the means by which they are imposed slightly. Ultimately, the federal enactment focuses more on the responsibilities of the mental health professionals who work with persons with psycho-social disabilities and less on detailing the substantive, non-derogable rights of those persons as active users of the mental health system. Similarly, due to the

[23] Modificación Ley 22,431 14-nov-2001 Boletín Oficial del 13-dic-2001, Número: 29795, Página 1.

[24] CH Acuña and L Built Goñi, *Políticas sobre la discapacidad en Argentina. El desafío de hacer realidad los derechos* (Editorial Siglo XXI, 2010).

[25] Accesibilidad de Personas con Movilidad Reducida 15-mar-1994 Boletín Oficial del 12-abr-1994, Número: 27868, Página 1.

[26] Decreto 914/1997 Reglamentación de los artículos 20, 21 y 22 de la Ley No 22,431 modificados por su similar No 24,314 11/9/97.

[27] F Bariffi, 'Human Rights and Disability: Reinterpreting Disability within the OAS in the light of the CRPD' in C O'Mahony and G Quinn (eds), *Disability Law and Policy: An Analysis of the UN Convention* (Clarus Press, 2017).

[28] Ley Nacional de Salud Mental 25-nov-2010 Boletín Oficial del 03-dic-2010, Número: 32041, Página 1.

federal structure of the country, laws of this type must be recognised by the provinces.[29]

On 1 October 2014, the National Congress approved a new comprehensive Civil and Commercial Code, which entered into force in August 2015.[30] The new Code partially includes the supported decision-making model enshrined in Article 12 CRPD. The provisions laid down in Articles 31 to 50 of the Civil and Commercial Code establish a new regime regarding the limitation and restriction of the legal capacity of persons with disabilities. This new legal regime contemplates the coexistence of two models, that is, the supported decision-making model (restricted capacity), and the substitution model (incapacity).[31] The Argentine Civil and Commercial Code, is among the few federal laws which are directly applicable to both the national and the provincial levels. This is possible pursuant to Article 75(12) CN.[32]

III. THE ROLE OF THE NATIONAL GOVERNMENT VIS-À-VIS SUB-NATIONAL ENTITIES IN SELECTED AREAS

A. Concept of Disability

As in most jurisdictions, Argentina requires a certification in order to consider an individual as a person with a disability. This recognition is accredited in the 'single disability certificate' (*Certificado Único de Discapacidad* – CUD), which allows the holder to benefit from both non-discriminatory remedies and social protection schemes. The assessments are carried out according to the International Classification of Functioning, Disability and Health (ICF).

The concept of disability is enshrined in Article 2 of Act No 22,431 of 1981. This Act, which in many parts is still in force, was adopted under Argentina's last military regime (1973–82). The Act aims to create a 'comprehensive system for the protection of the disabled' (*Sistema de protección integral de los discapacitados*)

[29] F Bariffi and M Smith, 'Same Old Game but with Some New Players – Assessing Argentina's National Mental Health Law in Light of the Rights to Liberty and Legal Capacity under the UN Convention on the Rights of the Persons with Disabilities' (2013) 31 *Nordic Journal of Human Rights*.

[30] Código Civil y Comercial de la Nación Ley 26,994 01-oct-2014 Boletín Oficial del 08-oct-2014, Número: 32985, Página 1.

[31] F Bariffi, 'Restricción a la capacidad y capacidad civil. Tensiones constitucionales y Código Civil y Comercial' (2016) 77 *Derecho de Familia. Revista Interdisciplinaria de Doctrina y Jurisprudencia.*

[32] Article 75 reads as follows: 'Congress is empowered: … 12. To enact the Civil, Commercial, Criminal, Mining, Labour and Social Security Codes, in unified or separate bodies, provided that such codes do not alter local jurisdictions, and their enforcement shall correspond to the federal or provincial courts depending on the respective jurisdictions for persons or things; and particularly to enact general laws of naturalisation and nationality for the whole nation, based on the principle of nationality by birth or by option for the benefit of Argentina; as well as laws on bankruptcy, counterfeiting of currency and public documents of the State, and those laws that may be required to establish trial by jury.'

covering areas such as social security, prevention, health, education, transport and built environment. According to Article 2 Act No 22,431, a person is 'disabled' when they are suffering from a permanent or prolonged functional alteration, either physical or mental, that in relation to their age and social environment implies considerable disadvantages for their family, social, educational or labour integration. Clearly under the influence of the medical model, the concept of disability in Argentina's cornerstone legislation is inconsistent with the corresponding definition of the CRPD. Article 3 specifies that the existence of the disability, its nature and its degree, as well as the possibility of rehabilitation of the affected person, will be certified by a governmental agency, currently the National Disability Agency (*Agencia Nacional de Discapacidad* – ANDIS).

Regarding the division of powers among levels of government, Article 27 indicates that the National Government:

> will propose to the provinces the adoption within their jurisdictions of normative regimes that establish similar principles to those of the present law. In the act of adhering to this law, each province will establish the agencies that will be in charge at the provincial level, of the activities provided for in [A]rticles 6, 7 and 13 above. They will also determine the scope of the rules contained in [A]rticles 8 and 11 of this law with regard to public bodies and provincial companies, as well as with respect to public or private domain assets of the provincial state and its municipalities.

This provision outlines with clarity the complexities of the federal system in the implementation of disability rights. The law acknowledges that provinces are not directly bound by their provisions unless they 'adhere' to the Act or establish their own legislation with similar principles. Coordination between the Federation and the provinces is essential as the obligations enshrined in the Act require allocation of resources (budget) and involve shared and concurrent competences. The references to specific Articles highlight the main areas of provincial autonomy. Article 6 deals with health and social assistance, Article 7 with mental health, and Article 13 with education. Similarly, Article 8 deals with governmental quotas (affirmative action) and Article 11 with public procurement and public domains.

While it cannot be attributed to this Act but rather to the Argentine constitutional system, Article 27 shaped a model of decentralisation for disability laws and policies in all subsequent normative developments. According to this model, both Federation and provinces are competent to adopt legislative and political measures about most disability related issues within their own jurisdictions. This has allowed the proliferation of diverse provincial legislations and policies are not always harmonised or synchronised with the national administration. The most evident proof of this are the asymmetries between provincial jurisdictions and the Federation in assessing and awarding the disability certificate. For this reason, in 2001, Act No 25,504 created the CUD as a way to unify and ensure territorial equality. In the first country report review,[33] the CRPD Committee outlined:

> The Committee acknowledges the progress represented by the introduction of the Single Disability Certificate. However, it notes with concern that the certificate has not yet been rolled out nationwide and that there are disparities in the criteria used for its issuance.

Argentina has indicated before the CRPD Committee that the concept of disability included in both the CRPD and the OAS Disability Convention are part of the domestic legislation pursuant to their respective Acts of Approval. While this is indeed the case, in practice these definitions do not have any practical application in either law or politics. The gateway to access any disability right or benefit, including anti-discrimination protection, is the CUD. Without this administrative certification an individual is left behind the protection of the legal framework, in clear breach of the CRPD.

The adoption of the CUD was a major step towards a federalisation of governmental measures in relation to disability rights obligations. It showed how harmonisation between federal and provincial competences is possible when all entities share not only legislative powers but also the need to tackle asymmetries causing serious implementation problems between jurisdictions.

In February 2022, the Federal Government announced a law reform process to adopt a new comprehensive disability Act to replace Act No 22,431.[34] According to the public information of the National Disability Agency the adoption of the new legislation will be carried out through a federal consultation process in light of Articles 4 and 33 CRPD. The government has also announced that this new legislation will adopt an intersectional and intercultural perspective and will be underpinned by the social model of disability. It will be a law that promotes universal designs for all environments and that understands the person with disabilities as an active subject of life in society in all its aspects, inter alia, education, employment, health, social protection, accessibility, political participation and autonomous and independent life.

This law reform process also reveals a clear impulse towards centralisation of disability rights. The public announcement also acknowledges, as a central aspect of the new comprehensive disability legislation, that instances of plural and federal dialogue will be generated as well as exchanges gathering the contributions and opinions of civil society, people with disabilities and their families, organisations of and for people with disabilities, and public entities, such as unions, universities, and all key sectors.

[33] CRPD Committee (n 18) para 9.

[34] Agencia Nacional de Discapacidad (ANDIS), 'Nueva Ley de Discapacidad' www.argentina.gob.ar.

B. Non-Discrimination and Equality

As indicated above, the core statutes on disability were released way before the adoption of the CRPD and therefore are inspired by the old medical model paradigm. For this reason, Acts Nos 22,431, 24,901 and 25,504 do not include anti-discrimination provisions and do not deal with inclusive equality or denial of reasonable accommodations. Some provisions may support affirmative action – such as quotas or free transportation – but there is no explicit reference to equality and non-discrimination.

The main anti-discrimination legislation in Argentina is Act No 23,592 on 'discriminatory acts', enacted in 1988.[35] The Act contains only seven Articles and adopts a narrow approach towards discrimination. Article 1 indicates that:

> Whoever arbitrarily prevents, obstructs, restricts or in any way undermines the full exercise on an equal basis of the fundamental rights and guarantees recognized in the National Constitution, will be obliged, at the request of the victim, to annul or cease the discriminatory act, and to repair the moral and material damage caused. For the purposes of this article, discriminatory acts or omissions will be considered if they are determined for reasons such as race, religion, nationality, ideology, political or union opinion, sex, economic position, social condition or physical characteristics.

Whereas this definition of non-discrimination follows, to a great extent, the human rights standard formula, it falls short of the CRPD standards for different reasons. Firstly, it does not include express reference to disability as a ground for protection from discrimination, even though the enforcing body, the National Institute to Combat Discrimination, Xenophobia and Racism (*Instituto Nacional contra la Discriminación, la Xenofobia y el Racismo* – INADI), reports disability as the main ground of discrimination cases.[36] Secondly, the Act does not include further provisions to address all forms of discrimination, but rather provisions to criminalise serious discriminatory acts when they are committed 'for persecution or hatred of a race, religion or nationality, or with the aim of destroying in whole or in part a national, ethnic, racial or religious group' (Article 2). Lastly, Argentina's Anti-Discrimination Act is an old-fashioned statute, clearly aimed at 'direct' discrimination such as 'hate crimes' or 'hate propaganda', but does not cover other forms of discrimination such as indirect discrimination, structural discrimination, inversion of the burden of proof, or other disability-related measures such as accessibility and reasonable accommodations.

[35] Medidas contra Actos Discriminatorios 03-ago-1988 Boletín Oficial del 05-sep-1988, Número: 26458, Página 1.

[36] Instituto Nacional contra la Discriminación, la Xenofobia y el Racismo (INADI) and Ministerio de Justicia y Derechos Humanos – Presidencia de la Nación, 'Discapacidad y No Discriminación' Documentos temáticos INADI (2012) www.argentina.gob.ar.

As indicated by Argentina during the first review process before the CRPD Committee, Act No 23,592 prohibits discriminatory acts, and the INADI is responsible for developing national policies to combat all forms of discrimination, xenophobia and racism, and for promoting and implementing federal and cross-cutting public policies in coordination with civil society aimed at achieving a diverse and egalitarian society.

The INADI has set up a complaint centre which receives and reviews complaints from individuals or groups who consider themselves victims of discriminatory practices. When the Institute has concluded an investigation of an administrative case involving a complaint of discrimination, an opinion is drafted. This consists of a report based on the evidence considered during the investigation and the relevant legislation. In its report, the Institute states its conclusion as to whether or not there has been discriminatory behaviour or omissions that violate Act No 23,592 on discriminatory acts.[37]

The inconsistencies between this anti-discrimination legislation and the obligations set forth by the CRPD were noted by the CRPD Committee in the list of issues to the Initial State Report:

> Given that there are a number of different anti-discrimination regulations, please indicate which national regulations have been used for the specific purpose of incorporating the concept of 'discrimination on grounds of disability' into general legislation, with particular reference to Act No. 24,013 on employment, Act No. 23,592 on discriminatory acts, Act No. 20,744 on employment contracts, Act No. 26,206 on education, Act No. 24,901 on the system of basic services and Act No. 26,657 on mental health. Please specify if 'denial of reasonable accommodation' is defined as a form of discrimination. Please indicate what percentage of reported cases of discrimination result in the imposition of penalties for the commission of acts of discrimination against persons with disabilities.[38]

The state response seems elusive and ambiguous. On the one hand, Argentina affirms that the definitions of 'disability-based discrimination' included in both the CIADDIS and the CRPD are part of its domestic legislation, and therefore, enforceable before local courts. On the other hand, Argentina quotes specific provisions contained in diverse statutes in areas such as employment (Act 24,013 and Act 20,744), education (Act 26,206), or mental health (Act 26,657) which include non-discrimination clauses. While these provisions are relevant for non-discrimination purposes, they are evidently insufficient to ensure and protect disability rights as recognised by the CRPD.

In the Concluding Observations to the initial report, the CRPD Committee noted:

> with concern that neither the concept of reasonable accommodation nor recognition that the denial of such accommodation is a form of discrimination are explicitly

[37] 'Dictámenes del INADI' www.argentina.gob.ar.
[38] CRPD Committee (n 8) para 4.

> included in anti-discrimination laws or in the laws on, among other things, employment, health and education. It also wishes to express its concern at the lack of simplified judicial and administrative remedies that would allow persons with disabilities to report cases of discrimination on grounds of disability. The Committee is concerned at the lack of information on measures and actions designed to address the specific situations of persons with disabilities who belong to indigenous peoples and of deaf-blind persons.[39]

The most recent State Party report submitted to the CRPD Committee does not seem to include any new and relevant information on this matter. Civil society, through a Joint Shadow Report, reaffirms that 'the current anti-discrimination legislation – Acts No. 23,592; 24,782 and 25,608 – has not explicitly included denial of reasonable accommodation as a form of discrimination on grounds of disability, nor has provided for multiple discrimination either'.[40] For this reason, the government has indicated that:

> Legislation is being drafted to amend the Anti-Discrimination Act (Act No. 23,592) so that it will cover more forms of discrimination and other socially vulnerable groups that are subject to discrimination, given the close relationship between the principle of non-discrimination and vulnerable persons or groups. The Secretariat for Human Rights and Cultural Pluralism has produced reports on the alignment of this draft legislation with the Convention in order to ensure that the amended law will be in compliance with the international treaties to which the State is a party.[41]

Strictly speaking, equality and non-discrimination is a shared competence between the federal state and the provinces. In fact, some provinces have their own non-discrimination legislations. For example, the City of Buenos Aires adopted an Act Against Discrimination in 2015 which basically includes and expands the provisions set forth at federal level.

But with the adoption of the first Anti-Discrimination Act by the National Government in 1988 and the reform of the CN in 1994 (Articles 43 and 75(23) CN), a shift toward the federalisation of this matter became inevitable. For example, since 2008, the INADI has under its competences created a Federal Council for Anti-Discrimination Public Policies (*Consejo Federal de Políticas Públicas Antidiscriminatorias*), to promote the dialogue and exchange between the provincial governments, the Autonomous City of Buenos Aires, and the nation, in order to propose and carry out the design and implementation of policies against discrimination in the country.

Similarly, in 2022, a new Bill to replace Act 23,592 was submitted to the National Congress (*Cámara de Diputados*). The Bill expands the narrow character of the current Act and recognises the federal competence in relation to any

[39] CRPD Committee (n 18) para 11.

[40] SN Funes (ed), 'Joint Shadow Report' (1 August 2017) www.ohchr.org.

[41] CRPD Committee, 'Combined second and third periodic reports submitted by Argentina under article 35 of the Convention, due in 2018' CRPD/C/ARG/2-3, 5 March 2019, para 56.

discriminatory act in the territory. The Bill indicates that the provisions of this law are of public order and mandatory compliance throughout the territory of the nation.

C. Accessibility

Act No 22,431, on the comprehensive protection system for the disabled, already included in 1981 chapter IV, which dealt with differentiated transportation and architecture, and was amended in 1994 by Act No 24,314 on Accessibility for Persons with Limited Mobility.[42] The amended chapter IV introduces three new provisions (Articles 20–22) to deal with the accessibility of the physical environment. The chapter aims at removing physical barriers in urban architectural and transport areas. This includes public buildings, as well as private buildings of public use, transport vehicles and premises, and housing. For the purposes of this law, accessibility is understood as the possibility for people with reduced mobility to enjoy the adequate conditions of safety and autonomy as a fundamental element for the development of activities of daily life without restrictions derived from the physical, urban, architectural or transport environment for their integration and equalisation of opportunities.

Since this amendment dates back to 1994, the obligations set forth are quite restricted in both substantive and subjective elements. Regarding the latter, the Act specifies 'people with reduced mobility', excluding any other impairment like 'sensory' or 'cognitive'. Regarding the former, the Act restricts its application to the physical environment excluding other areas such as 'relations with the public administration', 'communication', or the 'digital environment'.

In order to ensure compliance with these accessibility requirements, the regulation of this Act created a Monitoring and Advisory Committee (*Comité de Asesoramiento y Contralor*) with the purpose of monitoring Articles 20, 21 and 22, submitting complaints against breaches of these requirements, providing technical advisory services for the correct implementation, and proposing harmonisation criteria.[43] Moreover, in 2017 the federal administration launched a National Accessibility Plan aimed at creating and proposing:

> through participatory action and in coordination with the different areas and jurisdictions of the National Public Administration, of the Autonomous City of Buenos Aires, provincial and municipal, with competence in the matter, and with the Organizations of the Civil Society, especially Non-Governmental Organizations of, and for, people with disabilities, of public policies aimed at the full social inclusion

[42] Accesibilidad de Personas con Movilidad Reducida 15-mar-1994 Boletín Oficial del 12-abr-1994, Número: 27868, Página 1.

[43] Decreto 914/97, Apruébese la Reglamentación de los artículos 20, 21 y 22 de la Ley No 22,431 modificados por su similar No 24,314.

> of people with disabilities, in light of the principles and obligations set forth in the Convention on the Rights of Persons with Disabilities approved by Act No. 26,378.[44]

While the accessibility provisions in the main disability Act are restricted to the physical environment, other thematic legislation includes specific accessibility requirements in relation to transportation, to information and communications (including information and communication technologies and systems), and to other facilities and services open or provided to the public, including by private entities, both in urban and in rural areas.[45]

In the first country report review, the CRPD Committee noted:

> with concern that, despite the establishment of the Advisory and Monitoring Committee, the State party does not have effective mechanisms for overseeing and evaluating compliance with accessibility legislation in all the areas covered by the Convention or for regulating and monitoring the imposition of sanctions for non-compliance. The Committee is also concerned about the challenge posed by the State party's federal structure in terms of the achievement of full accessibility for all persons with disabilities in every province and municipality in its territory.[46]

During the second country report review (ongoing), civil society, in a joint shadow report, has pointed out the tremendous difficulties of implementation and effectiveness of accessibility requirements derived from territorial decentralisation:

> Regarding architectural and infrastructural barriers, current Accessibility Act No. 24,314 – whose adoption is still optional to provinces – is far to be accomplished, and the ad hoc Monitoring Committee doesn't play its role. In Córdoba Province, the Accessibility Office (Under-Secretariat of Disability, Rehabilitation and Health Inclusion) it is not competent to intervene on complaints and claims. In the Autonomous City of Buenos Aires, there are serious irregularities, inter alia: explicit exceptions to accessibility (commercial stores), different requirements for school buildings, depending on its public or private management, and the absent governmental control generates a false and risky accessibility in public road.[47]

In order to tackle the shortcomings derived from the Argentine federal system, Act No 24,314 introduces in Act No 22,431 a new Article 27, which provides that the provinces 'will be invited to adhere to and/or incorporate the contents of Articles 20, 21 and 22 hereof into their respective regulations'.

In short, accessibility is likely the most troublesome dimension of disability rights in the Argentine federal landscape for three main reasons. Firstly,

[44] Decreto 868/2017, Créase 'Plan Nacional de Discapacidad'.

[45] See eg Act No 25,635 on free land transport for persons with disabilities; Act No 25,643 on accessible tourism; Act No 26,522 on audiovisual communication services; Act No 26,619 on public procurement; Act No 26,989 on Braille instructions in commercial aviation; Act No 26,285 on waiver of property law to ensure access of blind persons to written texts; or Act No 26,653 on accessibility to web pages.

[46] CRPD Committee (n 18) para 9.

[47] Funes (n 40).

accessibility is not enshrined as a single right, but rather as isolated obligations set forth in specific laws and regulations in relevant areas such as transport, housing, urban planning, audiovisual communication services, or web accessibility. Secondly, each of those areas is independent in terms of territorial competences and thus needs to be coordinated individually with each province. Lastly, the coexistence of different levels of government inevitably creates intergovernmental coordination problems which require inter-jurisdictional negotiations.

In fact, the CN does not clearly specify through which mechanisms these interactions between levels of government should operate, especially with regard to relations between the national, provincial and municipal Executive Powers. Therefore, the articulation is left to *ad hoc* coordination processes that may result from a national, sub-national or joint initiative.[48]

For this reason, the creation of 'federal councils' was the natural response to the need to institutionalise mechanisms for intergovernmental coordination of public management, especially since the greater decentralisation of powers to the provincial levels that occurred in the 1990s. There are currently more than 40 federal councils in Argentina, with the participation of representatives of the nation and the provinces, operating in a multiplicity of thematic areas (internal security, public function, housing, industry, tourism, disability and others). This does not mean, however, that the main public policy coordination decisions are made in these areas as different national administrations have different strategies for relations with provincial governments. In fact, 'bilateral' instances, of the nation dealing with each province separately, are common in numerous areas.[49]

The National Accessibility Plan – now under review – is the main and perhaps the only framework to address accessibility as a comprehensive and coordinated strategy between different levels of government.

D. Participation

One of the most innovative aspects of the CRPD is related to participation. Usually, when we talk about participation, we focus on the political dimension rather than on the civic dimension. By contrast, the Convention acknowledges that persons with disabilities continue to face barriers in their participation as equal members of society and violations of their human rights in all parts of the world, and that participation of persons with disabilities in both the public and social life is essential for their effective inclusion.

[48] AM Hernández, 'Veinte propuestas para fortalecer el federalismo argentino' (2016) 49 *Boletín Mexicano de Derecho Comparado*.

[49] F Jaime et al, *Introducción al análisis de políticas públicas* (Universidad Nacional Arturo Jauretche, 2013) 42–43.

Participation of persons with disabilities in political and public life in Argentina has improved since the adoption of the CRPD.[50] Persons with disabilities are more frequently visible as participants in political parties and in public office. However, the level of inclusion and effectiveness of participation is far from ideal. Key electoral legislation still requires harmonisation with the CRPD, and most of the adopted measures to ensure 'accessible voting' rely on lower administrative regulations, in the best-case scenario, or on isolated political decisions.

Act No 26,571 deals with political parties aiming at the democratisation of the political representation, transparency and electoral equality. Article 57 requires political groups to add subtitles to messages transmitted in public spaces, Article 72 repeals part of the provision excluding 'demented' persons who have not been declared incompetent by a court from voter registration lists, Article 73 repeals the provision excluding 'deaf-mutes' from voter registration lists if they are unable to express themselves in writing, and Article 105 requires enforcement authorities to adopt measures to guarantee accessibility, confidentiality and privacy for the exercise of political rights by persons with disabilities.

The provisions set forth by Act No 26,571, and especially Article 105, has opened the door for the implementation of various measures to ensure voting rights of persons with disabilities. This includes the adoption of protocols for accessible voting, sign language interpretation support, priority voting, or assisted vote.[51] However, the National Electoral Code (*Código Electoral Nacional*) still excludes persons declared legally incompetent from the official electoral roll (*Padrón Electoral Nacional*). This was observed by the CRPD Committee in the Concluding Observations to the first country report, which recommended review of the Electoral Code and introduction of the necessary amendments to bring it in line with the CRPD, particularly with respect to legal capacity and the exercise of the right to vote on an equal basis for those declared legally incompetent.[52] In the second country report, Argentina indicated that although Bills to amend the Electoral Code are before Congress, none has yet been adopted.[53]

The evident incompatibility between the Electoral Code and the CRPD was brought to the attention of the CSJN. In the case *F.H.O. s/ artículo 152ter*,[54] which concerned a person declared incompetent by a court, and consequently excluded from electoral rolls, alleged a violation of Article 29 CRPD. The Federal Court overruled lower court decisions and reinstated voting rights to the applicant in light of the international human rights standards.

[50] F Bariffi, 'Reconocimiento y ejercicio de los derechos de participación política y en la vida pública de las personas con discapacidad' in A Kraut and G Sosa (eds), *Derecho y Salud Mental, Tomo I* (Rubinzal-Culzoni, 2020).

[51] ANDIS, 'Voto accesible' www.argentina.gob.ar.

[52] CRPD Committee (n 18) para 48.

[53] CRPD Committee (n 41) para 285.

[54] CSJN, Fallos: 341:745.

In the Argentine federal system, electoral competence is one of the matters that allows the provinces to preserve their own capacity for determination, within the framework of the CN. This allows the coexistence of various electoral systems, and electoral bodies of various formats, which have practically no relationship with each other, except in specific cases.[55] In accordance with the so-called 'federal electoral rule', the nation is responsible for setting the rules related to the election of national authorities – according to the delegation made by the provinces for the election of national deputies (Article 45), national senators (Article 54) and president and vice-president of the Nation (Articles 94 *et seq*); while it guarantees the provinces the establishment of their institutions and the election of their authorities without the intervention of the Federal Government (Article 122); subordinating both these and the nation to the full validity of a representative and republican system of government.

Although the original constitutional text did not foresee communication channels between national and provincial electoral norms and authorities, both electoral praxis and legislative development determined, in some cases, the forms of linkage between operative and normative orders, which in theory should not be related.

This is the case of 'simultaneous elections' which allows provinces to hold their own elections under the same national authority.[56] Although this is framed in the so-called coordination federalism, there is no real coordination, given that, on each occasion, the application of the law and the competence of the electoral bodies are exclusive. In these cases, a dialogue between institutions does not operate, but rather there is an application of different legal precepts by electoral bodies that do not cooperate with each other, and that limit their actions to the exchange of information. A review of the federal coordination mechanisms in electoral matters, beyond the constitutional limitations that have been described, requires a federal agreement on political rights and electoral guarantees. Likewise, the complexity of the electoral reality requires true horizontal and vertical dialogue between electoral bodies with different competences and minimum levels throughout the national territory and with respect to all levels of the state, to ensure quality levels of democracy and citizenship.[57]

IV. IMPLEMENTATION OF ARTICLE 33 CRPD

As discussed in the Introduction to this volume,[58] Article 33 CRPD embodies the obligation upon States Parties to designate or establish national implementation and monitoring mechanisms.

[55] A Tullio, 'El federalismo electoral argentino como régimen de autonomía institucional' (2016) 10 *Revista Mexicana de Derecho Electoral*.

[56] Ley 15,262 Simultaneidad de Elecciones Nacionales y Provinciales 10-dic-1959 Boletín Oficial del 20-abr-1961, Número: 19511, Página 11.

[57] Tullio (n 55).

[58] D Ferri, F Palermo and G Martinico, 'Introduction: Conceptual and Methodological Approaches', in this volume.

Between the first and second country revision before the CRPD Committee, Argentina restructured governmental agencies with competences on disability issues. As indicated by the State Party in the latest country report:

> With a view to ensuring that public policy on disability is appropriately positioned in the institutional and administrative hierarchy, the National Disability Agency (ANDIS) has been established. This body will assume the responsibilities of the National Advisory Commission on the Integration of Persons with Disabilities (CONADIS), the National Welfare Benefits Commission (with regard to disability pensions), the National Rehabilitation Service and the Federal Health Inclusion Programme. In addition, it will undertake other missions and functions as a legally and financially independent body that reports directly to the General Secretariat of the Presidency.[59]

A. Focal Point

The goal pursued by Article 33(1) CRPD with the designation of one or several government focal points for the application of the CRPD is twofold. On the one hand, it ensures that there is an adequate place for disability on the political agenda of the State Party, making the issue visible in such a way that it forces governments to give it impetus and an adequate place. On the other hand, the designation of one or more focal points is useful as an administrative tool to streamline and centralise all the institutional actors involved in disability rights policies, or in other words, such an organisation is required that can transform the social-contextual model of disability into reality.[60]

ANDIS was created in 2017 to replace the former CONADIS (*Comisión Nacional Asesora para la Integración de las Personas con Discapacidad*). The Agency is designed as a decentralised body within the orbit of the Secretary of the Presidency. According to the constituent regulation, ANDIS:

> will be in charge of, the design, coordination and general execution of public policies on disability; the preparation and execution of actions aimed at promoting the full exercise of the rights of persons with disabilities; and, the coordination of the processes for granting disability pensions pursuant [to] Acts No. 25,869 and No. 26,928 throughout the national territory.[61]

The functional structure includes an Executive Director with the support of serval sub-directorates, two Committees and a Council. The Advisory Committee (*Comité Asesor*) consists of non-governmental organisations of persons with disabilities. The Technical Committee (*Comité Técnico*) provides

[59] CRPD Committee (n 41) para 6.

[60] F Bariffi, 'Aplicación y seguimiento nacionales a la luz del artículo 33 de la CDPD' in P Rosales (ed), *Convención Internacional sobre los Derechos de las Personas con Discapacidad (ley 26.378) Comentada* (Abeledo-Perrot, 2012).

[61] Decreto de Necesidad y Urgencia 698/2017 – Se disuelve la CONADIS. Se crea la Agencia Nacional de Discapacidad (ANDIS) que reemplaza a la CONADIS.

support to ANDIS in mainstreaming strategies between national ministries and other decentralised sectors of the government for the implementation of the CRPD from an inclusive approach. The Federal Council on Disability (*Consejo Federal de Discapacidad*) serves as coordinating mechanism to mainstream strategies between the Federation, the provinces and municipalities.

ANDIS reports directly to the Presidency, avoiding the institutional rank shortcomings of its predecessor, CONADIS. Likewise, in light of the functions entitled by the constituent regulation, the Agency has the necessary powers to become the federal focal point to implement the CRPD.

ANDIS is a body with direct competences at national level – policies and legislation – and indirect competences in the implementation of the CRPD at provincial and municipal levels.[62] Each province has a specific focal point with similar competences. Furthermore, a Coordinating Committee for Programmes for Persons with Disabilities (*Comité Coordinador de Programas para Personas con Discapacidad*) was created under Act No 25,730 which allocates funds to promote different projects that improve the quality of life of people with disabilities and their families in line with the rights established in the CRPD. ANDIS chairs this coordinating body.

B. Coordination Mechanism

Under the scope of ANDIS there are two coordination mechanisms. On the one hand, the Advisory Committee as the mechanism to coordinate and mainstream strategies between national ministries and other decentralised sectors of the government, and, on the other hand, the Federal Council on Disability as the mechanism to coordinate and mainstream strategies between the Federation, the provinces and municipalities. This Council also has the purpose of promoting the permanent interrelation of governmental and non-governmental entities.

The Federal Council on Disability was created in 1996 under Act No 24,657 with the purpose of:

> preserving the key role of the provinces and municipalities in the implementation of national policies on comprehensive prevention-rehabilitation and equalization of opportunities for people with disabilities, and in the planning, coordination and execution of aspects that involve the joint action of the different spheres.

The Federal Council on Disability gathers on a regular basis in meetings called 'assemblies'. These meetings are chaired by ANDIS and include representatives for each province. The deliberations are open and decisions are adopted

[62] Eg the Directorate for the Promotion of the Rights of Persons with Disabilities within the Province of Buenos Aires (Decreto 510/2021), or the Commission for the Full Participation and Inclusion of Persons with Disabilities in the Autonomous City of Buenos Aires (*Comisión para la Plena Participación e Inclusión de las Personas con Discapacidad* – COPIDIS); Ley No 447.

by simple majority of votes.[63] The working rules also foresee the creation of commissions in order to study or address specific matters.

One of the latest developments of the Federal Council on Disability was the creation of the so-called '*Plan Accesar*' (Comprehensive Plan for the Promotion and Protection of the Rights of Persons with Disabilities at Local Levels)[64] in order to support municipal governments in the implementation of initiatives to make cities accessible and inclusive and allow the enjoyment of all human rights of people with disabilities in their territories. To this end, the *Plan Accesar* promotes the creation of accessible and inclusive environments, in coordination with municipal governments and considering the characteristics of each territory.

C. Independent Mechanism

As it is well known, Article 33(2) CRPD sets forth two specific obligations upon States Parties. Firstly, to designate, if there is no such mechanism in place, an independent body to promote, protect and supervise the provisions of the CRPD, and, secondly, the obligation to comply with, in the establishment of this body, certain minimum standards that guarantee its stability and independence, known as the Paris Principles.[65] As Quinn points out, these functions of promotion, protection and monitoring must be assigned to organisations that are genuinely independent of the state. National human rights institutions are called upon to become a key driver in ensuring proper implementation.[66]

Designation of the national monitoring independent body in Argentina has long been troublesome. During the first country review before the CRPD Committee, the information provided by the government failed to distinguish between national implementation and national monitoring. The State Report indicates that the 'creation of the National Disability Observatory was proposed as the implementation and coordination mechanism to facilitate related action in different sectors and at different levels (Art. 33(1) CRPD)'. In its Concluding Observations the CRPD Committee noted with concern that the National Disability Observatory is a subsidiary body under the governmental structure in violation of Article 33(2) of the Convention and the Paris

[63] A list of the records of the meetings can be consulted at: www.argentina.gob.ar/andis/estructura/consejo-federal-de-discapacidad.

[64] Plan Integral para la Promoción y Protección de los Derechos de las Personas con Discapacidad en el ámbito local, Resolución 1200/2021 Agencia Nacional de Discapacidad.

[65] Principles relating to the Status of National Institutions (the Paris Principles), General Assembly Resolution 48/134, 20 December 1993.

[66] G Quinn, 'Resisting the "Temptation of Elegance": Can the Convention on the Rights of Persons with Disabilities Socialise States to Right Behaviour?' in O Mjöll Arnardóttir and G Quinn (eds), *The UN Convention on the Rights of Persons with Disabilities. European and Scandinavian Perspectives* (Martinus Nijhoff Publishers, 2009).

Principles.[67] This was also pointed out by civil society in a joint shadow report.[68]

The existing national monitoring mechanism which might fall within the Paris Principles standards is the National Ombudsman Office (*Defensoría del Pueblo de la Nación*) which has constitutional rank (Article 86 CN), functions and has the budget to act independently. While this body promotes and protects the rights of groups in situations of vulnerability, and more specifically, persons with disabilities, it has not formally assumed the national monitoring functions outlined under Article 33(2) CRPD.

The failure to acknowledge and designate an independent monitoring body at national level has clearly had influence on the provinces. Both under the CN and under the CRPD itself, provinces have competence to designate their own independent monitoring bodies and yet such steps have not been taken.

V. CONCLUDING REMARKS

The reform of the CN in 1994 and the inclusion of the core human rights instruments in the constitutional text and their corresponding constitutional status is an important milestone. The CRPD also enjoys the highest rank within the federal state and the sub-national entities.

This brief analysis of the Argentine experience shows the complexities of the federal system in the domestic implementation of disability rights as enshrined in the CRPD and other universal and regional human rights obligations.

Whilst Argentina has taken several steps to improve the equal application of the CRPD in the whole territory of the Republic, including the creation of several coordinating bodies between the Federation and the sub-national entities, solutions do not seem to tackle the core problem of federal governance and the constitutional division of powers, ie the 'coordination federalism' which shifts the conversation from a legal towards a political perspective.

Human rights issues as such, are clearly a primary competence of the federal state in all of its branches of government. At legislative level, the National Congress has approved and turned most relevant human rights treaties into federal Acts and amended existing federal Acts to harmonise them with international obligations. At the executive level, the national administration has adopted the necessary regulations and adapted or created national bodies to implement and monitor human rights obligations. At the judicial level, the

[67] CRPD Committee (n 18) para 51.

[68] Funes (n 40): '[T]he Disability Observatory, created by Decree 806/2011, is not an autonomous body, given the fact that it hierarchically depends on the CONADIS. As mentioned, CONADIS is part of the National Executive Branch of government. The Decree does not include any provision mandating the participation of civil society organisations; and, in particular, of persons with disabilities and the organisations that represent them'.

CSJN has coined and consolidated a doctrine emphasising the key and ultimate role of the federal court as guardian of human rights protection and its control of constitutionality.

But the structure of the Argentine federal system dates back to the original text of 1853. These provisions, inspired by the American constitutional system, and in the liberal positivist view of the time, do not consider the peculiarities of post-UN Charter international human rights law obligations. As a result, the protection and promotion of human rights, and more specifically, of disability rights mandated by the CRPD, has failed to increase de facto exercise of national powers into a sort of 'federal-pre-emption'. Sub-national entities still retain their autonomous powers and the harmonisation process is erratic and inconsistent.

The Argentine federal state has managed to consolidate a system to incorporate human rights obligations into the national structure, with a predominant role of the federal court as ultimate interpreter of the constitutional and conventional rights and guarantees recognised in the text through judicial review remedies. However, this arrangement soon faces the limitations of the constitutional division of powers between federated states when it comes to implementing measures dealing with areas or competences either shared or retained by provinces and municipalities.

It appears clear from this analysis that the existing Argentine federal system was not thought to deal with international human rights obligations, especially when they enshrine social and collective rights. Provinces retain many autonomy powers to address key areas of disability rights locally such as inclusive equality, accessibility, education, health or employment. Consequently, federal decentralisation has become a major barrier to implement the CRPD at domestic level. The need to rethink and review Argentina's federal arrangement seems pressing.

13

Brazil

The Long Road to Citizenship for Persons with Disabilities*

GILBERTO MA RODRIGUES AND PALOMA BREIT

I. INTRODUCTION

BRAZIL IS ONE of the countries of the 'Global South' that committed strongly to the UN Convention on the Rights of Persons with Disabilities (CRPD). The country signed the Convention on 30 March 2007 and ratified it on 1 August 2008.[1] It also signed and ratified, on the same dates, the Optional Protocol to the CRPD (OP-CRPD) and accepted the investigation procedure (individual complaints) provided for in Articles 6–7 of the same Protocol.[2] Further, Brazil was able to elect the senator for the state of São Paulo, Mara Cristina Gabrilli, as one of the members of the Committee on the Rights of Persons with Disabilities (CRPD Committee), the body that monitors the implementation of the CRPD, during the 11th Conference of States Parties in 2018, with a mandate from January 2019 to December 2022.[3] Senator Gabrilli's presence in the CRPD Committee has had important consequences for the public debate on the implementation of the CRPD in Brazil,[4] as will be discussed below.

* The title to this chapter is inspired by the reference book on Brazil's citizenship history by José Murilo de Carvalho, *Cidadania no Brasil: o longo caminho* ('The Long Run to Citizenship in Brazil') (Civilização Brasileira, 2001).

[1] Office of the United Nations High Commissioner for Human Rights (OHCHR), 'Ratification, Reporting & Documentation for Brazil' www.tbinternet.org.

[2] OHCHR, 'Acceptance of Individual Complaints Procedures for Brazil' www.tbinternet.org.

[3] Senator Mara Cristina Gabrilli (Brazilian Social Democracy Party, *Partido da Social Democracia Brasileira* – PSDB, mandate 2019–27) is one of the most important political activists on the rights of persons with disabilities. Before being elected senator in the state of São Paulo, she was a congresswoman of the same state in the Chamber of Deputies (2011–19), a period in which she was Rapporteur on the Federal Law No 13.146/2015 (Brazilian Law for Inclusion of Persons with Disabilities). According to her biography, she has been quadriplegic since 1994, after a car accident (www.maragabrilli.com.br).

[4] Senator Mara Gabrilli's appointment to the membership of the CRPD Committee by Brazil's government is in line with the motto 'nothing about us without us'.

The internalisation of the CRPD in the legal order of Brazil was accomplished through a special procedure provided for in the Federal Constitution of 1988 (*Constituição da República Federativa do Brasil de 1988* – CF-88) as amended in 2004 by means of a comprehensive constitutional reform.[5] The special procedure provided for in Article 5(3) establishes that human rights treaties approved by a qualified quorum are equivalent to amendments to the Constitution, thus receiving constitutional status.[6] This means that the CRPD has the same level as constitutional norms in Brazil. Namely, the Congress approved the CRPD through Legislative Decree No 186/2008, and after its international ratification, the President of the Republic promulgated Decree No 6949 of 25 August 2009, which made it effective from then on.[7] It must be emphasised that only two international agreements have constitutional status in Brazil and both relate to the rights of people with disabilities.[8] In this way, the norms that emanate from the CRPD have superior force to all the international human rights norms to which Brazil has committed itself in the last three decades, since Brazil's re-democratisation in the 1980s and the approval of the Federal Constitution of 1988.

In order to implement the CRPD and to update concepts and existing legal interpretations about people with disabilities, Federal Law No 13.146/2015 was approved (Brazilian Law of Inclusion of Persons with Disabilities), which in its initial part declares to be 'intended to ensure and promote, under equal conditions, the exercise of rights and fundamental freedoms by people with disabilities, aiming at their social inclusion and citizenship'.[9] According to the opinion of LA David de Araujo, a constitutional law scholar specialised in the rights of persons with disabilities, 'Law No. 13.146/2015 has not only the character of an ordinary rule, but of a rule of integration of a constitutional rule'.[10]

Notwithstanding the country's international commitment to the CRPD and the constitutional status of this Convention as well as the Federal Law No 13.146/2015 that implemented it and systematised disability issues, it is important to note that the rights of persons with disabilities still face a long

[5] LAD de Araujo, 'A proteção internacional dos direitos das pessoas com deficiência e a ordem interna nacional' in CF Campilongo, A de Azevedo Gonzaga and AL Freire (eds), *Enciclopédia jurídica da PUC-SP* (Pontifícia Universidade Católica de São Paulo, 2021).

[6] Art 5(3) of the Constitution of the Federal Republic of Brazil (Federal Constitution): 'International human rights treaties and conventions on human rights approved by both Houses of the National Congress, in two different voting sessions, by vote of three-fifths of their respective members, shall be equivalent to Constitutional Amendments' (CA 45, 2004) (Federal Supreme Court, 2020).

[7] de Araujo (n 5).

[8] The CRPD and the World Intellectual Property Organization's (WIPO) Marrakesh Treaty to Facilitate Access to Published Works for Persons Who Are Blind, Visually Impaired or Otherwise Print Disabled (2013).

[9] Brazil, Presidency, Law 13.146 (6 July 2015) www.planalto.gov.br.

[10] de Araujo (n 5).

road and are not fully realised at the federal, state and municipal levels in Brazil, and in the private sector, especially in the field of public policies.

This chapter aims to demonstrate that despite the advances brought by the CRPD in Brazil, its implementation has faced difficulties. Governmental and non-governmental sectors have struggled to adopt the new conceptual paradigm of the Convention. Moreover, in recent years, the autonomy and effectiveness of the mechanisms provided for in Article 33 CRPD have diminished, due to regressive policies regarding civil society's participatory mechanisms and the limited national human rights agenda of the government of President Jair Bolsonaro. These difficulties at the federal level negatively impact on the coordinated, systematic and homogeneous implementation of the CRPD in the states, Federal District and municipalities.

Following this introduction, section II will briefly examine the three-tiered structure of the Brazilian Federation and the division of legislative and executive powers, and in relation to the rights of persons with disabilities, demonstrating that there is a concurrent competence (Union, states and Federal District) and a common one (among all entities, including municipalities), which implies a greater degree of coordination and articulation between the Union and states, the Federal District and municipalities. Section III will analyse the main axes of the Convention regarding the concept of disability, non-discrimination and equality, accessibility and participation based on the validity of the CRPD and the Federal Law No 13.146/2015, which integrated and regulated the CRPD in the domestic legal order, the advances, challenges and obstacles to its implementation at the national and sub-national levels, both at the government level and in the private sector. Section IV will deal with the implementation of Article 33 CRPD, addressing how the country still deals with the focal point, the coordination mechanism and the framework/independent mechanism in an insufficient manner, and how the critique and action of a Brazilian member of the CRPD Committee contributed to the public debate and the possibility of moving forward to establishing an independent mechanism, with real and effective capacity to coordinate and monitor the implementation of the CRPD. Finally, the concluding remarks will summarise the perceived impacts that the CRPD and its regulation by the CF-88 have produced, as well as what can and must be done to shorten the long road to citizenship for persons with disabilities in Brazil.

II. DIVISION OF COMPETENCES

A. The Brazilian Federation and the Division of Competences

The Brazilian Federation was officially instituted with the adoption of the Republic and presidentialism in 1889, and with the division of powers and institutional arrangements set out in the Constitution of 1891.[11] The Constitution embedded some of the general historical characteristics of the Constitution of 1824, elaborated under the influence of the French constitutional model, with strong centralisation in the figure of the emperor, and which remained in force throughout the parliamentary monarchical regime (1822–89) following independence from Portugal. In the monarchic model, the central government retained most of the legislative and executive powers, and the provinces had residual powers. This system was largely transposed to the Republic, conceived as a federation by decentralisation, approving a new constitution with direct inspiration from the United States and Argentine constitutionalism, but without the same autonomy of its states and provinces. With a new decentralised drapery of the Republic, due to pressure from the regional agrarian elites, the states gained more autonomy, but the Union remained the formal and material protagonist of the competences foreseen in the Constitution.

This original matrix of the Brazilian Federation went through different periods throughout the twentieth century, with successive constitutions (1891, 1934, 1937, 1946, 1967), and doses of more or less centralisation, until the approval of the current Federal Constitution of 1988. This Constitution was approved during the first government of the democratic transition (1985–89), after 20 years of civil-military dictatorship (1964–85). With respect to the new federal system of the CF-88, its main feature is the political and juridical decentralisation, with the formal recognition that the municipalities are federated entities, thus inaugurating a three-tier federation in the country (Union, states, municipalities and Federal District).[12] It is important to emphasise that in this process of political-constitutional update, the Union maintained a wide range of legislative powers, leaving to the federal states and Federal District residual legislative powers and to the municipalities some exclusive powers. When characterising the federal system of the CF-88, Celina Araujo states that, 'few constitutional powers are allocated to the states and municipalities … At the same time, states and municipal governments now enjoy considerable administrative autonomy, responsibility for policy implementation'.[13]

The decentralisation operated by the CF-88 was mainly in the concurrent and common competences, through the cooperative federalism model. According to GMA Rodrigues, '[i]n the Brazilian federal system, "common competencies" are related to executive concurrent powers and "concurrent competencies" to legislative powers'.[14] In this way, states have concurrent legislative competence

[11] C Souza, 'Federal Republic of Brazil' in J Kincaid and GA Tarr (eds), *Constitutional Origins, Structures and Change in Federal Countries* (Mc-Gill Queen's University Press, 2005) 77–102.

[12] GMA Rodrigues, 'Les villes sont-elles des unités constituantes dans le fédéralisme brésilien?' in F Mathieu, D Guénette and A-G Gagnon (eds), *Cinquante Déclinaisons de Féderalisme Théorie, Enjeux et Études de Cas* (Presses de l'Université du Québec, 2020) 443–51.

[13] Souza (n 11) 84.

[14] GMA Rodrigues, 'Concurrent Power and Local Interest in Brazil's Federalism' in N Steytler (ed), *Concurrent Powers in Federal Systems. Meaning, Making, Managing.* (Brill-Nijhoff, 2017) 206.

to regulate at the state level, based on the general parameters of the Union (*Paramount*) – being able to go beyond to expand rights, but not to reduce them. Further, all federated entities exercise common competence, in a set of specific areas fixed in the constitutional text. In this model, the Union plays the role of coordinator of national policies in the various areas of common competence.

Each of the 26 federal states has its own state constitution. State constitutions were approved after the CF-88 (mostly in 1989) and regulate the competences concurrent to the Union and common to the Union and the municipalities.[15] The municipalities have an organic municipal law, which regulates competences common to the Union and the states and exclusive to the municipalities,[16] and the Federal District (Brasília, *Distrito Federal* – DF), which contains elements common to the states and municipalities, also has an organic law.[17]

B. Division of Competences and Federal Coordination

In this way, since the CF-88, with the design of a federation with a cooperative profile, the Union has started to exercise the function of national coordinator of public policies through its ministries and secretariats, as well as through collegiate bodies – the national councils – which were created or updated with consultative and deliberative functions, and modelled on governmental participation and with members of civil society. Except for very specific and punctual cases, states and municipalities do not participate in these national councils but assume a central role in the dialogue and articulation with the state councils created with the same purposes for the same policies at the state level. Further, state councils play a similar role with municipal councils within their territory and jurisdiction.

Although the cooperative federalism design of the CF-88 demanded robust intergovernmental relations for the political and administrative exercise of the Union's coordination in the various areas, there was no significant development of executive branch bodies under the Presidency of the Republic to carry out this task. Intergovernmental relations occurred at some sectoral levels with a more

[15] Art 25 of the Federal Constitution, 'The Federated States': 'The states are organized and governed by the Constitutions and laws they may adopt, in accordance with the principles of this Constitution'.

[16] Art 29 of the Federal Constitution, 'The Municipalities': 'Municipalities shall be governed by an organic law, voted in two rounds, with a minimum interval of ten days between the rounds, and approved by two thirds of the members of the municipal council, which shall promulgate it, observing the principles established in this Constitution, in the Constitution of the respective state'.

[17] Art 32 of the Federal Constitution, 'The Federal District': 'The Federal District, which may not be divided into municipalities, shall be governed by an organic law, voted in two rounds, with a minimum interval of ten days, and approved by two-thirds of the Legislative Chamber, which shall enact it, in accordance with the principles set forth in this Constitution'.

technical component, especially in the area of health, with the Unified Health System (*Sistema Único de Saúde* – SUS). The government of President Lula da Silva (2003–10) began an initiative to strengthen intergovernmental relations, with the creation of the Secretariat of Institutional Relations, equivalent to a ministry, and the creation of the Federative Articulation Committee (*Comitê de Articulação Federativa* – CAF),[18] for direct relations between the Union and the municipalities, making use of the participation of the three national associations of municipalities that cover almost all of the 5,570 municipalities in the country, aiming to articulate public policies in several areas of common competence. This structure of coordination and political articulation was maintained through the government of President Dilma Rousseff (2011–16) but was then weakened under the government of Michel Temer (2016–18) and disappeared under the government of Jair Bolsonaro (2019–23), which proved to be averse to dialogue and federal articulation, and adopted, for most of its mandate, a discourse and practices against the Federation.[19] In this period of Bolsonaro's government, it is worth highlighting that, in response to a lawsuit filed by an opposition political party in the Supreme Court in April 2020, states and municipalities had their full autonomy recognised to act to prevent and combat the Covid-19 pandemic, in the absence of coordination and federal actions, and in the face of the president's attempt to hinder states and municipalities acting according to science and WHO protocols, including in relation to the purchase and production of vaccines.[20]

Based on this design of division of competences, and incipient intergovernmental relations based upon cooperative federalism, the national policy for people with disabilities fits into this framework, where the federal legislation is paramount and the Union exercises national coordination before the states and municipalities.

C. The Division of Competences from a Disability Perspective

Disability is addressed, in the CF-88, in a fragmented way, in different parts that cover different aspects, especially with regard to ensuring the application

[18] The Federative Articulation Committee (*Comitê de Articulação Federativa* – CAF) was first created in 2003 by an agreement between the Union and the three national associations of municipalities – CNM, ABM and FNP aiming to be an intergovernmental mechanism to foster cooperative federalism, specially related to common competences of Art 23 of the Constitution. In 2007, through a federal Decree, President Lula transformed the CAF into an institutional body in the Ministry of Institutional Relations. F Abrucio and EJ Green, 'The Federative Articulation Committee in Lula's Government: Obstacles in Territorial Cooperation' (2018) 33 *Revista Brasileira de Ciências Sociais*.

[19] GMA Rodrigues and VE de Oliveira, 'Brazil and Covid-19. The President Against the Federation' (*UACES Territorial Politics*, 5 June 2020).

[20] GMA Rodrigues et al, 'Brazil and the Fight Against Covid-19: Strengthening State and Municipal Powers' in N Steytler (ed), *Comparative Federalism and Combatting the Pandemic* (Routledge, 2021) 239–57.

of the equality principle to persons with disabilities. The Constitution provides for provisions on non-discrimination, accessibility, equality and participation, in areas such as labour, public administration, social welfare, education, family, children, youth, and the elderly. Table 1 shows areas and respective provisions of the CF-88 that are related to the rights of persons with disabilities.

Table 1 Federal Constitution and Rights of Persons with Disabilities

Rights of Persons with Disabilities/ Federal Constitution	Non-discrimination/ Equality	Accessibility	Participation	Concurrent competences (legislative)	Common competences (executive)
Fundamental Principles	Art 3				
Fundamental Rights, Guarantees	Art 5				
Individual, Collective Rights					
Social Rights	Art 7				
Competences				Art 24	Art 23
Public Administration	Art 37				
Social Assistance	Art 203, IV, V		Art 203, IV		
Education	Art 208, III, V				
Family, Children, Young People and Senior Adults	Art 227, para 1, II	Art 227, para 1, II; para 2			
General Provisions		Art 244			

The protection of persons with disabilities, like other human rights norms in the CF-88, is a common competence, expressly defined as such in Article 23(II), among the Union, the states and the municipalities, which reads: 'Article 23. The Union, states, Federal District and municipalities have the collective power: … II – to provide for health and public assistance, for the protection and safeguard of handicapped people'.[21]

The system for division of competences in the CF-88 ensures the Union, the states and the Federal District the concurrent legislative competence to regulate the issue of people with disabilities. Article 24(XIV) provides: 'Article 24. The Union, states and Federal District have the power to legislate concurrently on: … XIV – protection and social integration of handicapped people'.[22]

[21] Federal Constitution (n 6).
[22] Ibid.

Blauth and Vieira analyse how Brazilian state constitutions deal with the rights of people with disabilities, from five categories: health, education, work, accessibility and leisure.[23] We highlight here some important findings of these authors that shed light on the theme at the state level. Based on the research of Blauth and Vieira, Tables 2A and 2B indicate how each of the constitutions of the 26 Brazilian states[24] determines the rights of people with disabilities in the five categories analysed.

Table 2A Rights of Persons with Disabilities in Brazilian State Constitutions by category/policy area, based on Blauth and Vieira (2019), adapted and translated by the authors

Categories	AC	AL	AM	AP	BA	CE	ES	GO	MA	MG	MT	MS	PA
Health	X	X	X	X	X	X	X	X	X	X	X	X	X
Education	X	X	X	X	X	X	X	X	X	X	X	X	X
Leisure	X		X	X			X	X		X	X		X
Labour	X	X	X	X	X	X	X	X				X	X
Accessibility	X	X	X	X	X	X	X	X	X	X	X	X	X
Total	5	4	5	5	4	4	5	5	3	4	4	4	5

Table 2B Rights of Persons with Disabilities in Brazilian State Constitutions by category/policy area, based on Blauth and Vieira (2019), adapted and translated by the authors (continued)

Categories	PB	PR	PE	PI	RJ	RN	RO	RR	RS	SC	SE	SP	TO
Health	X	X	X	X	X	X	X	X	X	X	X	X	X
Education	X	X	X	X	X	X	X	X	X	X	X	X	X
Leisure		X	X		X				X			X	X
Labour	X			X	X	X	X				X	X	
Accessibility	X	X	X	X	X	X	X	X	X	X	X	X	X
Total	4	4	4	4	5	4	4	3	4	3	4	5	4

Analysis of the data shows that only 31 per cent of the state constitutions cover all five categories of the survey. However, all 26 state constitutions deal with

[23] RSM Blauth and RS Vieira, 'Análise das Constituições Estaduais Brasileiras e seu Conteúdo Quanto aos Direitos das Pessoas com Deficiência' (2019) 5 *Revista de Direito Sociais e Políticas Públicas* 119.

[24] These are the 26 federated states in alphabetical order. Table 2A: Acre (AC); Alagoas (AL); Amazonas (AM); Amapá (AP); Bahia (BA); Ceará (CE); Espírito Santo (ES); Goiás (GO); Maranhão (MA); Minas Gerais (MG); Mato Grosso (MT); Mato Grosso do Sul (MS); Pará (PA). Table 2B: Paraíba (PB); Paraná (PR); Pernambuco (PE); Piauí (PI); Rio de Janeiro (RJ); Rio Grande do Norte (RN); Rondônia (RO); Roraima (RR); Rio Grande do Sul (RS); Santa Catarina (SC); Sergipe (SE); São Paulo (SP); Tocantins (TO).

education, accessibility, and health. Blauth and Vieira conclude that 'although the State Constitutions have addressed the analysed categories … few states have established significant norms that ensure the right of the persons with disabilities'.[25]

D. Division of Competences and Judicial Protection of Rights of People with Disabilities

From the point of view of the Brazilian Federation, judicial power is divided into Union justice (which includes the justice of the Federal District) and state justice. Each federal state has its own state court, as is common in federations. The municipalities do not have a judicial branch.[26]

The rights of people with disabilities, in light of the common competences in Article 23 CF-88, are an equal competence of the Union's courts and the courts of the federal states.

The protection of the rights of people with disabilities as collective rights before the courts is the competence of the Public Prosecution Office (*Ministério Público*), which includes the Public Prosecution Office of the Union (Federal Public Prosecution Office and Federal District Public Prosecution Office) and of the Public Prosecution Office of the states. These are independent institutions which play an essential role in protecting the rights of people with disabilities in Brazil.

Regarding this specific action of the Public Prosecutor's Offices for the judicial defence of the rights of people with disabilities, the National Council of the Public Prosecutor's Office (*Conselho Nacional do Ministério Público* – CNMP), a body provided for in the CF-88 and which 'acts on behalf of the citizen by carrying out the administrative, financial and disciplinary supervision of the Public Prosecutor's Office in Brazil and its members, respecting the autonomy of the institution',[27] has a Working Group on People with Disabilities and a Special Action Centre for Accessibility, whose work has been guided by the new CRPD conceptions. Based on the activities developed in these two bodies, a Guide for Action by the Public Prosecutor's Office – Persons with Disabilities[28] was prepared, the most recent edition of which came out in 2016, updated in accordance with Federal Law No 13.146/2015 (the law that integrates the constitutional norm of the CRPD, as mentioned above). This document, which has

[25] Blauth and Vieira (n 23).

[26] For a detailed structure of the Judiciary in the Brazilian Federation, see GMA Rodrigues, MA Lorencini and A Zimmermann, 'The Supreme Federal Court of Brazil: Protecting Democracy and Centralized Power' in N Arouney and J Kincaid (eds), *Courts in Federal Countries: Federalists or Unitarists?* (Toronto University Press, 2017) 103–34.

[27] Conselho Nacional do Ministério Público (CNMP), 'Apresentação' (2015) www.cnmp.mp.br.

[28] CNMP, 'Guia de atuação do Ministério Público: pessoa com deficiência' (CNMP, 2016).

national reach and for all spheres of the Federation, details the rights of people with disabilities with regard to accessibility, non-discrimination and equity (right to accessibility, to priority service, to public tender, to inclusive education, to health, to supported decision-making and to guardianship). In addition, it indicates which extrajudicial and judicial procedures the members of the federal and states' prosecutor offices should undertake to defend the rights of people with disabilities.

Another important body for the protection of the rights of people with disabilities, and, more generally of those people whose socio-economic conditions do not enable them to hire a lawyer (ie, at least a quarter of the Brazilian population, about 50 million people),[29] is the Public Defender's Office. Like the Public Prosecutor's Office, there is the Union Public Defender's Office and the Public Defender's Offices in the states. However, these bodies have fewer human and financial resources than the Public Prosecutor Office, and their existence is more recent, which makes their work less comprehensive and, in many cases, their resources are insufficient to meet the great demands that exist.[30]

III. THE ROLE OF THE NATIONAL GOVERNMENT VIS-À-VIS SUB-NATIONAL ENTITIES IN SELECTED AREAS

A. Concept of Disability

The definition of disability rests within the competences of the Union. The term 'person with disabilities' was incorporated from the CRPD. It has been in force in the country since 2009 and is regulated by Federal Law No 13.146/2015.

Looking behind and tracing a brief contemporary history of the legal concept of disability in the constitutional sphere, it is worth recalling that the Federal Constitution of 1967, approved under the regime of civil-military dictatorship (1964–85), used the term 'exceptional' to refer to people with disabilities, within the scope of education. Under its validity, the Constitutional Amendment No 12 was also approved, which for the first time recognised and guaranteed some rights to those it called 'disabled'. Coincidence or not, Amendment No 12 was not incorporated into the main body of the Constitution, as is the procedural practice, but was separate at the end of the text, resembling what would be the very segregation to which these people were subjected at the time.[31]

[29] Instituto Brasileiro de Geografia e Estatística (IBGE), 'Síntese de Indicadores Sociais. Uma Análise das Condições de Vida da População Brasileira' (IBGE, 2017).

[30] Federal Law No 13.146/2015 regulates the right of persons with disabilities to access to justice and defines that the Public Defender's Office and the Public Prosecutor's Office must act to guarantee this right. See Art 79(3) Federal Law No 13.146/2015.

[31] LAD de Araujo, 'Direito das pessoas com deficiência' in CF Campilongo, A de Azevedo Gonzaga and AL Freire (eds), *Enciclopédia Jurídica da PUC-SP* (Pontifícia Universidade Católica de São Paulo, 2022).

Before the CRPD came into effect, the official terminology adopted to define people with disabilities was 'persons bearing deficiencies'.[32] This term is considered derogatory by people with disabilities, disability rights activists and experts on the subject.[33] It refers to a medical conception that was prevalent in Brazil until the advent of the Convention, and that was replaced by the CRPD. However, despite the normative force of the Convention and the Federal Law No 13.146/2015 that regulates it, the expression still exists in federal, state, and municipal norms that have not been changed or updated so far. This is one of the many obstacles on the 'long road' ahead to implement the CRPD.

Regarding the conception and definition of what a person with a disability is, Federal Law No 13.146/2015 incorporated the matrix of the CRPD. In Article 2 the law states:

> A person with a disability is considered to be one who has a long-term physical, mental, intellectual or sensory impairment that, in interaction with one or more barriers, may obstruct his or her full and effective participation in society on an equal basis with others.

This new multidimensional and social conception of persons with disabilities had already been incorporated through the CRPD into the country's legal system and was subject to the conventionality control, despite such control still being incipient in the Brazilian legal system.[34] However, with the federal law which, as stated, has the character of a norm integrating a constitutional rule, states, municipalities, and the Federal District are obliged to follow and adapt their legislation to the new concept. In this sense, there is a 'centralisation' of the concept of disability.

A crucial aspect of this new concept of persons with disabilities is the assessment of the disability, which in many cases gives the legal recognition that an individual is a person with a disability. Article 2(1) of Federal Law No 13.146/2015 states the terms in which such an assessment should be carried out, indicating that '[t]he assessment of disability, when necessary, will be biopsychosocial, carried out by a multi-professional and interdisciplinary team'.

It is not only in organs of the federal administration that difficulties and resistance to the full implementation of the CRPD and Federal Law No 13.146/2015 are encountered. Surprisingly, they still exist in the judiciary

[32] In Portuguese: *Pessoas portadoras de deficiências*, which implies that the person with a disability has the possibility to 'carry' the disability or not.

[33] In Brazil, the UK disability studies influenced those who preferred the term disabled to the expression people with disabilities, which instead ended up prevailing in the country, although there is still a predominantly biomedical view. There was an 'importation' of the CRPD expression, without, however, a real debate in the community of people with disabilities. See D Diniz, *O que é deficiência* (Brasiliense, 2007).

[34] The conventionality control, as the possibility to enforce international norms through judicial control, has evolved in the last years in legal demands, but still is not applied widely in the states.

branch of the Union. LA David de Araujo points out that one of the organs of the judiciary that maintains a norm with the old and outdated conception of persons with disabilities is the Superior Court of Justice (*Superior Tribunal de Justiça* – STJ).[35] In fact, the STJ has not changed precedent No 377, which states: 'The monocular vision bearer is entitled to compete, in public competitions, for the vacancies reserved for the disabled'.[36] This precedent of the STJ posits that a disabled person who has been recognised with a visual impairment on one eye has the right to apply for reserved posts (within the quotas) for people with disabilities in public competitions. The precedent maintains that proof of the disability results only from a report produced by a medical expert. LA David de Araujo explains that:

> the medical evaluation, in isolation, is ruled out. Any judicial decision based only in an opinion, by an expert only, even if very well supported, is null and void. Because the person with [a] disability has the right to have his or her full potential valued.

In the case of the STJ, precedents (*Súmulas*) guide all courts and judges, federal and state, to follow the same path. This precedent brings with it a serious problem of an outdated interpretation of the courts throughout the Brazilian Federation, in a crucial point related to the concept of disability which was changed radically by the CRPD and Federal Law No 13.146/2015.

The CRPD and Federal Law No 13.146/2015 also changed the way the census and mapping of people with disabilities in the population is carried out. Since the advent of Federal Law No 7853/1989, it has been mandatory to include people with disabilities in the demographic census, which has been conducted by the Brazilian Institute of Geography and Statistics (*Instituto Brasileiro de Geografia e Estatística* – IBGE) every 10 years (1991, 2000, 2010). This regular occurrence of the census was interrupted partly because of the difficulties generated by the Covid-19 pandemic and partly because of budget cuts under the government of Jair Bolsonaro. In the demographic census of 2010, 45.6 million people with disabilities were surveyed in the country, taking into account the WHO conceptual framework 'International Classification of Functioning, Disability and Health' (ICF).[37] This number would correspond to 23.9 per cent of the total Brazilian population.[38] From an analytical rereading of the data of people with disabilities in light of the recommendations of the Washington Group, based on the CRPD scheme, made by IBGE, the population of persons with disabilities

[35] In Brazil, the Superior Court of Justice (*Superior Tribunal de Justiça* – STJ) is the court of final instance of appeal for non-constitutional issues. The Supreme Federal Court (*Supremo Tribunal Federal* – STF) is the court of final instance in disputes involving constitutional law.

[36] STJ, *Súmula* 377, DJe 5 May 2009.

[37] World Health Organization (WHO), 'International Classification of Functioning, Disability and Health' (World Health Organization, 2001).

[38] Instituto Brasileiro de Geografia e Estatística (IBGE), 'Main Results – General Characteristics of the Population, Religion and Persons with Disabilities' (2010) www.ibge.gov.br.

fell to 12.7 million, equivalent to 6.7 per cent of the total population.[39] The most recent research, applying the methodology of population mapping of people with disabilities according to the CRPD, from the National Health Survey (*Pesquisa Nacional de Saúde* – PNS), identified 17.3 million people two years of age or older with some type of disability in the country.[40] This number is equivalent to 8.4 per cent of the Brazilian population, which is currently estimated by the IBGE at almost 215 million people.[41]

B. Non-Discrimination and Equality

Non-discrimination and equality is the theme that received the most attention in the Constitution.[42] Federal Law No 13.146/2015 aligned existing norms with the CRPD.[43] The protection afforded to persons with disabilities by this law applies to all federated entities, and includes affirmative action and quota systems in public competitions, access to higher education in federal and state universities, through affirmative action and quotas, as well as the private sector, in relation to mandatory hiring of persons with disabilities.

It is worth mentioning that the most relevant decision of the Supreme Court on non-discrimination and equality so far has been in the Direct Action of Unconstitutionality (ADI 5357) filed by the National Confederation of Educational Establishments (*Confederação Nacional dos Estabelecimentos de Ensino* – CONFENEN) in 2015. The action sought a declaration of unconstitutionality of Article 28(1), which prohibits private educational institutions from 'charging additional amounts of any nature in their tuition, fees and enrolment in compliance with these determinations'. The Supreme Court unanimously dismissed the case in 2017, upholding the CRPD and Federal Law No 13.146/2015 in its entirety.[44] This decision reinforces the centralisation of disability issues and is in line with a historical trend of the Supreme Court in protecting human rights.[45]

C. Accessibility

There is a consensus among scholars in the field of human rights in Brazil that the implementation of accessibility, with its instrumental character, is most

[39] IBGE, 'Nota Técnica' (January 2018) www.ibge.gov.br.
[40] IBGE, 'Pesquisa Nacional de Saúde (PNS) 2019' (6 October 2021) www.censos.ibge.gov.br.
[41] IBGE, 'População' (19 May 2022) www.ibge.gov.br.
[42] See above Table 1 Federal Constitution and Rights of Persons with Disabilities.
[43] Federal Law No 13.146/2015 Arts 4–8.
[44] STF, ADI 5357.
[45] Rodrigues, Lorencini and Zimmermann (n 26).

important to guarantee all the other rights. At the same time, scholars recognise it is the most difficult to realise, since it implies the adoption of universal design in practically all sectors of daily life – in public and private buildings, in public transportation and in digital media – but also reasonable accommodation where needed in particular cases. According to LA David de Araujo, to ensure that public entities comply with this obligation to guarantee accessibility, the Federal Law of Administrative Improbity[46] was amended, which regulates the actions and responsibilities of public managers at all levels of the Federation, thus 'one more behaviour that can be characterised as administrative improbity was included: failing to comply with the accessibility requirements set forth in the legislation'.[47]

This is due both to a deep-rooted discriminatory culture and to the lack of knowledge of the CRPD and of Federal Law No 13.146/2015, on the part of public managers, but also of private managers. In public administration, the biggest difficulties occur in the municipalities, in many cases with allegations that there is no budget for the necessary adaptations.

D. Participation

Participation of people with disabilities in political and public life in Brazil is regulated by Federal Law No 13.146/2015[48] and is affected by the representation of persons with disabilities' interests in national, state, and municipal councils for people with disabilities; and through the action of the Superior Electoral Court (*Tribunal Superior Eleitoral* – TSE) and the Regional Electoral Courts, which are mandated to foster accessibility of polling places.

With regard to participatory councils, in addition to the National Council for the Rights of People with Disabilities (*Conselho Nacional dos Direitos da Pessoa Portadora de Deficiencia* – CONADE), at the national level, each of the 26 states has its council, and in 2014 there was a network of more than 580 municipal councils of persons with disabilities in the country.[49] The councils are an important institutional channel of agency especially for civil associations representing the interests of different segments of people with disabilities, although it is not always the people with disabilities themselves who exercise representation.

[46] Federal Law No 8.429/1992.

[47] de Araujo (n 31).

[48] Federal Law No 13.146/2015 Art 76.

[49] The Superior Electoral Court (*Tribunal Superior Eleitoral* – TSE) is a permanent branch of the Union's judiciary – unlike many countries, where the electoral body is only active during election periods. The TSE has regional headquarters in the states, which allows it to act in a capillary manner.

One of the problems that the councils face, within the Brazilian reality, is the lack of budget, the lack of autonomy in relation to the Executive Branch, and the governmental centralisation in the management of the councils, including a formal parity participation, which in practice proves to be ineffective in many cases, due to the power of the Executive Branch to indicate, accredit the members, and manage the meetings and referrals. What happens with many national councils in fact is that they cannot be too critical or against the government without suffering retaliations to their regular functioning.

With regard to polling places, access was increased by Resolution No 23.381/2012 of the Superior Electoral Court, which 'instituted the Program of Accessibility in Electoral Justice', which presented several measures to guarantee the right to vote for people with disabilities. These measures are applied in electoral zones that have jurisdiction over certain territories, usually one or more neighbourhoods in the cities.

From the federal perspective, as a rule and in accordance with the federal principle, the Union does not exercise direct administrative control over the implementation of federal or international norms in the states and municipalities. The Federal Public Prosecutor's Office and the Union Public Defender's Office can exercise judicial control over the implementation of the CRPD. It is also up to the state law enforcement agencies, the state public prosecutors and the state public defenders to carry out this control in the states and municipalities. In this sense, the division of powers has not been impacted any differently than how the system of implementing federal laws already works.

IV. THE IMPLEMENTATION OF ARTICLE 33 CRPD

To explain how Brazil carries out the implementation of Article 33 CRPD it is illustrative to begin this section by commenting on the proposal of Federal Senator Mara Gabrilli, member of the CRPD Committee (2019–22).[50] On 31 March 2022, Senator Gabrilli presented Bill No 795/2022 in the Federal Senate that '[c]reates the National Institution for the Rights of Persons with Disabilities [*Instituição Nacional dos Direitos das Pessoas com Deficiência* – INADE]'. Senator Gabrilli aimed to set up '[a]n independent institution that could defend our rights and the protagonism of people with disabilities'.[51]

[50] In 2018 Senator Mara Gabrilli was elected by the state of São Paulo to the Federal Senate for the Brazilian Social Democracy Party (PSDB) for an eight-year term (2019–27). Initially the senator supported the election of President Bolsonaro and his government, but became critical of the president in the face of his policies contrary to human rights that negatively affected the rights of people with disabilities. She became the vice-presidential candidate on the ticket of the presidential candidate, Senator Simone Tebet, in the 2022 presidential elections.

[51] Senator Mara Gabrilli, 'Senadora Mara Gabrilli propõe a criação de órgão público de pessoas com deficiência' (29 April 2022) www.maragabrilli.com.br.

The proposed Bill aims to fill several gaps in the implementation of Article 33 CRPD by the Brazilian state and to address the dismantlement, by the government of President Jair Bolsonaro, of CONADE, the main federal body entrusted with coordinating, monitoring, and evaluating the National Policy for Persons with Disabilities.[52] In fact, Brazil currently has a formal focal point for the CRPD, has an ineffective coordination mechanism and does not have an independent national authority as defined by the CRPD. In the following subsections we will analyse each of these points.

A. Focal Point

Under the government of President Fernando Henrique Cardoso (1995–2002), the structure of the Federal Government included a National Secretariat for Human Rights, created in 1997 and attached to the Ministry of Justice. Through it the country participated, for example, in the implementation of the commitments and recommendations of the Vienna Conference and Plan of Action 1993 and in the preparatory work of the Durban Conference 2001. With the government of President Lula da Silva (2003–10), a new government structure was approved, including the creation of the Special Secretariat for Human Rights, with the status of a Ministry, which continued in the same way during the government of President Dilma Rousseff (2011–16).[53] The government of President Michel Temer (2016–18) retained the Secretariat and under the government of President Bolsonaro (2019–23) it was kept with the status of a Ministry but changed its focus, as the Ministry of Women, Family and Human Rights (*Ministério da Mulher, da Família e dos Direitos Humanos*),[54] gaining a new conservative and reactionary outlook, in its title and in its actions.[55]

The Human Rights Secretariat, in its different variations as a federal agency since 1997, has been consolidating and gaining relevance within the country and, in practice, has assumed the role of focal point for Brazil's international actions and representations at international conferences and before international protection and monitoring mechanisms at the UN and regional organisations.

However, the Ministry of Foreign Affairs (*Ministério das Relações Exteriores* – MRE), through its Department of Human Rights and Social Issues,[56]

[52] In that regard, Senator Gabrilli declared: 'When we started watching the increasing fragilization of CONADE, which had its activities suspended for about a year due to pure omission by the federal government … we realized that we had to propose INADE'. Senator M Gabrilli, ibid.

[53] Secretaria de Direitos Humanos da Presidência da República, 'Carta de Serviços' (October 2014) www.gov.br 7.

[54] Law No 13.844, 18 June 2019.

[55] See the website of Ministério da Mulher, da Família e dos Direitos Humanos at www.gov.br/mdh.

[56] Presidencia da República, Decreto No 11.024 (31 March 2022) www.planalto.gov.br.

has historically maintained great ascendancy over Brazil's international actions and representations in the human rights field, in many cases assuming the role of the country's main interlocutor before the human rights bodies of the UN system and regional systems. Regarding foreign policy for human rights at the multilateral level, the MRE, 'in coordination with the Ministry of Women, Family and Human Rights and other federal bodies [is responsible for] forwarding periodic reports on the promotion and protection in the country of the rights enshrined in these treaties'.[57] Thus, with regard to the CRPD, there has been no change in the pattern of international representation of the country on human rights issues. The current focal point of the CRPD, according to Article 33, is the National Secretariat for the Rights of Persons with Disabilities in the Ministry of Women, Family and Human Rights.[58] The coordination of policies related to the rights of persons with disabilities and the implementation of the CRPD involves two federal bodies: the National Secretariat for the Rights of Persons with Disabilities (*Secretaria Nacional dos Direitos da Pessoa com Deficiência* – SNDPD) in the Ministry of Women, Family and Human Rights, which 'is responsible for exercising the central coordination of different sectors (Article 14(II), Decree No 7.256/2010)'[59] and CONADE, as a collegiate body with multisectoral participation from government and civil society.

However, during the government of President Bolsonaro, human rights in Brazil have been deconstructed, suffering severe restrictions with notorious setbacks in various sectors, caused by the actions of the government itself. This deconstruction has also occurred in foreign policy, an area in which the country has built a good reputation over the last 30 years, since Brazil's return to democracy in the 1980s. This loss of the country's international reputation has greatly affected the implementation of Brazil's international commitments and the dialogue with international human rights monitoring and protection bodies. Various allegations of human rights violations have been made against the Bolsonaro government in different bodies of the UN system. Further, the High Commissioner for Human Rights has expressed great concern about the deterioration of human rights protection in the country.[60] Dozens of charges of crimes against humanity and genocide have also been filed against President Bolsonaro at the International Criminal Court (ICC), which is unprecedented.

[57] Ministério das Relações Exteriores (MRE), 'Política externa de direitos humanos' www.gov.br/mre.

[58] This information was confirmed to the authors by the Department of Human Rights and Social Issues of the Ministry of Foreign Affairs, by an e-mail of 4 July 2022.

[59] J Dias, 'Artigo 33. Implementação e Monitoramento Nacionais' in Secretaria Nacional de Direitos Humanos (ed), *Novos Comentários à Convenção sobre os Direitos das Pessoas com Deficiência* (SND, 2014) 214.

[60] OHCHR, 'Brazil' (2022) www.ohchr.org.

B. Coordination Mechanism

The Ministry of Women, Family and Human Rights entertains horizontal coordination with other ministries and federal secretariats, in relation to cross-cutting matters such as justice, citizenship, education, health, labour and others. This coordination could also occur at the political level with the Human Rights Secretariats of the states and municipalities, but, as mentioned above, Brazil has no institutional mechanisms for intergovernmental relations between the Union and the states in most areas of public policy, and the advances in this direction that took place in the Lula da Silva and Dilma Rousseff governments have been abandoned by the Bolsonaro government. At the same time, the animosity created by President Bolsonaro during his government against governors, aggravated during the Covid-19 pandemic, has not provided any kind of effective coordination from the Federal Government in the field of human rights.

CONADE, a collegiate body with the participation of the Federal Government and civil society, is officially the national coordination mechanism.[61] It also includes a commission for monitoring the implementation of the CRPD and its implementing law, and exercises a certain degree of coordination with other state and municipal councils. This coordination occurs through direct contact with the state and Federal District councils on the rights of persons with disabilities, and through the National Conferences on the Rights of Persons with Disabilities, held every four years since 2006, organised by CONADE, with the participation of representatives from the networks of state and municipal councils.[62] For the reasons already mentioned, both the historical lack of institutional intergovernmental coordination mechanisms and the abandonment of the few mechanisms that have been created, and the intergovernmental conflicts caused by President Bolsonaro, in addition to the difficulties arising from the Covid-19 pandemic, the coordination activity under Article 33 CRPD has been greatly impaired since 2019.

C. Framework/Independent Mechanism

Brazil does not have an ombudsman to act as an independent public agent in overseeing and monitoring the defence and implementation of human rights norms. In Brazil, the Federal Public Prosecutor's Office (*Ministério Público Federal* – MPF), a branch of the Executive, has this ombudsperson-like function and enjoys functional independence in the exercise of its constitutional functions. Unlike an ombudsman, normally elected directly by the population or by the Parliament, its equivalent in Brazil – the Attorney General of the

[61] This information was confirmed to the authors by the Department of Human Rights and Social Issues of the Ministry of Foreign Affairs, by an e-mail of 4 July 2022.

[62] National Conferences were held in 2006, 2008, 2012 and 2016. In 2020 it was not held due to the constraints of the Covid-19 pandemic.

Republic (*Procurador-Geral da República* – PGR) is chosen by the President of the Republic and approved by the Senate. His term of office is two years, and he may be reappointed for a second two-year term by the same parliamentary procedure.

Since the CF-88, the MPF has acquired central attributions related to the protection of diffuse and collective rights, including human rights and environmental law. The MPF is also responsible for the protection of minorities, including indigenous peoples and persons with disabilities.

Within the structure of the MPF, the Federal Prosecutor's Office for the Rights of the Citizen (*Procuradoria Federal dos Direitos do Cidadão* – PFDC) acts as the national human rights authority at the international level.[63] Since 2013, the PFDC has been a member of the Ibero-American Ombudsman Federation (*Federación Iberoamericana del Ombudsman* – FIO),[64] an international organisation established in 1995 in Cartagena de Indias, Colombia, which brings together some 20 Ibero-American countries.[65]

Although the PFDC is the Brazilian body which exercises the functions of a national human rights authority, it does not fulfil the requirements of Article 33 CRPD. Moreover, since the government of President Bolsonaro, the head of the MPF, who is serving his second term, shows great alignment with the president, avoiding or refusing to open investigative proceedings that could incriminate the president. Notwithstanding the guardian role that the MPF plays as an ombudsperson for the wide range of human rights, its main function is the protection of human rights, but it does not encompass the promotion and monitoring of human rights. Therefore, despite institutionally being independent, it does not fit the profile of the body recommended by Article 33 CRPD.

Joelson Dias, who was a member representing the Brazilian Bar Association (*Ordem dos Advogados do Brasil* – OAB) of CONADE, believes that this Council 'partially fulfils the function required by [Article 33(2)] of the Convention, since it is not an independent body'.[66] It must be acknowledged that CONADE is not an exception, since in Brazil, national public policy councils are not independent, neither from an organisational nor budgetary point of view. Like other councils, CONADE, as a collegiate body, is linked to the minister, although it is not subordinated to them. But when one checks the composition of CONADE one can clearly see that the Federal Government – through other ministries and government agencies – holds at least half of the seats, which makes its independence difficult. Not infrequently, civil society representatives vote in line with the government – whether by conviction or co-option – which further reinforces the collegiate body's lack of independence. From a budgetary perspective, the

[63] Ministério Público Federal, 'Procuradoria Federal dos Direitos do Cidadão' www.mpf.mp.br.

[64] Procuradoria Federal dos Direitos do Cidadão (PFDC), 'Federação Iberoamericana de Ombdusman' www.mpf.mp.br.

[65] Federación Iberoamericana del Ombudsman (FIO), 'Federación Iberoamericana del Ombudsman' www.portalfio.org.

[66] Dias (n 59) 215.

council is totally dependent on the ministry and has no autonomy to receive and manage the resources for its operation.

During President Bolsonaro's government, there were attempts to extinguish most of the national councils and to radically intervene in their structure and composition, in a move to dismantle the social participation built over more than three decades in the country. The attempt to extinguish councils was partially barred by the Supreme Court, which ruled that councils approved by law could not be extinguished by decree.[67] However, interventions in the composition of the councils have been occurring, as the mandates of the representations are about to end, and the government has the prerogative to maintain or change the representations.

According to the Department of Human Rights and Social Issues of the Ministry of Foreign Affairs, '[t]he mechanism provided for in Article 33(2) CRPD has not yet been established, but there are studies underway at the SNPDP and a bill in this regard'.[68]

V. CONCLUDING REMARKS

The CRPD has had a significant impact on the legal and public policy spheres in Brazil. The CRPD was incorporated with a special procedure equivalent to a constitutional amendment, inaugurating a mechanism of the CF-88 that was designed to give greater value and effectiveness to human rights treaties. Furthermore, at the substantive level, the CRPD changed the terminology and the concept of disability, with important consequences to ensure the dignity of people with disabilities, with impact in all federal, state and municipal regulations. This impact is the same as a constitutional rule that is mandatory for all states and municipalities.

Accessibility, non-discrimination and equity and participation are regulated at the federal level by the Federal Law No 13.146/2015. The major obstacles to fully realise the rights provided for in the CRPD are not of a legal or normative nature, but of insufficient public policies, especially in the states and municipalities, where the exercise of rights remains impeded or implemented in a partial and unequal way. Accessibility, for instance, is insufficiently implemented due to a lack of priority in most state and municipal policies – most local authorities argue there are no financial resources to implement universal design in buildings and other public facilities. Other accessibility resources, such as translation into sign language (*Libras* language, in Brazil), can be more easily implemented by the states and municipalities.[69]

[67] GMA Rodrigues, 'Brasil. Reducción de Espacios Civicos en America Latina y el Caribe, Policy Brief' (CRIES/Stanley Center for Peace and Security, 2021).

[68] Department of Human Rights and Social Issues of the Ministry of Foreign Affairs, e-mail sent to the authors on 4 July 2022.

[69] In fact, there are several initiatives underway regarding the inclusion of deaf people. Free courses in Libras are offered by various state and local governments. Similarly, there are also initiatives at the

The impact of the CRPD, and the law that regulated it as a constitutional norm, has also determined a significant increase in legal disputes related to the rights of people with disabilities in the country. According to the annual report of the National Council of Justice (*Conselho Nacional de Justiça* – CNJ),[70] legal disputes related to human rights increased by 46 per cent over 2019. On a quantitative scale, the subject with the second-highest number of human rights legal disputes in the country in 2020 was people with disabilities, with 4,173 cases.[71] Figure 1, extracted from the 2021 National Council of Justice Report, lists the most common human rights issues arising in cases before the courts (both federal and state). Of the 15 subjects listed, the most frequent was social assistance and the second subject was persons with disabilities.

Figure 1 Most In-Demand Human Rights Issues in 2020

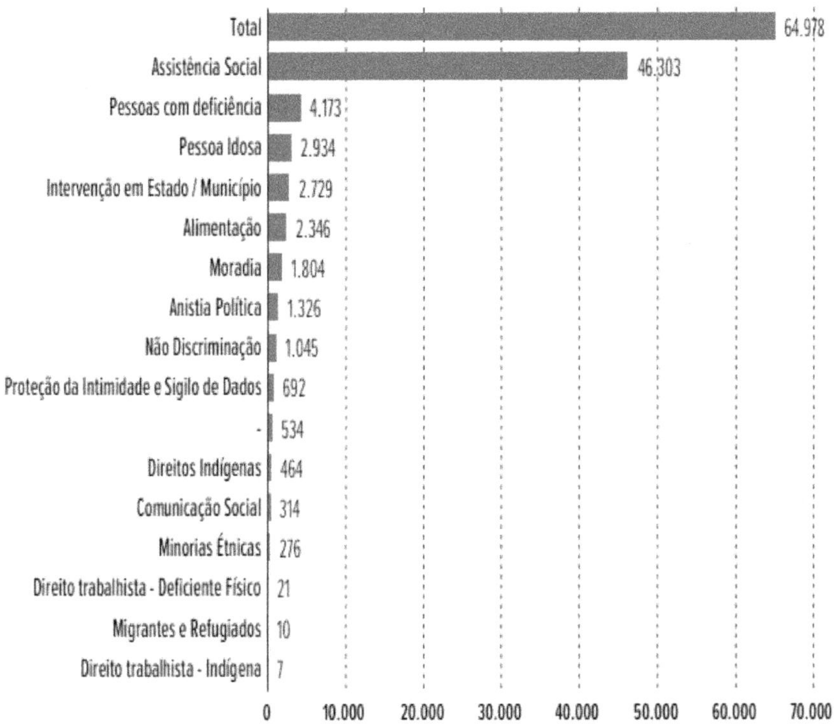

Source: CNJ 2021.

federal, state and municipal levels to draft laws that make the teaching of Libras mandatory from elementary school, for the inclusion of deaf people in society from an early age, and to have more listeners fluent in Libras.

[70] Conselho Nacional de Justiça (CNJ), 'Justiça em Números – 2021' (CNJ, 2021).

[71] According to the methodology applied in this report, these cases do not include health and education.

Regarding the implementation of Article 33 CRPD, the country has not yet been able to advance so that the focal point acts in a comprehensive and inclusive manner, and even less has it been able to affect the federal coordination that Brazil demands for its 26 states, the Federal District, and 5,570 municipalities. Indeed, states and municipalities have implemented the CRPD and Federal Law No 13.146/2015 by their own means and with their own structures, as it is constitutionally mandatory. However, the expected federal coordination, which is crucial for an equitable implementation, does not exist in practice.

Moreover, there is still no clear definition of the independent mechanism. The current structure adopted, supported by CONADE, is not independent but is subordinate to the Federal Government, and is still quite fragile, incomplete and insufficient. On this point, the Bill by Senator Mara Gabrilli, member of the CRPD Committee, proposed in March 2022 in the Federal Senate, has launched a necessary public debate that may result, in a few years, in a new and more effective structure that aligns with the requirements of Article 33(2) CRPD.

There is, finally, a great challenge posed in the implementation of the CRPD in a country with many socio-economic inequalities, both from a regional, gender and ethno-racial perspective: the challenge of advancing the rights of persons with disabilities in all regions and territories of the country and within all socio-economic spheres of the population in the states and municipalities. Given the deep legacy of Brazil's historic regional and ethno-racial socio-economic inequality, there is a great risk that the implementation of the CRPD will direct resources and actions to wealthier sectors of the territories of the cities, of the country, and of the population, to the detriment of the vast majority of millions of people with disabilities who are poorer and in more vulnerable socio-economic conditions.[72]

[72] Former President Lula won the October 2022 presidential election against the then-President Bolsonaro and, since taking office for his third term on 1 January 2023, the area of human rights has regained importance in Lula's government, with the recomposition of the Ministry of Human Rights and Citizenship, the emphasis on social participation in federal councils and the protection and promotion of diversity, both domestically and in foreign policy. A concrete example that Lula intends to restore the focus on human rights for persons with disabilities occurred on the very day of his inauguration, when he revoked Decree n 10.502/2020 approved by Bolsonaro, which regulated educational segregation – contrary to the principle of non-discrimination in Art 5 CRPD.

14

Mexico

Disability Rights in Mexican Federalism

IRENE SPIGNO

I. INTRODUCTION

MEXICO SIGNED THE UN Convention on the Rights of Persons with Disabilities (CRPD) and its Optional Protocol on 30 March 2007, and ratified them in December of the same year, thereby undertaking the obligation to protect and promote the dignity and rights of persons with disabilities, in pursuit of a global and inclusive society. The role of Mexico in the drafting and approval of the CRPD was key. On foot of the proposal submitted in 2001 by the Mexican delegation the UN General Assembly decided to establish a special committee that examined proposals for the elaboration of a wide and comprehensive international convention, in order to promote and protect the rights of persons with disabilities.[1]

Thanks to the constitutional reform of 10 June 2011, in Mexico the provisions of the CRPD, as an international human rights treaty, have the same hierarchical value as the Mexican Constitution.[2] However, in spite of this constitutional status, the implementation of the CRPD has represented a significant challenge for both the Federal Government and the states, in light of the paradigm shift in the promotion and protection of the rights of persons

[1] N González Martín, 'United Nations Convention on the Rights of Persons with Disabilities' (2008) 8 *Mexican Yearbook of International Law* 527–40. See Resolution adopted by the General Assembly of the United Nations A/RES/56/168, 19 December 2001.

[2] R Ortega García, 'The Hierarchy of Human Rights Treaties in the Light of the Constitutional Reform of 10 June 2011' (2015) 15 *Mexican Yearbook of International Law* 495–537. On the hierarchy of human rights treaties before the constitutional reform of 2011, see J Carpizo, 'The Mexican Constitution and the International Human Rights Law' (2012) 12 *Mexican Yearbook of International Law* 799–858.

with disabilities imposed by the CRPD.[3] Mexico has to align with the vision of disability embedded in the CRPD, which incorporates the 'social model' in Mexican law.[4]

The attempt to align with this model has in fact provoked an important paradigm shift in Mexico, which was part of the broadest process of mainstreaming human rights in all government action. The General Law for the Inclusion of People with Disabilities (*Ley General para la Inclusión de las Personas con Discapacidad* – LGIPD),[5] entered into force in 2011, provides relevant legal elements for the harmonisation of national legislation with the CRPD and seeks to address the rights of people with disabilities and promote their comprehensive development and equal opportunities. Mexico has made significant efforts and advances, both at the federal level as well as at the state level, which is reflected in the relevant regulatory apparatus in the protection of the rights of persons with disabilities, as well as in the case law of the Supreme Court of Justice of the Nation (*Suprema Corte de Justicia de la Nación* – SCJN). For some years now, the SCJN has been incorporating the social model of disability into its case law, referring to the CRPD to further the protection of the rights of people with disabilities.[6] However, despite these advances, the view that a person with a disability is someone who must be 'protected' still persists in many parts of Mexico. The latter view leads to the restriction of autonomy and reinforces a 'paternalistic' vision, in accordance with the medical model.[7]

In April 2022, the Committee on the Rights of Persons with Disabilities (CRPD Committee) issued its Concluding Observations (COs) on the second and third periodic report for Mexico. Those COs, after acknowledging the significant progress achieved by Mexico, highlighted concerns about gaps in federal laws regarding the rights of people with disabilities, and about the derogatory language used in these legislative texts, indicative of stereotypes and prejudices.

In the following pages, I will first analyse how the rights of people with disabilities have been dealt with by Mexican federalism (section II). Subsequently, the concept of disability at the federal and state levels (section III) and the implementation of the CRPD with reference to non-discrimination and equality, accessibility and participation in the Mexican legal system (section IV) will be discussed. After examining the implementation of the mechanisms provided for

[3] C Parra-Dussan, 'Convention on the Rights of Persons with Disabilities: Background and its New Approaches' (2010) 16 *International Law* 347–80.

[4] H Sandoval et al, 'Disability in Mexico: a Comparative Analysis between Descriptive Models and Historical Periods Using a Timeline' (2017) 59 *Salud Pública de México* 429–36.

[5] *Ley General para la Inclusión de las Personas con Discapacidad* (LGIPD), Official Gazette of the Federation 30 May 2011.

[6] Center for Constitutional Studies of the Supreme Court of Justice of the Nation, 'Derechos de las personas con discapacidad' (2020) 5 *Cuadernos De Jurisprudencia*.

[7] SD Barbosa, FV Salazar and J Beltrán, 'The Medical Model as a Disability Generator' (2019) 19 *Latin American Journal of Bioethics* 111–122.

in Article 33(1) CRPD (section V), some final remarks will discuss the future Mexican agenda on disability (section VI).

II. MEXICAN FEDERALISM AND DISABILITY

Mexico is a federal state and is made up of 32 federated entities. Federalism in Mexico was first adopted in 1824; throughout the nineteenth century it suffered several crises that tried to reverse the federal model and turn Mexico into a centralist state.[8] The federalist model was chosen in the current Constitution of 1917, in which the delimitation of the competences and powers that correspond to each of the levels of government is established mainly in three constitutional Articles. First, Article 73 sets out the competences of the Congress of the Union to legislate, and defines what matters must be regulated by the Federation.[9] These matters can be regulated through three types of laws. First, federal laws are adopted when only the federal authorities have powers in the matter. Secondly, general laws are approved if concurrent powers exist between the state governments and the Federation and indicate what corresponds to each one.[10] Finally, national laws intervene when there is a need for regulations to be the same throughout the country and these are applied by both sub-national authorities and the Federal Government. National laws have direct application throughout the national territory regardless of the order of government involved, but they are limited to the scope of competence established in the Constitution. Although the general law is the source of the distribution of powers, the national law is limited only to developing the distribution of powers previously given by the Constitution or other legal systems. Article 124 of the Constitution states that all powers not expressly granted to the federal authorities are understood to be reserved to the states.[11] Finally, Article 115 of the Constitution indicates the powers that correspond to the municipalities, and they refer above all to the provision of territorial public services.

[8] J Barragán Barragán, *Introducción al federalismo. La formación de los poderes en 1824* (National Autonomous University of Mexico, 1978); J Zoraida Vázquez and JA Serrano Ortega (eds), *Práctica y fracaso del primer federalismo mexicano (1824–1835)* (El Colegio de Mexico AC, 2012); J Zoraida Vázquez, 'Un viejo tema: el federalismo y el centralismo' (1993) *Historia Mexicana* 621–31.

[9] M Carbonell, 'El federalismo en México: principios generales y distribución de competencias' (2003) *Anuario de Derecho Constitucional Latinoamericano* 379–396; VM Rangel Cortés, 'El Congreso de la Unión y el proceso de centralización legislativa en México' (2021) 71 *Revista de la Facultad de Derecho de México* 121–52.

[10] O Gutiérrez Parada, 'Qué caracterizamos bajo la locución "leyes generales": tratados internacionales de derechos humanos y estructura jerárquica del sistema jurídico mexicano' (2012) *Congreso Redipal* 1–29.

[11] J Carpizo, *Comentario al artículo 124 constitucional, in Derechos del pueblo mexicano. México a través de sus constituciones* (Chamber of Deputies-LV Legislature/Miguel Ángel Porrúa, 1994) 953–59.

This structure shows that the drafters of the Constitution considered that federal powers should be limited to the competences explicitly indicated in Article 73, while the remaining powers would remain in the hands of the states. However, Article 73 of the Constitution has been reformed 77 times from 1917 to date, becoming the constitutional norm that has undergone the most modifications.[12] These reforms show a clear trend towards expanding the power of the Federation through the extension of concurrent powers, in substance extending the powers of the Federal Government in matters that originally were vested in the states. This centralising trend seems to be even stronger nowadays.[13]

The Mexican Constitution does not refer to disability as a matter attributed to the Federation or to the states. Being an issue with many facets that range from human rights to health, infrastructure, public policies and development, it falls within the concurrent powers between local governments and the Federation, falling within the exclusive jurisdiction of the Federation in all cases related to the matters indicated in Article 73 of the Constitution. In that connection, in 2011 the Congress of the Union approved the LGIPD, to incorporate the norms foreseen in the Convention into the Mexican legal system and to regulate the different competences of the Federation and states.[14] The LGIPD establishes the National System for the Development and Inclusion of Persons with Disabilities, made up of the agencies and entities of the Federal Government, the governments of the states and municipalities, as well as the individuals or legal entities of the social and private sectors that provide services to people with disabilities.

Likewise, the LGIPD creates the National Council for the Development and Inclusion of Persons with Disabilities as a decentralised public body, with its own legal personality and assets, which, in order to fulfil its powers, will enjoy technical and managerial autonomy, to formulate policies, actions, strategies and programmes derived from the same law.

In addition to the LGIPD, at the federal level, the Federal Law to Prevent and Eliminate Discrimination was also amended in 2014, to include a wider perspective on disability, making reference to disabilit*ies* (emphasis added) rather than to disability, and in the same year the Federal Telecommunications and Broadcasting Law of 2014 was approved, whose chapter II is entirely dedicated to the rights of users with disabilities.[15] The Mexican federal system has

[12] JC Zaragoza, 'The Metamorphosis of Mexican Federalism. Towards Asymmetric Federalism?' (2022) 12 *Latin American Yearbook – Political Science and International Relations* 155–72.

[13] J Cárdenas Gracia, 'México a la luz de los modelos federales' (2004) 37 *Mexican Bulletin of Comparative Law* 479–510; F Tortolero Cervantes, 'El primer eje del poder presidencial en México. Un federalismo centralizador' (2018) 17 *Ianus* 111–36.

[14] See generally and for comparison with US regulations ES Prieto Armendáriz and SP Saladin, 'A Comparison between the Ley General para la Inclusión de las Personas con Discapacidad and the Americans with Disabilities Act' (2012) 14 *Perspectivas sociales* 31–43.

[15] G Ortiz González, 'Telecomunicaciones: más beneficios y derechos a los usuarios' (2015) 28 *Quid Iuris* 17.

also a set of norms and public policies, protocols and guidelines, which have the objective of promoting and protecting the rights of people with disabilities, as indicated in the Convention.[16] However, these efforts have not been enough to overcome the medical model, which still treats disability as a disease that must be treated.

At the state level, in all entities of the Republic, there are laws for the protection of the rights of persons with disabilities. However, not all of them respect the standards provided for in the CRPD, since, as the Mexican state itself has pointed out in the initial report presented in 2011 to the CRPD Committee, some of these state laws referred to people with disabilities with derogatory language by using the term 'people with different abilities' or 'disabled'.[17] In addition, some state laws limited the concept of accessibility to physical accessibility, thus adopting a much more restrictive approach than that adopted by the CRPD.

III. THE MEXICAN UNDERSTANDING OF THE CONCEPT OF DISABILITY

In Mexico, the first definition of disability is found in the regulations approved in 2005,[18] before the signing of the CRPD. Article 2, section IX, of the General Law of Persons with Disabilities defined a person with a disability as:

> [a]ny person who has a physical, mental or sensory deficiency, whether of a permanent or temporary nature, that limits the ability to perform one or more essential activities of daily life, which can be caused or aggravated by the economic and social environment.

Since 2006, the year in which the CRPD was approved, the concept of disability has been redefined. The CRPD proposed understanding disability as a social construction, and is premised on the idea of equitable access to human rights. The 'social model of disability' focuses on the interaction between people with disabilities and their environment, mainly in terms of mobility, free communication and access to information. People with disabilities face certain barriers and greater challenges to access education, employment, the formation of their own

[16] See the 2014–2018 National Human Rights Program; the National Program for the Development and Inclusion of Persons with Disabilities 2014–2018; the National Labor and Employment Program for Persons with Disabilities 2014–2018; the National Program for Equality and Non-Discrimination; the Integral Program for the Prevention, Attention, Punishment, and Eradication of Violence against Women; the Prevention, Rehabilitation, and Social Inclusion Program for People with Disabilities; the Special Migration Program, Protocol for the Administration of Justice in Cases Involving Persons with Disabilities; see also, the Comprehensive Care Program for Victims 2020–2024 and the adoption of the Charter of Sexual and Reproductive Rights of Persons with Disabilities of 2018.

[17] As in the case of the states of Campeche and Nayarit.

[18] Published in the Official Gazette of the Federation on 10 June 2005.

companies, quality health, among others. Therefore, they face disadvantages compared to the population without disabilities.

This paradigm shift purported by the CRPD implied for Mexico a profound change in the design, execution and evaluation of public policies aimed at promoting, protecting, respecting and guaranteeing human rights for this social group. The LGIPD aimed to incorporate the spirit of the Convention into national legislation. In fact, the LGIPD contains a very broad definition of disability, understood as 'the consequence of the presence of a deficiency or limitation in a person, which, when interacting with the barriers imposed by the social environment, may prevent their full and effective inclusion in society, on equal terms with others'.[19] The LGIPD also defines the different types of disability, distinguishing between physical,[20] mental,[21] intellectual[22] and sensory[23] disabilities.

Compared to the 2005 definition, the new formulation attempts to incorporate the social model favouring the full and effective inclusion of people with disabilities in society. Further, in order to pursue this objective of full inclusion, the LGIPD created the National Council for the Development and Inclusion of Persons with Disabilities and the National System for the Development and Inclusion of Persons with Disabilities, as an institutional coordination mechanism to monitor the public policies on disability of the Federation and the states. Likewise, different government programmes have been adopted at the federal level, such as the National Program for the Development and Inclusion of Persons with Disabilities 2014–2018 and the National Work and Employment Program for Persons with Disabilities 2014–2018.[24] In the National

[19] Art 2 LGIPD, fraction added at the Official Journal of the Federation on 22 June 2018.

[20] Art 2, section X LGIPD defines physical disability as 'the sequel or malformation that derives from a condition in the neuromuscular system at the central or peripheral level, resulting in changes in movement control and posture, and that when interacting with the barriers imposed on it by the social environment, can prevent its full and effective inclusion in society, on equal footing with others'; fraction added at the Official Journal of the Federation on 22 June 2018.

[21] Ibid section XI: 'Mental disability. To the alteration or deficiency in the neuronal system of a person, which, together with a succession of events that they cannot handle, triggers a change in their behavior that hinders their full development and social coexistence, and that when interacting with the barriers that the social environment generates, can prevent their full and effective inclusion in society, on equal basis with others'; fraction added at the Official Journal of the Federation on 22 June 2018.

[22] Ibid section XII: 'Intellectual disability. It is characterized by significant limitations both in the structure of reasoned thought, and in the adaptive behavior of the person, and that by interacting with the barriers imposed by the social environment, can prevent their full and effective inclusion in society, on equal basis with others'; fraction added at the Official Journal of the Federation on 22 June 2018.

[23] Ibid section XIII: 'Sensory disability. It is the structural or functional deficiency of the organs of vision, hearing, touch, smell, and taste, as well as the structures and functions associated with each one of them, and that when interacting with the barriers imposed by the social environment, can prevent their full and effective inclusion in society, on equal terms with others'; fraction added at the Official Journal of the Federation on 22 June 2018.

[24] The objective of this programme is to disseminate and promote the labour rights of people with disabilities with full respect for their dignity, equality and non-discrimination.

Development Plan for 2013–2018, disability is mainstreamed. This Plan seeks to eliminate inequalities also through the establishment of comprehensive schemes of care for people with disabilities that promote the detection of disabilities, and rehabilitation. Further, the plan provides for designing and executing strategies to increase the productive inclusion of people with disabilities through job training schemes and linkages with the productive sector, and to ensure the construction and adaptation of public and private space to guarantee their right to accessibility. However, these programmes are still at their initial stage and remain to be evaluated. In addition, it is possible to find regulations related to disability in different areas, such as the rights of children and adolescents,[25] telecommunications,[26] transport,[27] tourism and others. Many of those are based on a conception of people with disabilities according to the still prevailing medical model.[28]

The SCJN has also been very critical of the approach still adopted in many regulations,[29] stating that the concept of disability included in the Convention is not a rigid concept, but conveys a dynamic approach that allows for adaptations. Therefore, the Court insists on the idea that the responsibility of the Mexican Republic is to eliminate 'socially created barriers that impede [the] enjoyment of human rights, [as well as] adopt the measures that are pertinent so that [they can exercise] in the legal capacity as much as possible'.[30]

The concept of disability adopted at the state level often refers to the physical, sensory, cognitive-intellectual, and psychosocial impairments that a person experiences and make it difficult for them to function adequately in the social environment. Some states (Durango, Guerrero, Jalisco, Nayarit and Nuevo León) make reference also to the economic environment. If we compare these concepts with the one included in the LGIPD, we see that there is no clear reference to *equality of conditions* as one of the first barriers caused by disability.

[25] The Mexican regulatory framework on the rights of persons with disabilities is also integrated by the General Law on the Rights of Children and Adolescents, which provides for the right to inclusion of children and adolescents with disabilities, requiring the adoption of affirmative actions. It reiterates that discrimination includes the denial of reasonable adjustments and provides for specific measures to achieve substantive equality for children and adolescents with disabilities.

[26] The Federal Telecommunications and Broadcasting Law also promotes that users with disabilities have access to closed telecommunications services and that strategies are generated to guarantee broadcasting on equal terms with other users and audiences, in accordance with Arts 199 and 257, respectively. Also, in order to have a real equality of opportunities.

[27] Some local public transportation laws recognise the rights of persons with disabilities, such as the processing of vehicle licence plates (Art 22 of the Transit and Transportation Law of Coahuila) or dignified conditions for specialised and accessible public transportation (Art 40 of the Transit and Transportation Law of Coahuila).

[28] Committee on the Rights of Persons with Disabilities (CRPD Committee), 'Concluding observations on the combined second and third periodic reports of Mexico' CRPD/C/MEX/CO/2-3, 20 April 2022, para 11.

[29] Supreme Court of Justice of the Nation (SCJN), First Chamber, Direct *Amparo* under Review 44/2018, 13 March 2019. In this case, the Court produced an easy-to-read version of this sentence. Similar reasons in AR 1368/2015, AR 702/2018 and in ADR 8389/2018.

[30] Ibid 48, para 3.

However, states do recognise this outcome when they provide the definition of 'person with disability'. That is, at the state and federal levels, two distinct concepts are mentioned: disability and person with a disability. When referring to a 'person with a disability', local laws, in line with general Mexican federal dynamics, fully replicate the definition of the General Law in Article 2, section XXVII.

The states of the Mexican Republic adopt very different measures[31] and unfortunately many of them are only of a welfare nature, since they provide rehabilitation services and donation of technical aids, neglecting actions that promote the participation, development, and empowerment of persons with disabilities. At the state level, therefore, it is necessary to consolidate institutions dedicated to the inclusion of people with disabilities, where through effective participation, challenges are identified and strategies are proposed for their empowerment, always under the guarantee of access to human rights. Similarly, the state administrations in each of their dependencies must work to include people with disabilities in all their government programmes for the population.

At the state level, the experience of the Constitution of Coahuila should be highlighted. The constitutional reform proposed in December 2021 incorporated different human rights charters into the Constitution. In particular, chapter X of Title Five of the Civil Rights Charter (*Carta de Derechos Civiles*) incorporates comprehensive protection of the rights of persons with disabilities at the local level, establishing that all persons with any type of disability have the right to benefit from the measures, affirmative actions and reasonable adjustments that guarantee, in an intersectional way and under transversal policies, their autonomy, their social and professional integration and their participation and inclusion in the community. In addition, it is specified that children and adolescents with disabilities will enjoy those rights, taking into account the principle of the best interests of the child. With reference to the definition of reasonable adjustments, the same provision defines them as the possible and effective modifications and adaptations obtained through the process of dialogue between those involved, which do not impose a disproportionate burden, when required in a particular case, to guarantee persons with

[31] There are states such as Guanajuato (Art 14 Ley para Prevenir, Atender y Eliminar la Discriminación en el Estado), Jalisco (Art 32 Ley Estatal para Promover la Igualdad, Prevenir y Eliminar la Discriminación en el Estado de Jalisco), Tlaxcala (Art 61 Ley para las Personas con Discapacidad del Estado de Tlaxcala), Zacatecas (Art 58 Ley para la Inclusión de las Personas con Discapacidad), and Colima (Art 11 Ley para la Integración y Desarrollo Social de las Personas con Discapacidad del Estado de Colima), which have had institutes or councils dedicated to the inclusion of people with disabilities for more than two administrations. However, most states leave public policy on inclusion in the hands of the National System for the Comprehensive Development of the Family. There is also a great deal of variety and diversity with respect to the coordination of institutional work due to the lack of cross-cutting strategies. Zacatecas is the exception of all and stands out for the existence of strong coordination between institutions (Art 6, section XXII Ley para la Inclusión de las Personas con Discapacidad).

disabilities the enjoyment or exercise of all human rights, on equal terms with others. The proposed reform indicated among the duties of the state that of guaranteeing the rights of persons with disabilities, through the adoption of the necessary measures, affirmative actions and reasonable adjustments for all types of disabilities in order to achieve the full enjoyment and exercise of their rights, as well as the assumption of all relevant legislative measures to modify or repeal existing laws, regulations, customs and practices that constitute discrimination against them. Further, the constitutional reform proposed to include a provision on the promotion of research and development of universally designed goods, services, and equipment. Finally, it requires the realisation of close consultations in the elaboration and application of legislation and policies to make effective the applicable regulations and the processes of decision-making on issues related to people with disabilities (Art 207).

The proposed reform is an example for the other states of what it means to incorporate this comprehensive protection of the rights of people with disabilities in local laws. The Articles of the *Carta de Derechos Civiles* serve as a model so that the authorities can protect and guarantee the rights of people with disabilities at the local level. Thus, international commitments can be better fulfilled at the state level.

IV. THE IMPLEMENTATION OF THE CRPD IN SELECTED KEY AREAS

A. Mexican Legislation on Non-Discrimination and Equality

Article 1 of the Mexican Constitution prohibits any discrimination based, inter alia, on disability. The transformation of Mexican legislation to ensure the right to equality and non-discrimination of persons with disabilities in the country had already begun before the entry into force of the CRPD. This guarantee was incorporated into the Constitutional Charter for the first time in 2001, with reference to the prohibition of discrimination against 'people with different abilities',[32] an expression rephrased in 2006 to 'disabled people',[33] and later replaced in the 2011 reform[34] by 'disabilities'. As of the constitutional reform of 2001, 12 states amended their local constitutions, in which they expressly prohibited discrimination or referred to the right to equality.[35]

In 2003, the Federal Law to Prevent and Eliminate Discrimination was approved, and later amended in 2014. The regulations, in their original version, contained only three references to disability: in Article 4, where it was specified

[32] Published in the Official Gazette of the Federation on 14 August 2001.
[33] Published in the Official Gazette of the Federation on 4 December 2006.
[34] Published in the Official Gazette of the Federation on 10 June 2011.
[35] Likewise in Chiapas (Art 9, section XV), Coahuila (Art 7 and Art 7-D, the latter one was added in 2022), Durango (Art 5), State of Mexico (Art 5), Hidalgo (Art 4), Michoacán (Art 1), Morelos (Art 1), Nuevo León (Art 1), San Luis Potosí (Art 7), Tabasco (Art 2), and Yucatán (Art 2).

that for the purposes of this law, discrimination shall be understood as any distinction, exclusion or restriction that, based on, among other things, disability; in Article 11, which included minors with disabilities as recipients of the measures implemented by public bodies and federal authorities aimed at promoting access to child development centres; and in Article 13, a specific rule with reference to positive and compensatory measures in favour of equal opportunities for people with disabilities to be carried out by public bodies and federal authorities, within the scope of their competence. After the 2014 reform,[36] the Federal Law to Prevent and Eliminate Discrimination established that discrimination shall mean any distinction, exclusion or restriction based, among other reasons, on disability, and listing the discriminatory behaviours that are prohibited. In addition, this law establishes the positive and compensatory measures that public bodies and federal authorities must adopt to enhance equal opportunities for various groups that historically have faced vulnerability. Similarly, 17 federated entities have approved state laws to prevent and eliminate discrimination and include disability as a ground of discrimination.

At the state level, the constitutions of 28[37] states have anti-discriminatory clauses; however, only 25[38] expressly recognise disability as a basis of discrimination. At the legislative level, all federal entities have a local anti-discrimination law that lists disability as a prohibited ground of discrimination.[39] In addition, in Guanajuato, Guerrero, Jalisco, Morelos, Nayarit, Nuevo León, Puebla, Quintana Roo, Sonora, Tabasco and Veracruz, the denial of reasonable accommodation is recognised as discrimination.[40]

[36] Published in the Official Gazette of the Federation on 20 March 2014.

[37] Baja California Sur (Art 7), Campeche (Art 7), Chiapas (Art 9, section XV), Chihuahua (Art 4), Mexico City (Art 4), Coahuila (Arts 7 and 7-D), Colima (Art 1), Durango (Art 5), Guanajuato (Art 1), Guerrero (Art 5), Hidalgo (Art 4), Jalisco (Art 4), State of Mexico (Art 5), Michoacán (Art 1), Morelos (Art 1), Nayarit (Art 7), Nuevo León (Art 1), Oaxaca (Art 4), Puebla (Art 11), Querétaro (Art 3), Quintana Roo (Art 13), San Luis Potosí (Art 7), Sinaloa (Art 4 bis), Sonora (Art 1), Tabasco (Art 2), Tlaxcala (Art 14), Yucatán (Art 2) and Zacatecas (Art 21).

[38] Baja California Sur (Art 7), Campeche (Art 7), Chihuahua (Art 7), Mexico City (Art 4), Coahuila (Arts 7 and 7-D), Colima (Art 1), Guanajuato (Art 1), Guerrero (Art 5), Hidalgo (Art 4), Jalisco (Art 4), State of Mexico (Art 5), Michoacán (Art 1), Morelos (Arts 1 and 19), Nayarit (Art 7), Nuevo León (Art 1), Oaxaca (Art 4), Puebla (Art 11), Querétaro (Art 3), Quintana Roo (Art 13), San Luis Potosí (Art 7), Sinaloa (Art 4 bis), Sonora (Art 1), Tlaxcala (Art 14), Yucatán (Art 2) and Zacatecas (Art 21).

[39] Secretary of Foreign Affairs, 'Response of the Mexican State to the request for inputs for the preparation of an analytical study by the Office of the United Nations High Commissioner for Human Rights (OHCHR) in compliance with resolution 37/22 of the Human Rights Council (UNHRC)' (2019) 1–20.

[40] Art 8 Ley para Prevenir, Atender y Erradicar la Discriminación en el Estado de Guanajuato; Art 11 Ley para Prevenir, Combatir y Eliminar la Discriminación en el Estado de Guerrero; Art 7 Ley Estatal para Promover la Igualdad, Prevenir y Eliminar la Discriminación en el Estado de Jalisco; Art 11 Ley para Prevenir y Eliminar la Discriminación en el Estado de Morelos; Art 13 Ley para Prevenir y Erradicar la Discriminación en el Estado de Nayarit; Art 7 Ley para Prevenir y Eliminar la Discriminación en el Estado de Nuevo León; Art 6 bis Ley para Prevenir y Eliminar la Discriminación del Estado Libre y Soberano de Puebla; Art 9 Ley para Prevenir, Atender y Eliminar la Discriminación en el Estado de Quintana Roo; Art 9 Ley para Prevenir, Combatir y Eliminar Actos de Discriminación en el Estado de Sonora; Art 12 Ley para Prevenir y Eliminar la Discriminación

However, despite these important advances brought about after the ratification of the CRPD, it is still necessary to align federal and state orders with the CRPD as interpreted by the CRPD Committee, to counter the persistence of the medical approach to disability.[41] This need has also been highlighted by the SCJN when affirming the unconstitutionality of regulations that require, among other things, medical certificates to reissue a disability permit or licence to drive motor vehicles to people who have been diagnosed with an impairment. The SCJN has held that those regulations do not comply with the duty of the state as such to promote the social inclusion of people with disabilities and violate their rights to dignity, equality, and non-discrimination.[42]

The SCJN has identified several violations of the principle of equality and non-discrimination with reference to the right to work in cases in which, for example, people with disabilities are unduly excluded from job offers,[43] when they are asked for documentation, such as authorisation certificates not required from other people,[44] to guarantee access under equal conditions in terms of the number of work placements for people with disabilities.[45] Finally, the Court has played a seminal role in guaranteeing the right of children and adolescents with disabilities to a nursery service with child development centres that are establishments where temporary care, food and, where appropriate, initial education are provided to minors with disabilities.[46]

en el Estado de Tabasco; and Art 6 Ley para Prevenir y Eliminar la Discriminación en el Estado de Veracruz de Ignacio de la Llave.

[41] These regulations are complemented by mechanisms that provide specific budget lines on equality and non-discrimination that contemplate the incorporation of reasonable accommodations for the inclusion of people with disabilities in the population, as an objective of social programmes considering accessibility in transversal approaches of gender equality, youth, disability, and ethnicity. In addition, the Federal Expenditures Budget contemplates the application of resources for the care programme for people with disabilities in the health sector and indicates that the Federal Executive may include other programmes that must be subjected to operating rules, promoting principles of equality, non-discrimination, best interests of children, integrity and family integration, gender equality, social inclusion, self-determination of indigenous communities, protection of the environment, protection of life, health and integrity of people. With the evidence received, it resolves claims and complaints for alleged discriminatory acts committed by individuals or by federal authorities in the exercise of their functions.

[42] More in detail, on the rights to equality and non-discrimination of people with disabilities, see the Unconstitutionality Action 96/2014 and its accumulated 97/2014 of 8 November 2016.

[43] See SCJN, Direct *Amparo* under Review 1387/2012, 22 January 2014.

[44] See the Action of Unconstitutionality 89/2015, 15 May 2017.

[45] In *Amparo* under Review 146/2018 of 20 June 2018, the SCJN pointed out that the binding standard was 2 per cent of the workforce in the public sector with people with disabilities in the state of Baja California, and not 3 per cent, as the appellant maintained, since this percentage responded to a recommendation without binding force.

[46] Also with reference to the protection of children and adolescents with disabilities, the SCJN has ruled in the Unconstitutionality Action 86/2009 of 2 October 2015, promoted by the National Human Rights Commission to request the declaration of invalidity of various Arts of the Public Health Law for the state of Baja California, in particular Art 147, related to child development centres and stays for being discriminatory by depriving children with disabilities of the fundamental right to the nursery service.

B. Mexican Legislation on Accessibility

In Mexico, the first official effort to make public buildings accessible dates back to the late 1990s, when the Interinstitutional Group without Barriers was created as part of the civil society's impulse against the Mexican Social Security Institute (*Instituto Mexicano del Seguro Social* – IMSS). This group was the spearhead for various institutions seeking to make their facilities accessible to people with disabilities and began to adopt strategies that, although they have had visible results, have not been able to be quantified.[47] Despite the lack of statistical information regarding the actual accessibility of all properties, it can be noted that Mexico is still at the beginning and has only adopted initial steps to make these facilities accessible to people with motor disabilities.[48]

Although accessibility for people with visual and hearing disabilities has been enhanced, public institutions face financial obstacles that prevent them from implementing accessibility features. Another challenge is represented by the lack of unified approach when it comes to technical specifications established in the three orders of Government. In 2011, some efforts made by the National Council for Science and Technology (*Consejo Nacional de Ciencia y Tecnología* – CONACYT) and the National Council to Prevent Discrimination (*Consejo Nacional para Prevenir la Discriminación* – CONAPRED) were made, but without translation into best practices.[49] At that time, 17 federated entities[50] contemplated in their legislation provisions to facilitate access for people with disabilities, to buildings and other facilities open to the public. In the main public and private higher education institutions in the country, there were subjects, programmes, or adaptations, both architectural and curricular, to allow the inclusion of people with disabilities or to teach subjects related to the topic.

[47] Federal Government of Mexico, 'National Program for the Development of Persons with Disabilities 2009–2012' (2009) 164.

[48] According to data from the Secretariat of Social Development, almost 40 per cent of people with disabilities have a motor disability. Recommendations are still being made to the Mexican government to adapt public places, from the moment of their planning to their construction and possible adaptations to ensure accessibility for persons with disabilities and provide them with a friendly environment. See Secretaría de Desarrollo Social, 'Diagnóstico sobre la situación de las personas con discapacidad en México' (Gobierno de México, 2016) 84.

[49] Particularly in 2011 the National Council for the Development and Inclusion of Persons with Disabilities (*Consejo Nacional para el Desarrollo y la Inclusión de las Personas con Discapacidad* – CONADIS) was created as an institution responsible for directing and coordinating public policy to protect and respect the rights of persons with disabilities. However, although CONACYT and CONAPRED were already conducting annual diagnoses of the situation of persons with disabilities, CONADIS did not yet have a *consolidated* national programme to implement. The first steps began to be taken in terms of visibility, but the section on enforcement and protection of the human rights of persons with disabilities was still in its very early stages. See CONAPRED, 'Personas con Discapacidad' (CONAPRED, 2011; 2012; 2013; 2014; 2015; 2016; 2017).

[50] Baja California, Chiapas, Chihuahua, Colima, ex Federal District (*Distrito Federal* – DF), Durango, Hidalgo, Michoacán, Morelos, Nuevo León, Oaxaca, Querétaro, Tabasco, Tamaulipas, Tlaxcala, Veracruz and Zacatecas.

In 2014, the CRPD Committee noted that the Mexican legislative framework on accessibility for persons with disabilities did not address all the aspects contemplated in Article 9 CRPD.[51] The CRPD Committee was also concerned that Mexico did not have specific mechanisms for evaluating compliance with accessibility regulations in all areas considered by the Convention. It recommended the state should speed up the process of regulating accessibility, including the establishment of monitoring mechanisms, and sanctions for non-compliance with accessibility laws. Further, the CRPD Committee recommended the adoption of measures to ensure that accessibility plans include existing buildings and not just new ones, as well as the design and implementation of a National Accessibility Plan applicable to the physical environment, transportation, information in communications, including information and communication technologies and systems, and other services and facilities open to the public or for public use.[52]

The LGIPD considers accessibility in the principles that must be observed by public policies and facilities in educational and work centres and grants, fiscal incentives to individuals and corporations that adapt their facilities to enhance participation of persons with disabilities and adhere to public policies on the matter.

A series of policy plans related, for example, to the General Law on Human Settlements, Territorial Planning and Urban Development,[53] considers promoting social inclusion through measures that prevent discrimination, segregation or marginalisation of people in a situation of vulnerability and also contemplates universal accessibility.[54] Similarly, the General Tourism Law[55] promotes the provision of accessible tourist services.[56] However, Mexico's regulatory framework on accessibility for persons with disabilities still does not contain binding legal instruments that implement accessibility in all the areas covered by Article 9 CRPD.

Even though it was modified in April 2022 to better align with the CRPD, and it gives special emphasis to rights such as the right to health,[57] labour rights,[58]

[51] CRPD Committee, 'Concluding observations on the initial report of Mexico' CRPD/C/MEX/CO/1, 27 October 2014, para 19.

[52] Ibid.

[53] Published in the Official Gazette of the Federation on 28 November 2016.

[54] General Law on Human Settlements, Territorial Planning and Urban Development, Art 4, particularly fraction II.

[55] Published in the Official Gazette of the Federation on 17 June 2009.

[56] General Tourism Law, Arts 18 and 19.

[57] Arts 7–10 LGIPD, where the need to design and implement adequate and specialised health programmes as well as the creation and strengthening of care facilities to ensure the human rights and dignity of people are highlighted.

[58] Ibid Art 11 that underlines the fighting for the prohibition of discrimination in the hiring of persons with disabilities, establishes the guarantees of remuneration, reinsertion, continuity, stability, and training and execute public policies for the specialised inclusion of all persons regardless of their disability.

the right to education,[59] accessibility and housing,[60] public transportation and communications,[61] sports, recreation, culture and tourism,[62] and access to information,[63] the LGIPD should be further modified. Binding regulations to guarantee accessibility should also be adopted. It would also be necessary to review the complaint and monitoring mechanisms so that effective remedies are defined in cases where the established rules are not respected.

The SCJN has also ruled on issues related to accessibility, declaring the unconstitutionality of several Articles of the Mobility Law of the Federal District that contained narrow definitions of accessibility, limited to physical accessibility in relation to people with limited mobility.[64]

In terms of accessibility, the criteria and standards developed by the Court are also important with reference, for example, to accessibility of air transport and the carrying of devices necessary to people with disabilities, which may be incompatible with the technical and safety specifications of an aircraft. In that regard, the Court stated the obligation of airlines to guarantee boarding, mobility during the flight and descent of people with disabilities in adequate conditions, without restricting or preventing the person's access to the flight.[65]

[59] Ibid Arts 12–15 that establish the obligation to design the National Education System to develop special and inclusive education programmes, the adequacy of all educational levels for persons with disabilities and the establishment of accessibility mechanisms such as absolute gratuity. Moreover, they provide for the inclusion of education in Braille and sign language, at analogue and digital level and the establishment of scholarship systems.

[60] Ibid Arts 16–18 provide for the obligation to progressively adapt public spaces, promote coordination among the three levels of government to implement programmes in the areas of accessibility, urban development, and housing and guarantee decent housing for people with disabilities.

[61] Ibid Arts 19–20 establish directly to the Secretary of Communications and Transportation the duty to promote access to public transportation and the use of technologies with universal design to facilitate inclusion at the social level, the development of road education programmes and the establishment of a differential pricing programme in favour of persons with disabilities.

[62] Ibid Arts 24–27 contain indications to create programmes with administrative, technical, human, and financial support to promote the practice of different sports and cultural disciplines for people with disabilities and, in the area of tourism, to facilitate and adapt the means of national transportation for transfers within and outside the country.

[63] According to Art 32 LGIPD, the implementation of mechanisms for the consultation of information in a simple, timely manner and at no additional cost that meets the needs of each person according to their different disabilities is ordered.

[64] See SCJN, Action of Unconstitutionality 96/2014 and its accumulated 97/2014, 11 August 2016.

[65] See SCJN, Second Chamber, *Amparo* under Review 388/2018, 17 October 2018. In particular, the case arose from an injunction filed by an airline that considered the unconstitutionality of several Articles of the Civil Aviation Law, as well as the Federal Consumer Protection Law. Specifically, it was Art 47*bis*, section I, in relation to 47*bis* 1 of the Civil Aviation Law, which provides for the mandatory transportation of the instruments required by people with disabilities. See also SCJN, *Amparo* under Review AR 579/2018, AR 583/2018, AR 635/2018, AR 392/2018 and in the AR 717/2018.

C. Participation of People with Disabilities in Mexican Legislation

The CRPD recognises participation as a cross-cutting general principle. It also articulates participation in specific obligations.[66] In the Mexican context, participation in political and public life is particularly relevant. The Mexican Constitution establishes that Mexican citizens, without any distinction, can vote and be voted for positions of popular election, having the qualities established by law. Article 4 LGIPD states that all people with disabilities will enjoy the rights established by the Mexican legal system without discrimination. Regarding the political participation of people with disabilities, Mexico has regulatory instruments so that people with disabilities can exercise their right to vote. In 2003, the General Council of the then Federal Electoral Institute (*Instituto Nacional Electoral* – INE) approved an agreement that provided that all Civil Service officials, as well as local and district councillors, were obliged to seek the eradication of conditions that caused discrimination.[67] In addition, the General Council of the INE has also made agreements that have had the result of facilitating the casting of the vote by people with disabilities.[68] The use of the Braille mask has been incorporated and, in the 2006 elections, special lamps were designed so that citizens who use wheelchairs and people of short stature could cast their vote.[69]

Some political parties also incorporated in their statutes the promotion of the participation of persons with disabilities. National delegates and the Electoral Tribunal of the Federal Judicial Branch initiated in 2011 the Institutional Program of Accessibility for Persons with Disabilities[70] in order to promote and protect the human rights of persons with disabilities in regard to their right of access to electoral justice and the exercise of their electoral political rights.

[66] See Art 3 on General principles, Art 19 on Living independently and being included in the community, Art 24 on Education, Art 29 on Participation in political and public life, and Art 30 on Participation in cultural life, recreation, leisure and sport, Convention on the Rights of Persons with Disabilities (CRPD).

[67] Agreement CG/28/2003 of the Federal Electoral Institute.

[68] Ibid.

[69] Agreement CG/201/2005 of the Federal Electoral Institute.

[70] The Electoral Tribunal of the Judiciary of the Federation (*Tribunal Electoral del Poder Judicial de la Federación*) became one of the first public institutions to implement technological adaptations so that people with disabilities could easily access the information contained in its official website, in order for them to fully exercise their political-electoral rights and actively participate in the country's political decisions. During the presentation of this programme, representatives of the Legislative Branch, the National Council for the Development, CONADIS and CONAPRED highlighted the initiative of the Electoral Tribunal to implement mechanisms in its webpage for persons with disabilities to easily navigate the institutional portal. Some of the improvements presented were navigation through voice commands, screen readers and sounds. Thus, people with disabilities will be able to learn about the work carried out by the Superior Chamber and the Regional Chambers of the Electoral Tribunal of the Judiciary of the Federation.

Since 2001 people with disabilities have held managerial positions within the Federal Government.[71] The existence of civil servants with disabilities at the highest level in the office of the Presidency allowed the country to promote the CRPD within the United Nations system. However, the CRPD Committee highlighted that people with intellectual and psychosocial disabilities were denied the right to vote and that electoral procedures, facilities and materials were not accessible.[72] In this respect, Mexico was asked to modify the provisions of the Federal Code of Electoral Institutions and Procedures to guarantee the right to vote for all persons with disabilities. It was also recommended to ensure that electoral procedures, facilities, and materials were accessible, in both urban and rural areas.[73]

Article 225 of the LGIPD on electoral procedures establishes requirements that must be met by the places to locate the voting booths, highlighting easy and free access for the electorate.[74] In addition, in 2017, the General Council of the INE approved an agreement[75] by which the Protocol for the Inclusion of People with Disabilities as Civil Servants and Officers of Polling Station Boards was issued. The Protocol creates the conditions to make effective the right of people with disabilities to participate in the integration of polling station boards. It also establishes criteria for the preparation of materials that favour the participation of people with disabilities and the selection of accessible spaces for the installation of voting booths, as well as the possibility that people with disabilities can be accompanied by a trainer, electoral assistant, a poll worker or official or a person they trust. These measures have been complemented by SCJN case law. The Court in the Action of Unconstitutionality 38/2014 and its accumulated 91/2014, 92/2014, 93/2014 of 2 October 2014, declared the unconstitutionality of the restriction of the right to active suffrage to people with intellectual and psychosocial disabilities, including those who are under guardianship or curatorship regimes, in order for them to be able to exercise their right to vote and be elected and participate fully in the leadership of public affairs. Thus, in the 2015 manual for poll workers,[76] any provision that referred to preventing the access of people deprived of their mental faculties to the polls was eliminated. More recently, in the electoral process of 2019, the Electoral

[71] Government of Mexico, 'Response to the Study on participation in political and public life of persons with disabilities of Human Rights Council resolution 16/15' (2015).

[72] CRPD Committee (n 51) para 56.

[73] Given such urgency and substantial need to reform electoral rules in Mexico, this Code was abrogated and in its place a new General Law of Electoral Institutions and Procedures was issued on 23 May 2014. This law recognised the right to vote of persons with disabilities in Art 8; and the accessibility of polling places in urban and rural spaces in Arts 253 and 255.

[74] New Law published in the Official Gazette of the Federation on 23 May 2014.

[75] Agreement CG/161/2017 of the Federal Electoral Institute.

[76] Federal Electoral Institute, 'Polling Station Official's Manual for the 2014–2015 Electoral Process' (INE, 2015). This instrument is no longer in force. It has received a series of updates in 2017 and 2021, changing its name to 'Guide for the polling station official'. And its content has only been updated in terms of human rights, never any regression in this regard.

Tribunal of the Federal Judicial Branch, in collaboration with local electoral courts and related authorities, civil society organisations, people with disabilities, academics and defenders of electoral political rights, carried out workshops on rights and access to electoral justice for people with disabilities.[77]

However, the CRPD Committee, in its 2022 COs, expressed concern that people with intellectual and psychosocial disabilities are still denied their rights, since the voting procedures continue to be inaccessible.[78] Likewise, concern is expressed about the possibility of people with disabilities, and in particular women with disabilities, to participate in public and political life.[79]

As regards, on the other hand, the issue of the participation of persons with disabilities in cultural life, recreation, leisure, and sport provided for in Article 30 CRPD, multiple activities have been developed. Among those, the Marrakesh Treaty to Facilitate Access to Published Works for Persons Who Are Blind, Visually Impaired, or Otherwise Print Disabled was ratified on 29 July 2015. As a consequence, Article 148 of the Federal Copyright Law was modified, to provide that:

> [l]iterary and artistic works already disclosed may be used, provided that the normal exploitation of the work is not affected, without the authorization of the holder of the economic right and without remuneration, invariably citing the source and without altering the work, only in the following cases: (VIII) Publication and representation of artistic and literary works for non-profit purposes for persons with disabilities.

Authorised or recognised entities may avail themselves of the provisions of this section, under the terms of international treaties signed and approved by Mexico, for the cross-border exchange of copies in accessible formats, including their importation.[80]

V. THE IMPLEMENTATION OF ARTICLE 33 CRPD IN MEXICO

With regard to Article 33(1) CRPD, Mexico has designated as focal point the National Council for the Development and Inclusion of Persons with Disabilities, a decentralised public body with economic and legal autonomy, which establishes public policies promoting human rights of people with disabilities.

In compliance with Article 33(2) CRPD, in February 2011, the Government of Mexico presented to the Secretary-General of the United Nations and the

[77] The first course was held on 5 December 2019. In the following years its corresponding editions were also held, although both courses on 22 November 2021 and 2 May 2022 were held online due to the Covid-19 health emergency. The programmes are available on the website of the Electoral Tribunal of the Judiciary of the Federation. See Tribunal Electoral, 'Curso los Derechos Político-electorales de las personas con Discapacidad – modalidad en línea' (2 May 2022) www.te.gob.mx.

[78] CRPD Committee (n 28) paras 64 and 65.

[79] Ibid.

[80] This section was added on 17 March 2015 and amended on 1 July 2020 to be as cited here.

United Nations High Commissioner for Human Rights, the designation of the framework in charge of promotion, protection and supervision of the application of the CRPD, which includes the National Human Rights Commission (*Comisión Nacional de los Derechos Humanos* – CNDH) and the 32 public organisations for the protection and defence of human rights in the states. However, in 2014, the CRPD Committee urged the National Human Rights Commission and the 32 state human rights entities to define the structure, goals, indicators and resources of the mechanism for its work, and required Mexico to strengthen the National Commission so that it can carry out its mandate effectively and independently.

On 3 December 2015, the CNDH was established as a national monitoring mechanism for the Convention and on 17 June 2016, it entered into a general collaboration agreement with the 31 public human rights agencies to create an instrument for the independent national monitoring mechanism. Currently, according to the First National Mechanism Report 2018–2019, all states have implemented their corresponding division in the local agencies.[81] On 12 June 2017, the Regulation of the CNDH law was reformed, including Articles related to the structure of the mechanism, forming a General Council, and a Government Commission.[82]

The most delicate points highlighted by the same CRPD Committee are about the national and state mechanisms implemented to apply the Convention, including the budget and its allocation between 2015 and 2019. The same budget-type problems affect the National Council for the Development and Inclusion of People with Disabilities. In this sense, the national mechanism to apply the Convention is the National Program for the Development and Inclusion of Persons with Disabilities,[83] which sets the objectives and guidelines that public institutions at the federal and state levels must comply with.

The National Human Rights Commission is governed by the Paris Principles and is part of the Global Alliance of Human Rights Institutions. In December 2016, it obtained re-accreditation for a period of five years, with status from the office of the United Nations Commissioner. However, despite the fact that the CNDH complies with the Paris Principles and follows up on compliance with each of the recommendations it issues, for which it requires information from the authorities on the actions that each of them carries out

[81] Comisión Nacional de los Derechos Humanos (CNDH), 'First Report of the Independent National Monitoring Mechanism 2018–2019' (CNDH, 2020).

[82] The board shall be composed of 10 persons with a certain prestige in society, Mexicans in full exercise of their rights, and at least seven of them must not hold any position as public servants. Its functions are to establish general guidelines for the Commission's actions; approve the Commission's internal rules and regulations; give its opinion on the draft annual report of the president of the Commission; and give its opinion on budgetary matters and the handling of money within the Commission.

[83] See Gobierno de México, 'National Program for the Development and Inclusion of Persons with Disabilities 2014–2018' (30 April 2014) www.gob.mx.

to attend to the points recommendations embodied in each recommendation, it has not yet achieved full implementation. The Committee has expressed its concerns regarding the existence of complexities and the existence of many gaps in focal points and coordination mechanisms and especially in regard to their mutual interaction. The recommendation addressed to Mexico makes reference to 'the current system of focal points and coordination mechanisms at all levels of government, and [establishment of] a transparent system with sufficient funding, defined competences, and mutual interaction'.[84] In fact, despite the establishment of an independent mechanism for monitoring the implementation of the CRPD in Mexico, the structure of said mechanism, as well as its functions and activities, have not been sufficiently defined with reference to the promotion, protection and monitoring of the rights recognised in the Convention both at the federal and state levels, especially with reference to the participation in said mechanisms of women with disabilities.[85] In the same way, the CRPD Committee recommended that Mexico develop a strategy to ensure that both the CNDH as well as the state commissions, as part of the independent monitoring mechanism of the Convention, define the structure, objectives, indicators, and resources of this mechanism. Finally, it was recommended that the CNDH be strengthened so that it can fulfil its mandate effectively and independently and so that persons with disabilities (particularly women with disabilities) and the civil society organisations that represent them are more involved for greater participation in both the implementation and monitoring of the Convention.

VI. WHAT'S NEXT? SOME CONCLUDING REMARKS

Mexico protects the rights of persons with disabilities, and since the ratification of the CRPD it has enacted very progressive laws and programmes. In Mexico, the implementation of the CRPD reflects the general dynamics of Mexican federalism, which is rather federal on paper but with extreme centralising tendencies. The states tend to do nothing more than replicate what is done at the federal level, with only a few exceptions.

This is evident due to the fact that, despite all the efforts made to include the social model of disability at the federal level, the medical model still permeates Mexican governance structures and society. To embrace the human rights model and eliminate the medical, rehabilitation and social assistance model to achieve the inclusion of people with disabilities has probably been the main challenge for Mexico thus far.

[84] CRPD Committee (n 28) para 69.
[85] Ibid para 68.

The pending agenda remains very long: there is a lack of a National Plan to include people with disabilities in the community at the state and federal level, and Mexico should adopt administrative and financial policies to support them to live independently and in the community. There is concern about the inadequate allocation of the budget to implement the Convention at the federal, state and municipal levels, and the use of pejorative terms in relation to people with disabilities continues (especially at the state level).

The judiciary has protected the rights of people with disabilities by means of a new protocol adopting a disability perspective: this is the Protocol for Judging with a Disability Perspective[86] published in April 2022. The Public Defender's Office (a public institution made up of lawyers whose job it is to represent the people who have been accused of committing a crime) has raised awareness of disability among lawyers. However, it is necessary to take expeditious measures to put an end to the deprivation of legal capacity of people with disabilities. Further, it would be vital to adopt mechanisms to eradicate stereotypes based on gender and disability from the justice system, while requesting to guarantee that all procedures and trials are carried out with a gender and disability perspective.

Finally, there is still a significant protection gap, since, at the federal level as well as in some states and municipalities, laws that prohibit intersectional forms of discrimination against persons with disabilities and that recognise the denial of reasonable accommodation as a form of discrimination in all areas have yet to be adopted.

[86] This text of more than 300 pages is divided into four main sections: a chapter on disability from a human rights approach; another on the essential concepts for judging from a disability perspective; another on equality and non-discrimination and access to justice for persons with disabilities; and finally, a guide for judging from a disability perspective. In this regard, it discusses concepts such as self-recognition; reasonable accommodation; affirmative measures; formal, material and inclusive equality; discrimination; access to justice; legal capacity; duty of enhanced protection; intersectionality; cross-cutting obligations; among many others. See SCJN, 'Protocolo para Juzgar con Perspectiva de Discapacidad' (April 2022) www.scjn.gob.mx.

15

Governing the Rights of Persons with Disabilities in Federal Systems

Trends and Patterns

DELIA FERRI, FRANCESCO PALERMO AND GIUSEPPE MARTINICO

I. INTRODUCTION

THE UNITED NATIONS (UN) Convention on the Rights of Persons with Disabilities (CRPD) is the 'first human rights convention introduced in the new millennium'.[1] As noted in the Introduction to this volume, while the CRPD does not create new rights, it reformulates civil, political, economic, social and cultural rights in light of disability. It revolves around the principles of respect for the dignity, autonomy and independence, non-discrimination, accessibility and participation of persons with disabilities in all spheres of life. These principles, laid out in Article 3 CRPD and mainstreamed across the whole text of the Convention, apply in a cross-cutting way and craft a framework for implementation.

The CRPD encompasses a significant paradigm shift from a medicalised view to a social-contextual understanding of disability.[2] Furthermore, as discussed at the outset of the collective volume, the CRPD is said to embed the human rights model of disability.[3] In its General Comment No 6 on equality and non-discrimination, the UN Committee on the Rights of Persons with Disabilities

[1] C Conte, 'What about refugees with disabilities? The interplay between EU asylum law and the UN Convention on the Rights of the Rights of Persons with Disabilities' (2016) 18 *European Journal of Migration and Law* 331.

[2] As noted in the Introduction to this volume, while this terminology is not consistently used, Broderick suggests that the social contextual model entails a more refined elaboration of the 'pure' social model of disability (A Broderick, *The Long and Winding Road to Equality and Inclusion for Persons with Disabilities* (Intersentia, 2015) 77).

[3] T Degener, 'A New Human Rights Model of Disability' in V Della Fina, R Cera and G Palmisano (eds), *The United Nations Convention on the Rights of Persons with Disabilities: A Commentary* (Springer, 2017) 41.

(CRPD Committee) clarified that such a human rights model of disability is underpinned by the recognition of disability as a social construct and values impairments as aspects of human diversity[4] and one of 'many multidimensional layers of identity'.[5] It also acknowledges that human rights are interdependent, interrelated and indivisible. In that connection, the human rights model of disability is key to redressing the history of stigma, discrimination and segregation that people with disabilities have faced worldwide.

As highlighted by Series, the CRPD 'enshrines key tenets of contemporary disability scholarship and activism'.[6] Furthermore, Logan, former Chief Commissioner of the Irish Human Rights and Equality Commission, argues that the CRPD 'adopts a modern, forward looking model of disability, recognising persons with disabilities as primary stakeholders, active participants and equal partners in State action around disability'.[7] In that regard, the CRPD has been considered 'the most complex human rights treaty ever drafted'[8] because of the wide-ranging obligations that it includes and because it obliges States Parties to enact new legislation and policies that reflect the transformative potential of the CRPD and arise from participatory processes. In requiring domestic implementation and monitoring bodies, by virtue of its Article 33, the CRPD also obliges States Parties to set up new and effective governance structures. The complexity of the CRPD is also reflected in the fact that it is the first UN human rights treaty to be open for signature by regional integration organisations, and the first to be ratified by the European Union (EU).

Both scholarship and the CRPD Committee have so far documented an uneven progress in advancing disability rights. However, so far little has been said about the extent to which such uneven advancement is linked to domestic constitutional postures and federal structures. The preceding chapters of this volume, grouped following a geographic and a comparative logic and encompassing a range of European and non-European countries, have attempted to gauge the impact of the CRPD in selected federal systems. After a stand-alone chapter on the EU as a *sui generis* federal system, chapters followed an order of presentation based on historical duration of the federal experience, coupled with consideration of the historical evolution of the federal systems from traditional, and of more symmetric versus asymmetric status of sub-national entities.

[4] Committee on the Rights of Persons with Disabilities (CRPD Committee), 'General Comment No 6 on equality and non-discrimination' (2018) CRPD/C/GC/6.

[5] CRPD Committee, 'General Comment No 8 on the right of persons with disabilities to work and employment' (2022) CRPD/C/GC/8.

[6] L Series, 'Disability and Human Rights' in N Watson and S Vehmas (eds), *Routledge Handbook of Disability Studies* (Routledge, 2020) 72–88.

[7] E Logan, 'Establishing a Monitoring Framework in Ireland for the United Nations Convention on the Rights of Persons with Disabilities' (NUI Galway and Irish Human Rights and Equality Commission, 2016) Foreword.

[8] Conte (n 1).

The latter, ie non-European federal countries, were ordered along a scale based on the different legal and cultural traditions.[9]

On the basis of these cases studies, this final chapter aims to look at the impact of the CRPD on federal governance as a whole. By comparing the way in which the CRPD has been transposed into domestic law and implemented, it is possible to identify existing common centripetal tendencies and/or centrifugal approaches. In doing so, this volume situates the emerging field of disability law within the more established comparative federalism scholarship. It does so by following a path that mirrors the one followed by the authors of the preceding chapters. After a preliminary reflection on the status of the CRPD in the selected countries, it discusses the impact of the CRPD on the division of competences in a general fashion, and it then zooms in on the distinct areas that that have been looked at – ie, the concept of disability; non-discrimination and equality; accessibility; and participation. Furthermore, the chapter moves on to discuss the national implementation structures and the framework for national monitoring required by Article 33 CRPD. The closing section wraps up the discussion of trends and patterns in the states considered.

As discussed in the Introduction to this volume,[10] we left to chapters' authors the opportunity to qualify and self-define the federal system under consideration. Some authors hence highlighted the very centralistic stand of their countries (for example, India and South Africa). Further, we asked authors to refer to the national terminology of federalism, in order to enhance clarity and correctness. However, this comparative chapter deploys concepts such as *federal system* and *national* and *sub-national* (levels of) government as umbrella terms.[11] This choice allows to formulate the comparative analysis on the array of formal federations and other types of states (regional, devolved) and polities (EU) included in the volume.

II. A PREMISE: THE UNBEARABLE LIGHTNESS OF BEING … MONIST, DUALIST OR 'IN BETWEEN'?

Broadly speaking, the countries examined in the volume can be classified in three groups: monist, dualist or characterised by a special status granted to human rights treaties. However, in general, authors, while outlining at the outset the position of international law (and, specifically, the CRPD) within the hierarchy of sources of law, did not engage extensively with the interrelation between

[9] See D Ferri, F Palermo and G Martinico, 'Introduction: Conceptual and Methodological Approaches' in this volume.

[10] Ibid. See also F Palermo and K Kössler, *Comparative Federalism. Constitutional Arrangements and Case Law* (Hart Publishing, 2017) 7.

[11] Ibid.

national and international law, nor with the classification of the country as monist or dualist. In fact, in most cases, and regardless of the broadly accepted classification of a country as monist or dualist, the relationship between domestic legal orders and the CRPD presents itself as more nuanced and complex. This confirms what has already been highlighted by Waddington and Lawson in their study on the use of the CRPD in national courts, ie that States Parties to the CRPD 'display a great deal of variation in approach when it comes to incorporation of the CRPD at domestic level' and that 'great variation exists between the approaches of different so-called monist states, as it does between different so-called dualist states'.[12] Waddington in particular has observed that 'in reality state practice often exists along a continuum between the two extremes of pure monism and pure dualism'.[13]

Belgium is generally considered a monist system, where international law is seen as part of the domestic order without the necessity to incorporate its norms. Actually, Ghys *et al* highlight that the law ratifying the CRPD states that the Convention 'will have full effect' in the Belgian legal order. However, they also clarify that this does not mean the CRPD is directly applicable. In fact, according to the case law of the Belgian Court of Cassation, to be directly applicable, a provision of an international treaty must be sufficiently precise and complete,[14] and must impose on States Parties detailed and 'precisely expressed' obligations.[15] In this respect, Ghys *et al* recall the broad texture of the CRPD, and argue that it is unlikely to be declared directly applicable. This is particularly so, should the Belgian Court of Cassation follow the path of the Court of Justice of the European Union (CJEU) ruling in *Z v A Government Department*, where the Luxembourg judges held that 'the provisions of [the] Convention are not, as regards their content, provisions that are unconditional and sufficiently precise',[16] or the reasoning of the Italian Constitutional Court, which has defined the CRPD as 'programmatic'.[17] In fact, even German courts, that have recognised the potential for direct applicability of the Convention, have so

[12] L Waddington, 'The Domestication of the Convention on the Rights of Persons with Disabilities: Domestic Legal Status of the CRPD and Relevance for Court Judgments' in L Waddington and A Lawson (eds), *The UN Convention on the Rights of Persons with Disabilities in Practice: A Comparative Analysis of the Role of Courts* (Oxford, 2018).

[13] Ibid.

[14] See N Ghys, F Louckx and D Dumont, 'Belgium: The Quest for Equal Employment and Coherence in the Social Protection and Participation of Persons with Disabilities' in this volume, citing Court of Cassation (Cass) 10 mei 1985, *Arresten van het Hof van Cassatie (AC)* 1984–1985, 1230 and other decisions.

[15] Ibid Cass 21 april 1983, *Rechtskundig Weekblad (RW)* 1983–1984, 2315; Cass 11 mei 2001, *AC* 2001, 872.

[16] Case C-363/12 *Z v A Government Department* ECLI:EU:C:2014:159, para 90.

[17] Italian Constitutional Court Decision No 2/2016. For a comment on this decision see P Addis, 'La Convenzione ONU sui diritti delle persone con disabilità e la Corte costituzionale. Osservazioni a partire dalla sentenza 2/2016' (*Federalismi.it*, 17 June 2016).

far been rather cautious and found that only Article 5 CRPD is capable of being directly applicable.[18]

Several countries covered in this volume are usually classified as dualist, hence requiring an incorporation of the CRPD into the domestic legal order. Austria can be seen as a dualist country, where, as noted by Bußjäger, the CRPD must be implemented by law and is not directly applicable. Germany is usually understood as a dualist system. Welti recalls that the Federal Constitutional Court (*Bundesverfassungsgericht* – BVerfG) case law follows a dualistic approach to international law. However, he highlights that German courts and public authorities are obliged to take international treaties into account for interpretation and application of federal and *Länder* law. In a similar fashion, other authors suggest that actually 'the relationship between domestic fundamental values and international as well as supranational law in the German legal order is quite complex' and that, given that the Basic Law (*Grundgesetz* – GG) 'is mute on the rank and status of international treaties within the German legal order, the BVerfG 'had a lot of leeway in the development of its doctrine on the relationship between international and domestic law'.[19] Italy is usually seen as a country characterised by a strong dualist tradition, according to which the international and national legal systems are conceived of as autonomous. However, norms derived from international treaties may not be abrogated by referendum.[20] Further, Article 117 of the Italian Constitution provides that 'legislative power belongs to the State and the regions in accordance with the constitution and *within the limits* set by European Union law *and international obligations*' (emphasis added). The United Kingdom responds to a dualist approach, given that, as recalled by McCall-Smith, it 'requires incorporation of international law before it becomes binding on state actors at any level',[21] and so does Canada,[22] in which international treaties do not automatically enjoy prevalence over national law. In India, the dualist strategy is also codified in Article 253 of the Constitution, according to which the 'Parliament has power to make any law for the whole or any part of the territory of India for implementing any treaty, agreement or convention with any other country or countries or any decision made at any international conference, association or other body'.

[18] Waddington (n 12).

[19] N Petersen, 'Germany' in FM Palombino (ed), *Duelling for Supremacy. International Law vs. National Fundamental Principles* (Cambridge University Press, 2019) 89.

[20] Despite that, the Italian Constitution recognises a particular force to the laws related to international obligations. Art 75, para 2 (devoted to the referendum) states: 'No referendum may be held on a law regulating taxes, the budget, amnesty or pardon, or a law ratifying an international treaty'.

[21] However, the British legal order also presents a monist approach with regard to general international law which is seen as a part of the national law.

[22] 'Simply put, the matrix within which state affairs take place and according to which international law is understood postulates the existence of a normative "divide", a sort of dualist reasoning box. Thus the international legal plane is deemed distinct and separate from the national legal realms'. S Beaulac, 'Canada' in FM Palombino (n 19) 21.

However, when it comes to human rights law, the Supreme Court of India has allowed for unmediated implementation.[23]

The third group of 'in between' countries is the biggest and the most heterogeneous one. It comprises those systems that are characterised by a high level of constitutional openness to international human rights law or that, while being nominally dualist, do allow for direct incorporation of certain international obligations into the domestic law. Argentina has evolved from a dualist position to a context in which international human rights treaties enjoy constitutional supremacy, according to the current wording of the Argentine Constitution. Pure dualism was partly overcome in 1992 by several rulings of the Argentine Supreme Court of Justice of the Nation (*Corte Suprema de Justicia de la Nación* – CSJN),[24] and later with the constitutional reform of 1994, by which Article 75(22) was amended, giving constitutional status to human rights treaties. Brazil is a dualist system, and therefore international treaties have to be incorporated through national domestic measures. However, the situation partly changed in 2004, when Article 5(3) was revised by means of Constitutional Amendment No 45. This provision reads: '[i]nternational treaties and conventions on human rights approved by both houses of the National Congress, in two different voting sessions, by three-fifths votes of their respective members, shall be equivalent to Constitutional Amendments'.[25] South Africa, while being formally a dualist country, is well-known for its openness to the international system, since '[i]nternational law is, in many instances, directly enforceable in South African domestic law without the need for transformation by the legislature'.[26] In addition, all legislation must be interpreted compatibly with South Africa's international obligations if it is possible to do so.[27] Chigwata and Nanima suggest that such an approach to international law 'adds credibility to the application of international and regional law as sources of definitions of persons with disabilities'.[28] In Spain, international treaties need the intervention of a national legislative measure to enter into force, but they have a super-primary ranking. In this respect, scholars have argued that Spain is characterised by a moderate monism. Article 10(2) of the Constitution acknowledges a sort of interpretative priority to human rights treaties by stating that '[t]he principles relating to the fundamental rights and liberties recognised by the Constitution shall be interpreted in conformity with the Universal Declaration of Human

[23] A Dhanda, 'India: Disability Rights in a "Quasi" Federal Country' in this volume.

[24] For instance *Ekmekdjian v Sofovich* (1992) Supreme Court of Justice of the Nation (Corte Suprema de Justicia de la Nación – CSJN) Fallos: 315-1492 and consolidated in the decision 'Cafes La Virginia S.A' (1994) CSJN Fallos: 320:1166.

[25] See P Wojcikiewicz Almeida, 'Brazil' in FM Palombino (n 19) 10.

[26] H Woolaver, 'South Africa' in FM Palombino (n 19) 320.

[27] Ibid.

[28] TC Chigwata and RD Nanima, 'South Africa: Centralised Federalism and the Implementation of the CRPD' in this volume.

Rights and the international treaties and agreements thereon ratified by Spain'. Although this does not give human rights treaties a constitutional force *per se*, Article 10(2) is frequently mentioned as a signal of the constitutional openness which features in many post-WWII constitutions in Europe.[29] Mexico is normally seen as a dualist system (although some authors have questioned this classification),[30] but confers constitutional status to human rights treaties like the CRPD, as Spigno recalls in the introductory remarks of her chapter. The Ethiopian case is also rather intriguing. Sometimes Ethiopia is treated as a monist system,[31] because ratified international treaties form an integral part of the law of the land.[32] However, Fessha and Dessalegn posit that it 'is not clear and continues to be a subject of fierce academic debate whether Ethiopia follows the monist, dualist or intermediate approach in incorporating international treaties in the domestic legal system'.[33] In a somewhat similar fashion, other scholars argue that:

> Although the Ethiopian constitution favors for both dualistic and monistic methods of implementation of human right treaties, there are neither transformation into domestic laws including amendments and repeals as dualistic approach so demands nor any single translation and publication of the actual treaty provisions as the monistic approach so requires. This in result produced lack of human right treaty texts into one of the main vernaculars of the local languages, lack of access to international human right treaties and decisions, and led drafters and other officials in drafting process to focus only on constitution and other domestic laws.[34]

Finally, given its *sui generis* nature, the EU also departs from the usual schemes. According to the *Haegeman* doctrine, the agreements concluded by EU institutions benefit from a kind of 'automatic treaty incorporation'[35] into EU

[29] A Saiz Arnaiz, *La apertura constitucional al derecho internacional y europeo de los derechos humanos. El artículo 10.2 de la Constitución Española* (CEPC, 1999); P Carrozza, 'Constitutionalism's Post-modern Opening' in M Loughlin and N Walker (eds), *The Paradox of Constitutionalism: Constituent Power and Constitutional Form* (Oxford University Press, 2007) 169, 182.

[30] A Cisneros Aguilar, 'The Position of International Treaties in PRC and Mexican Law: Using the Chinese "Dialectical Model" to Implement and Enforce a Hypothetical Mexico-China FTA, as Related to Foreign Investment' (2018) *Arellano Law Review* 29, 36.

[31] Gemeda argues that '[t]hough Ethiopia is a monist State in which an international treaty becomes part of the law of the land by the fact that it is ratified by a domestic act, the status of application of treaties remains subject to controversy. It is, in fact, proved to be a myth that monism promote the applicability of international instruments in to domestic legal system. Courts in many traditionally dualist African countries use international law to a larger degree than explicitly monist countries like Ethiopia'. AG Gemeda, 'Domestic Implications of Concluding Observations of the Committee on the Rights of the Child: the Case of Ethiopia' (2016) *Haramaya Law Review* 33, 51.

[32] Art 9(4) of the Constitution of the Federal Democratic Republic of Ethiopia.

[33] TS Bulto, 'The Monist-Dualist Divide and the Supremacy Clause: Revisiting the Status of Human Rights Treaties in Ethiopia' (2009) 23 *Journal of Ethiopian Law* 132.

[34] L Worku, 'Legislative proposals and application of human right treaties in Ethiopia' (*Legislative Drafting Blog*, 9 June 2015) www.abyssinialaw.com.

[35] M Mendez, 'The Legal Effect of Community Agreements: Maximalist Treaty Enforcement and Judicial Avoidance Techniques' (2010) *European Journal of International Law* 83.

law, since the provisions of these agreements 'form an integral part of [EU] law'.[36] Further, international agreements are situated below the provisions of the Treaties, but above secondary EU law (regulations, directives and decisions). However, this does not mean that international agreements automatically have direct effect. Only those international provisions that are sufficiently precise and unconditional can be directly invoked. In fact, over the years, the CJEU transformed itself into the 'gatekeeper'[37] of the effects of the international agreements concluded by the EU, giving the Court the possibility of opening or closing the doors of their direct effects in EU law.

The wide suite of approaches to international law and the status of the CRPD in the selected jurisdictions, however, seem to have proved rather immaterial to the impact of the CRPD on domestic constitutional structures. None of the authors of the chapters included in this volume have reported any impact or changes on the formal articulation of competences as a consequence of the ratification of the CRPD, regardless of the level of openness of the country to international law. They all describe the system of distribution of competences between the federal level and the sub-national entities and underline that the constitutional relationship between the 'centre' and the 'periphery' has not been formally affected by the ratification of the CRPD, not even in those jurisdictions in which the Convention has been 'constitutionalised', such as in Brazil or Argentina.

The analysis carried out in these chapters, however, does confirm that, in almost all the selected jurisdictions, the CRPD has displayed a certain impact over the 'material' constitution when it comes to the division of competences, regardless the actual status of the CRPD in the hierarchy of sources of law, its direct or indirect incorporation into domestic law, and without any connection with regard to the monist, dualist or 'in between' characterisation of the country. As will be discussed in the subsequent sections, the CRPD, has determined a push – albeit uneven across the material fields considered – towards 'centralisation' of disability issues or, at least, towards a certain 'harmonisation'. Due to many reasons, in some of the countries considered, this phenomenon is engendered by the role of the judiciary, which has *de facto* adapted the formal distribution of powers to the impact of the Convention by relying on interpretative doctrines. Exceptions to these centralising patterns seem to be represented by Belgium and the United Kingdom – respectively a monist country and a dualist one. Another exception is Argentina, where, as mentioned above and as recalled by Bariffi, the CRPD 'is an integral part of the Constitution' and therefore federal or provincial laws may be subjected to control of constitutionality (judicial review) vis-à-vis the CRPD by all lower courts. Those exceptions,

[36] Case C-181/73, *Haegeman* ECLI:EU:C:1974:41.

[37] F Snyder, 'The Gatekeepers: the European Courts and WTO Law' (2003) 40 *Common Market Law Review* 313–67.

again, confirm the irrelevance of the domestic approach to international law when it comes to the constitutional impact of the CRPD.[38]

III. THE IMPACT OF THE CRPD ON THE DIVISION OF COMPETENCES

Often, the constitutions of the countries considered either proclaim the rights of persons with disabilities (eg Belgium) or include an obligation for the state to protect persons with disabilities (eg Italy). Sometimes they comprise disability as an explicit ground of prohibited discrimination. However, usually they do not enunciate 'disability' as such as constituting a distinct material field of competence. With the exception of the Indian Constitution, which allocates to the states the power of making laws and policies for 'the relief of the disabled and the unemployable', the absence of disability as a distinct stand-alone material field listed in competences catalogues has been highlighted by many authors, such as Bußjäger or Spigno. The latter scholar, in particular, emphasises that the 'Mexican Constitution does not refer to disability as a matter attributed to the Federation or to the states'.[39]

Across the jurisdictions considered, disability issues typically fall within and cut across different areas of competence. With regard to Brazil, for instance, Rodrigues and Breit argue that in the Brazilian Constitution disability is addressed 'in a fragmented way, in different parts that cover different aspects, especially with regard to ensuring the application of the equality principle to persons with disabilities'.[40] In a similar vein, Spigno highlights that '[b]eing an issue with many facets that range from human rights to health, infrastructures, public policies and development',[41] disability falls within the concurrent powers between local governments and the Federation. The fact that disability pertains to a range of enumerated areas of competences emerged strikingly also in countries such as Germany, Austria, or Canada. For instance, Bußjäger suggests that '[m]atters regarding the rights of persons with disabilities (in particular social aid, health care and education) are cross-cutting matters, which means that both the Federal Government and the *Länder* are, in principle, responsible for enacting legislation on those issues' and indicates that each provision of the CRPD should be carefully analysed to actually detect the extent to which either the

[38] This finding mirrors what Lawson and Waddington found in their comparative study of the use of the CRPD in domestic courts, whereby they 'identified a variety of different elements influencing the legal status of the CRPD, and different ways in which courts regarded the CRPD as relevant' but suggested that 'there is no indication in general that the distinction between monist and dualist systems was a particularly significant factor in this respect'. Waddington (n 12).

[39] I Spigno, 'Mexico: Disability Rights in Mexican Federalism' in this volume.

[40] GMA Rodrigues and P Breit, 'Brazil: The Long Road to Citizenship for Persons with Disabilities' in this volume.

[41] Spigno (n 39).

Federal Government or the *Länder* have the power to implement it.[42] A paramount example is the EU, where disability issues have been mainstreamed and addressed to a large extent within the shared competence on the 'internal market'.[43] In this respect, the volume somewhat confirms Cameron and Fraser's finding that disability, at least in the five federations they considered (Australia, Belgium, Canada, Germany and the United States), 'does not present itself as a relatively coherent policy field', and that 'the policy field in all of them is fragmented and uncoordinated'.[44] In terms more common to lawyers, this is to say that disability is a policy but not a competence field (or a jurisdiction), which means that dealing with it requires a strategic approach that is implemented by different actors as it crosses the constitutional division of powers among levels of government. The fragmentation of disability within multiple fields of competence coupled with the breadth of the CRPD make disability rights sit at the intersection of national and sub-national powers and therefore challenge constitutional contexts. In fact, as mentioned above, almost all the authors recorded an (uneven) impact over the 'material' constitutional division of competences.

A. The CRPD as Engine for Centralisation or Harmonisation

Overall, the CRPD has determined a push – albeit unevenly across the material fields considered – towards 'centralisation'. This is particularly evident in Spain, where González Pascual conceives of the CRPD as 'a trigger for the action of the State, a clear driver of centralisation', but also in Italy. The Spanish case is very telling of the competence creep operated via fundamental rights, since 'the outcome is the growing irrelevance of the regional powers in fields such as social welfare because regional statutes or regulations must follow the particularly exhaustive legislation of the State on constitutional rights'.[45] With regard to Italy, centralising trends prompted by the CRPD *per se* tally with general centralising trends attributable to the Italian National Recovery and Resilience Plan (*Piano Nazionale di Ripresa e Resilienza* – PNRR), enacted following the Covid-19 pandemic. The PNRR, as noted by Addis and Monti, actually seems to have amplified the centralising effect of the CRPD, given that it refers to the Convention multiple times as a global standard of protection for

[42] P Bußjäger, 'Austria: The Implementation of the CRPD in the Austrian Federal System' in this volume.

[43] D Ferri and A Broderick (eds), *Research Handbook on EU Disability Law* (Edward Elgar Publishing, 2020).

[44] D Cameron and V Fraser (eds), *Disability and Federalism: Comparing Different Approaches to Full Participation* (Institute of Intergovernmental Relations, 2001).

[45] M González Pascual, 'Spain: The Alignment with the CRPD through Centralisation' in this volume.

disability rights. This 'centralisation' is also blatant when it comes to the *sui generis* federal arrangement that characterises the EU, where 'the implementation of the CRPD has rather deeply affected the balance "between unity and diversity", provoking a centralising effect'.[46] More subtle, but still detectable in some areas (such as the concept of disability), is the centralising effect that the CRPD displayed in Brazil and Argentina.

Even where such centralisation of disability issues is not ostensible, the CRPD has been an engine of harmonisation across different levels of government, which entail the enactment of legislation aligning with, domesticating or implementing the CRPD at the national level followed by similar legislative processes at the sub-national level, or leaving to the sub-national entities only the power to implement national legislation within the boundaries of national legislation. This harmonisation, which reconciles tensions, bringing more uniformity and ironing out differences, is manifest in Mexico. Spigno contends that, in this jurisdiction, 'federated entities tend to do nothing more than replicate what is done at the federal level, with only a few exceptions', somewhat mirroring already existing centralising dynamics of Mexican federalism.[47] In India, the enactment of national legislation like the Rights of Persons with Disabilities Act (RPDA) has 'creat[ed] the same norms for the entire country', and Dhanda suggests that since 'the States are duty bound to implement the law made by the centre, possibilities of customization of the law only arise in the manner in which the law is implemented'.[48]

In several cases, authors treaded carefully and did not explicitly refer to centripetal dynamics, but did highlight, to varying degrees, that the CRPD prompted a more prominent role of the federal level compared to its sub-national entities. Welti suggests that 'the implementation of the CRPD has left marks in the German federal system', as some matters 'acquired a place on the federal agenda for the first time, because they were included in an international treaty and, accordingly, the Federal Government must be able to make statements at the international level, even if it cannot act in the respective field'.[49] A prominent role of the federal state in implementing the CRPD is very evident, for example, in India and in Ethiopia. In the latter country, the CRPD has been implemented mostly (almost exclusively) at the federal level. In this regard, Fessha and Dessalegn argue that a lot remains to be done 'by state governments, and they should use their law- and policy-making powers to protect and promote the rights of persons with disabilities'.[50] In a somewhat similar fashion, in South Africa,

[46] D Ferri and N Šubic, 'The European Union: Federal Trends in Disability Rights' in this volume.

[47] Spigno (n 39).

[48] Dhanda (n 23).

[49] F Welti, 'Germany: Is Cooperative Federalism Generating Multi-Level Barriers or Facilitating Multi-Level Inclusion?' in this volume.

[50] YT Fessha and B Dessalegn, 'Ethiopia: The Missing Relationship between Federalism and Disability' in this volume.

there have not yet been any 'significant independent initiatives from provinces and municipalities aimed at implementing the CRPD even though they have the room to do so'.[51] In that connection Chigwata and Nanima suggest that the CRPD has brought to the fore 'the centralised nature of South Africa's federal system' and that provincial and local governments remain largely 'implementers of national laws and policies even though there is scope for them to do more independent initiatives'.[52] Similarly, in India, all laws for persons with disabilities 'have been made by Parliament but the implementation responsibility of these laws largely resides with the states'.[53] In Austria, the Federation has played a key role in the development of disability policies, albeit at the expense of a dialogue with the *Länder*. In that connection, Bußjäger notes that 'the pressure for harmonisation' is expected to increase in Austria.[54]

B. Asymmetry and the Little Appeal of the Laboratory Theory

In Canada, where broad centralising trends are not detectable, the Federal Government has limited power to affect decision-making in disability-related areas falling under provincial and territorial jurisdiction. In this regard, Beaudry makes a case for more robust federal interventions, and recalls the quest for such 'stronger federal oversight' by the disability community. However, he does suggest that the CRPD has had a certain impact producing a '*de facto* harmonisation, albeit enduring divergences across levels of government and between regions remain'.[55]

An exception to the patterns identified – where authors claimed the lack of even subtle harmonisation – seems also to be represented by the United Kingdom and Belgium. In line with Beaudry's claims with regard to Canada, McCall-Smith and Ghys *et al* advocate somewhat for a more decisive harmonisation as essential to guarantee a full realisation of the human rights model of disability. Argentina is another exception, as there are no visible centripetal dynamics, albeit some harmonisation is in fact present when it comes to the definition of disability. In that regard, and in consonance with other authors, Bariffi notes however that 'federal decentralisation has become a major barrier to implement the CRPD at domestic level'.[56]

[51] Chigwata and Nanima (n 28).
[52] Ibid.
[53] Dhanda (n 23).
[54] Bußjäger (n 42).
[55] J-S Beaudry, 'Canada: A Federal Perspective on the Implementation of the CRPD' in this volume.
[56] FJ Bariffi, 'Argentina: Ensuring Disability Rights in the Context of an Anachronistic Federal System' in this volume.

More generally, however, the question arises as to the asymmetric potential of rules pertaining to the protection of fundamental rights, notably the rights of persons with disabilities. Fundamental rights protection has traditionally been a strong centralising factor in federal systems, beginning essentially in the second half of the nineteenth century with the social reforms put forward by Bismarck and with the incorporation of the Bill of Rights in the United States of America. In the 1930s the doctrine of the so-called 'laboratory federalism' was elaborated, initially by US Supreme Court Justice Luis Brandeis, and since then cultivated as a factor of potential differentiation.[57] The rationale behind it is that solutions found at sub-national level can be exported to other sub-national entities and ultimately to the national dimension if they prove valid, while the harming potential of wrong policies is limited, as they remain confined in the sub-national sphere. While this is valid for policies, the laboratory theory has had much less appeal, overall, in the field of fundamental rights. In general, the differential treatment of fundamental rights is associated with different levels of protection and is thus at odds with constitutional clauses granting the same standards in the whole national territory (see inter alia Article 72(2) GG). While providing additional protection in certain areas should not per se be considered a violation of equal protection and non-discrimination, the issue remains very slippery and open to potential abuses. The recent overruling of *Roe v Wade* and the abolition of the federal guarantee of the right to abortion in the US was carried out in the name of the protection of the rights of states,[58] and 'leaving' rights in the hands of sub-national units has indeed the potential to produce abuses. For these reasons, the asymmetric potential of federalism, which is paradoxically extremely developed in certain areas including notably the fundamental rights of certain minority groups like national minorities,[59] is much more limited when it comes to traditional fundamental rights and as a matter of fact has not been deployed in the analysed cases subsequent to the ratification of the CRPD.

IV. THE CONCEPT OF DISABILITY: A JOURNEY TO THE CENTRE ... ?

In its 2021 report, the Special Rapporteur on the rights of persons with disabilities highlighted that the CRPD 'embodies the culture shift to the human rights framing of disability and consigns the old paradigm of charity and welfare to

[57] See WE Oates, 'An Essay on Fiscal Federalism' (1999) 37 *Journal of Economic Literature* 1120; GA Tarr, 'Laboratories of Democracy? Brandeis, Federalism and Scientific Management' (2001) 31 *Publius* 37–46; J Sutton, *Who Decides? States as Laboratories of Constitutional Experimentation* (Oxford, 2021).

[58] *Roe v Wade*, 410 US 113 (1973), overturned by *Dobbs v Jackson Women's Health Organization*, No 19-1392, 597 US (2022).

[59] See inter alia TH Malloy and F Palermo, *Minority Accommodation through Territorial and Non-Territorial Autonomy* (Oxford University Press, 2015).

history'.[60] In fact, as several authors in the volume posit,[61] in order to fully implement the rights provided for in the CRPD, States Parties have to adopt the human rights model of disability which embeds the idea that disability is a social construct, and derives from the interaction with external barriers posed to an individual with impairments. Remarkable is the fact that the CRPD Committee makes a social-contextual approach to disability, conveyed in Article 1(2) CRPD, functional to the recognition that persons with disabilities are subjects of rights and rights holders.[62]

As noted by the Special Rapporteur on the Rights of Persons with Disabilities, the Covid-19 pandemic has 'painfully shown that the old paradigm that existed prior to the adoption of the Convention, by which persons with disabilities are treated as if they are invisible or in ways that reinforce unequal power dynamics, is still alive'.[63] In a similar vein, most recently, in its General Comment No 8 on the right of persons with disabilities to work and employment, released on 9 September 2022, the CRPD Committee has recalled its concerns on legal frameworks that 'still reflect an ableist approach to disability through charity and/or medical models, despite the incompatibility of those models with the Convention'.[64] However, most of the countries considered in this volume have indeed moved towards the adoption of a definition of disability akin to the conceptualisation laid out in Article 1(2) CRPD. Further, the notion of disability is probably the area where centralisation or harmonisation dynamics are most visible and generally widespread. In this respect, in spite of few exceptions, the impact of the CRPD on the distribution of competences is patent and the national government has become the centre of gravity when it comes to embedding the social-contextual concept of disability.

A. Centralisation Dynamics

Centralising trends are most evident in the EU, Italy and Argentina. Case law of the CJEU has consistently highlighted the need for an EU autonomous concept of disability in EU non-discrimination law which fully aligns with the CRPD. More notably, the CRPD has determined a spill-over effect in several other areas of EU law, from state aid to the broader remit of internal market legislation, determining a progressive erosion of Member States' power to adopt

[60] Special Rapporteur on the Rights of Persons with Disabilities, 'A/HRC/46/27: Rights of Persons with Disabilities – Report of the Special Rapporteur on the Rights of Persons with Disabilities' (19 January 2021) www.ohchr.org.

[61] See K McCall-Smith, 'The United Kingdom: Asymmetrical Challenges to Implementing the CRPD' in this volume.

[62] CRPD Committee (n 4) para 8.

[63] Special Rapporteur on the Rights of Persons with Disabilities (n 60).

[64] CRPD Committee (n 5).

diverse conceptualisations of disability. What Ferri and Šubic define as the 'Europeanisation of the concept of disability' is a growing centripetal dynamic which pushes towards more 'unity'. In Italy, Law No 227/2021 empowers the Government to adopt a definition of 'disability' consistent with Article 1(2) CRPD. In that connection, Addis and Monti highlight that this will entail a new 'uniform standard valid throughout the national territory'.[65] Argentine law, at present, incorporates what Bariffi defines as 'a medically inspired definition of persons with disabilities', which was adopted in 2001 at the national level with the intent of supporting a more uniform approach to disability across sub-national entities. That definition was already, as Bariffi suggests, 'a major step towards a federalisation' of disability issues. The ratification of the CRPD and the need to move away from the medicalised approach to disability have bolstered this trend. In February 2022, the Federal Government announced a law reform process to adopt a new comprehensive Disability Act which should adopt a social-contextual and intersectional perspective to disability. This 'law reform process also reveals a clear impulse towards centralisation of disability rights'.[66]

In India, Ethiopia and South Africa, while it is not possible to identify any centralisation dynamics prompted directly from the CRPD, some sort of 'centralisation' of disability definitions is perceivable, since those definitions exist in national laws and are applied across sub-national levels. In Ethiopia and South Africa, different and still rather medicalised conceptualisations of disability are included in national laws. In India the RPDA has opted for a more expansive definition of disability than its predecessor (ie, the Persons with Disabilities (Equal Opportunity, Protection of Rights and Full Participation) Act – PWDA), that seems to partially align with Article 1(2) CRPD. Section 2(s) of the RPDA defines a person with disability as 'a person with long term physical, mental, intellectual or sensory impairment which, in interaction with barriers, hinders his full and effective participation in society equally with others'.[67] However, the RPDA includes a schedule that specifies five broad categories of disabilities which mention as many as 21 impairments, and section 99 RPDA allows the central government to add to this list. Interestingly, the remaining medical undertone of the RPDA, while blamed by the CRPD Committee, has not been questioned by Disabled Persons Organisations (DPOs) which, as Dandha recalls, rejected the use of a generic human rights definition of disability and 'feel more secure in their entitlements if their condition is expressly named in the statute'.[68]

[65] P Addis and M Monti, 'Italy: Is the CRPD Engendering a Centripetal Dynamic in the Italian Regional State?' in this volume.

[66] Bariffi (n 56).

[67] Rights of Persons with Disabilities Act (RPDA), s 2(s).

[68] Dhanda (n 23).

B. Harmonising Trends

Harmonising trends can be identified in Spain, as well as (to a lesser extent) in Brazil and in Mexico. In Spain, national legislation adopted a CRPD-inspired human-rights approach which trickled down to regional legislation and permeated it. In Brazil, the definition of disability rests within national competences. The term 'persons with disabilities' was drawn from the CRPD and the conceptualisation of Article 1(2) CRPD was incorporated into Federal Law No 13.146/2015. All sub-national entities – namely states, municipalities, and the Federal District – 'are obliged to follow and adapt their legislation to the new concept'.[69] In this respect, even though Rodrigues and Breit speak about a form of centralisation, what they describe is a process of top-down harmonisation across different levels. In Mexico, the General Law for the Inclusion of People with Disabilities (*Ley General para la Inclusión de las Personas con Discapacidad* – LGIPD), which entered into force in 2011, aims to embed a social-contextual understanding of disability into national legislation, aligning with the CRPD. Despite this innovation, different (and medicalised) definitions still persist at both national and sub-national levels. In spite of a remaining patchiness, the LGIPD seems to enhance existing centralising Mexican federal dynamics.

In some instances harmonising trends, while detectable, are incomplete or at the very beginning. This is the case of Germany, Austria and also Argentina. In Germany, in 2016, paragraph 3 of the Disability Equality Act (*Behindertengleichstellungsgesetz* – BGG) was reformulated to better align with the CRPD. In the same year, the Federal Participation Act (*Bundesteilhabegesetz* – BTHG) reformed the Social Code Book Nine – Rehabilitation and Participation of Disabled Persons (*Sozialgesetzbuch* – SGB IX) and included in paragraph 2 SGB IX a nearly identical formulation.[27] Since 2016, in a sort of spill-over effect, Disabled Equality Acts of the *Länder* have started to be reformed. Welti highlights how, as of the time of writing this volume, 'Five of the 16 Acts have aligned with the conceptualisation of disability included in the CRPD and refer to "full and effective participation" of persons with disabilities'.[70] In Austria, harmonisation is still at the beginning and significant fragmentation is evident, as well as the persistence of medical approaches to disability in *Länder* legislation. However, the recent Austrian National Action Plan on Disability 2022–2030 (NAP Disability 2022–2030), will support a more uniform approach and a harmonising process. When it comes to Canada, Beaudry suggests that 'a great number of similarities' among disability legislations adopted by sub-national entities exists because those entities do not proceed in isolation and benefit 'from the insights that other legislatures developed when structuring disability-related norms'.[71]

[69] Rodrigues and Breit (n 40).
[70] Welti (n 49).
[71] Beaudry (n 55).

C. Asymmetries and Remaining Medicalised Approaches

No harmonisation is visible in Belgium, where the trend can be described as one of decentralisation. In fact, the ratification of the CRPD has not (yet) shifted the outdated, medical understanding of disability which is still prevalent in the federal legislation. A timid move towards a more social and CRPD-inspired definition is, however, detectable in Flanders and in the region of Wallonia. Similarly, in the United Kingdom, there is 'no harmony across the national and devolved governments' when it comes to their approaches to disability. McCall-Smith, in line with other scholars,[72] views section 6 of the Equality Act 2010 (EqA) as still rather reliant on the medical model. She suggests, however, that whilst devolved governments are bound by the EqA or the Disability Discrimination Act 1995 (DDA) and their medicalised approaches when it comes to enforcement, policies produced in Wales and Scotland have shifted to 'advance a social model of disability'.[73] In an asymmetric way, Northern Ireland has, instead, according to Mc-Call Smith 'narrowed its approach over that of even the central government'.[74] In these two countries, commitments to asymmetry and subsidiarity outweigh the pursuit of a more centralised approach.

V. NON-DISCRIMINATION AND EQUALITY: NOTHING NEW ON THE WESTERN FRONT?

Non-discrimination and equality are the cornerstone of the CRPD, and cut across all rights of the CRPD, which must be enjoyed by people with disabilities on an equal basis with others. While the CRPD embeds a rather capacious concept of equality – that of inclusive equality – thus far, the implementation of the Convention has been for the most part anchored to existing national equality legislation and underpinned by constitutional equality clauses which are included in all the national constitutions of the countries considered. As a consequence, several authors (for example Bariffi with regard to Argentina, or McCall-Smith with regard to the United Kingdom) find evidence that existing legislation falls short of the obligations of the CRPD. One of the most problematic aspects remains the implementation of the rights of persons with disabilities to be provided with reasonable accommodation in all spheres of life, as shown, for instance, in the chapter on South Africa.

[72] See among others A Lawson, 'Disability and Employment in the Equality Act 2010: Opportunities Seized, Lost and Generated' (2011) 40 *Industrial Law Journal* 359, 363. See also H Saunders, 'Difficult Distinctions in Anti-Discrimination Law: Disfigurement, Appearance and Disability' (2020) 20 *International Journal of Discrimination and the Law* 21–44.

[73] McCall-Smith (n 61).

[74] Ibid.

However, the need to implement the principle of inclusive equality (and more generally the CRPD) has led, in some cases, to far-reaching constitutional reforms at both the national and sub-national levels. In Belgium, a new provision on persons with disabilities was included in the Constitution in 2021. Inspired by the CRPD, Article 22*ter* grants persons with disabilities the right to full inclusion in society, including the right to reasonable accommodation. In the same year, the reform of the Constitution of Coahuila (Mexico) led to the incorporation of disability rights in chapter X of Title Five of the Civil Rights Charter (*Carta de Derechos Civiles*). In Spain, a constitutional reform of Article 49 is underway. If approved, this new provision should embed in the Spanish Constitution a proclamation that persons with disabilities are holders of fundamental rights 'in conditions of real and effective freedom and equality, without discrimination'.[75]

Aside from the constitutional reform processes that occurred in these countries, given the existence of well-established constitutional equality clauses and long-standing legislation, all authors in the volume highlight the limited impact of the CRPD on the federal layout when it comes to equality. This is so because the implementation of the CRPD has so far been embedded within existing legislation, with higher courts often taking the lead in enhancing disability rights through consistent interpretation or through application of the CRPD, already highlighted by Waddington and Lawson in their volume[76] and as emerges in Welti's and Spigno's chapters respectively on Germany and Mexico.

In several cases, authors highlight the leading role of the national level and the limited (or inexistent) contributions of sub-national entities in enhancing equality. This is the case of Spain and Italy, where non-discrimination and equality laws pertain to the national level and are generally highly centralised (also due to the strict reading introduced by the constitutional jurisdiction), but also that of Brazil, South Africa and Ethiopia. In the latter jurisdiction, while at the sub-national level, state constitutions provide protection against discrimination and rights of persons with disabilities in an identical way to that of the Federal Constitution, Fessha and Dessalegn highlight that there has been a reluctance of sub-national entities in legislating in this area. In South Africa, while the Constitution mandates all national and sub-national entities to implement laws and policies on non-discrimination and equality, Chigwata and Nanima argue that 'the national government has taken a leading role in establishing anti-discrimination laws and policies which are then implemented by provinces and municipalities'.[77]

Even where equality and non-discrimination legislation pertain to both national and sub-national levels, such as in Germany, Mexico, Argentina and

[75] L Cachón, 'Proposed Draft Reform of Article 49 of the Constitution, on the Rights of Persons with Disabilities' (14 December 2018) www.equalitylaw.eu.

[76] Waddington and Lawson (n 12) 478–79.

[77] Chigwata and Nanima (n 28).

Canada (albeit to a more limited degree), sub-national legislation generally mirrors (or sometimes expands) the provisions set forth at national level, making evident some kind of (voluntary) harmonisation. In Germany, in particular, according to Welti, 'a minority of *Länder* function as the avant-garde, then the federal legislation sets a standard and most of the *Länder* follow',[78] confirming that often sub-national entities are a test bed for normative innovation.

An initial nuanced centralising dynamic is evident in the EU. The Employment Equality Directive, adopted in 2000, remains the main piece of legislation that addresses discrimination, inter alia, on the ground of disability, and the CRPD has not been a sufficiently strong driver for the adoption of new far reaching non-discrimination legislation, which (if and when adopted) would significantly reduce the scope for autonomy of the Member States. However, the CRPD has supported an already existing interpretative trend extending the reach of the Employment Equality Directive, slowly but steadily eroding the room for manoeuvre of Member States. Within the context of the peculiar legal system of the EU (and of its not less peculiar federal system), this also represents a clear trend towards centralisation.

On the whole, with the exception of the United Kingdom and Belgium, the narrative emerging from all the chapters, to varying degree, seems to point to a centralised approach to equality for persons with disabilities. Where this is not the case, authors argue strongly for further harmonisation or uniformity in the alignment with the CRPD, to reduce territorial discrepancies which result in a compound inequality faced by people with disabilities in certain areas of the country.

VI. ACCESSIBILITY IN A MULTILEVEL LEGAL ENVIRONMENT

The CRPD lists 'accessibility' among the general principles, but mentions it in the general obligations and in other provisions devoted to specific rights. According to Article 9(1) CRPD, in order to:

> enable persons with disabilities to live independently and participate fully in all aspects of life, States Parties shall take appropriate measures to ensure to persons with disabilities access, on an equal basis with others, to the physical environment, to transportation, to information and communications, including information and communications technologies and systems, and to other facilities and services open or provided to the public, both in urban and in rural areas.

Moreover, this provision requires for accessibility measures to encompass 'the identification and elimination of obstacles and barriers' when it comes to the physical environment (eg buildings, roads, transportation and other indoor and

[78] Welti (n 49).

outdoor facilities, including schools, housing, medical facilities and workplaces) and information, communications and other services, including electronic services and emergency services.

The normative status of accessibility as right *per se* or a mere principle has been debated and is still rather controversial.[79] The CRPD Committee has thus far proffered inconclusive answers, referring to accessibility as a 'precondition for the effective and equal enjoyment of civil, political, economic, social and cultural rights by persons with disabilities'.[80] In general, the authors of the preceding chapters have not engaged with such normative status, but rather focused on key aspects of the implementation of Article 9 CRPD, highlighting that the breadth of accessibility obligations represent a challenge in federal states. Some authors also suggested that the controversial status of accessibility adds to such inherent complexity. For example, Bariffi notes that 'accessibility is likely the most troublesome dimension of disability rights in the face of the Argentine federal landscape' inter alia because 'accessibility is *not enshrined as a single right*, but rather as isolated obligations set forth in specific laws and regulations in relevant areas such as transport, housing, urban planning, audiovisual communication services, or web accessibility'.[81] All areas in which the entanglement of powers and jurisdictions may cause some overlap and potential conflict in federal dynamics.

In light of their complexity, the implementation of accessibility obligations, in the jurisdictions considered, pertains *de jure* to different levels of government and usually falls within different fields of competence enumerated within national constitutions. Thus, a degree of fragmentation remains and is highlighted by several authors. However, the CRPD has had a notable impact on the sharing of competences, prompting clear centralisation and harmonisation dynamics which coexist and overlap.

In some countries, despite the existence of accessibility legislation at the sub-national levels, centripetal trends are linked to the inclusion of accessibility duties and/or accessibility as a general principle in national disability laws. This is the case of Brazil that mentions accessibility in Federal Law No 13.146/2015 – Brazilian Law of Inclusion of Persons with Disabilities. This also occurs in Mexico, where the LGIPD:

> considers accessibility in the principles that must be observed by public policies and facilities in educational and work centres and grants, fiscal incentives to individuals and corporations that adapt their facilities to enhance participation of persons with disabilities and adhere to public policies on the matter.[82]

[79] A Broderick, 'Of Rights and Obligations: the Birth of Accessibility' (2020) 24 *The International Journal of Human Rights* 393–413.
[80] CRPD Committee, 'General Comment No. 2 on accessibility' (2014) CRPD/C/GC/2.
[81] Bariffi (n 56). Emphasis added.
[82] Spigno (n 39).

In India, section 40 RPDA confers the power of laying down the normative standards of accessibility of the physical environment, transportation, information and communications as well as appropriate systems and technologies, facilities and services in urban and rural areas on the central government.

In other instances, centralising trends are associated with the enactment of national accessibility laws. This is the case of Canada, having regard to the adoption of the Accessible Canada Act 2019, whose purpose 'is to benefit all persons, especially persons with disabilities, through the realization, within the purview of matters coming within the legislative authority of Parliament, of a Canada without barriers'.[83] As noted by Beaudry, some 'provinces have implemented legislation specifically addressing disability accessibility', while all of them have several laws or programmes related to accessibility. Treading carefully, Beaudry suggests that disability laws concerning inter alia accessibility 'are more likely to become more uniform across Canada'. However, we believe that the effects of a federal Act such as the Accessible Canada Act 2019 are those of enhancing the role of the central level and spurring a harmonised approach to accessibility. The approval of the Accessible Canada Regulations,[84] in 2021, which implement the Act (and admittedly only apply to federal departments and agencies and federally regulated sectors) may further enhance harmonisation, where provinces might include similar requirements in their own regulations.

In the European countries considered (Germany, Austria, Italy, Spain, Belgium), those centralising and harmonising trends are, as noted for example by Welti in his chapter on Germany, facilitated by the key role played by the EU. Accessibility of different means of transportation had been addressed extensively by EU legislation (both by means of directly applicable regulations and directives) long before the CRPD,[85] and had prompted not only a generally uniform approach across the EU, but also a broad harmonisation within Member States. In other areas, such as information and communication technologies or services, a portfolio of EU legislative and other instruments implementing the CRPD has been enacted, prompting a major role of the EU vis-à-vis its Member States. Ferri and Šubic suggest that in fact 'the CRPD has provoked a "quantitative shift" in the adoption of new harmonising legislation addressing accessibility' and that 'the capacity for Member States to conduct an autonomous policy to increase access appears rather limited'.[86] The EU, making use of Article 114 of the Treaty on the Functioning of the European Union (TFEU) on the internal market, has substantially centralised the implementation of Article 9 CRPD, and this in

[83] Accessible Canada Act, SC 2019.

[84] Accessible Canada Regulations: SOR/2021-241 13 December 2021 Canada Gazette, Part II, Volume 155, Number 26 www.gazette.gc.ca.

[85] See generally E Varney and A Pearson, 'Disability in EU Transport Legislation' in Ferri and Broderick (n 43).

[86] Ferri and Šubic (n 46).

turn has provoked at Member States' level either a centralisation or (at least) a harmonisation. The only area in which the EU has a very limited capacity is that of the built environment. However, in that regard, we note similar centralising (or harmonising) dynamics taking place to different degrees at the Member States' level. For example, Addis and Monti note that Italian regions approved regulations regarding accessibility, but within the mere purpose of furthering national measures. In Spain, while regions dealt with accessibility before the state, national legislation and policies are gaining momentum.

A (soft) centralisation (and harmonisation) dynamic is also occurring in Argentina, where national legislation on accessibility exists only in certain fields (such as the built environment) via the National Accessibility Plan. This Plan encompasses aims that are broader than accessibility, in that it endeavours to guarantee full inclusion to persons with disabilities in society. Notably this Plan aims also to achieve a high level of coordination across the territory. In both Ethiopia and South Africa, the national government has played a key role in the implementation of the CRPD. In particular, in South Africa, Chigwata and Nanima suggest that 'the formulation of the laws and policies relating to accessibility remains largely at the national level with a more "implementational" approach at the provincial and municipal levels'.[87]

The only exception to those trends seems to be (again) the United Kingdom, mostly because accessibility has remained a sectorial issue.[88] After Brexit, some accessibility provisions deriving from EU legislation have for the most part remained in place, as advocated by activists,[89] yet the future of accessibility in the United Kingdom remains uncertain and somewhat patchy. Lewthwaite and James also posit that a major concern will be the lack of supranational oversight, with the UK Government 'essentially monitoring its own performance'.[90]

While in most jurisdictions, the ostensible centralising dynamics have generally pushed towards an enhancement of accessibility, they also hampered the role of substantial entities and their ability to be laboratories of innovation in a domain in which there could probably be room for pushing innovation in universal design. However, even more significantly, the *de facto*, sometimes profound, remaining differences in the degree of implementation of accessibility obligations in the different sub-national jurisdictions are not considered as factors that might depend on different political choices made by the different legislators, but as factors hampering the equal enjoyment of the rights laid down in the Convention. Thus, like for asymmetry as a whole (as discussed above), any possible sub-national difference in accessibility requirements and policies that

[87] Chigwata and Nanima (n 28).
[88] McCall-Smith (n 61).
[89] Disability Rights UK, 'Brexit Manifesto' (21 June 2017) www.disabilityrightsuk.org.
[90] S Lewthwaite and A James, 'Accessible at last?: What Do New European Digital Accessibility Laws Mean for Disabled People in the UK?' (2020) 35 *Disability & Society* 1360–65.

indirectly impacts on the rights granted in the Convention is (or at least has the potential) to be seen as a violation of the obligation arising from Article 9 CRPD itself. This means, paradoxically and taken to the extreme, that where there is margin for differentiation, there is – at least potentially – also a margin for violation.

VII. FIFTY SHADES OF … PARTICIPATION

As mentioned above and in the Introduction to the volume, participation of persons with disabilities in all aspects of life is a key principle of the CRPD. It intersects inclusive equality, which embraces 'a participative dimension to reaffirm the social nature of people as members of social groups and the full recognition of humanity through inclusion in society'.[91] The principle of participation tallies with a general obligation to implement participatory decision-making processes in which persons with disabilities are co-producers of policies and legislation. Given the cross-cutting nature of this area, authors were asked to identify issues related to participation of persons with disabilities in decision-making but also in social life more broadly that could give an indication of the impact of the CRPD on the division of competences or on the nature of federalism in their jurisdiction.

With regard to this all-encompassing field, the impact of the CRPD on federal governance is far less clear, and possibly less evident. In many instances, however, national laws spell out the principle of participation (eg Mexico, Brazil) providing a general framework for participatory practices (including in political elections) across different levels. In some cases, those same laws stem from a participatory process. This is the case of the Indian RPDA whose enactment was preceded by a long law reform process, commenced in 2010, with the active involvement of civil society. Some authors refer to bodies that facilitate participation in public life created both at the national and sub-national level, giving rise to a sort of structural harmonisation. This is the case of the dedicated Commissioners in Germany, whose mandate is that or working toward equal living conditions of persons with disabilities in all parts of the society.

In several jurisdictions considered (eg, India, Mexico), there are obligations to consult with persons with disabilities at different levels of government when it comes to policy-making impacting on persons with disabilities. However, some centralisation dynamics which stem from the CRPD, albeit rather nuanced, are visible in some of the jurisdictions considered (eg, the EU, Italy, Spain). In the EU, the Commission's proposal to create a European Disability Card with a view to 'expand[ing] the scope of the mutual recognition of disability status

[91] CRPD Committee (n 4).

in areas such as labour mobility and benefits related to conditions of service provision', is a striking example of such centripetal trends. Some authors, such as Ferri and Šubic with regard to the EU and Fessha and Dessalegn with regard to Ethiopia, have also emphasised the role of policies and soft law, rather than binding law. In other countries, centralised national postures are replicated also with regard to the broad area of participation. In South Africa, for example, the national government 'has taken the lead in ensuring the participation of people with disabilities in social, economic and cultural activities' defining the legislative framework.

On the whole, procedures set up at the national level are often mirrored at the sub-national levels, and in some countries the national government has taken the lead in supporting political and social participation of persons with disabilities.

VIII. IMPLEMENTATION AND MONITORING IN MULTI-LAYERED ENVIRONMENTS

Article 33 CRPD 'is arguably the most comprehensive provision on national level implementation and monitoring ever included in an international human rights treaty'.[92] In fact, several scholars have highlighted that no other UN convention includes an explicit reference to domestic implementation,[93] the only example comparable to the CRPD being 'Article 3 of the Optional Protocol to the Convention Against Torture and Other Cruel, Inhuman or Degrading Treatment or Punishment (OPCAT), which requires states parties to designate or maintain a "national preventive mechanism"'.[94]

Article 33(1) CRPD identifies two key structures to ensure the realisation of the rights provided for in the CRPD. First, it requires a 'focal point', located within government, to support the implementation. Secondly, where necessary, it provides for the creation of a 'coordination mechanism', also located within government. While the setting up of the focal point is compulsory, the coordination mechanism is not (at least formally). Focal points and coordination mechanisms must be ingrained into existing constitutional structures, therefore being part of domestic public administration. De Beco and Hoefmans have

[92] M Birtha, 'Nothing about CRPD Monitoring without Us: Case Study on the Involvement of the Disability Movement in Policy-Making in Zambia' (2013) 1 *African Disability Rights Yearbook* 115–38; LFA Gatjens, 'Analysis of Article 33 of the UN Convention: The Critical Importance of National Implementation and Monitoring' (2011) 14 *SUR International Journal on Human Rights* 7.

[93] Ibid. See also G de Beco, 'Study on the Implementation of Article 33 of the UN Convention on the Rights of Persons with Disabilities in Europe' (United Nations Human Rights Office of the High Commissioner Europe Regional Office, 2011) 4.

[94] Ibid.

suggested that the focal point must be placed within national government.[95] Indicators related to Article 33 CRPD point to the need for 'legal and/or statutory appointment of one or more focal points within government (across all branches and levels of government, ministries, and sectors) with sufficient authority to mainstream the rights of persons with disabilities for implementation of the Convention'.[96]

Article 33(2) CRPD requires 'a framework, including one or more independent mechanisms' for the purpose of promotion, protection and monitoring of the implementation of the CRPD. To carry out those functions, as noted by scholars, States Parties can designate multiple existing bodies, or appoint one existing independent body, or create a new independent body. Independence entails full compliance with the Paris Principles.[97] If the framework does consist of multiple bodies, this would allow for an independent mechanism to be supported by other non-independent bodies. However, de Beco and Hoefmans argue that all bodies within the monitoring framework must be independent.[98] Finally, according to Article 33(3) CRPD, civil society, in particular persons with disabilities and their representative organisations must be involved and participate fully in the monitoring process.

Article 33 is probably the CRPD provision that has attracted more attention from a comparative perspective, giving rise to an array of grey literature[99] and scholarly articles.[100] Following the 2011 study for the Office of the High Commissioner for Human Rights, de Beco edited a volume discussing the implementation of Article 33 CRPD in several countries. Other works focused on the role of National Human Rights Institutions (NHRIs) in monitoring the domestic implementation of the CRPD.[101] Cognisant of this scholarly work, the authors in this volume and we, in this Section, do not discuss at length the

[95] G de Beco and A Hoefmans, 'National Structures for the Implementation and Monitoring of the UN Convention on the Rights of Persons with Disabilities' in G de Beco (ed), *Article 33 of the UN Convention on the Rights of Persons with Disabilities: National Structures for the Implementation and Monitoring of the Convention* (Martinus Nijhoff Publishers, 2013) 9, 23.

[96] Office of the High Commissioner for Human Rights (OHCHR), 'Article 33: List of Illustrative Indicators on National Implementation and Monitoring' (United Nations, 2020).

[97] See Ferri, Palermo and Martinico (n 9); European Union Agency for Fundamental Rights (FRA), 'Strong and Effective National Human Rights Institutions. Challenges, Promising Practices and Opportunities' (European Union Agency For Fundamental Rights, 2021).

[98] de Beco and Hoefmans (n 95).

[99] Irish Human Rights and Equality Commission and Centre for Disability Law and Policy, 'Establishing a Monitoring Framework in Ireland for the United Nations Convention on the Rights of Persons with Disabilities' (NUI Galway and Irish Human Rights and Equality Commission, 2016).

[100] C Caughey, 'Government Human Rights Focal Points: Lessons Learned from Focal Points under the Convention on the Rights of Persons with Disabilities' (2021) 39 *Netherlands Quarterly of Human Rights* 119–39.

[101] Eg E Kamundia and F Sidi, 'The Role of National Human Rights Institutions in Advancing Article 19 of the UN Convention on the Rights of Persons with Disabilities' (2020) 8 *African Disability Rights Yearbook* 52.

appropriateness of the structures created vis-à-vis the obligations of the CRPD or the human rights model of disability. Our analysis rather focuses on the impact that the implementation of Article 33 CRPD has had so far on federal structures, and which kind of dynamics it has spurred. It suffices to say that most authors highlight the complexity of implementing Article 33 CRPD in a multilevel constitutional context, and refer to the concerns expressed by the CRPD Committee in this regard.

A. The Focal Point(s) and Coordination Mechanism

In all the jurisdictions considered, focal points have been first placed at the national level, generally within the remit of a Ministry whose portfolio includes Social Affairs (such as in Austria and Germany), or, on occasion, within Ministries with competence on human rights. For example, in Brazil, the current focal point is the National Secretariat for the Rights of Persons with Disabilities in the Ministry of Women, Family and Human Rights. In some instances (eg, Italy and Spain), a specific unit within a national ministry is designated. In Spain, Gonzáles Pascual suggests that the main focal point is the General Directorate on the Rights of Persons with Disabilities, although competences relevant to disability are exercised also by other ministries. In other countries, the focal point is located within specific agencies or bodies at the national level, such as the Argentine National Disability Agency (*Agencia Nacional de Discapacidad* – ANDIS), or the Ethiopian National Implementation and Monitoring Coordinating Committee (NIMCC). Usually the composition of those bodies is mixed (and includes representatives of various ministries and DPOs), but do not comprise representatives of sub-national entities. In some instances, such as in Italy or Argentina, a scientific committee provides support to the focal point in order to ensure the adequate implementation of the CRPD, which might include the involvement of sub-national authorities.

With the exception of Canada in which (albeit with territorial differentiation highlighted by Beaudry) each province and territory has an office responsible for disability issues, which can be seen as acting as regional focal points, the creation of sub-national focal points has been slow and inconsistent, and often (such as in Germany and Austria) followed the setting up of a national focal point. In some cases (such as in Italy), there are no sub-national focal points. Hence, what emerges (often implicitly from all the chapters of this volume) is an initial strong centralising impact of the CRPD, coinciding with the designation of single national focal points (which do not include sub-national entities' representatives), subsequently mitigated by the creation of sub-national focal points, which tend to mirror national ones, giving rise to some sort of harmonisation.

The practice related to coordination mechanisms is quite inconsistent across the jurisdictions considered. While, as de Beco and Hoefmans suggest, 'federal or decentralised States may benefit from the establishment of a coordination mechanism',[102] not all countries have set up such a mechanism. The EU is probably the most blatant example of the lack of coordination mechanisms. However, in such a quasi-federal structure, omitting the creation of a coordination mechanism seems to be functional to the centralising dynamic in the implementation of the CRPD and the Europeanisation of disability rights, while potentially losing out on the benefits of learning from the experience of the Member States. In other countries, coordination mechanisms have been set up, but their efficacy is unclear. In Argentina, the Federal Council on Disability (*Consejo Federal de Discapacidad*) serves as coordinating mechanism to mainstream strategies between the Federation, the provinces and the municipalities. Further, a Coordinating Committee for Programmes for Persons with Disabilities (*Comité Coordinador de Programas para Personas con Discapacidad*) was created under Act No 25,730, which allocates funds to promote different projects related to the rights established in the CRPD. In some countries (for example in the United Kingdom and in Italy), the focal point and the coordination mechanism coexist or are conflated in the same (national) body, emphasising a tendency to centralisation. In Spain, the coordination mechanism National Council on Disability is merely a horizontal mechanism which ensures the coordination within the central government. In other countries there is an overlap with the independent mechanism. For example in Brazil, the National Council for the Rights of People with Disabilities (*Conselho Nacional dos Direitos da Pessoa Portadora de Deficiencia* – CONADE), as a collegiate body with the participation of the Federal Government and civil society, is officially the national coordination mechanism, but it also includes a commission for monitoring the implementation of the CRPD.

On the whole, while centripetal dynamics are detectable, these are overshadowed by an overall jumbled approach to the implementation of Article 33(1), and what seems to be a rather casual attitude on the coordination across different levels of government.

B. The Implementation of Article 33(2) CRPD

The implementation of Article 33(2) CRPD has undoubtedly proved problematic, namely with regard to the creation or designation of the independent mechanism(s) in the framework, in particular in countries where there were not NHRIs. In this respect, the criticism expressed by de Beco and Hoefmans and, rather vocally and consistently, by the CRPD Committee in its Concluding Observations is either conveyed or echoed by most authors in this volume. For example, Rodrigues and Breit note that, in Brazil, 'there is still no clear definition

[102] de Beco and Hoefmans (n 95).

of the independent mechanism' and the current structure of the framework 'is subordinate to the Federal Government, and is still quite fragile, incomplete, and insufficient'.[103]

In some countries (the United Kingdom, but also Mexico), the framework includes an array of sub-national entities, and can be characterised as truly federal governance framework. For example, the UK Independent Mechanism (UKIM), established to implement Article 33(2) CRPD, is comprised of the various independent statutory national equality and human rights institutions operating in the national and sub-national spheres. These include the Equality and Human Rights Commission (EHRC), the Scottish Human Rights Commission (SHRC), the Equality Commission for Northern Ireland (ECNI) and the Northern Ireland Human Rights Commission (NIHRC). The Northern Ireland Act created the NIHRC and the ECNI and the two operate together as the Independent Mechanism for Northern Ireland (IMNI) promoting and monitoring implementation of the CRPD.

Most notably, the implementation of Article 33(2) CRPD is however the domain in which some form of 'experimental federalism' has been seen. This is the case of Italy, where the absence of a proper NHRI and the stalemate of current legislative proposals on the issue in a state of permanent political instability, has been counterbalanced by an active role of regions. Addis and Monti refer to the important role played by some regional Ombudspersons,[104] who often use the Convention as a tool to enforce certain administrative policies,[105] or regional Guarantors that are charged with general anti-discrimination functions, as in the case of Friuli-Venezia Giulia (Article 10(1) Regional Law No 9/2014). In other regions, such as Puglia, Sicily, Campania and Lombardy, special bodies with the task to guarantee the application of the CRPD (ie a regional Guarantor of the Rights of Persons with Disabilities) were created, giving concreteness to a diffused (still incomplete) framework of regional independent mechanism.

IX. THE (LIMITED) ROLE OF COURTS

While the role of courts is key in determining nearly every issue pertaining to the everyday functioning of federal systems, as they adjudicate inter-governmental conflicts and more broadly interpret the scope of each jurisdiction,[106] it is striking to note that this has been much less the case with regard to the topic of this volume.

[103] Rodrigues and Breit (n 40).

[104] M Magri, 'Le autorità regionali di tutela dei diritti: il caso dell'Emilia-Romagna' (2017) *Istituzioni del federalismo*.

[105] Regione Emilia-Romagna Assemblea Legislativa, 'Sospensione idrokinesiterapia a persone con disabilità a Piacenza, Difensore civico ne chiede la ripresa' (22 January 2021) www.assemblea.emr.it.

[106] See E Delaney, 'Judicial Federalism in Comparative Perspective' in K Kössler and Y Fessha (eds), *Federalism and the Courts in Africa* (Routledge, 2021) 23.

Only a few cases are mentioned in the previous chapters, and some are very significant, but rather in defining the contours of the definition of disability or individual aspects of rights laid down in the Convention.[107] As already discussed by Waddington and Lawson in their book, courts also played a fundamental role in aligning the respective legal systems (and their approaches to the rights of persons with disabilities) to the CRPD, thus helping the enforcement of the Convention in the respective legal systems. As discussed by the authors in this volume, this has been notably the case in India, Mexico, Italy and South Africa, but also in Belgium. However, no significant case law is to be signalled with regard to intra-federal dynamics as far as rights of persons with disabilities are concerned. In other words, the conflict between different levels of government has not played out between national and sub-national governments in contesting the respective jurisdiction on issues pertaining to the (implementation of the) CRPD. At least not directly, since indirect contestations may always emerge as supporting arguments in conflicts over competences.

The limited, even insignificant, role of case law in federal conflicts around rights of persons with disabilities comes as no surprise. Although centralising and harmonising trends are visible in most jurisdictions, the relations between the levels of government have not yet been dramatically affected by the ratification of the Convention, at least not in terms of visibly shifting competences. Consequently even when subtle dynamics of centralisation, that occur under the surface, may erode the autonomy of sub-national entities, they do not give rise to conflicts. If nothing changes (or rather, nothing is perceived as changing), there is unlikely to be a challenge in courts. This does not downplay the importance of courts as umpires of federal conflicts. Rather, it shows the limited perception of the CRPD (and its rights) as a significant battleground for federalism in the analysed countries.

X. LESSONS LEARNED

The comparative review developed in this book first of all confirms that, from a methodological point of view, a purely formalistic approach is not conducive in the analysis of the impact of the CRPD on the federal structures of our case studies. Important as they are, the constitutional rules on dividing and sharing competences cannot provide an exhaustive basis for analysis, and this is due to a number of recurring elements in the perspective of the comparative law scholar.

All federal systems have experienced the inadequacy of a purely dual federalism which is based on a liberal vision of the relationship between centre and

[107] See eg the role of the Court of Justice of the European Union (CJEU) or the case law of the Supreme Court of Canada mentioned by Beaudry (n 55).

periphery.[108] This can be explained in light of the crisis of subject matter[109] and the impossibility of excluding the intersections between levels of government in certain areas. The complexity of policies, in particular, has led many federal systems to rethink the way competences are described by explicitly providing for competences that are either concurrent or shared. Unlike more recent federal constitutions, those of the classical federal systems do not refer to intergovernmental relations simply because coordination between governments was considered under the dual federalism paradigm as hardly necessary and the idea was that subject areas could be clearly delimitated and attributed to one level only.

In the case of Belgium and Spain, it should be added that the formal text of the national constitution does not have a monopoly on the distribution of competences, as the *Estatutos de autonomía* in Spain and special laws in Belgium must also be taken into account (and so are the Statutes of Autonomy of special regions in Italy). In Canada, the layered and incremental constitutional model in which the distribution of powers is set out in the Constitution Act of 1982 needs to be considered, alongside some norms included in the British North America Act of 1867. In the Canadian case, moreover, intergovernmental agreements, with a hardly amendable constitution,[110] have always played a role in supplementing the constitutional text. We also saw that all analysed systems show a certain amount of asymmetry, which is in line with comparative research suggesting the growing importance of asymmetrical dynamics in the main federal experiences,[111] although the implementation of the CRPD, with very few exceptions, limited them.

While, as a matter of fact, all the authors of the country reports began their analysis by describing the system of distribution of competences between the centre and the periphery, the analysis carried out confirms, in all the cases chosen, a clear impact of the Convention over the territorial 'material' constitution, no matter what the formal provisions suggest and regardless of the level of asymmetry known to the system. While centralising and harmonising dynamics are

[108] The US and Canadian federal constitutions reflect this approach, but over the years, the need to move towards cooperative federalism has emerged. See R Schütze, *From Dual to Cooperative Federalism: The Changing Structure of European Law* (Oxford University Press, 2009).

[109] N Steytler (ed), *Concurrent Powers in Federal Systems. Meaning, Making, Managing* (Brill, 2017).

[110] PH Russel, *Constitutional Odyssey: Can Canadians Become a Sovereign People?* (University of Toronto Press, 2004).

[111] C Tarlton, 'Symmetry and Asymmetry as Elements of Federalism: A Theoretical Speculation' (1965) *Journal of Politics* 861; R Agranoff (ed), *Accommodating Diversity: Asymmetry in Federal States* (Nomos, 1999); in particular see the essay by RL Watts, 'The Theoretical and Practical Implications of Asymmetrical Federalism' in Agranoff (above) 24; F Palermo, 'La coincidenza degli opposti: l'ordinamento tedesco e il federalismo asimmetrico?' (federalism.it, 7 February 2007) *www.federalismi.it*; G D'Ignazio (ed), *Integrazione europea e asimmetrie regionali: modelli a confronto* (Giuffrè, 2007); AM Russo, *Pluralismo territoriale e integrazione europea: asimmetria e relazionalità nello Stato autonomico spagnolo* (Editoriale Scientifica, 2010).

not consistent nor equally visible, in most countries the CRPD has contributed to a compression of sub-national entities' autonomy and powers. This confirms the general trend observed in federal countries, that the respect of international obligations undertaken by federal governments can trigger a centralising dynamic in the exercise of legislative powers.[112] In fact, the implementation of the CRPD confirms that rights tend to be – as the case of the US Bill of Rights teaches – vehicles of centralisation and, above all, instruments of transformative constitutionalism. In some cases, this centralising function of rights is manifested in an implicit manner through comparative case law that hinges on the principle of equality. In other cases it is made explicit in constitutional clauses capable of fostering a true and proper emptying of sub-national competences. The latter seems to be the case of Italy: Article 117 of the Constitution provides that the state (the centre) has exclusive legislative powers in the 'determination of the basic level of benefits relating to civil and social rights to be guaranteed throughout the national territory'. As suggested by Addis and Monti in their chapter, regional competences in the chosen field of analysis have been somewhat re-centralised thanks to this concept of 'basic level of benefits'. Similarly, the Spanish case, as González Pascual confirms, is very telling of the competence-creep operated via fundamental rights, since 'the outcome is the growing irrelevance of the regional powers in fields such as social welfare because regional statutes or regulations must follow the particularly exhaustive legislation of the state on constitutional rights'.[113] Interestingly, where centralisation dynamics or harmonising trends do not occur, the evolution of disability rights is hampered by lack of collaboration between the national level and sub-national entities.

[112] Ibid.
[113] González Pascual (n 45).

Concluding Remarks

Perspectives on Future Research

DELIA FERRI, FRANCESCO PALERMO AND GIUSEPPE MARTINICO

THE LAST CHAPTER has comparatively summed up the main findings of the volume and the research behind it. While this volume represents a new step in the still little-explored field of the intersection between federalism and disability law, further research is necessary to cast new light on and investigate this topic. As noted throughout the book, there is the need to further unpack the evolving implementation of the United Nations Convention on the Rights of Persons with Disabilities (CRPD) and the initial centralising dynamics unveiled in the volume.

Around the globe, disability law and policy has been transformed by the entry into force of the CRPD. Legal research has increasingly discussed not only the normative content of the CRPD itself, but also its domestic implementation, either focusing on distinct rights provided for in the Convention or presenting country case studies. The latter often engage in vertical comparison between the CRPD and national law, encompassing some sort of compliance analysis. Horizontal comparisons across the CRPD, international and regional legal instruments have also gained momentum. In some cases, those analyses also address post-colonial biases, the extent to which the CRPD represents a global and shared understanding of disability rights, trying to shed light on local influences and emerging global patterns. However, comparative analysis on the implementation of the CRPD is still narrow in focus and spectrum, evidencing disconnect between comparative law and disability law scholarships. For example, the role of courts in implementing the CRPD has been comparatively analysed by Waddington and Lawson,[1] and comparative analyses have been conducted mostly on the implementation of Article 33 CRPD.[2]

[1] L Waddington and A Lawson, *The UN Convention on the Rights of Persons with Disabilities in Practice. A Comparative Analysis of the Role of Courts* (Oxford University Press, 2018).

[2] G de Beco (ed), *Article 33 of the UN Convention on the Rights of Persons with Disabilities: National Structures for the Implementation and Monitoring of the Convention* (Martinus Nijhoff Publishers, 2013).

Almost no attention has been paid to the potential that federal arrangements can display in the implementation of disability rights, in facilitating matching of citizen preferences, accommodating diversity, leading to more efficient policy outcomes. By contrast, the somewhat recurrent lament about the complexity of implementing the CRPD in federal countries and the growing disappointment with the patchy realisation of disability rights in highly decentralised countries often disguise an undertone of dissatisfaction about decentralisation and federalism themselves, as it emerges from the present study. In other words, nothing in this volume proves that a federal system *per se* is an obstacle to the proper implementation of the obligations under the CRPD. Such obstacles rather can be found either in the unsatisfactory functioning of the multi-layered governance as a whole, or in the problematic approach to (certain) rights laid down in the Convention, but not in the combination 'federal system – CRPD'. To the contrary, the effects of the CRPD on federal structures have been indirect and 'unaware', as it has been *de facto* centralising the division of powers.

This book has filled a gap in current literature and tendered an analysis of the implications of the CRPD in federal countries, bringing federalism front and centre of each chapter. The comparative method has then been the key to gauge the potential of the CRPD to affect constitutional structures, and its actual effects on the sharing of competences in federal countries which present a multi-layered governance of disability issues. The final chapter of this collection has shown that the protection of disability rights has impacted on the level of integration among different territorial levels, and that the CRPD might *de facto* put the design, content, and form of decentralisation in federal countries under pressure. A detailed catalogue of competences has not been an effective shield to curb centralisation processes, especially in fields affecting fundamental rights and covered by international treaties, as it is the case of the rights of persons with disabilities. The final chapter has shown that original federal bargain included in national constitutions is moulded through implementing processes that often (albeit not always) place the national government front and centre. Further, centralising dynamics that are already present in countries like India, Mexico and South Africa are engendered by the CRPD.

Comparative federalism has been key to shedding light on the harmonising and centralising effects that the CRPD is slowly but steadily displaying in federal countries, and which has been disregarded by the Committee on the Rights of Persons with Disabilities (CRPD Committee) and scholars alike. In doing so, comparative federalism has offered the opportunity to show how conventional taxonomies are put under pressure, particularly the widely accepted unitary-federal dichotomy, including when it comes to disability rights.

This book, ambitious in its coverage and in its overall goals, is a starting point to embolden legal academics to abandon inward-looking approaches on the CRPD and embrace the critical potential of comparative federalism when engaging with the implementation process of the CRPD, in particular with regard to contentious and blurred areas of law, such as the definition of disability, that are heavily influenced by preconceptions, moral views and values. At the same time, it invites scholars of comparative federalism to look at the effects on federal systems by specific policies and rights, especially recent and less considered ones, like disability rights. Drawing on the comparative federalism literature would bring a recalibrated analysis and set of expectations when it comes to the implementation of the CRPD in multi-level systems. Comparative federalism can also contribute to reflecting on the different qualities that rule-making in national and subnational entities may display in the protection and promotion of disability rights.

Index

Please see individual countries for detailed information relating to that country

www.ingramcontent.com/pod-product-compliance
Ingram Content Group UK Ltd.
Pitfield, Milton Keynes, MK11 3LW, UK
UKHW020230290926
15470UKWH00002B/453

9 781509 962433